MOZART AND POSTERITY

Music Advisor to Northeastern University Press
GUNTHER SCHULLER

GERNOT GRUBER

Mozart &
Posterity

Translated by R. S. Furness

Northeastern University Press
BOSTON

Originally published in German as *Mozart und die Nachwelt*
Copyright 1985 by Residenz Verlag
First English publication in Great Britain by Quartet Books Ltd.,
London, in 1991
Translation copyright 1991 by R. S. Furness
First U.S. publication in 1994 by Northeastern University Press,
by agreement with Quartet Books Ltd.

Excerpt from W. H. Auden's "Metalogue to *The Magic Flute*" reprinted
by permission of Faber & Faber and Curtis Brown Ltd., New York;
copyright 1956 by W. H. Auden and Chester Kallman.

Library of Congress Cataloging-in-Publication Data
Gruber, Gernot.
[Mozart und die Nachwelt. English]
Mozart & posterity / Gernot Gruber ; translated by R. S. Furness.
p. cm.
Includes bibliographical references (p.) and index.
ISBN 1-55553-194-6
1. Mozart, Wolfgang Amadeus, 1756–1791—Appreciation. I. Title.
II. Title: Mozart and posterity.
ML410.M9G8713 1994
780'.92—dc20 94-6519

Printed and bound by The Maple Press, York, Pennsylvania.
The paper is Sebago Antique, an acid-free sheet

MANUFACTURED IN THE UNITED STATES OF AMERICA
99 98 97 96 95 94 5 4 3 2 1

CONTENTS

PREFACE

This book will investigate a prophecy which Goethe made over 150 years ago when he expressed the opinion that 'a creative force' radiated from Mozart's music 'which will continue from generation to generation and will be neither readily consumed nor expended'. I will seek it primarily in the history of ideas, which embraces very many different areas of relevant interest. When I spoke of my intention to my colleagues they kept asking me: 'How can you limit your theme?'; my reply 'Not at all' produced an embarrassed silence. I am well aware of my dilettantism, but it seemed to be defensible as I am not concerned with specifically musical, or literary, or artistic, or philosophical, or socio-historical topics but with general and comprehensive views on the phenomenon we call Mozart.

The material, however, had to be restricted in order to arrive at a readable and an easily comprehensible result. What to leave out was a bigger problem than what to put in. And an element of subjectivity is unavoidable in any process of selection. My intention is nevertheless to give a truly representative overall picture. I am not in a position to solve the difficulty of combining a discussion of Mozart's influence on the history of composition up to the present with a detailed examination of concrete musical analyses. I have left out the mass of data concerning the history of performances, printing and interpretation, and the huge amount of documentation relating to Mozart-Kitsch and light fiction, although these areas played a part in my survey. I felt a bibliography was unnecessary since the volumes of the *Mozart-Bibliography* are easily accessible, but I have ordered the literary references in such a way as to make them helpful for anyone wishing to study further. I finally gave up the idea of using illustrations: if I had wanted to use these as meaningful commentators on the text I would have needed another volume.

At a first glance the book may strike the reader as being loosely

vii

structured. The chronological division into four chapters more or less corresponds to Alexander Hyatt King's book *Mozart in Retrospect* (London 1955): it results from the historical evaluation and development of the topic. Was this something natural? I admit that I gave up reading the literature on the aesthetics of reception and also the idea of providing a solid theoretical basis when I started to write; the intellectual doubts were overlaid by the desire which slowly arose during my work on the material to give as true a picture as possible of the history of Mozart's influence. I wished neither to conceal the naïvety of this desire, nor simply to leave it at that, and so the following plan of action arose. I mixed documentation with critique, facts, data and a lot of quotations with judgements of my own; it was easy to separate one from the other. Of course, as the text developed there arose a network of utterances, allusions and questions, of associations and reflections from various specialties. I was fascinated by the idea of finding a thread which ran through the bulk of the material and of weaving it further. It was a thread which sometimes split, frayed, or at times grew into a strong rope. Difference in consistency would be expressed by structure and formulation. I felt that I was thus getting close to 'reality', closer than I would have done by sticking rigidly to a theoretical approach and by ordering the details into preconceived categories, a tidy but levelling process.

My main interests lie in Mozart's posthumous success in the decades around 1800 (a success story not easy to comprehend), in the false idea of a 'Romantic' Mozart and in the open question concerning the direction of today's Mozart reception, above all in the fascination and also the deep perplexity which has radiated from Mozart in the last two hundred years. The story of this desire to get to grips with a phenomenon such as Mozart gives a clear commentary on the history of genius which underlies it. So the history of reception consists mainly in a tension between history and the desire to transcend it; in other words, with that oscillating theme 'Mozart and posterity', that idea expressed in Hermann Hesse's *Steppenwolf* which was coined with Mozart in mind: 'In eternity there is not a world which comes *after* us [no *Nachwelt*], only a world which is *around* us' (a *Mitwelt*).

When the book first appeared at the beginning of 1985 it inadvertently became caught up in the rising *Amadeus* tide. I had expected something similar for 1991, but not for the Bach-Handel-Schütz year. This new edition takes into account the sensation caused by Milo Forman's film, the attendant circumstances, and also the intensive intellectual discussion about Mozart in most recent times. The ending of the book has been extended, as has the preface. Certain corrections have also been made.

I wish to thank the International Mozarteum Foundation and its collaborators for their asssistance, and Frau Sigrid Wiesmann, Herr Otto Biba, Herr Wolfgang Hildesheimer, Herr Wolfgang Rehm and Herr Wolfgang Ruf for the helpful support they gave to the unpublished manuscript.

Gernot Gruber
Munich
December 1986

MOZART AND POSTERITY

I

Before 1800

It is still a mystery why Mozart's reputation should have waned in the last years of his life, why he should have ended up in the shadows, outside 'public interest'. Perhaps one reason for this simply does not exist, despite the claim that it could be found sometimes here, sometimes there. There are many causes which seem reasonable – historical, political, social, psychological, musical or aesthetic. But factors that are without reason, apparently or actually groundless, may well have played a part: things that simply happen. After a trough in the waves there could well have been a crest – there is a lot of evidence that in the autumn of 1791 Mozart could have looked forward hopefully to a successful future. But his unexpected death gave the crisis of the preceding years a fatal, logical inevitability. For those who came after him the last phase of Mozart's life was to have the halo of an enigmatic catastrophe. Yet a decade after his death things were decided differently: the world of music knew that he was not simply a European phenomenon because he had been a child prodigy or because he had had outstanding success as a pianist. It knew that the work which he composed is to be reckoned among the highest achievements of Western culture.

Mozart was finally granted that recognition which his contemporaries had criminally denied him for years: almost every biography of Mozart finished with sentences to that effect. The biographers quite naturally use the fact that his work did finally triumph, and relatively quickly too. Indeed, among the avant-garde of our century this example of posthumous success served to emphasize the expectation of future triumphs, causing Stefan Zweig's somewhat mocking admonition to young artists: 'Be unrecognized for a while, or pretend to be – then you'll get friends.' It's obviously naïve to deduce a future recognition using the example of Mozart, Schubert, Bruckner or even Anton von Webern. But apart from this it is remarkable that in the vast amounts of Mozart literature there have been very few ideas on how it was that an unfairly treated genius became someone whose greatness was recognized.

Obviously the change in Mozart's standing during the 1790s represents an effective beginning in any account of his influence. But the temptingly simple formula, 'From the darkness of oblivion to the light of transcendental triumph', makes this change seem too spectacular. During his lifetime Mozart was only scantily regarded by the majority, by the public who eagerly noted the new fashions, but around the year 1800 he was esteemed by many influential personalities as one of music's great composers – yet these are not two isolated points which together create an incomprehensible contradiction. Rather it is the case that Mozart's posthumous success was latent in the work created during his lifetime; on the other hand the difficulties concerning the reception of his art did not disappear with the beginning of the nineteenth century. But what did change is fascinating enough: the apparent uncertainty when confronted by a phenomenon became a certainty *vis-à-vis* quality, a certainty which soon extended to the very characteristics of what this quality entailed.

To make this process plausible for the shaping of our consciousness of Mozart we must range a little further afield and discuss both tangible factors and imponderables as they interact. To give one example as illustration: a keen observer of musical life was the lawyer, musician and musicologist from Sondershausen, Ernst Ludwig Gerber. In his *Historical-biographical Encyclopaedia of Musicians*, which appeared in 1790, while Mozart was still alive, he was unable to reach any definite assessment of Mozart's achievements as a composer. Gerber came to the following conclusion:

This great master, in his early years, made such a deep and intimate acquaintance with harmony that it is very difficult for the unpractised ear to follow him. Even those more skilled in listening must hear his works several times over. It is indeed fortunate for him that he was still a young man when he reached his fulfilment among the charming and trifling muses of Vienna, otherwise he might well have suffered the same fate as the great Friedemann Bach, whose flight could only be followed by the eyes of a few surviving mortals. That Mozart still remains among the best and most skilful of our pianists is something of which I do not need to remind you.

In 1813, in his new encyclopaedia, Gerber freely admitted his earlier uncertainty and justified it by claiming: 'He was a meteor on our musical horizon, a phenomenon for which we were not prepared.'

For Gerber's critical (and later self-critical) considerations too there was one initial starting point, one which was named before him and after him, or which had a subliminal influence: Mozart's fame as a child prodigy. In the Europe of the 1760s the appearance of the two Mozart children had – apart from the sensation value – another highly relevant significance. Mozart and his sister Nannerl were living examples of that much discussed Baroque concept – and a leading one – of the miraculous, and of the modern Enlightenment ideas of *bonté naturelle*: they were admired either as signs of the grace of God or as inexplicable natural phenomena. Contemporary reports and even the letters of Leopold Mozart reveal these conceptions to be widely held. And there is something very touching in the report of the aged Goethe when he tells us that he 'clearly' remembered 'the little man with his wig and his sword'.

This fame as a child prodigy was a barrier, an impediment for the public at large to the acceptance of another Mozart. Mozart had been marvelled at since childhood, tested by musicians, discussed by philosophers, and pampered by half the princesses of Europe. He always knew how to succeed, and this superfluity of memories of childhood successes must surely not have been without consequences for his psyche. We do not know whether he was aware of this circumstance and its shaping significance. The correspondence between father and son gives us the impression that Wolfgang Amadeus Mozart moved through life like the Egyptian Joseph in Thomas Mann's novel and that there was a disturbing discrepancy between his naïve trust that everybody wished him only good and actual reality. Whether that was actually so, and why that was so, and whether Mozart was in fact so oblivious to reality, and what kind of reality he did in fact inhabit – these are fundamental questions which continually challenge us and belong to the 'creative force' of the phenomenon Mozart.

If we push these questions aside for the moment there appears all the more clearly a somewhat rigid framework to his career. According to this Mozart was able to carry over his fame as a prodigy into his adolescence; when he was about seventeen, however, he passed the climax of untroubled success; when he was twenty-five he freed himself from the unsatisfactory artistic prospects of Salzburg and from the direct influence of his father by moving to Vienna; in his first years in Vienna he reached new and lasting heights as a pianist and composer of keyboard music; from about the middle of the 1780s he had to accept negative criticism, above all of his chamber music but also of his operas; his hopes for an honourable post as *Kapellmeister* were not fulfilled; Mozart got into financial difficulties; public acclamation in Vienna was lacking until only shortly before his death. But why was Mozart so

7

hapless in his undertakings? Did he go about things in a half-hearted manner? Or was he incompetent? Was he not serious about getting a post? Didn't he realize that the post of court *Kapellmeister* was well and securely filled by Antonio Salieri? Had he not perhaps compromised himself somewhere? Did he have enemies? Was he not deceiving himself and his family? Did he really live, naïvely, in 'another world'? Our helplessness when confronted by these questions is seen in the conflicting answers which are part of his influence, but not a point of departure for its understanding.

What facts remain give us a sober history, indeed a dry one. Nothing is more indicative of Mozart's decline, and more important for the story of his influence, than the large gaps in our knowledge as well as in the knowledge of those who immediately followed him. We cannot expect otherwise since soon after Mozart's death, and with his growing fame, the legends began to circulate. It is surprising that many of the informants who had actually known Mozart and had consorted with him, published their memoirs very late – in some cases only after thirty or forty years – that is, the eyewitnesses (actual and ostensible) remained silent even when Mozart's fame was largely established. Why they should have done so is an area for speculation. Those who remembered him liked to give the impression that for decades nobody hit upon the idea of asking them about Mozart. The sceptic will assume that they knew perfectly well that if they waited for a certain length of time scarcely anyone could correct what they were saying. And the well-meaning observer will at least have to consider the fact that any attempt to remember what happened in the distant past easily succumbs to the temptation to weave fables. An important factor is also the question of whether or not anecdotes and disclosures about famous musicians were of any interest to the public. In the late eighteenth century this was certainly less the case than a century later. However that may be, the fact in all these memoirs is simply that they are more of a symptom than a source of information about who Mozart actually was.

The fact that these reports, although of doubtful historical veracity, should have survived so long and are even current today, has one of its causes in a most paradoxical phenomenon. Apropos of the lives of famous musicians of earlier ages, there is hardly a case where we have more exact information than with Mozart. For long periods of his life we have unbroken documentation and diaries; a great deal was preserved by Mozart, a most conscientious letter-writer. And yet the deeper motives remain shadowy; it is difficult to avoid mystification where Mozart the person is concerned. Even the rigours of historical source-research indirectly reinforce it; this is particularly noticeable in Mozart's last years. The contrast between artistic

8

heights and extreme misery which many biographers describe and which represents an extreme example of human tragedy is not present in the contemporary sources; only the financial difficulties and Mozart's begging letters to his lodge brother Michael Puchberg are on record. But where is the gambler? the revolutionary? the one who compromised? the roué? the man tormented by presentiments of death? the Mozart tangled in the machinations of Freemasonry? Most of his letters are basically happy, roguish, optimistic. Of course, this lightheartedness (which was perhaps only a façade) may be psychologically deciphered as something quite different, especially if one is prepared beforehand and knows what is behind it. But the plain fact is we know nothing definite about Mozart's situation and his state of mind.

I am in the fortunate position of not having to report how it actually was and what Mozart was really like. But history can help us at least to understand better the external causes of both Mozart's behaviour and the behaviour of those around him. One banal fact, already mentioned, is that the life, the personal qualities and even the sense of mission of an eighteenth-century composer excited much less interest than a comparable account of the personality of a poet like Klopstock or a philosopher like Rousseau (even if the latter, in his *Confessions*, liked to think of himself as a musician). Mozart's scant communications in letters about what 'really' moved him is not unusual in the context of the picture of the musician pertaining at that time (what is unusual is more the artificial way in which he deals with language). In contrast to the nineteenth-century cult of the hero and the compulsive craze for hectic musical jubilees of our age, the attitude to music in the eighteenth century generally gave no reason to elevate musical personalities on to a pedestal for permanent admiration.

Music was regarded rather as a fleeting art – and this in an entirely positive sense. The value of the experience of an individual musical performance was rated far more highly than the handing-down of masterpieces or *auctores classici*. If one leaves aside such examples of church music as Gregorian chant or the work and style of Palestrina, then there is a complete lack of venerable models. The popular discussions about the advantages of ancient and modern art were certainly heard in musical circles, but when antiquity was mentioned there were no models and therefore the debates had something insuperably abstract about them and could be of concrete use only in the advocacy of a particular contemporary stylistic direction: aesthetic reasoning completely dominated the historical interest. Music had a direct share in the wider historical dimension of art only through its texts or the subjects with which it was linked in vocal music and above all in opera. This (false, but effective) view of the relative ahistoricity of music also encouraged mobility in musical creation, the stimulus to make something new. The boundaries set for the search for originality (and now we come to a third prerequisite for reception) were determined by music's being anchored (not rigorously, but naturally), as regards its forms and its styles, in social functions of both a spiritual and a secular nature.

Music could support those aspects of life which demanded *gravitas*, or provide intellectual diversion, but it ran the risk of being regarded as something inappropriately difficult and consequently rejected as soon as it set itself up as an aesthetic subject in its own right. A spiritual trend like the so-called movement of *Empfindsamkeit* (sensibility) which broadly demanded a decidedly contemplative and inward-looking attitude towards music extolled its simplicity and necessarily rejected an increase in complexity in compositional technique. And finally that music which was subsequently and less happily known as *Sturm und Drang* and which burst the bonds of traditional restraint as, for example, in the fantasies of Carl Philipp Emanuel Bach – this music, with its profoundly existential and theoretical justification, sprang from northern and central Germany and not from the south German/Austrian cultural milieu.

A composer who wished to succeed would have to come to terms with facts like these. Mozart was certainly no newcomer to the sphere of what was considered musically appropriate; indeed his education and his experience since childhood had taught him just what was needed. Perhaps it was the very virtuosity with which he was able to manipulate his knowledge that prompted his imagination to compose works which in some, but by no means all, areas were too difficult for the ears of his contemporaries. This might seem a superficial explanation, but again, I am not concerned with locating the decisive cause. We simply have an abiding paradox. On the one hand, Mozart represented traditional basic beliefs: he knew about the functions of forms and styles; he quite naturally wrote for a definite audience (musician or listener); it would never have occurred to him to write an opera, say, without a commission and simply as a work in its own right; he sought the post of court *Kapellmeister* and did not wish to live as a free artist. On the other hand there are so many works in which, despite the fact that he should have tried to be successful, he ignored the necessary balance. He did it in such a way that it was only posterity which learned to recognize a qualitative difference.

In this apparent tension between convention and artistic consequence there is another aspect of the 'creative force' of Mozart's artistry. There may be all sorts of covert and problematic difficulties in our understanding here, but they become apparent in the most fleeting comparison with Joseph Haydn. There was much reciprocal stimulation and admiration, but Haydn always showed himself to be the more conciliatory, the man who better understood what the public wanted. The works of Haydn never received the same intensive criticism as did those of Mozart, and yet today nobody doubts the equality of stature of Haydn and Mozart. We point to Mozart's genius, a genius which followed its own path despite all the risks of failure, and we seek the obvious reason for the paradox in his compositional technique which we have mentioned, but this seems all too simple an explanation.

The reasons for the criticism are more understandable: they are more sharply articulated in the case of chamber music and opera. In both cases Mozart seemed to have sinned against the familiar conventions. Yet he does not stand alone here. The development away from *musique gallante* to what we call a classical string quartet comprises all in all a change in both demands and musical attitudes, a change which demanded much from the complacent expectations of the listening public. And yet, against this musical background, it is remarkable how skilfully the actual harbinger of this development, Joseph Haydn, was able to make his way seem plausible to both connoisseurs and amateurs and how Mozart, who closely modelled himself on Haydn particularly in the composition of string quartets, came up against difficulties.

The very influential Berlin composer and musicologist Johann Friedrich Reichardt, in his *Musikalisches Kunstmagazin* of 1782, criticized Mozart's instrumental music as being 'highly unnatural' because 'it is first very funny, then suddenly sad, and then again immediately funny': it consequently lacked unity of character. Observed more closely, the most extreme misunderstanding is to be found only *vis-à-vis* isolated examples in Mozart's work. An extreme case is the introduction to the so-called 'Dissonant Quartet' in C major, K. 465, a work dedicated to Haydn. Anecdotes, probably false, but nevertheless enlightening, were frequently heard. The printer Artaria was supposed to have had the 'defective' notes sent back to him; Giuseppe Sarti evaluated Mozart as 'the pianist with ruined hearing'; the amateur lover of music Prince Anton Grassalkovics from Bratislava is supposed to have torn up the score in a rage because of the many dissonances. According to the report of Georg Nikolaus Nissen, the publisher and composer Franz Anton Hoffmeister, who was friendly with Mozart, had such bad sales with the piano quartets K. 478 and K.493 that he paid Mozart the full royalties on condition that he should not compose the other four pieces which were stipulated in the contract and admonished him thus:

11

'Write in a more popular style, otherwise I can neither publish anything by you nor pay you.' The discrepancy between the demands of chamber music and the public's expectations is seen most clearly in the fact that in February 1785 at a musical evening when Mozart's Dissonant Quartet was being played, Joseph Haydn made the famous and authentic statement to Leopold Mozart: 'I tell you before God and as an honourable man: your son is the greatest composer I have known personally and by repute – he has taste and, above that, the greatest knowledge of composition.'

The opposition which Mozart the opera-composer had to face in Vienna above all consisted in the advocacy of certain prescribed models which lasted in some quarters for a long time and which, particularly in the 1780s, led to specific tensions. I mean here the arguments at court between a strong Italian tradition and the 'national *Singspiele*' expressly encouraged by Joseph II. Mozart was predestined to fall between two stools here. Compared to the Italian models his declamations in the singing parts were too *virtuoso*, not sufficiently *cantabile*, and the musical utilization of the orchestral parts so admired by posterity was considered unacceptable as it threatened to upset the traditional dominance of the voices. On the other hand, Mozart composed in a far too demanding operatic manner to be able to achieve the ideals of simplicity, popularity and accessibility associated with the German *Singspiel*. And Mozart's lively, agile, pathos-free style did not correspond to the German operatic ideals of Christoph Willibald Gluck (*Iphigenia in Tauris*) which were gaining ground with their 'particular boldness and strength of expression'.

But an all too extensive collection of quotations from negative critics would give a false picture. Mozart was actually never a completely misunderstood or disregarded composer: it was precisely the best musicians in his entourage who appreciated him most. His name may be found in popular accounts of his great contemporaries, although among these great men there are many scarcely known even to the historians of today. In some writings, some encyclopaedias where we might expect to find him mentioned, his name is inexplicably missing. All this betokens a high degree of arbitrariness and insufficient basic knowledge for a judgement of Mozart. This uncertainty in arriving at even a basic picture of the man is expressed in the image that his contemporaries made of him. This is found in the comments by Gerber that were quoted earlier and is defined by the discrepancy between the admiration for the genius's talents, his overwhelming wealth of imagination and the warning against false paths and lack of moderation. All in all his contemporaries saw in Mozart a *Stürmer und Dränger* of genius rather than a 'classical' artist reflecting on his art in the search for balance.

This picture – because it is so shifting – was easily changeable and subject to the intellectual metamorphoses prevalent at the end of the eighteenth century. What is more important is that it thereby received a shape which was more succinct, more terse. This change occurred with Mozart's death. Through death his life and work achieved something self-contained and clearly formulated. This self-contained quality produced first of all an understandable sense of consternation, not seen at the funeral ceremonies but certainly elsewhere. Friends and acquaintances helped the young widow, only twenty-eight years old, and took care of the children. Magnanimous sums arrived from abroad. A few days after Mozart's death the Emperor Leopold II granted Constanze an audience, and her petition for a pension was approved in a remarkably short space of time. In the middle of a flush of great successes in London Joseph Haydn heard of Mozart's death and expressed his shock in many letters and diary entries. Letters of condolence might well contain courtly exaggerations, but when writing to the wife of a Viennese doctor, Marianne von Genzinger, these artificialities fall away, and Haydn writes as follows: 'I look forward like a child to coming home and embracing my good friends. But how I regret that I shall not do this to the great Mozart: would it were otherwise and how I wish he had not died – posterity will not see another such talent for a hundred years.'

The sense of the irrevocability of what had happened seems to have called forth a clear formulation of Mozart's greatness. Haydn's statement did not reflect a general opinion but it suddenly had a greater chance of being generally accepted than his high opinion of the living Mozart. Most remarkable is the obituary published by Heinrich Bossler in the *Musikalische Korrespondenz* of the year 1792. Alongside the usual positive statements such as 'imaginative fire' and 'fruitfulness' we find the unusual sentence: 'Mozart's musical genius was musically completely mature.' As an anticipation of what was to come later we read a commemorative article from Prague, that town which had been the first to show enthusiasm for Mozart's work; the *Oberpostamtszeitung* of 17 December 1791 explains: 'His loss can never be made good. There are, and there will always be, masters of music, but to bring forth a master above all masters Nature needs centuries.' And completely separate from the normal run-of-the-mill judgements we find in this same article the first unambiguous description of Mozart as a classic: 'Everything that he wrote bore the clear stamp of Classical beauty. This is why he entrances us more and more each time, because one form of beauty develops from another, and this is why he will forever entrance us, for he will always appear in new guise, and these are the merits which belong to a classic. Or do his operas not demonstrate this?'

13

Indeed, in the first weeks after Mozart's death words were spoken and deeds were done which with hindsight look like seeds from which the later development of the Mozart image would spring, even if they appeared at the time to be only 'unrealistic' ventures into the unknown. The first sign was the following statement, entered by Constanze into Mozart's family album: 'What once you wrote on this leaf to your friend I now write to you, crushed with grief: Dearly beloved husband! Mozart, unforgettable for me and the whole of Europe! Now you are at rest, eternal rest!!! At one o'clock after midnight, between the fourth and the fifth of December of this year, he departed in his thirty-sixth year – oh, all too early – this good, but ungrateful world – oh God! For eight years we were joined by the tenderest bond, insoluble here on earth! Oh, if soon your deeply distressed wife, Constanze Mozart née Weber, could be joined to you eternally! Vienna, 5 December 1791.'

Even the authenticity of this text is a little unclear. Nobody denies that it is Constanze's hand, though the early date, the day of his death, is questionable. But the despairing cry of a distraught and helpless widow struck a chord. The exclamation 'unforgettable in the whole of Europe' scarcely corresponded to the actual reputation of the departed, yet it was to return, slightly modified and also intensified. The *Wiener Zeitung* of 7 December, in an announcement of his death, stated that 'he had climbed to the level of the greatest masters', and this announcement itself was echoed further. On 9 December it reappeared in a Hungarian newspaper, supplemented by the reference to 'a helpless widow with two orphans' and by the first attempt to see the myth of the *Wunderkind*, the child prodigy, which the father had exemplified, now re-enacted in the children. 'One of these little children, although still very small, already plays the clavichord in such a way that all who hear it are amazed.' Most obituaries attempted to link the fame of the child prodigy with the achievements of the mature composer, and this finds its most striking formulation in an epitaph which was published in the *Wiener Zeitung* of 31 December (although no gravestone was erected): *Qui jacet hic, Chordis Infans Miracula Mundi/Auxit; et Orpheum Vir superavit.*

Constanze could hardly have foreseen the impact her cries 'oh, all too early!' and 'this good, but ungrateful world' would have. To mourn one who has died particularly young, and to lament the times for not having appreciated him are in fact platitudes, but here they did lead to an effective mythologization. The yearning for union in death to which Constanze found herself transported is certainly not an anticipation of any *Tristan*-Romanticism, but it is difficult to differentiate between genuine exaltation and calculated cunning.

14

In her precarious situation Constanze was, quite understandably, anxious to get her hands on money, and not only the pension. She gave the autograph copy of the *Requiem* fragment to Joseph Leopold von Eybler, who was meant to complete the score, for only then could she be sure of getting the fee from the client. This was the impetus for the growth of interest in this work and its genesis, which rapidly became shrouded in mystery. A few days later Constanze offered copies of *La Clemenza di Tito* and *Die Zauberflöte* to the tenor Luigi Simonetti who was working in Bonn; she demanded an excessive price, and was unsucccessful. In a letter of January 1792 to Mozart's friend Michael Puchberg, Haydn promised to seek to organize charity concerts in London in aid of the widow and to give Mozart's eldest son free lessons in composition. What was important for Constanze was the sale in March 1792 of various autograph scores and a copy of the *Requiem* (was Franz Xaver Süssmayr, the second person engaged in finishing it, ready so soon?) to King Friedrich Wilhelm II of Prussia. As early as December 1791 the first concerts were organized for Mozart's dependants; whether or not Leopold II prompted a benefit concert in Vienna is uncertain, but we do know that a concert was put on in the National Theatre of Prague. The close link with Mozart's art felt by the citizens of Prague is seen in the funeral obsequies celebrated in St Nicholas's Church with magnificent pomp and a lavish requiem by Franz Anton Rosetti. Mozart's pupil Anton Eberl, who would later become for many years Constanze's friend and helper, composed with his poet brother Ferdinand a cantata *At Mozart's Grave* in which Terpsichore and the other Muses, accompanied by the Spirit of Germania and divers artists, lament the cruelty of the Fates. This first composition in Mozart's memory was to remain unperformed, but on 18 March the cantata *Mozard's Urn* (*sic*) by one Bernard Wessely (the libretto by Gottlieb Wilhelm Burmann) was performed in Berlin at a memorial concert. Already before this, on 31 January, a form of Mozart homage was chosen in Kassel (and a form which would be much imitated): a concert with works by Mozart which terminated in a final chorus as an apotheosis.

In consideration of all these activities it is surprising how long it took in Vienna before either an institution or a group of friends was prepared to put on at least a semi-official funeral service for Mozart. And if there *was* one it is remarkable that none of the papers of that time should have mentioned it. Only at the end of April 1792 did the Masonic lodge Zur Neugekrönten Hoffnung hold an address on Mozart's death, given by Karl Friedrich Hensler, together with a commemorative speech on the accession of a master. The text of the speech, and the poem which crowned it, are generally of an edifying tone, Mozart being praised as a benefactor.

Very quickly there emerged malicious rumours as well, suspicions and disclosures which were soon to prove of no less consequence. In the Berlin *Musikalisches Wochenblatt* of 31 December 1791 a correspondent from Prague first circulated the theory that Mozart had been poisoned: 'Because his body swelled up after death it was even believed that he had been poisoned.' Without expressly coming out into the open, the scribbler did nevertheless play with the idea of poison in a very sensational manner. The next sentence gives a mixture of true and false information: 'One of his last works was said to be a Requiem Mass which was played at his exequies.' Then follow digs at Vienna and Mozart: 'Now that he is dead the Viennese will at last know what they have lost. In his life he had to put up with much intriguing which his insouciant manner probably incited.' Such cheap journalism is only worth mentioning because posterity had to satisfy its curiosity largely from sources and formulations like these, which were fed by 'significant' suggestions. Even more macabre was a rumour concerning the attempted murder by the Viennese secretary Franz Hofdemel of his wife Maria Magdalena and his suicide on the day of Mozart's funeral. The couple were acquaintances of Mozart; Hofdemel had lent Mozart money in 1789 and his wife was supposed to have been Mozart's pupil. It was concluded from this that Hofdemel had attacked his wife because she was expecting Mozart's child. Frau Hofdemel did in fact give birth to a boy in the May of the following year, so this assertion, neither proven nor disproven, survived.

Naturally the consternation caused by Mozart's death gradually abated. This had positive results as well: the gutter press of those days, journals in the style of the promisingly entitled Viennese rag *Der heimliche Botschafter* (*The Secret Ambassador*), began to forget about Mozart. But promises made in the first shock of dismay were not honoured: Haydn was not very successful in his attempts to put on performances of Mozart in London, and when he returned to Vienna he never gave lessons to Mozart's son; Eybler soon gave up the attempt to complete the *Requiem*. Performances and benefit concerts for Mozart's family did not become the norm, and the sale of manuscripts to the Prussian king had no immediate consequences. In 1793 Constanze tried unsuccessfully to auction her husband's instruments.

In order to understand further developments we must realize that Mozart's growing influence was furthered by two factors. The first was the dedicated activities of certain individuals, of Constanze, Nannerl, friends and admirers; the second was more anonymous, more general, and vaguely describable in terms of 'formation of opinion' and 'dissemination of his work'. The activity of individuals runs the risk of remaining without resonance, yet on the other hand new possibilities might suddenly emerge without anyone's intention. That the individual should seek to exploit general tendencies as well as chance events seems just as reasonable as the fact that the anonymous aspects of a development can be influenced by the activities of individuals. This simple yet abstract parallelogram of forces looks more complex when viewed concretely, but also more vivid.

As far as individual activities are concerned it is those of the widow which are the most important and the most tangible. Many of Mozart's pupils and friends certainly put their energies at the disposal of his family and his work, but the reports that we have are sporadic and often nebulous. The patron in the most influential position was Gottfried van Swieten, son of Maria Theresia's personal physician; he was a diplomat, court librarian, founder of Viennese musical historicism and therefore of importance for all three classical composers, also librettist of Haydn's *Die Schöpfung*, etc. – but even his intervention remains unclear. It was probably van Swieten who helped Constanze at court; it is possible that it was he who first concerned himself with the children's education, but he did not assume any legal guardianship. How far private initiatives were primarily important for the performance of Mozart's work is seen in the case of Munich: the performances (not particularly frequent) in amateur concerts before the turn of the century were instigated in the majority of cases by singers who could be counted among Mozart's friends or at least acquaintances. In Graz we have to thank the Masonic brother Franz Deyerkauf and the Mozart enthusiasts Josef Bellomo and Eduard Hysel for organizing a concert in February 1793 with 'nothing but masterpieces of the immortal Mozart' and, as well as that, about seventy Mozart performances between 1791 and 1797. Personal contacts with the Mozart circle and personal commitment could also be of use in a wider sense, for example in the case of the Swedish count Frederik Samuel Silverstolpe who was *chargé d'affaires* in Vienna between 1796 and 1802. He got to know Haydn and Mozart's widow there and, on returning home, set about encouraging the performance of Viennese classics, particularly, as it so happens, of Haydn.

As a rule it must have been Constanze who was the one who sought assistance, with a lesser or greater degree of success; her financial difficulties and mental anguish must certainly have been very great. In the fifty years that she outlived her husband she did indeed come close to becoming a certain type of artist's widow (by no means extinct) – a mixture of grail-guardian and businesswoman, full of distrust. With Constanze the psychological causes lay in the discrepancy between that which she was and that which she represented; what was very likeable in her case (and for which she was later much reproached) was that she was quite carefree and

17

unconcerned about the interests of posterity and would have nothing to do with the growing hagiography. The cult of the genius began rather with Mozart's father, followed by his daughter Nannerl and then, in Constanze's place, her second husband, Georg Nikolaus Nissen. Constanze's efforts (and later Nissen's) were concentrated on the organization of concerts and concert-tours, the education and presentation of the children and all the matters dealing with the unpublished works.

An isolated success was the memorial concert organized by van Swieten in Vienna on 4 January 1793. In all probability it was there that Mozart's *Requiem* was performed for the first time, without the knowledge of the man who commissioned it. Things took a turn for the better only in 1794 when enthusiasm for Mozart had generally achieved a notable level. Constanze quite naturally tried to exploit these favourable conditions. In Prague conditions had always been favourable; Franz Deyerkauf must have been responsible for the two Graz concerts. The two Viennese concerts, at the end of 1794 and at Easter 1795, finally had the desired official status, the Emperor having permitted them to take place in the Kärntnertortheater and the Burgtheater. Constanze made full use of newspaper announcements and other notices.

In August 1795 Constanze embarked on a fairly long concert-tour accompanied by her sister Aloisia Lange and, to begin with, Anton Eberl. The goals were Berlin and Hamburg; on the way there and back they visited Prague and Leipzig, and we also know through concert announcements that they went to Dresden. Aloisia Lange also appeared in Hamburg whilst Constanze was in Berlin. The reason Constanze's only large enterprise of this sort did not take her to the south or to the west of Germany but to Saxony and Prussia is that she remembered Mozart's journey in the year 1789 and the favourable reception he received there. Friedrich Wilhelm II of Prussia, a man frequently denigrated by historians as a pleasure-seeking monarch, proved himself increasingly a Mozart admirer. Against the wishes of his theatre-director he recommended a performance of *Die Zauberflöte* and he was kindly disposed towards Constanze and permitted, for her benefit, a performance of *La Clemenza di Tito* at the Royal Opera House. In a handwritten letter His Majesty expressed himself in a most gracious fashion and spoke of the 'true pleasure which it gives Me to shew, by granting the wishes of the widow of Mozart, how much you, the widow, honour the talent of your deceased husband, and how you lament those dire circumstances which prevented him from harvesting the fruits of his work'. We may leave open the question as to whether or not this 'pleasure' was simply a result of the monarch's appreciation of art or to demonstrate to the

Viennese court how to set an example in dealing with one's subjects.
The preference given to lesser-known works, *La Clemenza di Tito*, the
Requiem and also *Idomeneo* (for whose printing Constanze had put an
advertisement in an 'Advance Notice' in May 1795), was not simply
speculation as to the public's desire for sensation but was an attempt to draw
attention to the hitherto unpublished work. The best insight into Constanze's
way of doing things is afforded by the *Requiem*: this, after all, was for her his
most important work. After Eybler had given up the attempt to finish it and
Süssmayr had taken over in the course of the year 1792, she did not
immediately give the score to Count Walsegg, who had commissioned it,
but had two copies made, one for herself and one for the publishers
Breitkopf & Härtel. She had further copies made of her own transcript to
offer for sale to highly placed persons. Abbé Maximilian Stadler must have
made a copy for himself before this. Count Walsegg gradually began to see
through Constanze's ruse and was quite naturally indignant. But by any
standards it was surely he who was guilty of theft of cultural property when
he wrote 'Requieum composto del Conte Walsegg' on his copy of the score
and had the work publicly performed as his own in Wiener Neustadt on 14
December 1793 in memory of his deceased wife. In the early days of
copyright, however, it was quite in order for a purchaser to treat the
acquired work with such liberty, and it was improper of Constanze to have
the *Requiem* performed on several occasions without informing Count
Walsegg. But piracy in matters musical was standard business practice at
that time. Constanze ran into difficulties only towards the end of the 1790s
when she entered into an agreement with Breitkopf & Härtel for the
planned *Oeuvres complettes* and wanted to sell the unpublished material. Yet
even this was finally settled. Constanze had contact with Breitkopf & Härtel
and also with the publisher André after the concert-tour of 1795/6; the sale
was a tactical masterstroke which, however, demonstrated Nissen's
cleverness rather than Constanze's. Above all it was the Leipzig publishers
who were interested in the unpublished work for their collected edition;
with one being played off against the other the Offenbach publisher Johann
Anton André had to pay the sum – very high for its time – of 3,150 florins to
get the autographs.
   With the children's education in mind Constanze had the tempting goal
before her of playing on the fame which her husband had enjoyed as a child
prodigy. Nothing is more telling here than the fact that she changed the
name of her younger son, who had been baptized Franz Xaver Wolfgang, to
Wolfgang Amadeus. When Constanze was staying with the children in
Prague in the spring of 1794 the nine-year-old Carl Thomas was supposed to

appear as a sacrificial victim in the opera *Axur*, an Italian version of Antonio Salieri's *Tarare*. Nothing came of this; Constanze then put out the following notice in the *Prager Neue Zeitung*: 'The boy Mozart, son of the immortal man whose divine harmonies will continue to entrance us, will, at the behest of His Excellency Baron van Swieten, his noble benefactor, and trusting in the spirit of the Bohemian nation, repair to Prague for his general education.'

So Carl Thomas came into the care of an old acquaintance of the Mozart family and a later biographer of Mozart – Franz Xaver Niemetschek – who later reported that 'Karl slept in my room for more than three years and was under my supervision.' During Constanze's journey the Niemetschek family also took in the younger son for half a year, and free of charge. Carl Thomas did not become a prodigy; perhaps it was because Constanze realized this that she sent him before finishing school to a business house in Livorno in 1798 to learn commerce. His brother first appeared on the stage in Prague when he was six with Papageno's *Vogelfänger* aria during a concert 'to give a small indication of his humble gratitude and to show that he was beginning to feel the need to emulate the great example of his father'. Even though the dream which Constanze presumably cherished of travelling with her children through Europe as the dear departed Leopold had, surrounded by jubilant crowds, did not come to fruition, then at least Wolfgang Amadeus the younger did have the prospect of a musical career.

Constanze surely did not have an easy time of it: not all her relations and acquaintances were well disposed towards her. The relationship between the Weber and the Mozart families – always a bad one – brought about a grave feeling of insecurity, part of the legacy left by her husband. Sister Nannerl felt herself to be the last member of the actual Mozart family and sought to preserve the memory of her brother in her own way. She represented what could be called the context of Mozart's life and work before his move to Vienna in 1781. The information which she gave was partly harmless and factual, and the publishers Breitkopf & Härtel turned to her from 1799 onwards with appropriate questions. Yet her role as informant could easily slide into the pursuit of polemical goals. Why Friedrich Schlichtegroll, the first man to write an obituary notice for Mozart, should have turned (via a middleman) to Nannerl and not Constanze – who never forgave him this *faux pas* – we do not know: perhaps he quite innocently became entangled in the fight between the two women.

Nannerl certainly responded with vigour and let Schlichtegroll have a lot of material which she amplified with memories of Andreas Schachtner, Salzburg musician and friend of the Mozart family. Her factual report limited itself to Mozart's Salzburg experiences; what she added consists of self-adulation and a brief, but effective, polemic. This was directed in a subliminal fashion at her brother, who had never grown to be a 'man', but hit Constanze fair and square: '... he could not manage money and married a girl who was quite unsuitable, against the wishes of his father, which explains the serious domestic disorders at the time of, and following, his death.' In this we hear the voice of someone who has been snubbed, someone who had not been able to follow her brother to the artistic heights and who had lost him as a human being; after the father's death there had been scarcely any correspondence between brother and sister. We do not know how far Nannerl exaggerated on the negative side in her characterization, but the consequences for the resulting Mozart image are all too obvious. Schlichtegroll removed the compromising comments on Constanze from his writing, but, despite the friendly words which he included in the obituary, she knew full well the source of the material and fought with all her power against the article when it appeared in 1793. She bought up all the six hundred copies of the reprinting in Graz in 1794, but this did not prevent its dissemination.

But more disturbing than these apparently unavoidable quarrels was the coolness felt towards Constanze by those people who were in themselves not averse to her. We have already mentioned Mozart's pupil Anton Eberl for example; as a composer and pianist, he did not simply devote himself to the memory of his teacher but worked for Constanze, accompanying her to north Germany. He broke off the journey prematurely, married shortly afterwards in Vienna and went with his wife to St Petersburg for a few years. Certain conclusions may be inferred; we shall avoid spreading new rumours about Constanze's love life. But a certain ill feeling did seem to arise at that time. Eberl fought against having works by him printed under Mozart's name and published warnings against this in 1798 under the title *Suum cuique*. There are no direct reproaches, but in an editorial note to one such warning in the Leipzig *Allgemeiner litterarischer Anzeiger* of 28 August 1798 we read some very spiteful words which could hardly have appeared against Eberl's will. We read of 'Mozart's widow' who 'has so little respect for her husband's ashes that she not only willingly lends her hand to all manner of illegal deeds but also is not ashamed of making similar suggestions here in Leipzig to a famous composer'. Even the good-natured Niemetschek made the following statement about the material which Constanze gave him for his Mozart biography: 'I could not use everything, partly because of the people still alive and partly because I did not believe what Mme Mozart said to me or showed me.'

As far as we know the contribution of Mozart's circle of relations and friends to his growing reputation is not that insignificant. We do not have new incentives, rather an intensification of already existing attitudes. Let us now look at the 'anonymous' side of early Mozart reception. It is obvious that the motives here will be still more difficult to comprehend. So we shall turn first to concrete facts and only later ask questions about the intellectual change of emphasis.

One change in his career, and one concerning the external conditions of his career as composer, should be mentioned at the start. For someone in Mozart's position an excellent appointment at court or with the church, despite all his negative experiences and his attempts to break out, did represent the best prerequisite for his reputation. Esteem, patronage and the ruler's protection encouraged the circulation of works through correspondingly good performances and printing, etc., and from the outset encouraged in the public – and this was equally important – a sense of positive expectation.

This old feudal structure was still very prevalent in the Austria of Mozart's day. At the same time, however, there appeared a counter-force in European musical life – the marketplace. Free enterprise gained, so to speak, an unofficial power over the dissemination and standing of musical works, but the entrepreneur was in turn vulnerable to the law of supply and demand. On the one hand the composer could free himself from feudal bonds and turn with his work to an anonymous public, but on the other hand he was dependent on both the taste and even the whim of this great anonymous entity. A statement of Joseph Haydn's documents this new situation, a statement which his confidant Griesinger communicated to the publisher Härtel: 'Haydn leaves it to you to decide to whom you should dedicate this edition; for his part, he dedicates it to the public.' If a composer made such high demands as Mozart then he would traditionally turn to a widely educated aristocracy or, consciously or not, would put his hopes in the cultural advancement of the bourgeoisie. It is clear that Mozart did not aim to exploit the chances offered by an emerging market. His father had judged the situation better when he admonished his son thus: 'Don't forget that which they call popular, that which will also tickle the long-eared ignoramuses!' With hindsight we see that Mozart's attitude, quite unpragmatic, had been proved right: his music did finally triumph whereas so much of the popular music of the 1780s was soon to be forgotten.

The rapid growth in this market for musical works and musical instruments further encouraged the awareness of a higher, superordinate idea: the general public. It was the institution of the concert which most manifestly gave the contemporaries the possibility of gaining admittance to

22

a public experience without the barriers of class simply by paying an entrance fee. Consideration for a wider public was also demanded here. As long as he could combine it with an immediate, actual awareness, Mozart possessed from childhood a fine assessment of the audience he was meant to address. In the piano concertos, for example, he differentiated between whether a work was meant for private or public performance, between movements which were simpler and others which possessed above all greater contrapuntal complexity. Yet he had no sense of how to manipulate an anonymous audience. And Viennese concert life, still in its infancy in his day, gave him little enough incentive to develop it.

The ever-wider spread of good, high-quality composition left tangible traces in the music market. Without wishing to overestimate the meaningfulness of numbers when evaluating a work of art it *is* perhaps helpful to have statistics about the dissemination of music according to composers, countries and genres, in order to make comparisons. The state of our knowledge allows us to cite certain tendencies. In the last third of the eighteenth century printed or handwritten copies of musical scores competed against each other. The places which were traditionally the most important centres for printing were Paris, London and Amsterdam. Around 1770 printing predominated in France, England and the Netherlands, whereas in other countries, especially Italy, Germany and Austria, copying was far more prevalent. From about 1780 printing spread further and came to Vienna. Leipzig became the vortex for the German music trade through its large music-copying works (J.G.J. Breitkopf and C.G. Thomas), through its fair and, increasingly, through the universally known publishers Breitkopf & Härtel. Church music and operas were usually hand-copied, whereas instrumental music and songs were printed (André, for example, printed 200 copies). This practice admittedly reflected a differing estimation of music, whether it was more traditional or more modern.

Obviously it is far easier for musicologists of today to get a clear picture of the production of printed music than of music hand-copied and circulated privately between producer and amateur collector. But we can distinguish certain characteristics for the dissemination of Mozart's work from printed music. The extensive lack of printed church music, oratorios, etc., is not surprising: even Joseph Haydn's masses, despite their fame, only appeared after 1800. The printing of the Masonic works (K. 471, K. 619 and K. 623) in 1792 had to do with Freemasonry and piety. It is in no way startling that not one of Mozart's operatic scores appeared in print before the end of the century. Noticeable, however, is the dissemination of the operas through piano arrangements – this is almost completely lacking with Haydn's operas. So we now have the following chronology: 1785 *Die Entführung aus dem Serail*; 1791 *Don Giovanni*; 1792 *Die Zauberflöte* and *Der Schauspieldirektor*; 1794 (?) *Così fan tutte*; 1795 *La Clemenza di Tito*; 1796 *Le Nozze di Figaro*; 1797 *Idomeneo*. Sections of *Il re pastore* and *La Finta Giardiniera* were printed in 1795; only *Die Zauberflöte* appeared in multiple editions before 1795. The mean variation of these numbers shows that before 1795 the public's interest was concentrated in the loosest sense on Mozart's *Singspiele*. Looking at the multiple editions of complete piano arrangements or of individual sections before about 1800 we have the following picture: at the top of the list we have *Die Zauberflöte* which was found three times as frequently as the following operas, which may be listed thus: *Così, Die Entführung, Don Giovanni, Idomeneo, Figaro, La Clemenza di Tito*, etc. These editions were printed by new or ambitious German publishing houses (Breitkopf & Härtel, Simrock, and Schott), rather than the Viennese publishers (*Die Zauberflöte* is a positive exception here). Very little appeared in the London houses. With the other vocal works (songs, choruses, etc.), the national boundaries are similarly sharply defined; dissemination after 1795 increased notably; what is remarkable before this is the publication of Mozart songs in anthologies for children.

The printing of Mozart's instrumental music before 1800 may be roughly listed as follows. Of the symphonies above a quarter were in print, mostly in parts. In comparison with Joseph Haydn the international distribution is much less. Apart from the symphony composed in Paris (K. 297) and the symphony K. 318, both of which appeared first in Paris, only German and Viennese publishers accepted the symphonic works – in the 1790s Johann André was the only one (and it is he we must thank for the publication of the late symphonies). Certainly it must have been the piano arrangements (by Johann Wenzel of Prague) of 1793 and 1794 (reprinted 1801) of the Linz symphony (K. 425) and the great E flat major (K. 543) which contributed to Mozart's growing popularity. The divertimenti and the serenades achieved more international interest among publishers in the 1790s; the frequently printed Divertimento K. 563 occupied a special position here, whereas *Eine kleine Nachtmusik* (K. 525), later to become so popular, remained unprinted. Mozart's dances and marches went through many editions (above all in Vienna, and even elsewhere outside Germany). The wind and violin concertos were passed by (the exception being the violin concerto K. 268 which appeared with André, although the authenticity of this concerto is dubious). The piano concertos found a lot of interest; above two-thirds were already printed in the eighteenth century: K. 413, K. 414 and K. 451 were preferred, also abroad, whereas the rest were almost all on offer by German and Viennese publishers. The chamber music appeared in its entirety in the 1790s and in a much greater quantity and a more international representation than might have been expected from the frequently sharp criticism of the 1780s. The string quartets, especially, appeared individually and in collected editions by both English and French publishers. A 'Collection complette des Quatuors, Quintetti, Trios et Duetti', appearing from the Viennese publisher Artaria between 1790 and 1808, established Mozart's reputation as a composer of chamber music. While the wind chamber music was very little noticed, the chamber pieces for piano were very frequently printed, to the disadvantage of the larger compositions (piano quartets and particularly quintets); the emphasis lay most heavily upon piano trios and the constellation preferred by Mozart – the sonata for piano and violin (the first works here were already printed in London and Paris in 1764). Similarly favourable is the situation with the works written purely for piano.

One very characteristic phenomenon of the times, and one which is now almost unknown to us, was the publication of musical periodicals which grew increasingly popular after the 1780s. These gave the buyer the opportunity to catch up on music he had heard in a concert or at the opera without stretching his technical abilities if he were a musical amateur. The selection and arrangement of the pieces also assured their popularity. Mozart's music was taken up by these periodicals increasingly after his death; compositions for piano, and also songs, were preferred, as were the piano reductions of his operas.

We get an idea of their importance for the increasing cultivation of family music in middle-class homes when we look, for example, at the twenty-five handwritten music books of a citizen of Saarbrücken. Written between 1789 and 1800 and preserved by chance, they contain mostly piano pieces which were easy to play, but also sentimental songs, by Mozart and others, which had been copied out of musical periodicals. The numerous 'collections' of piano pieces, songs and arias, etc., had the same function. Their link with the world of concerts and operas is partly obvious from the titles: the Berlin publisher Johann Karl Friedrich Rellstab published, in 1788, a 'New Selection, arranged for voice and piano, of those Arias from Operas upon the National Stage which are Particularly Pleasing'. The fashion for variations which emerged in the late eighteenth century also found an early expression here: in 1792 Rellstab brought out an – admittedly incomplete – 'Collection Complette des Variations de Mozart'.

The flood of arrangements which, with an eye to the future, set in during the 1790s, also served to popularize Mozart. The serious Mozart fan of our times might wrinkle his nose at such trivializations, but he cannot deny that the educational value of an arrangement that one might oneself play is equal to listening to music on stereo. And looking at it from a business point of view the growing demand was answered by the correspondingly large selection on offer. Leaving quality aside, the range was extensive: arrangements made not only for piano but for all the instruments and combinations imaginable – violin, flute, guitar, as solos, in duets, with and without piano, for wind instruments – i.e. 'harmonies' for two oboes, two clarinets, two bassoons and two horns (these were very popular). Excerpts from Mozart's operas, also his dances, provided the choicest material; it was Vienna and the German-speaking countries which were to the fore here.

From dry statistics from the world of printing we can glean a certain amount of information. As far as the cultural-geographical distribution is concerned we can see the following picture: the chamber music had an international appeal balanced with a national popularity when associated with the traditional publishing houses: it was more strongly represented than many old prejudices concerning its complexity would have us believe. The vocal pieces (also the operas) remained for the time being restricted to German publishers; the dances were published above all in Vienna (Mozart's activities as court composer lay primarily in this field). The weighting – sometimes extremely disparate – between the different genres of instrumental music can be attributed neither to the differences in quality nor to those of technical complexity: the reason for the wide dissemination of piano works of all kinds (solos, concertos, chamber music for small ensembles) lay in the esteem which Mozart enjoyed in his lifetime both as a pianist and as a writer for the piano. I cannot explain the fact that the concertos for strings and woodwind were ignored, or why interest in the symphonies was so sparse; perhaps a striking enough cause for drawing attention to this group of compositions was lacking. The Offenbach publisher Johann André attempted to remedy this. His commitment did not simply spring from a selfless devotion to Mozart's music but from the canny insight of a businessman on the make who saw the need to turn to areas which had not yet been explored; he was also convinced of the quality of Mozart's music.

What we lack when we attempt to profile the spread and distribution of Mozart's work are standards of comparison. For Parisian publishers, for example, he did not even figure among their favourites: his work had to compete with that of well-established names like Haydn, Pleyel, Carl Stamitz, Vanhal and Rosetti. We do have a clear view of André's German activities. Before 1800 there were 118 Mozart items in the catalogue, which put him in second position, the first being occupied by Ignaz Pleyel with 226. Playing with numbers like this shows how dominant the Vienna circle was – and Pleyel belonged to this circle – in the list that follows: Joseph Haydn (82), Hoffmeister (70), Gyrowetz (65), Wranitzky (54). Johann André himself (50) did much better than, say, Muzio Clementi (25) or François Devienne (25). As well as German patriotism there was another impetus: the publisher André also furthered the career of the musician André. Composers with this dual function were generally remarkably successful; Hoffmeister belonged to this category, as did Pleyel (but only from 1797). We find a similar picture when we look at the production of the Mainz publisher Bernhard Schott. The following distribution may be seen from the publisher's catalogues from 1779 to 1797: Pleyel (41), Sterkel (33), Mozart (20), Vogler (20), Hoffmeister (10), Dalberg (8), Dittersdorf (8), Joseph Haydn (8), Clementi (7), Grétry (7). Composers from the Viennese circle also dominate here; the frequency of the editions of Johann Franz Xaver Sterkel's works had local reasons.

Another valuable source of information is the sales catalogues of the Breslau dealer Franz Ernst Christoph Leuckart from the years 1787 to 1792 which give us an insight into a typical situation. Breslau was not one of the leading music centres, but it was certainly worthy, and the public's interest reflected this. Sales catalogues have an extra advantage in that they tell us more about what the public wanted than about the taste of the publisher himself. The musical favourites in Breslau (local patriotism was not a factor) were Pleyel (named 481 times in six years), and Hoffmeister (368); those beaten, so to speak, included Joseph Haydn (134) and Mozart (83) – the latter certainly did better than Dittersdorf (25) and Vanhal (21). In contrast it is noticeable how Mozart beat Haydn in 1787 and 1792. Six of the eighteen numbers of *Die Zauberflöte* were already offered in 1792, even though it was not performed in Breslau until 25 February 1795.

Of the 83 Mozart items 24 came from operas, the other preferences included all sorts of piano music, then chamber music (particularly sonatas for violin and piano, also piano trios), and finally orchestral music (only dances and piano concertos); the symphonies appear nowhere. So the picture we get from Leuckart's catalogue corresponds to the one gained from publishers in general. But – and we must stress this again – the accuracy of the numbers should not deceive us as to their contingency and their fragmentary character. And yet, from today's standpoint, they do document some rather strange facts, among them that Pleyel was a more popular instrumental composer than Mozart. Perhaps students of the piano still know his name; it scarcely ever appears on concert programmes today, even

27

though for the music lover Arthur Schopenhauer a flute concerto by Pleyel belonged in the standard repertory together with Mozart and Rossini, bearing witness in the middle of the nineteenth century to this composer's memory.

A 'list of ancient and modern music, copied and engraved' which the music dealer and publisher Johann Traeg brought out in 1799 gives us further information concerning the spread of Mozart's popularity. Traeg ordered his catalogue according to the old custom (but in marked reversal of the sequence) according to 'Chamber-musick, Theatre-musick and Church-musick'. On the basis of the genres singled out as examples we can outline Mozart's position in numbers (but because the inconsistencies in Traeg's catalogue are not resolved the numbers given have only an approximate value): with the symphonies listed Haydn is at the top (111), before Dittersdorf (34), Pleyel (30), Mozart (19), Gyrowetz (18), Vanhal (13), Wranitzky (10); with the piano concertos Mozart (13) holds first place, followed by C.P.E. Bach (10), E.W. Wolf (8), Haydn (7) and Vanhal; with the violin concertos Mozart still had a low rating (with 1), whereas Dittersdorf leads (12), Anton Stamitz (10), Vanhal (7), Viotti (5); with the string quartets, Handel arrangements (23) surprisingly beat Haydn (13), Mozart (12), Pleyel (12), Wranitzky (10) and Cambini (9); with piano sonatas, the sequence is as follows: Haydn (34), Mozart (25), C.P.E. Bach (25), Clementi (11), Kozeluch (9), Handel (5); with piano variations we have Mozart (18), Gelinek (7), Philipp Carl Hoffman (7), Kirmair (7), Beethoven (6) and Haydn (5); the most popular dance compositions were obviously by Bock and Gyrowetz. In the sphere of 'Theatre-musick' Starzer and Joseph Weigl dominated with ballet and pantomime; with *Singspiele* and melodramas we have, ranged alongside Mozart, Benda, Grétry, Haydn, Hiller and Winter in approximately the same representation. With selections from German-speaking operas arranged for voice and piano, Mozart leads (13), and after him come Wenzel Müller (9), Hiller (4), Hoffmeister (4), Weigl (4), Grétry (3), Dittersdorf (2), Salieri (2), Schenk (2) and Wranitzky (2); with operatic selections in foreign languages we have Mozart (6), Gotifredo Jacopo Ferrari (4), Cimarosa (3), Martin (3), Salieri (3) and Weigl (3). With 'Odes and Songs for Voice and Piano' we have Zumsteeg (9) and Bornhardt (8) before Mozart (7), Haydn (6), Müller (6), Reichardt (6), Schulz (6), Sterkel (6) and Neefe (5). With church music Mozart's position varies: with the masses he has nine items, even more than Haydn (8), but takes second place to Cajetan Freundthaler, a musician completely forgotten today; under the rubric 'Oratorios, Graduals, Offerings in the score or parts' Mozart does not have a place among the most frequently offered composers: here we have Handel in first place (17), then Freundthaler (11), Monn –

presumably Matthias Georg – (6), Joseph (5) and Michael Haydn (4). All in all it is remarkable how the various imbalances in the reception of Mozart towards the end of the nineteenth century smoothed the way to a general appreciation of his *oeuvre*; of course, Traeg's list reflects only the Viennese situation.

We may now confirm these findings from the – albeit rather meagre – information about Mozart peformances. Today's custom, whereby musical institutions can justify their activities by progress reports, statistics and so on, was then unknown, so the historian does not have this useful source of information. Reports by correspondents in the musical journals and belletristic publications which were only just coming into prominence at that time give sporadic accounts of outstanding occurrences. The situation is worst with church music: only the handwritten scores with a few performance dates give an idea of the distribution and popularity of Mozart's works. With operas we are in a much better position: behind this institution we have as a rule the court with its venerable institutions and its newer enterprises, and prestigious events always excite attention, attention which is reflected in publicity.

The situation is most confusing in that field which seems to us today to be sharply defined – the interplay between private amateur music and the world of the concert, with a fixed number of seats, season tickets and professional know-how. The old *musica da camera*, understood as an intellectual diversion at court, had experienced a fragmentation with the rise of the bourgeoisie and the concomitant market forces whose reality is not sufficiently grasped by positing an alternative between private and public music-making. The rule is simple: unusual events (whether of an official and prestigious character or of a musical nature) are more likely to enter history than 'normal' events. The spread of music-making which took place in a private to semi-public sphere of society was certainly mirrored in the rapidly advancing publication of music, but scarcely in the reports of performances, let alone statistics.

Even during Mozart's lifetime a concert-industry had begun to establish itself in Vienna. Subscription concerts had existed for some while, but there were far more concerts *al fresco*, and in casinos and restaurants; in short, concert life depended on favourable opportunities, chance happenings and the initiative of individuals. Not until 1831 was there in Vienna a building intended solely for concerts (there had been one in Hamburg since 1768, in Leipzig since 1781). The orchestras consisted mainly of dilettanti and professional musicians hired from somewhere or other. For a more or less elevated tier of society various exclusive concerts were organized in the palaces of nobles or in middle-class houses. This situation was not

29

particularly Viennese, even if the development in the towns of central and northern Germany, and above all in the European cultural centres (London and Paris), began some decades earlier. This was also valid for the 'musical societies' which became increasingly important as centres of middle-class musical cultivation, and appropriate above all for helping the 'new spirit' in music and music-making to gain a sense of security and continuity.

Mozart's position in the early history of European concert life is more easily defined specifically than globally. In Paris and London, the old centres of music-making, other composers were to the fore. Joseph Haydn played a much more important role in London after the passing of the Johann Christian Bach generation. Although two symphonies by Mozart, a piano quartet and the six string quartets dedicated to Haydn did turn up in London programmes in 1788, Mozart's music remained unpopular until the turn of the century. Impresarios like Bach/Abel and Salomon did take the odd symphony into consideration; Johann Wilhelm Hassler and Johann Nepomuk Hummel played two piano concertos in 1792. Vocal numbers appeared very seldom in the various other musical events, string quartets hardly at all.

The revolutionary events of 1789 had brought with them certain restrictions in Paris, but also new impulses. The Berlin musician Johann Friedrich Reichardt reported that Parisian orchestras were the finest in Europe. The longstanding conflicting preferences for either Italian or German instrumental music were decided in favour of German; in 1801 a correspondent reported that 'Paris . . . seeks above all in its concerts to play German music.' It was Haydn's symphonies above all that were admired, particularly for their originality; Mozart stood very much in his shadow, only sporadically performed before the turn of the century. Even a Mozart admirer of the status of Luigi Cherubini achieved little, as he had fallen out of favour with Napoleon.

The trail-blazing function of Haydn's symphonic music in London and Paris became an exemplary model. When the Leipzig *Allgemeine Musikalische Zeitung* wrote in 1802 that Haydn's music would be exalted 'from Lisbon to Petersburg and Mosko [sic], from beyond the ocean to the Arctic sea', then Mozart was necessarily relegated to second place, even although his work did finally come into its own. And we do actually find a Mozart performance in America before the turn of the century: a symphony was played in Charleston, South Carolina, in 1797, and a piano sonato had been played by the pianist Alexander Reinagle, who was of Austrian descent, at a concert in Philadelphia in 1786.

Mozart's music had been fostered early in Sweden. Thanks to the commitment of personalities like Frederik Samuel Silverstolpe and the

German musician Joseph Martin Krause (known as 'the Swedish Mozart') there was considerable interest in the instrumental music of the Viennese circle. It is the preponderance of the symphonies (from 1789 onwards) which is unusual in the Mozart reception in Stockholm. We can prove that there were thirty-five Mozart performances during the 1790s. These included eleven symphonies and five piano concertos but only a few vocal works. The last were generally overlooked at first outside German territory because of the language barrier; what *was* sought was the novelty of the instrumental music.

Whereas Haydn's international fame as an instrumental composer preceded the patriotically tinged admiration for his personality, Mozart's reputation developed somewhat differently. Thanks to the printers and music-makers we can see a very respectable international spread of his instrumental music, a distribution, however, that was bolstered by the 'older' genres (divertimento, sonata for violin and piano) and tending to exclude the symphony, which was felt to be rather modern. But the positive change which appeared at the same time had many a motive, and was not solely restricted to Mozart's work. One important motive was German patriotism, which turned against foreign infiltration and was entirely compatible – astonishingly so – with enlightened ideas which had also been taken from abroad. The opponent against which patriotism had to fight was basically Italian music which had had a dominating position since the sixteenth century. Patriotic, influential musicians (such as Johann Adam Hiller who was active in Leipzig, Berlin and Breslau, and the later Thomas-cantor August Eberhard Müller) had been successfully concerned since the 1780s to reduce the proportion of Italian music in their programmes in favour of German. This was more easily achieved in some places than others, depending on how strong the Italian tradition was. The Italians were most powerful in Vienna itself: this explains the reason why the prerequisites for a change in receptivity were more readily found in northern and central Germany than in Vienna, that city close to the south, where the musical changes were in fact taking place.

But this may sound like a one-sided preference for the role of Viennese music in a process which is indeed complex. What we can say with certainty is that a contrast was forming in about the middle of the eighteenth century between the north and the south. Differences in matters of musical taste have always had to do with the style of music as well as more general cultural and political matters. The former is difficult to pin down to tangible and historical facts, but the latter cannot be overlooked. Throughout the Seven Years' War (1756–63) the political conflict between Prussia and

31

Austria had worsened; this was of significance for Austria which had been defeated militarily – and it also affected music. In an essay which appeared in 1766 in which there are obvious digs at 'People in Germany' we hear for the first time of 'Viennese musical taste'; Joseph Haydn is praised as 'the darling of our nation'. There was no mention yet of Mozart, who was only ten at the time.

In an autobiographical sketch of 1766, that same Haydn complained that, 'In chamber music I have had the good fortune to have pleased almost all the nation – except the Berliners.' Even if it was Leipzig rather than Berlin which was important for the advancement of German concert-life – the signs for the victory of the Viennese musicians were not favourable. But the fact that they *did* triumph must surely have musical rather than political reasons. A difference in generation may also have played its part: after the Bach sons and the Mannheim circle, after musicians such as Hasse, Graun and also Hiller, there was a hiatus which the Viennese could fill. Events in Leipzig were significant and may have acted as an example: at the first concert in the new Gewandhaus a symphony by Johann Christian Bach was played, as well as works by his contemporaries who are completely forgotten today. Under Johann Gottfried Schicht's direction the pro-grammes (twenty-four concerts a year!) were reorientated to take in the Viennese, whereby it was Haydn who dominated; from 1790 onwards we meet Mozart symphonies, at first played occasionally, then in ever-increasing numbers. They were frequently played from 1793 onwards in the Leipzig 'Dilettanti Concerts'. Even in Berlin tastes began to change, a trend initiated at the highest level. We have already spoken of Friedrich Wilhelm II's high regard for Mozart's music; his greatest favourite from 1787 onwards was admittedly Carl Ditters von Dittersdorf who did, in fact, belong to the Viennese circle. We have to thank the spread of publishers' activities for this tendency, a spread already acknowledged.

The success of Viennese music was probably influenced by the increase in the number of concerts. These institutions which, incidentally, pointed the way ahead, encouraged the search for a new repertoire, and the Viennese manifestly provided this more readily than the others. And we cannot over-emphasize Haydn's importance as a focus here. As the self-awareness of the middle class in general, as well as the growth of concerts, was established earlier in north and central Germany rather than in Vienna, we get the paradoxical circumstance – paradoxical when we consider the political situation – that the originality of the music from Vienna was recognized earlier in Prussia and Saxony, and taken up far more emphati-cally, than in Vienna itself.

That modernity was preferentially associated with two genres – symphony and oratorio: Mozart did not appear in either as a leading spirit. There was Haydn in the one case, and Handel in the other. Looking back to Handel was probably a result of London's exemplary position: the concerts of the British capital, in their monumental Handel festivals, reflected the economic power and the cultural glory of the country, and the Germans could only look with envy on these performances. Haydn was most impressed by the oratorios that he saw there, and the Abbé Vogler reported that he once heard five hundred singers and four hundred instrumentalists in Westminster Abbey. In addition, Handel's oratorios are of a completely different order from the pietistic, sentimental offerings of a Graun, a C.P.E. Bach or a Reichardt.

As neither the intellectual nor the institutional prerequisites were present, the search for the new could advance only gradually; the first performance of the *Messiah* in Germany, in Mannheim in 1777, ended in uproar. An about-turn was achieved by a memorable performance in Berlin Cathedral in 1786 with the participation of the royal orchestra, then again by performances in 1787 and 1788 in Leipzig and Dresden respectively. The choirmaster Johann Adam Hiller showed forward-looking initiative here by strengthening the choruses in the English manner, thereby achieving a monumental grandeur. Hiller had arranged the *Messiah* as Mozart had done, bringing it in line with the contemporary sound; he hoped to reform the composition of cantatas in his Handel-retrospective.

The foundation of the Berlin *Singakademie* at the beginning of the 1790s under Karl Fasch also served to encourage high-class choral singing. The continuity of Handel performance in Vienna is uncertain, although performances of the oratorios were initiated by van Swieten and began quite early between 1788 and 1790 with Mozart's arrangements of the *Messiah, Alexander's Feast*, the *Ode to St Cecilia* and *Acis and Galatea*. But the exclusive offerings of the Palais Lobkowitz were very different from Hiller's monumental performances; Mozart's arrangements were occasionally revived during the 1790s. The concerts which were most appropriate for these works, those of the 'Tonkünstler-Sozietät', performed Handel oratorios only after 1820, although choruses by him were heard in 1792, as well as other oratorios, cantatas, etc.

Mozart's *Davidde penitente* (based on the magnificent fragment of the C minor mass, and performed in 1785) belongs in the series of oratorios which put the traditional Baroque offerings in a new light. It was also fitting, considering the style of the 'Sozietät' concerts, that Mozart's *La Clemenza di Tito* should have been given a concert performance in 1795. These concerts, incidentally, gave many of the works of Haydn, Süssmayr and Salieri, etc., but scarcely anything by Mozart. The work of his which *did* correspond to the emotive, dramatic musical taste most closely was the *Requiem*. It was Hiller's involvement which confirmed this particular interpretation. Hiller had got to know it through Constanze Mozart's Leipzig sojourn; he headed his copy of the work with the words '*Opus summum viri summi*', and in a letter to Ernst Ludwig Gerber he called the *Requiem* 'the last, but also the greatest of Mozart's works'. Of particular significance for the tone of middle-class concert life is the fact that Hiller translated the text into German, thereby consciously freeing it from a religious nexus and reworked it as a concert piece with ethical demands; an attempt to see a continuous link here to a work like Brahms's *Ein Deutsches Requiem* is entirely justified. Hiller performed the work for the first time in Germany in the Leipzig Gewandhaus on 20 April 1796; it is also axiomatic for any attempt to see it in context with the Handel Renaissance to recall that the first performance it ever had, on 4 January 1793 in Vienna, was organized by van Swieten. It was surely also not by chance that the first of the great works performed in London was the *Requiem* (successfully, 20 February 1801), followed by *La Clemenza di Tito* (a failure, rather, in 1806).

In the field of music theatre the centre of gravity is different, and far more favourable for Mozart: the recognized paradigms do not come from Haydn or Handel, but from Mozart above all. Actually, this is relevant only to German-speaking countries; outside these Mozart's operas were only sporadically performed and seldom successfully. (Only in 1818 did Thomas Busby, in his *General History of Music*, name Mozart as the pinnacle of operatic music, as Haydn was the pinnacle of the symphonic.) In Copenhagen *Così fan tutte* was performed in 1798 (as an opera far less expensive to produce than others); *Le Nozze di Figaro* was produced in Paris in 1793 (Beaumarchais's popularity obviously played a part); *Così fan tutte* was produced in Trieste in 1797 (probably for the same reasons it was chosen in Copenhagen) – an early and successful Italian production mounted on a stage of a town which at that time was Austrian. In this political, or at least cultural, world centred on Austria we find other places with early productions: Budapest, Bratislava, Warsaw, Riga, Hermannstadt (Sibiu), etc. The productions in Amsterdam were quite frequent (*Die Entführung* in German in 1791, in Dutch in 1797; *Don Giovanni* 1794, *Die Zauberflöte* also 1794). We may consider the *Don Giovanni* production in St Petersburg (1797) and the *Figaro* in Monza (1787; probably 1788 in Florence) as rarities.

It is surely not extravagant to see the spontaneous success of *Die Zauberflöte* as being the most important driving force in the complex weave of Mozart's growing posthumous fame. The sensational quality of this success seemed to trigger off something else. One could, when talking of the development of the German *Singspiel*, talk about a kind of blockage in its fulfilment, a blockage which was freed, as if Horace's maxim of the *delectare prodesse* which had been discussed for decades suddenly found its object. Yet despite this, the contemporaries articulated their reactions to the novelty of *Die Zauberflöte* in a variety of ways. The identification with this opera – or should we not talk about the fashionable, modish desire to be consistent with everything? – appears in such droll examples of Manichaean, exaggerated interpretation as the Jacobin one of 1792, with its scheme of good and evil (here the Queen of the Night is associated with the reign of Louis XVI, Pamina appears as 'Freedom as the Daughter of Despotism', Tamino as 'the People', Sarastro as 'Wisdom of a Better Legislation' and the priests as 'the National Assembly') or the Masonic interpretation (the parallels drawn between the Queen of the Night and the Empress Maria Theresia – who persecuted the Freemasons – Tamino and Joseph II, Pamina and the Austrian people, Sarastro and the Grand Master Ignaz von Born) or in the no less comical Passau transcription into a knightly milieu of the year 1795 (whereby Tamino is portrayed as 'a wandering Knight . . . in spangled armour fighting a serpent with broken blade').

Mozart had already been successful in the *Singspiel* in 1782 with *Die Entführung aus dem Serail*, but this story is not entirely free of contradictions. The divertingly popular components, which the public loved, were soon joined by enlightened, didactic and patriotic elements which aroused suspicions of interference from above, as there had been in the 'national *Singspiele*' of Joseph II. A prime example of a naïvely simple insistence, an attempt, as it were, to hammer home a message full of the ideas of the Enlightenment, is seen in the libretto of Mozart's *Zaide*: anyone who knows this work will appreciate *Die Entführung* all the more and realize how advanced the composition techniques have become. If we also see in the *Singspiele* of central Germany a swing away from folk-like simplicity to the operatic, then we must admit that Mozart went much further. *Die Entführung* made him known as opera composer to a very wide audience (performances in 1783 in Prague, Leipzig, Frankfurt am Main and Bonn, in 1784 in Mannheim, Salzburg, Schwedt, in 1785 in Dresden, Munich, Kassel, and so on), but at the same time the difficulties and the extravagance of his score were criticized. On the one hand *Die Entführung* appeared on the stage at exactly the right time – the hopeful beginning of Joseph's 'national *Singspiele*' and the advancement of new theatrical enterprises (Schikaneder, Böhm, Seconda, etc.), in the southern German/Austrian area – and on the other hand its taxing compositional demands came too early, and ten years later the fashion for Turkish operas had passed. So it was only *Die Zauberflöte* which set the tone for a 'German Opera', the designation given by Mozart in his catalogue of works.

Between *Die Entführung* and *Die Zauberflöte* stand the masterpieces written in Italian, *Le Nozze di Figaro* (1786), *Don Giovanni* (1787) and *Così fan tutte* (1790). It is well known how badly these works were received by the Viennese public: for four years after its first productions *Don Giovanni* was not performed in Vienna. The dissemination outside Vienna was considerable, and yet it must be admitted there were certain limits. In north Germany productions of Mozart operas were thin on the ground: the first *Die Entführung* was seen in Rostock on 5 July 1786, then followed *Don Giovanni* in 1789 in Hamburg (a town not noted for its tradition of opera) and, in Berlin, *Figaro* and *Don Giovanni* in 1790. Performances of *Figaro* and *Così fan tutte* are generally fewer than those of *Don Giovanni*. People had long puzzled over why it should be that the Viennese public rejected these three operas, and why *Don Giovanni* was preferred elsewhere. One reason might have been the preference for the mystical aura of opera rather than critical realism. But a warning must be given against discerning causes for a rejection where perhaps inducements for a positive reception were simply lacking; the unusual dramatic structure of *Figaro* could not have been a particularly negative factor, especially as *Don Giovanni* is just as lacking in conventional form.

The patriotic aspect is the most striking of the motives for a positive reception of Mozart's operas. The great enthusiasm that the citizens of Prague felt for Mozart and which reconciled him to his Viennese disappointments certainly reflects well on the culture and the openness of the citizens of that town but also on the patriotism of the Germans in Prague. Mozart was also a factor in the struggle against the Czech national movement in Brno, but with less success. The gradual, growing self-awareness of the Germans did not exclusively develop in opera alone, but also and above all in the *Singspiel*. The bourgeois ideals of sincerity and simplicity, making deep inroads into aristocratic culture, overlap with the attempt to create something specifically German in the field of art. The unusual demands made by Mozart's operas fitted in well with this desire for something new, but a compromise was needed to deal with them. Nothing proves the aristocratic element in Mozart's art – that dash of 'superiority over the world' – better than the corrections which first made his work popular.

The manner in which Mozart's operas were translated into German is very informative. In what was supposedly the earliest German *Don Giovanni* translation (that of Christian Gottlob Neefe of 1788; the first printed one is that of Heinrich Gottlieb Schmieder, Frankfurt am Main, 1789), Don Giovanni becomes a certain Hans von Schwänkereich, Donna Anna becomes Miss Marianne, Don Ottavio a Herr von Frischblut and Leporello becomes Fickfack; Masetto becomes Gürge. In Christoph Friedrich Bretzner's German version of Così fan tutte (which becomes Women's Faithfulness or The Girls from Flanders) the three ladies are known as Lottchen, Julchen and Nannchen. Every translator had to show the white flag, as it were, in those passages which showed the character in extreme situations. The brief but unqualified outburst of sensuality in Don Giovanni's so-called 'champagne aria' caused difficulties in any attempt to approximate a Singspiel tone. Friedrich Rochlitz (1801) found an acceptable compromise: 'Open the cellars! Bring me the barrels. Now we shall drink, so splendid and free. Bring me the maidens, Quietly, Quietly, I wish to dance, so bring them to me! In all the fun I'll angle me one . . . A girl in my arms, forget the alarms . . .' In later translations the tone becomes even more like that of a governess, as in Franz Grandaur's version (1868): 'Now to a party, Let us be happy, for all my guests like drinking the wine! Look at the maidens, Don't let them leave me, Have a good time . . . Pink pretty mouths, I kiss them and kiss them, Use now your chances, Frankly and well!'

Trivialization such as this is justified when we consider the needs of touring companies performing before middle-class audiences who had paid for their tickets, but less so with translations used at courtly theatres. A great many were in circulation, influenced by local considerations and differing expectations. Propriety and decency, both practised in everyday life, should be confirmed by what was seen on the stage: a watered-down philosophy of Enlightenment such as was successfully advocated by Adolf von Knigge in his book Über den Umgang mit Menschen of 1788 (he had also translated Figaro) permeated many a production. The explosive force of those images which showed human beings under threat was tamed and made harmless: this caused difficulties not only in the champagne aria (in a Berlin production of 1790 it was simply given to Leporello to sing) but other works too needed substantial moderation. Figaro and Così fan tutte were regarded as being particularly tricky; ambiguities and irony had to be smoothed out even if this ran the risk of making the action implausible and invalidating the music's subtle commentary.

It would, however, be an exaggeration to claim that Figaro and Così fan tutte were ignored: the distribution of productions is not markedly different from those of Don Giovanni, and the printed versions (excerpts for piano, individual numbers and arrangements) show how at least parts of the music were appreciated. And if we regard the efforts undertaken for appropriate translations as a criterion for the interest shown in these works then it is surprising that *Così fan tutte* was translated eleven times between 1791 and 1797. There were also express admirers of *Figaro* and *Così*: one reviewer for the Berlin journal *Musikalische Monatsschrift* wrote about an arrangement of the latter work ('So do they all') in 1792 that 'After *Le Nozze di Figaro*, an opera which . . . takes precedence over all Mozart's theatrical works, this opera is unquestionably the most excellent.'

Although we run the risk of giving an all too subjective impression it is possible, after hunting through the material at hand, to give a rough idea of the popularity of the individual operas. The popularity curve of the *Singspiele Die Entführung* and *Der Schauspieldirektor* sinks somewhat after about 1795; *Don Giovanni*, on the other hand, rises, as does *La Clemenza di Tito* towards 1800; *Figaro* and *Così fan tutte* are well represented in the middle of the 1790s and only dip considerably round the turn of the century; interest in *Idomeneo* increased towards the end of the century; from 1792 onwards *Die Zauberflöte* held a clear and lasting lead.

Its success story brought many surprises: it was immediately successful in Vienna, a city where Mozart had had little luck with his operas. This was probably due to the fact that Schikaneder's stage appealed to levels of society other than that of the court theatre. And it is also remarkable how quickly *Die Zauberflöte* became famous in places where it had not even appeared: the music market had, of course, been prepared for a phenomenal success. Papageno's music and that of the three boys was especially popular. *Die Zauberflöte* had the chance of reaching out to the sort of wide audience which perhaps the figure of Leporello could attract in *Don Giovanni*, but which *Figaro* and *Così fan tutte* could never hope to achieve. Despite its 'baser' elements in keeping with the tradition of popular Viennese theatre, *Die Zauberflöte* impressed such illustrious spirits as Goethe, and this rootedness in the Viennese tradition did not prevent it from spreading throughout the whole of Germany.

It was about 1794 that the success of *Die Zauberflöte* reached its first climax. The opera had been played in all the most important theatrical centres before then (Leipzig, Frankfurt am Main, Munich, Dresden, Mannheim, Weimar, Berlin and Hamburg) and was accessible to everyone in piano excerpts and arrangements. A wave of songbooks hit the market; the Weimar arrangement by Christian August Vulpius appeared simultaneously in two editions and was frequently reprinted. At this time *Die Zauberflöte* was often known as a *Singspiel*; this trend, however – the tendency to conceive of all Mozart's operas as *Singspiele* – shifted towards the end of the century in favour of a more classical definition, manifesting itself from 1793 onwards in the description of *Die Zauberflöte* as a 'heroic-comical' opera. The work's fame is seen in the many and varied attitudes which it engendered: if the local conditions were right it was even adopted by the 'opposing' Italian side. Giovanni de Gamberra translated the libretto into Italian (for Dresden and Prague, both 1794) and changed the dialogues into recitative. The enthusiasm of the citizens of Prague, an enthusiasm transcending national boundaries, is seen in the fact that there was also, and probably as early as 1794, a version in Czech as well as the German and the Italian versions. Even the continuous tinkering with Schikaneder's libretto (which began with Vulpius and continued in Peter von Braun's arrangement of the work 'in a German form') should not be understood just as a criticism but also as an involuntary compliment to Schikaneder's theatrical instincts. Imitations immediately followed on the heels of the work's triumph: Schikaneder tried to cash in on his own success by writing an opera *Das Labyrinth oder Der Kampf mit den Elementen, der zweyte Theil der Zauberflöte* (*The Labyrinth or The Battle with the Elements: The Magic Flute Part Two*), and it is known that Goethe also (even though the content had quite a different direction) latched on to the success of *Die Zauberflöte* with his own version of *Part Two*. And the influence that the opera had on the further development of the magic-opera genre is incalculably varied.

Germany had been seized by a veritable *Zauberflöte* craze. And, indeed, next to *The Beggar's Opera* in London and Beaumarchais's *Mariage de Figaro* in Paris it became one of *the* theatrical sensations of the eighteenth century. Even after two centuries we can still detect something of the vitality of its impact when we read one of the reports which appeared in the August number of the Weimar *Journal des Luxus und der Moden* (1794):

For a few years now it has been incessantly performed on all stages and booths where one and a half throats, a couple of fiddles, a curtain and six bits of scenery were available; it has pulled in the spectators from miles around like the magic drum of a shaman which attracts the faithful, and it has filled the box offices. For our engravers and our music dealers it has been a veritable gold mine of Potosi, for it is obtainable at all manner of fairs and market-places, all manner of music dispensaries, in its entirety, or in sections, in individual arias and fragments, in piano reductions with and without song, in variations and in parodies, printed or hand-copied. It has given bread and livelihood to our town-band, our Bohemian musicians, our ballad-singers and minstrel-lads, for in all the fairs, the spas, the gardens, coffee-houses, inns, balls and serenades, wherever there

39

is a fiddle, there you will hear nothing but *Die Zauberflöte*, and, indeed, it has been transplanted on to the barrels of the hurdy-gurdy players and on to the magic lantern shows. It is found on all the pianos of our twanging, banging novices; it has given our lads – both large and small – Papageno pipes and our ladies new fashions, coiffures and headbands, new muffs and purses *à la* Papagena; it has presented us with a young offspring which the ever-ready, beloved German desire for imitation has made of it – the Magic Zither. It has, in short, produced in Germany a commotion, an activity, a titillation and a joy.

The success of the work and the spreading Mozart craze are inextricably related. In places which initially had reservations about Mozart, *Die Zauberflöte* was a truly pioneering work. In Rostock, for example, the first city in north Germany to have seen any of his operas, he was largely disregarded for a long time, and Dittersdorf, Grétry, Salieri, Gluck and Benda were preferred. Yet it was *Die Zauberflöte*, in 1795, that turned the tide. Prague was certainly a place favourable to Mozart, even after his death. When we read in a report from Prague of the year 1794 that 'since the existence of Mozart's operas, no other, fundamentally, has succeeded', we can draw no general conclusions, but the future drift will point in this direction. A polemical article appeared in Chemnitz in the year 1795 and criticized the 'widespread idolization' of Mozart, and the following assertion – perhaps somewhat exaggerated – is made: 'In this year of our Lord 1794 nothing must be sung or played, and nothing must be received with acclaim which does not carry the all-powerful talismanic name of Mozart on its brow. Operas, symphonies, quartets, trios, duets, piano pieces, songs, even dances – everything must be written by Mozart if it seeks to earn general applause.' The neologism 'mozartizing' which we find in this article – just three years after Mozart's death! – speaks for itself. Mozart's music seems at any rate to have taken over some ostensibly exemplary function even though it is not clear what 'mozartizing' actually consisted of. This is true of the Prelude and Cadenza '*alla* Mozart' which Muzio Clementi published as early as 1787 in his London collection of *Musical Characteristics*. His motives were commercial ones, and in this respect bore witness to the popularity of Mozart's piano compositions. We must say of Clementi that he avoided unambiguous quotations: what he offered was a brief juxtaposition of commonplace, hackneyed phrases which could be associated with certain of Mozart's piano pieces (K. 414, K. 415, K. 485, etc.). But Clementi never so much as tried to do what was crucial, that is, to work on these phrases, to process them as Mozart would have done, to grasp their formal implications.

And what do we make of the reproach levelled against Süssmayr, that he 'cursed his true teacher, Mozart, yet copied from him'? And what about the praise given to Peter von Winter's opera *Fratelli rivali*, that it 'bears the tender impression of Mozart's spirit'? To claim that, say, the Slovenian composer Johann Baptist Novak should have written his *Figaro* (1790) under the influence of Mozart's example, or that Mozart's *Figaro* should have stood godfather to the first Polish popular opera, Jan Stefan's *The Cracovians and the Mountain People*, are rather unsubtle assertions.

It is difficult to express in words what we actually mean when we talk about an atmosphere favourable to Mozart reception. Contemporary formulations and the abstract nature of how they come down to us have something deceptively certain about them. We thus read in letters, documents and reports of the 1790s many flattering comments about 'the great Mozart' and his work. Let us take just one example to illustrate this. An 'Imperial and Royal Bohemian-Austrian Agent of the Court', one Augustinus Erasmus Donath, writes the following in a report about Emanuel Aloys Förster: 'With reference to his work upon the piano forte, the great master Mozard [*sic*] often provided him with the public testimonial that the latter was, after him, Mozard, the strongest and most accomplished master. Furthermore, let all musicians do justice to him and let him know that Emanuel Förster Esq. should always be placed between Haydn and Mozard in composition setting.' Is Förster then of equal rank with Haydn and Mozart, a genius who has been unfairly neglected? When Donath wrote this report Mozart had just died and Förster had applied to succeed him in the post of court musician. Donath boosted Förster's reputation with this comparison: he referred to Mozart's personal judgement, to the objective 'all musicians' and showed suitable piety in his praise of Mozart. Yet because he was supporting Förster's application his big words have something threadbare about them. When Johann Albrechtsberger in a similar situation praised Joseph von Eybler as 'the greatest genius since Mozart' the same question marks are appropriate. And when in the *Musikalische Korrespondenz* of Speyer (30 November 1790) the string quartet K. 499 and the piano quartet K. 493 are on offer, and we read of the 'fire of imagination, of precision', of the 'fame of one of the greatest musicians in Germany', we hear very clearly the interests of the publisher Hoffmeister and only vaguely any appreciation of Mozart's difficult string quartets. We find the same in Artaria's announcement in the *Wiener Zeitung* of 7 January 1792, where 'the quartets which were recently received with such acclaim [i.e. K. 575, K. 589, K. 590] . . . are still available'.

The fact that a literature on Mozart was gradually increasing is in itself an indication of the interest which he was arousing. But with these utterances we have before us a by no means conceptual condensation of the reality of Mozart's influence but rather one particular reality, a literary one. Mozart starts to play a role in aesthetic discussion, in north Germany especially, but scarcely in Vienna. And as with Beethoven's last work a few decades later – it was not primarily a question of finding an adequate understanding of it, but above all of finding access to it.

The fashionable 'haze of Enlightenment' that in the 1780s and 1790s extensively enveloped the citizens in literary criticism and visions of the future should not deceive us as to its inconsistencies. Although the enlightened aims of the German *Singspiel* were very favourable to Mozart's reputation we should by no means overlook the fact that the success of his operas threatened to burst the idea of the form itself. One example of the irritation felt at *Die Zauberflöte* is given by the Hamburger Johann Friedrich Schink in the *Dramatische Monaten*: 'Our musical taste has grown more sophisticated. In opera we are no longer interested in such things as common sense. We are bored by the light simplicity of Hiller's song, we need cavortings and the leaps of tightrope walkers.' Schink noticed that there had been a change, and we hear again the old objection to Mozart's operatic music, namely, that it was contrived and difficult. The same mode of thinking – this time in a sharper formulation – is found in *Teutschlands Annalen des Jahres 1794*. Starting out from the existence of a Mozart craze the anonymous author turns to stern criticism which actually contains nothing new: Mozart, we read, was certainly gifted but was still in his 'years of ferment': he had written symphonies which had much 'fire, pomp and radiance', but in comparison with Haydn's they were lacking in 'simplicity . . . clarity and definition'; the vocal works had 'far more weaknesses', they were unnatural, a 'badly seasoned sustenance'.

There are no fixed topoi in the writings of the apologists: they look for appropriate words but find that the natural apologia is in Mozart himself. Schink not only criticized Mozart but published in his *Hamburgische Theaterzeitung* (7 July 1792) a complimentary report about the *Singspiel*-like setting of *Figaro* and the 'spirit of delight and levity' that was found in his music. Carl Spazier, writing in the *Musikalisches Wochenblatt* (Berlin, 25(?) February 1792) detected in Wranitzky's *Oberon* a 'contrived affected fullness' which he contrasted with the 'genuine, original unartificial wealth of ideas' which he found in Mozart. In another place (the Berlin *Musikalische Monatsschrift* of November 1792), Spazier speaks of Mozart's *Don Juan* as a work 'where there are single arias which have more inner value than whole operas by Paisiello'. In the same publication an anonymous writer finds that such extravagant praise of *Don Juan* is 'highly exaggerated and one-sided' and is of the opinion that an expert would find Mozart to be 'neither a correct, far less an accomplished, artist'. An isolated case is the Prague obituary (in the *Oberpostamts-Zeitung* of 17 December 1791) which was probably the first account to classify him as a Classic: the common reproach that Mozart was 'too rich in ideas' is here taken up and skilfully turned into its opposite:

Everything that he wrote bears the clear stamp of Classical beauty. That is why he pleases more and more each time, because one beauty develops from another; that is why he will always please us, because he will always appear new to us, and these are the advantages of a Classic. Do his operas not prove this? And do we not hear them for the eightieth time with the same pleasure as we did for the first?

Such controversial partisanship in musical and aesthetic journals scarcely reaches beyond the level of the *bon mot*. In spite of this the reproaches which were uttered demonstrate an extremely shallow concept of 'common sense'. But Mozart's music, even in a work like *Die Zauberflöte* which is supported by so many of the ideas of the Enlightenment, transcends any simplistic affirmation, whether it be of the Enlightenment or not, because of the profusion of its ideas and a liveliness which, working from within, upsets the traditional portrayal of emotion. Behind a divertingly packaged didacticism Mozart reaches, through his music, an illusion of spontaneity and, at a deeper level, an effect which, in the spirit of the Enlightenment, dissolves all prejudices. The discrepancy between this element of aesthetic freedom and a phraseology which was associated with the Enlightenment and which, in its turn, had been reduced to a prejudice, was not considered in the Mozart literature prior to 1800. It was the other discrepancy that arose, namely, that those ideas which, with hindsight, seem suitable in an attempt to grasp the essence of Mozart's art have been formulated with no express reference to his work.

The discrepancy is moderated only in the aesthetic ideas of Christian Gottfried Körner. This Leipzig patrician and academically qualified lawyer, a much-talented man concerned to further and support the aesthetic aims of his life-long friend Friedrich Schiller, could well have got to know Mozart personally at the house of his sister-in-law, Dora Stock, who made the famous silverpoint drawing of the composer. In any case, he saw in Mozart a leading musician, and he granted him (in a letter to Schiller) a special status where universality of expression is concerned: 'The names of Gluck, Haydn,

43

Mozart and Bach will always remain honourable. But the character of German music shows more dignity than charm: perhaps Mozart was the only one who was great in the comic as well as the tragic modes.' In his essay written on Schiller's instigation for the *Horen*, 'Concerning the representation of character in music', he does not mention Mozart, but must have included him in the views expressed. Körner envisages a musical ideal which lay in a higher mean somewhere between the Baroque portrayal of emotion with its uniformity and the 'incoherent tangle of passions' found in the music of the *Sturm und Drang*. He postulates, in succinct concepts, a 'character' for instrumental music which would not consist of uniformity but a 'unity in variety'. Here Körner introduces an early starting point for a classical aesthetic of music in his essay, which would never have been formulated without Schiller's great essays on aesthetics, written between 1793 and 1795.

Schiller never wrote in great detail on music as an artistic form, but he *did* write some very remarkable things on it. His views are expressed most radically in the letters entitled *Über die ästhetische Erziehung des Menschen*. In the twenty-second letter he rejects the preoccupation with 'individual effects' and postulates the following: 'The more general the mood and the less limited the direction . . . the more notable is the genre . . .' It was the underlying relationship between the arts which prepared the way. Here Schiller, however, when talking about music, reaches a pronouncement which sounds almost classical: 'In its highest fulfilment music must reach *form* and exert its power on us with the tranquil power of antiquity.' He names no examples, but we most readily think of the contemporary cultivation of Handel, of the operas of Gluck and of Mozart's *La Clemenza di Tito* or the *Requiem*.

But Schiller goes still further, turns against the limitations imposed by 'the specific character of artistic genres' and even sees in that genre which was so important for him – tragedy – 'no absolutely free category', as it has as its aim the expression of the emotive. We seem to read here an absolutely striking description of Mozart's music drama (which of course it is not) when he writes: 'The most frivolous object must be treated in such a way that we feel like moving from the same to the starkest earnestness.' At the most extreme point of this train of thought we read the sentence: 'The content, no matter how sublime and universal it may be, always has a limiting effect on the spirit, and only from the *form* may we expect true aesthetic freedom.' The consequence of such a view, when referring to music, seems to have as its goal an absolute music, with a Classical emphasis. Even that proximity of all the arts which was, in principle, sought with a transcendence in mind, has much in common with the Romantic concept of the 'Poetic' which was formulated later; but the idea of a '*Gestalt*', and above all the goal of 'aesthetic freedom', in the sense of the 'inviolability' of the spectator or listener, are no longer reconcilable with the 'endless yearning' of the Romantics. The simple reason why we are mentioning such ideas is the fact that, in the 1790s, and before the separate development of Classicism and Romanticism, there was an enhancement, a revaluation of the status of music above its social function which provided a pattern that enables the listener to tackle Mozart's instrumental music from its 'difficult' side. This model turned against the older conception of music as a mere diversion (Sulzer, for example, sees instrumental music as a 'charming and pleasing tittle tattle which does not occupy the heart'), but also against the bourgeois notion of a moralizing, emotive aesthetic.

Let us not be misunderstood here: the concentration of this train of thought has nothing to do with Mozart, and Schiller's musical interests are more concerned with the vocal rather than the instrumental; as far as opera was concerned he spoke with enthusiasm only about the works of Gluck, particularly his *Iphigenie auf Tauris*. In the correspondence with Goethe on generic boundaries Schiller makes a reference (on 29 December 1797) to 'a certain confidence *vis à vis* opera'. He was once more concerned, he writes, to link the mode of tragedy as closely as possible to the postulate of 'aesthetic freedom' – and here he accords music a special position. 'Through the power of music and through a freer harmonic stimulation of the senses, opera tunes the soul to a higher level of conception; in pathos, in emotionalism itself, a freer play is found because music accompanies it, and the element of the marvellous which is tolerated in this genre must necessarily make us more indifferent to the subject matter.' Schiller was certainly thinking of Gluck – but here is Goethe's reply (30 December): 'The hope which you had of opera you would have seen fulfilled in a higher measure recently in *Don Juan*; yet this piece stands there quite isolated, and Mozart's death has frustrated any prospect of something similar.' Schiller's letter of 2 January 1798, however, makes no reference to Goethe's pointed allusion to Mozart.

What becomes apparent here is not only a difference in musical taste between Goethe and Schiller but the strange fact that Schiller's aesthetic opinions, to which Goethe expressly reacted, led to a combination with very differing paradigms. No sooner has Schiller moved, in his reflections, in the direction of concrete entities than music is seen in relation to tragedy, and opera is considered tragic, possessing the traditional features of *opera seria* (the reference to the 'marvellous'): a charitable interpretation might see it as *eroico comico*. Thus his Classicistic theory of drama touches upon that tendency towards the 'sublime' that we find also in the realm of music in the 1790s.

This appeared as we have already seen in the wave of oratorios, also in opera and in symphonic music. We see various characteristics in Mozart's operas which support this: on the one hand we get those aspects which are fondly considered 'under Gluck's influence' (especially in *Idomeneo*, and also in the simple emotionalism of chorus and marches, particularly in *Die Zauberflöte*), and on the other, the earnest and expressive reference to an older tradition (we have an extreme example of this in the 'Men in Armour' scene in *Die Zauberflöte*). Seen from this point of view, Mozart's last opera, *La Clemenza di Tito*, was no aberration, neither was it an anachronistic relapse, but this *opera seria* (and *Idomeneo*, to a lesser extent) could be seen as being progressive in the sense of being part of an up-to-date Classicism in opera. The printings and the data concerning performances bear this out; Constanze Mozart's feelings about this, around 1795, were the right ones, and Mozart himself contributed to it in the last years of his life. An anonymous report from Prague, written for the *Allgemeines Europäisches Journal* of 1794, has some very pertinent things to say about Mozart and about *La Clemenza di Tito*: 'A certain Greek simplicity, a still sublimity suffuses the music, and the heart is touched so gently, but all the more intensely ... in short, Gluck's sublimity is here combined with Mozart's originality, his flowing emotion and his rapturous harmony.' Our author, dazzled by an ideal, finally claims: 'Experts are in doubt whether or not *La Clemenza di Tito* might even be greater than *Don Giovanni*' – an evaluation that strikes us today, after two hundred years of Mozart study, as almost absurd.

The history of theatre production would supply a clear picture of this intellectual change of emphasis. Even if we do not have much in the way of illustrated material for Mozart's operas from the eighteenth century then at least certain prominent stages in the development are recognizable. *Figaro, Don Giovanni* and *Così fan tutte* were performed in a contemporary setting in Mozart's lifetime, that is, in a fairly plain *Louis-Seize* style. No authentic pictures remain of the decorations and costumes of the first performance of *Die Zauberflöte* or of *La Clemenza di Tito*: it is uncertain whether the copperplate engravings of *Die Zauberflöte* by Josef and Peter Schaffer of the year 1795 were based on the first performance. Pamina and Tamino appear in contemporary dress; Sarastro and his followers, in the first finale, have costumes that look as though they had come from one of the Turkish operas; the priests' architecture is classical. Older copperplate figurines for the Leipzig production of 1793 correspond in their simplicity to the *Singspiel* conventions.

But in 1793 Joseph Quaglio produced a very elaborately decorated *Die Zauberflöte* in Munich, filling the Baroque stage with a Classicistic and

Egyptian-like background (obelisks, and so on). Iffland's production in the Mannheim National Theatre on 29 March 1794 (its first performance there) created a sensation by its cost; Iffland used the three-act *Singspiel* version by Vulpius. The figurines of Franz Karl Wolff which were illustrated in the *Rheinischer Merkur* (1794 and 1795) show that the tone was decidedly Classical: Sarastro wears no beard, and appears in a tunic adorned with hieroglyphics; Tamino appears as a Roman youth with sandals and a tunic whose hem is embroidered with a meander-pattern. A famous climax to this Roman, monumental style of production is found in the Frankfurt *La Clemenza di Tito* of 1799 with décor and costumes by Giorgio Fuentes of Milan. It is significant that Schikaneder also fell in with this style of production with his new Viennese production of *Die Zauberflöte* in 1798 with magnificent decorations by Vincenzo Sacchetti. The desire for unadorned greatness, clarifying and sublimating the fashionable antique grandeur of the times, is seen in a sketch which has been preserved of the appearance of the Queen of the Night which Lorenzo Sacchetti probably drew for a production of *Die Zauberflöte* in the Viennese Kärntnertortheater in 1801.

As a theatre director, Goethe represented another tendency: his interests in the realm of music-theatre were in the 1780s primarily directed towards the *Singspiel*. A Mozart experience (*Die Entführung*) in 1791 radically altered his views and led to some characteristic consequences in his cooperation with the Berlin composer Johann Friedrich Reichardt. As a person and as an educated and many-sided man, Reichardt stood closer to Goethe than any other musician. He was a fervent admirer of Handel, respected Gluck, whom he had met in Vienna, for the 'noble simplicity' of his earnest operas and despised Mozart for a long time, reproaching him for his 'slavish imitation of Italian, conventional forms' and his 'blending of disparate characters and styles'.

Reichardt particularly disapproved of *La Clemenza di Tito* and the *Messiah* arrangement, which appeared in print in 1802; he assumed the classical stance which was close to Schiller's musical taste but which led to differences of opinion with Goethe. For the *Singspiel* which he and Reichardt planned together, *Claudine von Villa Bella*, Goethe (by exhorting himself) indirectly encouraged Reichardt to 'give up all poetic inhibitions after the noble manner of the Italians'. At the Weimar production of 1795 (it had already been given in Berlin in 1789) Goethe was inwardly disappointed. It was only much later that he did indeed refer to his objections to the 'excellent' Reichardt: 'The instrumentation, more suited to the taste of an earlier time, is a little weak.' In spotting a weakness in Reichardt's music Goethe was taking his measure from Mozart.

47

Goethe's Weimar theatre is at the furthest possible remove from the sensational and magnificent productions of the times. His theatre is modest, for economic reasons as well as from a deep conviction. An amusing account of the weaknesses and shortcomings of a provincial stage is given by the singer Caroline Jagemann in her memoirs of the Weimar *Die Zauberflöte* productions of January 1794:

> Whereas the three angelic boys in Mannheim's *Die Zauberflöte* (as in all other theatres) were sung by pretty girls in pretty costumes, here in Weimar they used three lads from the seminary, clumsy peasant boys wearing brick-red cotton jerseys with sleeves so wide that they looked like great flaps of skin, also tunics which were not exactly clean and neither short enough to hint at a Greek costume nor long enough to conceal their dirty boots; their unkempt mops were adorned with crude wreaths painted in a uniform red which denoted roses, and their cheeks were daubed in purple and looked like Easter-eggs. But no pen can describe their acting: they held their palm-leaves stuck in front of them like sceptres and sometimes beat time with them.

Goethe chose Baroque costumes not only for reasons of economy and the desire to reuse what was already on hand, but to demonstrate his awareness of the tradition to which he felt *Die Zauberflöte* belonged. This theory of Goethe's 'Baroque subconsciousness' which breaks forth in *Faust II*, and the role which *Die Zauberflöte Part Two* plays in this supposed predisposition has triggered off in German studies an eloquent head-on conflict between rejection and acceptance.

Did Weimar have anything to do with Vienna? Is Goethe's fragment simply one of many peripheral works or is it an important beginning for a new dimension of the genre? From a superficial point of view it could be claimed that Goethe was cashing in on the popularity of *Die Zauberflöte*, or on the fame of its dramatic line-up; his intention (which certainly seems alien to posterity) to let a musician named Paul Wranitzky set the libretto to music fits in with current attitudes, the attitudes of a theatrical practician. This collaboration would certainly have taken place if the negotiations had not foundered on Goethe's excessive demand for a fee of 100 ducats. We can only speculate on what ulterior motives he may have had at the back of his mind. But if we are to bestow a heightened significance on Goethe's *Die Zauberflöte* fragment we must also accord Goethe a deeper insight into Mozart's music, for this insight, to use Hofmannsthal's words, had the effect that Goethe – in contrast to Schikaneder – gave the material of *Die Zauberflöte* nobility and depth.

Hans Georg Gadamer, Arthur Henkel and also Walter Weiss see the kernel of Goethe's conception in an utterance of Pamina's which occurs in a repetition of the fire and water trial (Pamina and Tamino are passing through fire and water to their child who has been imprisoned in a cavern): 'And human love and human power/Are greater still than wizardry.' Goethe here, without doubt, is emphasizing a 'moral, human characteristic' that overcomes trust in the flute's magic power: this is a fundamental belief of the Enlightenment which does not appear at the appropriate place in Schikaneder's libretto but which received an echo in the fact that Pamina and Tamino do pass the final test united in their love. Mozart's music expresses this decisively. It does not express the journey through fire and water in the usually blaring music of storm and tempest, neither is it simply the charm of the flute's sweet tone which conquers the elements; Mozart shapes the flute's march into a kind of improvisation (a motif which we have already heard in Pamina's invitation 'Play thou the flute, it leads us on a dreadful path', is seized by Tamino who dissolves it into a sequence of ever smaller units). Pamina's trust in the magic of the flute is combined in a musical symbol with Tamino's spontaneous action. And it is precisely this musical aspect which is to be seen as the starting point of Goethe's change of emphasis from magical to human.

Goethe was certainly the first of the leading intellectual personages of Europe to have grasped the essential nature of Mozart's music, even though his Mozart experience was more concealed, separate from the idea of music he had found represented by Zelter and Reichardt. That opera which had triggered off significant reverberations in Goethe was regarded by most of his contemporaries as a naïve work, 'as that which it is, namely a pretty peepshow, a ragout of sense and nonsense, spiced by charming music and precious decoration'. To reduce it to the simplest common denominator – what is unusual in Goethe's attitude is that he did not simply see Mozart as representing the 'sublime', but neither did he relegate him to the position of outsider.

In any case, in the 1790s neither Mozart's operas nor those works which could be grouped with the new oratorios were unreservedly compatible with the category of 'the sublime'. It was most difficult of all to reach a corresponding understanding of the symphonies, basically because their circulation was inadequate. When, in the *Allgemeine Musikalische Zeitung* (Leipzig, 1801) Carl Philipp Emanuel Bach is hailed as a second Klopstock; when Ludwig Tieck deals with the Macbeth overture of his brother-in-law

Reichardt; when, somewhat earlier, Schubart praises the 'symphonic homogeneity' of the symphonies of Christian Cannabich and never mentions Mozart or Haydn – then this points to a variety of things, among them not only the persistence of the head-on conflict in musical taste and a discrepancy between idea and object, but also the doubtfulness of those stylistic concerns which are circulating today, as a search for a sublimity in orchestral music which borrows its categories from Kant or Klopstock will find itself confirmed more readily in music which is assigned to the *Sturm und Drang*.

It certainly comes as no surprise that vocal music lent itself to sharper definition than instrumental music which had no text or scenery to assist the understanding and whose content was less familiar. Körner's intellectual approach should be appreciated all the more here. But the actual prerequisite for an adequate connection between idea and object was the awareness which became increasingly strong of the extraordinary quality of the music of Haydn and Mozart. We see how this began to alter existing positions in Christian Friedrich Daniel Schubart's essay *Ideen zu einer Ästhetik der Tonkunst*, written probably in 1784–5; the work was published only after his death in 1791. There is practically no reference to Mozart in the detailed accounts of the music of his day: the editor, Ludwig Schubart, finds it necessary to excuse the fact that 'the great epoch which the immortal Mozart has brought forth in the music of our day' remained unexplored. But we do meet a change of emphasis in the original text in certain later corrections: the entry on Haydn begins with the sentence: 'A musician of great genius who recently, with Mozart, has written epoch-making music.' We also read the following, a comment on the unsatisfactory use of trombones: 'Mozart has also helped us here – since his work most of the new operas do use trombones.'

Another example, and a much clearer one, is found in the composer Heinrich Christoph Koch who was also probably the most important music theorist of his age. Born seven years before Mozart and somewhat traditional in his outlook, Koch nevertheless reacted strongly to the change in instrumental music. In his *Musikalisches Lexikon* (1801) he finishes the article on the divertimento with the comment: 'For a while now it has had to give way somehow to the quartet and the quintet after these sonata forms have been so worked and perfected by Haydn and Mozart.' Far more significant is a remark by Koch in his *Versuch einer Anleitung zur Composition* (1793). When explaining the different genres Koch, wherever possible, took quotes from Sulzer's *Allgemeine Theorie der schönen Künste*, a source which was not exactly modern. In the section 'On the Quatuor' Koch came to discuss the most recent developments in this musical form and mentioned the great popularity of Haydn, Pleyel and Hoffmeister but finally praised Mozart above all, whose quartets 'amongst all the modern four-voice sonatas correspond most nearly to the actual form of the quartet and whose music is unique because of its remarkable fusion of *legato* and free styles and in its treatment of harmony'.

Unfortunately without going into detail, Koch gives a positive and exemplary portrayal of those string quartets dedicated to Haydn, those which had been most severely criticized up till then. Koch therefore was able, and indeed very early, to explain the alien quality of Mozart's instrumental music as a structural phenomenon; Heinrich Bossler anticipated him somewhat by explaining, in 1790, that the quintet K. 593 had been written 'according to the strict rules of composition' and singling out the minuet in the quartet K. 589, with its complex contrapuntal structure, for high praise.

Koch begins his discussion of the 'Quatuor' with the comment that 'it is at present the favourite of small musical groups', implying, although not saying, that the interest in this form had shifted to the more complicated chamber music. The appropriate works by Haydn and by Mozart were widely circulating, thus justifying Koch's observation. In other words – a process was underway and needed explanation. One aspect that we should not underestimate is the enormous spread of Mozart arrangements: these contributed in no uncertain manner. There were 'external' reasons – the way music was marketed, the rise of the middle classes, and so on; fashion also played its part, and the success of *Die Zauberflöte* had shown the way. The Viennese publisher Artaria and Johann Julius Hummel in Berlin had brought on to the market, in 1792, arrangements of this opera for flute, and a mass of arrangements for all manner of instruments soon followed. Other Mozart operas shared in the success; it goes without saying that adaptations for family music were well underway, particularly with the obvious 'hits'. In many places the arrangements met with approval before the operas themselves had been performed locally; in the case of arrangements of overtures for piano, *Die Zauberflöte* and *Don Giovanni* were not preferred to actual opera performances and the piano reductions, whereas they were in the case of *Così fan tutte, La Clemenza di Tito* and *Figaro*.

These symptoms betray a tendency to uncouple the music from the opera, and Mozart's successes in the field of opera led indirectly to an interest in his instrumental works. And so even before 1800 the ground is being prepared for an understanding of the esoteric idea of absolute music, and this from a low point in Mozart reception, so to speak. We may seek reasons for this assumption, but it had a tangible background and led to definite results: Friedrich Rochlitz, for example, arrived at a train of thought in an essay which appeared in 1801, a train of thought which led to the rejection of imitation in music by claiming that the vocal parts in music 'were simply means to a general purpose – were instruments'. We have here the concept of 'pure music' and a defence of the musicality of operatic scenes, for the 'uninterruptedly flowing music', by and through itself, served the idea of the whole. And Arthur Schopenhauer, an extreme advocate of abstract music, did not see his ideal confirmed in string quartets, as we might think, or in symphonies, but in operatic music, where music transcends its function as regards text and drama. The actual reason for this curious idea lies in the philosopher's own music-making: like numerous other dilettanti of the early nineteenth century, Schopenhauer as a flautist occupied himself by preference with the opera music of Mozart and, later, Rossini. He identified music with the ideal, and sought long to fathom its essence – but he did so by using 'mere' arrangements.

Had the personality of Mozart not been forgotten for the moment because of the great success of the work? His memory was much honoured, but the image of the person remained pale. Were memories not suppressed? Yet psychological probing, given the paucity of our information, would give an all-too-simple judgement. But however it was – it is incomprehensible that (to give just one irritating example) it was only after the reproachful report of an Englishman travelling through Europe, a report printed (in 1799) in Christoph Martin Wieland's *Neuer teutscher Merkur* about Mozart's unknown grave in Vienna, that his widow, with Nissen and Griesinger, sought in vain to find it.

The first biographers invite criticism simply because their temporal proximity to Mozart teases our curiosity without satisfying it. The first among them is Friedrich Schlichtegroll. He did not go down well with Constanze Mozart, nor with the learned scholars who came after him. Schlichtegroll was no music expert, but a highly esteemed professor, privy counsellor, member of the Academy of Sciences in Munich and extremely well educated – this we see in all that he wrote about Mozart. Between 1791 and 1806 he composed *Obituaries of Remarkable People*; as is usual with such writings Schlichtegroll first wrote a character description, then a life history; what was lacking was the personal contact with the deceased. What interested him in Mozart was something different from what was described in other critical writings: Mozart was, for him, an example of the Enlightenment's idea of a man.

Schlichtegroll is certainly also attracted by the sensational, by the 'memory of those human beings with unusual powers and potentialities for individual accomplishments'; he described 'phenomena which we all admire', 'masterstrokes, *pièces de résistance*', but by and large his various examples led him to what was universally human, to an admiration for 'the limitless compass of the human spirit'. When discussing Mozart, Schlichtegroll admired 'the inexhaustible fecundity of his ideas', the musical universality, the early, rapid development of talents (the word 'magician' is heard already, but without Schlichtegroll's being in any sense aligned with Romanticism).

The subsequent life-history emphasizes Mozart's pre-Vienna stage; this corresponds to the author's interest in 'the miraculous talents and the early development of the same' and the memory (which was still alive) of Mozart's time as a prodigy; we also see the kind of information that Schlichtegroll had at his disposal. Mozart is described as being small, unprepossessing and 'constantly fidgeting'. Schlichtegroll does not, in fact, use the word 'genius', and yet his obituary begins with an endless series of discussions in which Mozart is regarded as an *exemplum classicum* or touchstone for the concept of genius. A gap is said to separate the two halves of Mozart's personality: he was 'early a master in his art', 'in all other circumstances a child', 'at the piano he was a higher being', he was 'a human being who was always distracted, always dallying'. Even if these character-istics came in fact from Nannerl, they do strikingly illuminate the incomprehensible, the boundless aspects of the human greatness of mind which Schlichtegroll strove to visualize. At the same time, the thesis concerning the incompatibility of life and art emerges here, of an artistic existence 'parallel to life', an idea which has become highly topical recently through Wolfgang Hildesheimer.

The only biographer who would have known Mozart personally, and perhaps quite well, was Franz Xaver Niemetschek, a university professor and philanthropist; he was made an honorary citizen of Prague for his social work and, together with his wife, looked after Mozart's family. He may therefore be seen as a far more committed apologist for Mozart's cause. His book, which appeared in Prague in 1798, may be seen as a biography, but was also the first attempt to summarize or recapitulate the reception history of Mozart in the 1790s. The title itself, *Leben des k.k. Kapellmeisters Wolfgang Gottlieb Mozart*, explains the very purpose of the book, a purpose which the author also set forth in his preface, namely, on the basis of enthusiasm for Mozart's music to draw attention to the composer himself. A subtitle further explains that Mozart's life would be portrayed 'from original

53

sources', and at the end he identifies these as personal contact with Mozart's family), the testimonies of witnesses, and information given by Mozart's widow; Schlichtegroll's obituary is acknowledged as a source of information about Mozart's youth.

Yet Niemetschek's book is a disappointing biography. For a start, he chose an anecdotal mode of representation which Friedrich Rochlitz was to continue in his serialized account for the *Allgemeine Musikalische Zeitung* of Leipzig in the same year, 1798, the so-called 'Authenticated Anecdotes from W.G. Mozart's Life', an anticipation, so to speak, of a Biedermeier literary fashion. The 'shadowy messenger' appears, as do gripping pictures of Mozart's presentiment of death: yet Niemetschek also speaks of an 'unexpected death'. His apologia is also bound up with his eulogy for Prague and his praise of German patriotism – interesting, certainly, for any reception history. Niemetschek by no means ignores the difficulties which Mozart suffered in his later Viennese years; he seeks, rather, to account for them in a quite specific manner. According to Niemetschek, 'Mozart did indeed have quite a considerable income, but the financial sources were unreliable and disordered, and because of his wife's frequent confinements, and her protracted illnesses, Mozart, being in a city like Vienna, had to starve.' But it was not his 'fault', 'unless his character was blameworthy, upright and open as it was, and incapable of fawning and sycophancy. But he was only a German.' It was, then, the intrigues of the Italian singers in Vienna who made his life so difficult to bear. 'This craven band of wretched creatures remained in full activity until the early demise of the immortal artist.' And Niemetschek counters the reproach – acknowledged to be justified – that Mozart 'could have known the value of money better' with the quotation from Horace: '*Quid tu? nullane habes vitia?*' and adds the disarming question: 'And are you Mozarts then, in any art?' He thus sought to gloss over the darker sides in Mozart's life to moderate – in contrast to Schlichtegroll – the contrast between art and life.

Niemetschek's description of Mozart's person overlaps with that of Schlichtegroll: he too speaks of an 'unprepossessing appearance' and links this with 'over-exertion from childhood onwards'. We also read: 'But in this unprepossessing body there dwelt an artistic genius which nature only rarely bestows upon its favourites.' This vindicatory use of an artistic maxim seems characteristic for Niemetschek, often appearing and demonstrating a particular intention behind the biography. Niemetschek was concerned above all to understand the Mozart phenomenon, a phenomenon known personally to him; it was not just his bounden duty but a different motivation, and one touching his own creativity.

54

His view of life was exactly the same as Schlichtegroll's. Such sentences as, 'The early development and the rapid maturity of this creative genius call forth the greatest admiration in the student of human nature,' or, 'The student of human nature will not be surprised to see that this rare and unique artist was not such a great man in the other aspects of his life,' adequately confirm this. Five distinctive features of genius are differentiated in the case of Mozart: 'the uniquely rapid course of his development', the 'high degree of perfection', his musical universality, the 'newness and originality of his works' and his 'incomprehensible ease of composition'. Niemetschek's attitude of mind is made transparent when he comes out against the Romantic idea of the artist in the second edition of his book (1808), against the idea, that is, of the 'instinctive nature' of Mozart's talent, by emphasizing the importance of 'education and practice'. As early as 1798 he turned against the reproach that Mozart possessed no higher education by asking the rhetorical question:

Who indeed may define the limits of his own mental faculties so precisely as to be able to assert that Mozart, apart from his art, had no other talents or capabilities? I know that the genius of art is increasingly placed among the lower, or aesthetic faculties of the soul, but we also know that the arts, and particularly music, frequently call for perspicacity, judgement and insight into the nature of things, and this must be assumed in Mozart's case all the more readily as Mozart was no ordinary mechanical virtuoso in one instrument but embraced the whole world of music with a remarkable power and skill.

When discussing this well-defined, enlightened philosophy – enlightened indeed in its repeated praise for the Emperor Joseph II – I would wish to put forward the assertion that Niemetschek succeeded in drawing up a picture of Mozart as a Classic (as an evaluative and a factual judgement) before any of the premises existed for a Romanticizing vision. Prague's favoured position as a bulwark of tradition enabled him to formalize the Classical qualities of Mozart's work all the more easily. In Prague a tradition of staging performances was established early, and this had never been interrupted as it had, say, in Vienna. We cannot test how far the cultivation of original tempi, etc., was preserved there, but we *do* know that many of the singers and musicians who worked with Mozart were still active there, and that despite all the expressions of German patriotism Mozart's Italian operas were performed predominantly in Italian, more so than anywhere else.

Niemetschek started from the current notion that was certainly valid at that time: 'Among all the fine arts it is music which, above all others, is the slave of fashion and ephemeral taste.' In order to overcome this transience, a 'focus of coordination' was necessary, an 'institution' which could cultivate it, and a corresponding 'theory'. Yet Mozart's music, without these preconditions, could transcend transience. 'How much power, and how much Classical substance must lie in Mozart's music if its effect marks an exception to these requirements?' The symphonies, he claimed, were 'true masterpieces of instrumental music . . . full of surprising transitions and possessing such a swift, fiery pace that they excite our expectation for something sublime.' The 'beauty' of Mozart's music increases the more frequently we listen, and this is the 'test for Classical worth'. He continues: 'Who can express in words that which is new, original, captivating, sublime, and resonant in his music?'

Niemetschek finds the elements of the 'new' in the Mozartian syntheses, the 'original' is seen in Mozart's 'economy linked with appropriate extravagance'. In *La Clemenza di Tito* he admired the 'fusion of the highest compositional art with charm and grace'; he also saw how, in general, 'the greatest multiplicity was combined with the strictest simplicity'. In the vocal music 'the purest expression of sensitivity was paired with the individualism of the person and his situation'. He sees the reasons for Mozart's operatic successes in his 'sure and refined ability to gauge exactly each character's personality, situation and sensitivity: *reddere convenientia cuique*'. In Niemetschek's vocabulary, attitudes and intentions Mozart, as the details quoted have shown, is hailed as nothing less than a paradigm for what is known as Classicism in a musico-aesthetic sense. I surmise, incidentally, that Niemetschek was the author of the anonymous obituary which appeared in the *Prager Oberpostamts-Zeitung* of 1791 and also of other reports in Prague in which the 'Classical' element is emphasized in Mozart's music.

But it is not only biographies that give information on the various attitudes to Mozart's personality. The fact that commemorative compositions and memorial services were by no means absent in the late 1790s – indeed, they increased in their geographical distribution – points to a slowly developing Mozart cult. Especially interesting is the text of Carl Cannabich's cantata *Mozarts Gedächtnisfeyer* (1797), and for three reasons: firstly, the topos of the 'peak and crisis of life's trajectory', a theme very popular since the murder of Johann J. Winckelmann, here receiving drastic presentation. Secondly, the mixture of emotion in Mozart's music (which hitherto had been regarded as problematic) is now singled out for praise: 'It is, alas, only too true/That he alone perceived the way/To combine with mild gravity/The happiness of fancies gay.' A musical quotation from the

Pamina/Papageno duet from *Die Zauberflöte* ('Man and wife . . .') was here appended. This line must have been quite well known, for it was the inscription on a bust of Mozart which we find engraved on a copper print of the early nineteenth century. The work finally assumes the unmistakable character of a prayer (in the form of an accompanying recitative): 'Oh thou who art free of bonds/Dissolved in harmony/And hovering in an aether pure/Inspire, if us thou hearst/Our hearts and spirits joined!' The obvious tendency which we meet in memorial works, that is, the tendency to elevate consecration into an aesthetic religiosity, points forward into the nineteenth century.

The first statues also point forward to a practice that was to come. In 1792 Mozart's Masonic brother, the music-dealer Franz Deyerkauf, erected the first Mozart monument, in Graz. He had it built in his garden as a personal memorial (and perhaps also as a form of 'temple of friendship', similar to those already built by Frederick the Great in the park at Sanssouci), not suspecting that he was here anticipating the cult of the hero. In 1799 the Weimar *Journal des Luxus und der Moden* and shortly after the *Allgemeine Musikalische Zeitung* of Leipzig reported that a Mozart statue, worked by the royal court sculptor Klauer, had been erected 'by Wieland's *Olympia* in the park at Tiefurt near Weimar'. Mozart was honoured as an opera-composer with a lyre, the masks of comedy and tragedy and references to both *Die Entführung* and *La Clemenza di Tito*. Symbolic, however, for the refusal to bestow eternal status on Mozart was the fact that the statue was made of clay, and obviously did not last long. A few decades later it was recast in more permanent material.

The memory of Mozart now also came to be associated with significant dates. A silver coin (designed by Carl Emanuel Baerend) was struck to commemorate the fifth anniversary of his death (1796). More commemorative coins, less valuable, began to circulate as the celebrations became more extensive. Yet it says much for the taste of the age that this, the first devotional object relating to Mozart to be duplicated, is a miniature made of precious metal.

II

1800–1830

Mozart in the age of German Classicism and Romanticism; Mozart and *l'Empire*; Mozart's operas and the craze for Rossini; fame in Europe following fame in Germany – these are the different facets of the prevailing image of Mozart in the first third of the nineteenth century. But these key words do not give a chronological sequence; their succinctness can only be partly justified, and there are great divergences between them. Yet the picture that we do have is not a diffuse one: a clear trajectory may be discerned. Mozart's posthumous success was stabilized in Germany around the year 1800, and many aspects of his work were gaining an international reputation. A naïve enthusiasm for Mozart was giving way to a more intellectual reaction: Mozart had become an ideal, an ideal which played a role in the artistic and ideological endeavours of the day. His musical style was much emulated, yet at the same time the more modern techniques in composition parted company with him, those techniques which, around 1830, excited musical interest more than he or his contemporaries did. That aesthetic change of direction around 1830, the end of the age of Goethe, of Viennese Classicism and of Romanticism in the strict sense of the term means that the vitality of his music had become problematic; a polarized partisanship was to follow.

In the year 1800 Friedrich Rochlitz replied to an anonymous reviewer in the *Allgemeine Musikalische Zeitung* of Leipzig who had claimed that 'in *Don Juan* we find the most sublime and the tenderest melodies' by asserting that Mozart's greatest achievements lay 'in the higher forms of instrumental music, above all in quartets and concertos, and not in opera; a form in which – at least abroad – he finds not a few opponents, and perhaps always will'. It may simply here be a case of contradictory aesthetic views which tend towards exaggeration, but Rochlitz's argument does succinctly mirror the state of Mozart reception. In the same year, 1800, this journal published a comprehensive review of the first volumes of Mozart's *Oeuvres complettes*, brought out by Breitkopf & Härtel. In 1801 it printed a call for the foundation of a 'Society for the Promotion of Music' under whose aims the following (third) point was made: 'That a canonic standing be awarded to the musical ideas of the best musicians of all ages and peoples, and that this status be elevated to a rule for instruction of all practising musicians.' These three newspaper cuttings have something fundamental in common: they outline what is meant by the definition of Mozart's fame. Higher instrumental music, and opera – these very genres in which Mozart was exposed to the sharpest criticism – are now accorded the rank of greatness; the question of priority was open to discussion. The complete edition of Mozart's works is a visible witness to a 'canonic standing' for music after the model of literature: this canonization referred specifically to the work of Haydn and Mozart and placed this *oeuvre*, in a somewhat ahistorical manner, alongside the work of Handel and Bach. This process may be called modern to the extent that it ran parallel to the reorientation of the literary canon, moving from the authors of antiquity to those of more modern times; the historical dimension of music here approached that of literature. And the conceptual parallel between Viennese Classicism and Weimar Classicism has its justification here (although other factors also play a part).

The idea of bringing out an edition of Mozart's work stemmed from the little known Brunswick publisher Johann Peter Spehr who advertised a 'Collection complette' at the Leipzig Easter fair of 1797. Spehr put the Leipzig firm of Breitkopf & Härtel in a tight spot here. But even if his edition was started earlier, the Breitkopf edition was the one which was the most highly esteemed and a publishing event on the heels of which followed other *Oeuvres complettes* (of Mozart, Haydn, Clementi, Dussek, etc.). None of them were 'complete', but it was Breitkopf's Mozart edition which reached the greatest degree of comprehensiveness. The juvenilia was largely ignored: the public's interest was focused on the works of the Viennese period. This was the characteristic pattern which lasted for a very long time, without interruption; old predilections, however, dating from Mozart's time, remained in evidence. Breitkopf first of all gave preference to works for solo piano and piano concertos, then sonatas for violin and piano, and songs; a series of string quartets and the printed musical score of *Don Giovanni* reflected the new tastes of the time. Other editions of Mozart's work, such as those of the Viennese publishers Steiner, Haslinger and the *Magazin de l'imprimerie chymique*, of Simrock in Berlin and Pleyel in Paris, restricted themselves by and large to piano and to chamber music. But the instrumental parts of the late symphonies, of the most important wind concertos and also of many works belonging to the older genres, such as divertimento, serenade, cassation and so on, were available by about 1810. The Mozart scholar Alexander Hyatt King calculated that soon after 1820 about two-thirds of Mozart's entire *oeuvre* was on offer by a flourishing music trade at home and abroad.

We may dispense with a detailed description of the publishing statistics. The mass of prints and copies was enormous and, in contrast to the practice of the late eighteenth century, there is a fundamental difference: those publishers who gave a powerful boost to the dissemination of Mozart's work each followed particular aims which became lost in the eager production of pieces which were for the most part already popular. Even the Offenbach publisher André who had been a most commendable sponsor and enthusiast fell in line with this and only published a few 'new' works from the Mozart manuscripts which he had obtained. Only the *Oeuvres complettes* and valuable bibliophile editions were able to introduce additional perspectives; the *Don Giovanni* score which we have already mentioned is relevant here, as is that curiosity which appeared from André in 1829 – a print of the overture to *Die Zauberflöte* 'which accords exactly with the composer's manuscript as he sketched, instrumented and completed it'.

Even if the numbers given by Hyatt King could well be expanded – and indeed considerably – they do at least give us some insight. For the period 1792 to 1830 Hyatt King lists 121 publishers who were turning out Mozart's work: 34 in 19 German cities, 14 in Vienna, 37 in Paris, 23 in London, 2 each in Edinburgh, Liverpool and Manchester, 4 in Prague, 3 in Amsterdam and 1 each in Copenhagen and Milan.

It is not an exaggeration to say that Mozart's music was ubiquitous in all sorts of arrangements. The extent and the complexity of this trade in Mozart's music could easily be documented by lists spread over pages, but it would be difficult to get a representative let alone comprehensive picture. A good illustration, however, of the extent of this tendency is provided by a joke announcement of an imaginary Viennese 'Musical Arrangement Institution' which appeared in the *Berlinische Musikalische Zeitung* of 1806. I shall give extracts here (even if Mozart's name is accidentally missing):

At Veitl's shop in Vienna, Steigbahn no.1703, the following may be obtained for the first time –

a. Hiller's *Hunt*, arranged for seven flutes and six horns: 2 florins

b. The *Madcap* by Méhul, for four trombones and an obbligato Turkish drum: 2 florins *c.* Cherubini's *Water-Carrier*, for guitar and bass-bassoon: 4 florins

d. Kauer's *Maid of the Danube*, quintet for three piccolos, flutes, and Jew's harp and two sets of double-drums: 2 florins seven crowns.
We will also be glad to take in orders for excerpts from operas and oratorios for as many instruments as one may wish to have; new instruments may also, if desired, be invented, and the jockeys trained on the spot.

The attitudes of the recipients of this kind of music were indeed varied in their expectations; the inventor of the joke advertisement obviously wanted to poke fun at the fashionable and rather shallow desire for unusual and incompatible instruments. The flute, a favourite instrument of the time, was most prevalent: Jean Paul, in his *Flegeljahre* (1804/5), was probably inspired by arrangements for the flute to wing his imagination heavenwards in a Romantic flight of fancy: 'Dearly I love the flute, the magic wand which transfigures our inner world when touching it: a divining rod which opens up the inner depths.'

Mozart's omnipresence called forth, and was reflected by, parodies as well, parodies in the older, more serious, sense as well as the newer persiflage, even though it is sometimes difficult to decide how to understand them. An – admittedly extreme – example is seen in the religious parodies from the Silesian cloister at Grissan (today Krzeszów): from 'Ah che tutta in un momento' (*Così fan tutte*, no. 18) we get 'Alma redemptoris mater'; from 'Non mi dir, bell'idol mio' (*Don Giovanni*, no. 25) we get 'Ave Jesu qui sacratum'; and from 'Beware thee 'gainst the wiles of women' (*Die Zauberflöte*, no. 11) we get 'Regina coeli laetare'. If one finds it unacceptable to use the term parody in this elevation of the secular, then the best thing to do would be to take these earnest – and by no means infrequent – examples lightly. As examples of operatic parodies which were intended as persiflage let us take a very obvious one, and a very recondite one: in 1818 Carl Meisl put on in the Viennese Theater in the Josefstadt a farce with song and dance, with music by Wenzel Müller, under the revealing title *The Magic Flute Travesty*. In 1817 there appeared in London (and in New York in 1819) the first English Mozart parody: *Don Giovanni or A Spectre on Horseback!* by Thomas Dibdin. The subtitle speaks worlds: 'A comical-musical-tragical-pantomimical-burlesque-sensational magic farce'.

The dissemination and the canonization of Mozart's works are two separate tendencies: the latter, logically speaking, presupposes the former. Beyond the sphere of German culture the work had, obviously, to establish itself on a sufficiently large scale. This happened under different conditions,

64

conditions which were determined, first, by the national traditions at hand and, second, by that topicality which again brought them into contact with the relevant developments in Germany. Let us start with this: I shall give it a fairly detailed depiction, one which is entirely appropriate and remains true to the facts.

The demand for a better basis, both practical and aesthetic, for music-making which received a much sharper definition after 1800 was realized in the flourishing music societies, choirs and similar institutions which characterized middle-class life at the time. At the same time, as a result of the extinction of the Holy Roman Empire and the removal of the Napoleonic threat, a cultural and national upsurge was experienced in Germany in which art achieved a special status in the struggle for an inner self-assertion. Music above all was suited to promote a sense of national identification, even transcending political differences. But it is not a work of Mozart's which stood at the zenith here, but Haydn's *Die Schöpfung*. Its performances had something unforgettably sublime about them, they were an outlet, as it were, for the longing for greatness – either in the patriotic Austrian sense, as it was in the famous performance of 27 March 1808 in the Great Hall of the University of Vienna (and in the presence of the aged Haydn), or in the national German sense, as was seen in the unadorned fervour of its first performance in Leipzig in 1801. It became apparent – as it had earlier – that Mozart's works did not lend themselves easily to the emotiveness of an ideological statement. His music spoke only indirectly to this fashionable tendency, in the form of the Handel arrangements, or else in the *Davidde penitente* (in Hiller's version). At the time of its foundation, in 1812, the 'Gesellschaft der Musikfreunde des österreichischen Kaiserstattes' put on Mozart's arrangement of Handel's *Alexander's Feast* in a very tendentious manner. The frequent performances of Mozart's *Requiem* at funerals bestowed an aura of patriotic dignity. The poet Friedrich Gottlieb Klopstock was given a funeral such as no German poet had had before him: he was laid to rest in a magnificent ceremony in Hamburg on 22 March 1803; Mozart's *Requiem* was played at the burial ceremony. This work was also heard at the unveiling of a memorial to the anti-Napoleonic patriot Heinrich von Collin (who had died in 1811) on 1 September 1812 in Vienna, as it was at the funeral ceremony for the dowager queen on 5 March in Berlin's National Theatre and also, between the years 1808 and 1810, in Schloss Ludwigslust at the annual memorial ceremonies in honour of the deceased Duchess Louise von Mecklenburg-Schwerin. But the use of the *Requiem* on state occasions also seems to have established itself very early outside Germany: we hear it in France and in the winter of 1812/13 in Naples at the funeral of a French general. It became more and more customary to perform the *Requiem* at official acts of mourning, as was the case for such composers as Beethoven and Chopin.

War and economic difficulties – in 1811 Austria experienced national bankruptcy – had a detrimental effect upon musical life. We read about a 'crisis in concert life around the year 1800' in the literature. As well as the external factors there may also have been inner reasons for the setback. The apparently irresistible rise in the number of concerts given at the end of the eighteenth century led finally to a surplus, a glut which brought a dislocation in its train. In Berlin and Vienna, and even more so in the smaller cities, there were complaints about empty concert halls. The *Allgemeine Musikalische Zeitung* of Leipzig in 1807 reduced the problem to a simple formula: 'Decline in prosperity, decline in art.' This also affected the reception of Mozart's music in concerts. Mozart's Vienna symphonies were by now well known, and they were also appreciated but, as always, they were less popular than his piano concertos. The reasons must lie in the increasing popularity of the piano, which made Mozart's piano concertos standard works in the repertoire, and also in the fact that Haydn was still regarded as the master of the modern symphony, particularly in Paris, the centre of orchestral culture.

With opera the situation was similar. The laments concerning the stagnation of both interest and choice were universal: in Vienna they were, quite rightly, extreme. Apart from *Die Zauberflöte*, Mozart's operas had almost disappeared from the Viennese stages in the 1790s. A Viennese correspondent to the *Berlinische Musikalische Zeitung* reached the sober conclusion in 1805 that, 'The most remarkable thing that I have to report to you from here for your newspaper is the fact that I have nothing to report that would in any way warrant its being accepted.' With the breaking up of the Italian opera troupe in 1806 there was, however, a considerable upsurge of interest in German opera, and above all in Mozart's. Prague again became an important factor as far as continuity was concerned, particularly because the inhabitants clung to the original versions, and especially to their great favourite *Don Giovanni*. This is indeed remarkable, as, at the same time, the work was revalued and reinterpreted in north and central Germany (it was translated in 1801 by Rochlitz, the score was printed, there were various interpretations), and a definite German, nationalistic tendency is apparent which seeks to free itself from the Italian operatic tradition.

The equation of the decline in prosperity with the decline in artistry contradicts that of the rise of the middle classes and their sense of national edification. Wilhelm von Humboldt saw the unity of artistic enjoyment and

66

the appreciation of higher things in national life, and here attributed to music a popularizing function: 'But through which of the arts is this achieved, spreading down to the lowest classes, and in such a purer, a more powerful and a lighter way, if not through music?' The practice of making music arrangements is also given a higher status here. This sense of something changing, something moving, could only survive as an inner energy, for which the performance of Haydn's *Die Schöpfung* gave emphatic markers (the optimism of this work stood, did it not, in contrast to the plight of the age).

The usual descriptions concerning the decline of the world of the Rococo and the rise of a new age smack of empty phrases. A telling picture – although also a negative one – of an actual change which did occur is given by Mozart's birthplace, by Salzburg itself. Salzburg, which had always been in a precarious situation between Bavaria and Austria, met its end as a spiritual principality in the vortex of the Napoleonic wars. Lacking a university, or court, or any higher authority, and after the migration of the old-established aristocracy, the city which had once been the site of a glorious tradition sank to the status of an insignificant district capital in the Austrian dukedom upon the Enns. We get a glimpse of the cultural lethargy of the city in the fact that – inconceivable as it may appear – neither Mozart's name nor his work is once mentioned in a Salzburg newspaper during the first two decades of the nineteenth century. This spiritual deracination of Mozart's memory in his own birthplace may serve as a symbol for his historically conditioned alienation (which is not to be confused with the philosophical problem of the 'alienation of genius').

Similarly, the fact that Constanze and Georg Nissen moved to Copenhagen in 1810 means that not one of Mozart's family was living in Vienna any more. The artistic continuity of the family which was sought through the promotion of his sons was not to be upheld. The elder son, Carl, lived in Milan from 1805. Through Haydn's intervention he was able to study music with the director of the Conservatoire, Bonifazio Asioli, but was not successful. Carl spent the rest of his life as a Neapolitan, and later an Austrian, civil servant and a committed Mozart admirer in Milan. His younger brother, Wolfgang Amadeus, had a series of brilliant teachers in Vienna, but Haydn was not among them.

The intention behind the concert given by the thirteen-year-old Wolfgang Amadeus on 8 April 1805 in Vienna, to celebrate Haydn's seventy-third birthday, is obvious. But the attempt to latch on to the already existing myth of 'Haydn and Mozart' bore little fruit. The younger Wolfgang Amadeus was very ambitious and, according to a statement by

Beethoven, ostensibly very vain; as a composer, however, he was never able to escape from his father's shadow. He led the life of a travelling piano virtuoso, as many another far more famous musician of the age. The wish for a prestigious and prominent position was granted to the son just as little as it had been to the father; his longest involvement in any local musical life was in Lemberg, Galizia. The Danish painter Hans Hansen, a friend of the Nissen couple, had already done a portrait of the two boys in 1798; he spoke of a 'tableau of brotherly tenderness'. When we stand in front of the picture in Mozart's birthplace in Salzburg it is difficult not to read into it what it does not contain: melancholy, and a slight feeling of awkwardness at the fate of two who were born too late. Franz Grillparzer must have experienced something similar when he wrote his poem 'At the grave of Mozart's son', when we read: 'It was your father's name/Which destroyed the source of your vitality . . ./The name which to you was a companion in pain,/Is now transformed to joy.'

As I said at the beginning of this chapter, I do not wish to stick premature labels like 'Classicism' or 'Romanticism' on to the structural changes to which the Mozart image was exposed at that time, but rather attempt to describe it on the basis of three characteristic features: firstly a much stronger reflective quality in the approach to the music; secondly an idealism, and thirdly the extent to which it comes under the rubrics 'sublime' and 'heroic'.

Obviously we can only surmise what sensations were projected into Mozart's music if his contemporaries articulated their interest in a graphic, concrete manner. The growth of reflection, of thinking about music, has various aspects, but all of them have as a common prerequisite the method of using something which is no longer completely axiomatic, a certain conscious distance, or an insight into the complexity of the work as a suspense-creating factor in interpretation. And the simple fact that literary music criticism was now gaining in quantity and, above all, in intellectual substance bears witness to this metamorphosis. The awareness of the uniqueness of Mozart's music was stimulated by a nascent historicism. The canonization of a repertoire and its historical awareness are two different things, yet a repertoire which was growing and consolidating itself could awaken curiosity for its history. In the year 1818, for example, Carl Maria von Weber justified his interest in Die Entführung aus dem Serail thus: 'There is, perhaps, no more important matter for a lover of the arts than to observe the historical development of those great spirits who moulded and dominated their age.'

Usually it is the Viennese circle around Gottfried van Swieten, a circle whose members included Haydn and Mozart, which, through its deliberate cultivation of the music of Handel and Johann Sebastian Bach, is credited with the inception of a musical historicism. Mozart's arrangements of Bach's fugues and Handel's oratorios – however significant they may have been for his own compositions – are not the result of some historical awareness; on the contrary, they were instigated by an awareness that it is necessary to make these older works comprehensible, as it were, for contemporary musical creativity. In the background there is always the consciousness that the music was somehow different. A few years later this relationship between distance and the conquest of distance begins to shift somewhat; Mozart's Handel arrangements were performed in several places in the early nineteenth century – but they met with criticism. When the *Messiah* was performed (and on several occasions) in December 1804 in the Royal Opera House in Berlin, one reviewer (probably Reichardt) praised the 'tranquil greatness' and the 'inner radiance' of Handel's work, but found that 'these rare qualities' had been harmed by Mozart's 'destructive additions'. And in 1805 a performance in Hamburg was criticized with the same historical arguments.

We see a similar change in the creation of the stage-sets used in opera. The passage of time obviously led to a certain distancing. *Le Nozze di Figaro* was set in the 1780s, hence the costumes and interiors were different from those of the early nineteenth century. In Mozart's lifetime *Don Giovanni* was given a contemporary setting; it was only after the turn of the century that we get historical reminiscences of the Italian Renaissance as, for example, in Anton de Pian's stage-sets for the Viennese production of 1810. The fairy-tale timelessness of *Die Zauberflöte* and its richness of associations, was restricted and reduced to a rational historical framework: we now find a series of Egyptian-like settings, the most famous of which was that created by Karl Friedrich Schinkel for the Berlin production of 1816. Schinkel's success brought forth many imitations; Goethe, too, rejected the old sets of 1794 and, in 1817, appointed Friedrich Beuther who designed a historicizing architecture. (A Classical Greek design was planned, but Egypt won the day.) The historical verisimilitude of the stage-sets was often linked with a certain monumental severity; we find this both in the Renaissance of de Pian and the dark, magnificent colours of Schinkel's Egypt.

Not only historical veracity but other features of the dramatic stage were carried over into the genre of opera. Before 1800 the singing-roles in Mozart's operas were often filled by actors: the first Papageno was Schikaneder, that is to say an actor. The aim of this kind of casting did obviously not have the music in mind, but was more concerned with the action and the emphasis on the realistic and on farcical elements. After 1800 the concept of the *Singspiel* became less convincing: the result was travesties of Mozart's operas, and the inclusion of fantastic biographical scenes (like Joachim Perinet's *Jupiter, Mozart and Schikaneder*) which represented a more reflective attitude to Mozart, an alienating approach to such successful works as *Die Zauberflöte* or *Don Giovanni*.

There were also performances which reflected the world of popular comedy and which put their trust in spontaneous stage effects: a playwright, Johann Nestroy, made his debut as Sarastro in 1822. There were also the newer interpretations in opera which turned against the old *Singspiel* form. When Friedrich Rochlitz inserted whole scenes into *Don Giovanni* (as well as brooding meditations from the Don himself) he was attempting to stress the drama at the expense of the action. Or as a contemporary tersely put it: 'The action is there to develop the character of the personages; the personages are not there only to enliven the action.' The figure of Leporello, usually over-emphasized, is now downplayed. Papageno and Papagena, both wearing severly cut Egyptian costumes and surrounded by archaic, monumental scenery, must have felt very out of place with their jokes and their natural behaviour (the Milan production of 1816 was an extreme case of this).

The agile, open structure of Mozart's operas was felt to be in need of correction. The ending of *Don Giovanni* provides the best known example of the imposition of an improvement which – for almost a century – was felt to be necessary: Rochlitz cut the final sextet (Friedrich Lippert had done the same in the Berlin production of 1790) and thereby, at a decisive moment, removed the *giocoso* aspect of Mozart's *Dramma giocoso* (Mozart even referred to it as an *opera buffa*) in order to bring the tragedy to a sensible end with the destruction of the hero. There was a tendency to bridge the gulf between splendid music and inferior libretti: Johann Gottfried Herder expressed this very emphatically in his *Adrastea* of 1801. 'How deeply we regret, wondrous Mozart,' he wrote, 'to see you in your *Così fan tutte*, your *Figaro*, your *Don Juan* . . . The notes transport us to heaven, but the sight of the scenery puts us in purgatory, if not deeper.' These intrusions seem at first glance to be at the expense of the music; they also most certainly detract from the musical side of the *buffa* sphere. Yet, furthermore, the switch of attention from the action to the feelings, thoughts and passions of the protagonists must have thrown a stronger light on the music itself. The dramaticization of the opera displaced (paradoxically, and yet also consistently) the singing actor and encouraged the development of the singer's creative power.

Critical reflection was also found in the approach to instrumental music. In an essay from the year 1805 an author who signed himself 'C.F.' hinted at

70

one of Schiller's central concepts by using the title *Etwas über sentimentale und naive Musik* (Touching Upon Naïve and Sentimental Music). Naïve music, apparently, 'expressed, in the greatest simplicity and calm, the gentle feelings of a heart which is in harmony with itself, free of the turmoil of powerful affections and passions, a heart which is at peace'. Only traces of this naïvety is found in sentimental music. 'In this music the soul seeks on many paths to envisage its beautiful goal, and to approach it. The bashful soul divines its imminent assuagement, and reaches out even more.' Behind the old problem of rationally understanding the mixture of emotions in music our author suspects that a composer has gained an insight into things which are incompatible, causing him to yearn for some beautiful goal. 'Most, and the best, music of modern times is sentimental . . . Jos. Haydn, Mozart, Emanuel Bach, Reichardt, Zumsteeg, Beethoven, Cherubini and other masters.' It seems that Schiller's aesthetic writings have opened the way to Romantic longing.

What characterizes the metaphysical quintessence of this 'beautiful goal' is that it is indescribable. The biblical metaphors of light and darkness which were used *ad nauseum* in the Enlightenment to portray a secularized, rational expectation are now applied in a very different way to describe Mozart's art. The light of his music is juxtaposed with a disagreeable present. Opposed to this present is the historical past, and, at the same time, a hope for the future. The conservative Niemetschek inserted the following passage into the second edition of his book (1808): 'After the turmoil of the newest composers how gladly we listen to the sublime, clear, so simple melodies of our favourite! How pleasing they are to our soul – it seems as if we had been transported from a chaotic confusion, out of dense darkness, into light and serenity.'

In a diary entry (14 June 1816), after having been to a concert, Franz Schubert continues to portray – and even more emphatically – this vision of a golden age in Mozart's music, a vision frequently extolled in later writing:

A clear, light, beautiful day like this will remain with me throughout my life. As from afar, the magical tones of Mozart's music resound in my senses. How indescribably powerful – and yet so gentle – was it impressed in my heart by Schlesinger's masterful playing. So it is that these beautiful imprints remain in the soul, untouched by time and circumstance, exerting a beneficial influence upon our lives. In the darkness of this life they show to us a light, clear, lovely goal, which we hope and trust we shall gain. Oh Mozart, immortal Mozart – how many, oh how infinitely

71

many of these beneficient impressions of a lighter, better life have you not donated to our souls.

To see the past in a more colourful, clearer and more immediate way than in the flux of the present is not exclusively a Romantic tendency, but lies deep within us all. And, with all the convulsions that Europe suffered in the decades around 1800, it is a fact that the potential for creating contrastive images must have been particularly great. How difficult it was to establish a conceptual framework may be seen in the 'Romantic' quotations given above. Niemetschek's attitude was a humanistic one. It is impossible to classify Schubert; in the Vienna of his time Romanticism was not a dominant reference-point. That German-Austrian nationalism into which music had been drawn was unreal in its political stipulations and idealistic in its aims: otherwise the amalgamation of German nationalism and Romanticism in the case of Mozart would scarcely have been possible. The different nature of the goals was not only the result of their metaphysical quality but part of a historical development which led from an experimental phase about the year 1800 to a conceptual clarification in the 1820s and 1830s.

We can detect a growing concretization of musical opinions within literary Romanticism. The evaluation of instrumental music in the sense of 'an idea of absolute music' was a matter of concern above all to Wilhelm Heinrich Wackenroder and Ludwig Tieck. On a less speculative level, we find similar premisses in the musical receptivity of the 1790s. Tieck expressed the tendency most clearly in his essay 'Symphonien' when he writes the following of instrumental music: 'It improvises playfully and without aim, and yet expresses that which is higher; it follows its dark urges and, in its triflings, expresses that which is most profound, most miraculous.' But the high-flown ideas of the early Romantics were based upon that which, to our way of feeling, consisted of something more simple: the music of Stamitz, Cannabich and Reichardt. Around 1800 there was as yet no Romantic music, and surprisingly enough it was not the work of Haydn or Mozart which provided the model, at least not *expressis verbis*. It is difficult to understand this when looking on the history of musical reception: if, to use a phrase of Emil Staiger's, Romanticism was 'invented on the pavements of Berlin' it could not avoid Mozart's music. But the fact that it *did* can be grounded in the antiquated clichés of non-musicians or musical ignoramuses attempting to deal with music; it also demonstrates the fact that the potential for reflection and idealization far exceeded the structural basis of the musical subject.

The growing proximity of the poetic and the musical was a phenomenon of the age and also of the musical literacy of the poets involved. A change may be detected in a developmental process within the writer Tieck which found its fulfilment in the young writer-musician Ernst Theodor Amadeus Hoffmann: in his 1813 novella *Don Juan* Mozart is the inspirer of poetic fantasies. Hoffmann achieved a unity of poetical form and musical structure in his famous reviews, but their fitting object is in fact Beethoven's instrumental music; there is no more talk of 'playfulness' or 'trifling'. For Hoffmann (as previously for Tieck and later for Eichendorff) Mozart is important as a composer of operas, not so much of instrumental music.

The idealization of music aimed basically to move towards a religious content; this was sought in all the genres but obviously provoked a discussion of church music. As early as Tieck, Mozart gets bad marks in this context. In *Phantasus* one of the speakers doubts whether Mozart 'could ever have written truly spiritual music, just like the rest of the moderns'. And in his essay 'Alte und neue Kirchenmusik', Hoffmann speaks of the 'infectious plague of secular, splendid frivolity', and refers to Mozart's masses as being 'almost his weakest works'. Some years later Hoffmann tones the rigour down somewhat and in the second volume of the *Serapionsbrüder* (1819) lets even the conservative Cyprian attribute to Haydn, Mozart and Beethoven a characteristic – that is, modern – religious style. Hoffmann does not only transfigure what lay in the remote past – he also sought in the music of his day a hope for the future: this can only be found in that one particular case which stands out from the ordinary, that one particular object which is worthy of idealization. Hoffmann's identification with an ideal as the result of a previous alienation is very clearly seen in the essay which we have already mentioned: 'Alte und neue Kirchenmusik'. For after he has put forward a negative criticism of Mozart's music, one which is unique in his writing, he immediately switches to an emphatic praise of the *Requiem* which is a work standing on its own, incomparable: 'Who is not seized by the most fervent piety, by the holiest ecstasy which radiates from it? His *Requiem* is indeed the highest work which modern church music has produced.' Only the 'tuba mirum' is criticized by Hoffmann as being 'oratorio-like', but otherwise everything corresponded to his ideal of church music: 'It is worship pure and simple, miraculous chords that speak of the Beyond, which *are* the Beyond in their remarkable dignity and force.' This ideal had prompted Hoffmann to compose his own *Requiem* in 1805, a work which – and surely this is no accident – he never performed.

The tendency to excessive effusiveness is not only found in utterances about music, but, more tangibly, in operatic productions themselves. Let two examples serve. The figure of the Commendatore in *Don Giovanni* is a

73

good starting place for any interpretations which set out to emphasize the supernatural. In an alabaster-relief of the scene in the cemetery, which survived from a Viennese production of, probably, 1789, the Commendatore is standing on his memorial slab; Joseph Quaglio represented him in a similar fashion in his Mannheim production, also of 1789. In many productions of the early nineteenth century the figure sits upon a horse and is 'transported' on to a pedestal, as though both horse and rider were a monument. Something similar (as regards the scenery) is found in the first appearance of the Queen of the Night in Die Zauberflöte. The sudden eruption of the nocturnal element is a challenge to the imagination of any stage designer. In both Schikaneder's production and in Goethe's at Weimar the Queen of the Night is positioned on a solid, movable construction; in Joseph Quaglio's Munich sets of 1793 she is a remote figure, enthroned upon clouds and garlands. Twenty-five years later, also in Munich, Simon Quaglio emphasized the threatening quality of the Queen, enthroned upon clouds, before the crescent moon and beneath a star-strewn canopy, by introducing rags of cloud and a group of elongated, ghostly shapes. Schinkel chose yet another form of exaggerated awesomeness in his Berlin production of 1816 by having the clouds open to reveal a radiant, glittering cosmos. Both of these tableaux became famous exemplars.

To understand these purely and simply as symbols of Romanticism *per se* is tempting, as they manifest the ambivalence of the 'spirit world', poised between the dangerous and the elevated. From a stylistic point of view they also provided examples for the admittedly blurred contrast between Romanticism and Classicism. But let us draw the attention to certain facts of the case which muddle the chain of associations. Neither the poets nor the musicians of Romanticism were preoccupied by a demonic *Don Giovanni* or a mythological *Zauberflöte*. There was just as much interest in Mozart (and in operatic circles even more) as a 'comic Romantic', as the non-Romantic Reichardt strangely, but aptly, commented. This attitude has much in common with the earliest reception of Mozart, particularly with *Die Zauberflöte* and the translation of Mozart's *opera buffa* into a German milieu.

The enormous success of this work brought with it all manner of consequences, and some of these were far-reaching. With reference to Goethe, Norbert Miller described the genre of magic opera with the composite formulation 'Weimar-Romantic-Theatre'. Schikaneder continued in the tradition of theatre-as-illusion, with appropriate costumes and decor, and this was closer to the roots of opera than Goethe's late solution with his Helena act in *Faust II*. Both had little success with composers who tried to follow in Mozart's footsteps, but it was only Goethe who realized

74

the impossibility of trying to find a worthy alternative. Schikaneder, however, for a long time cleverly avoided the trap into which many an impresario had fallen, that is, of trying to latch on immediately to a theatrical success; it was only when his troupe began to lose popularity with the public that he dared to launch his sequel to Die Zauberflöte, called Das Labyrinth, with music by Peter von Winter.

Winter was a respected composer, and enjoyed a certain amount of fame after his death, but was completely forgotten in the later nineteenth century and is remembered today as an eclectic composer, significant from a historical point of view. Schikaneder, in his libretto, revived the familiar characters, groupings and situations in a well-ordered manner; Winter attempted, similarly, to re-awaken in the audience identification with the music. His Mozart quotations did indeed create such an atmosphere of familiarity, as everyone would have recognized them, but I cannot quite make out what he was trying to offer to musical connoisseurs, or whether his music was a 'study of Mozart's musical technique'. I must also admit that I was very disappointed with a performance of Das Labyrinth which I saw in the Cuvilliés Theater in Munich a few years ago, not only because Mozart's operas are incomparable but because Winter made very few demands on himself. And the audience of the time probably was displeased to have to watch a kaleidoscope of transfers taken from a well-known pattern. Das Labyrinth did not have the success that was expected; Winter turned away from Schikaneder and returned to Munich. And now came a decisive turning point – he realized the impossibility of ever being a successor to Mozart and began, in his own way, to translate into reality that greater emphasis on music for the dramatic sujet, an emphasis which Mozart had encouraged. He turned to the magic world of Shakespeare's The Tempest and hence contributed to the precursors of Romantic opera.

Of course, the attempts of Winter and others to explore new terrain were partly superseded by arrangements of Mozart's own works: a good example is given by the history of the performances of Così fan tutte in Berlin. The early version, more of a Singspiel, did not catch on with the audiences; success was only achieved by Georg Friedrich Treitschke's arrangement in 1805. The work's piquant aspect, that is the weakness of Fiordiligi and Dorabella, was neutralized by Treitschke who placed the threads of the action in the hands of Alfonso the magician and Despina as his subject spirit. Hence magic and morality are fused in a way which is typical of the German Romantic opera. Alfonso becomes a kind of Prospero, and Despina a kind of Ariel: Così fan tutte now enters the sphere of Shakespeare's The Tempest. It was, probably, Clemens von Brentano who was the first in the sphere of literature to translate the ideal of the unity of Mozart's operas and Shakespeare's comedies into reality with his *Ponce de Leon*.

Tieck had already translated *The Tempest* in 1793 and written on Shakespeare's treatment of the miraculous. His brother-in-law, Reichardt, pleaded in vain in 1798 for him to arrange *As You Like It* as an opera libretto. Tieck then wrote a 'musical fairy tale' with the title *Das Ungeheuer und der verzauberte Wald (The Monster and the Enchanted Forest)* but distanced himself from Reichardt as a composer as the latter, 'schooled in the style of Gluck', had no knowledge of 'the fantastic'. These causes of friction in the collaboration of two friends contains *in nucleo* an ideological conflict: it was Tieck, the modern artist *par excellence* at the turn of the century and not the traditional Reichardt, who was initially an admirer of Mozart. In his memoirs he stylized his veneration for Mozart in the following anecdote: before the performance of an opera, in 1789, he held an animated conversation about Mozart's operas with a stranger in Berlin – it later transpired that the friendly gentleman was Mozart himself.

Despite this picture of an uncomplicated enthusiasm for Mozart, Tieck's Mozart reception was more complex, partly adhering to older habits and partly anticipating a model that would remain in force until Richard Wagner – or even Ferruccio Busoni. Tieck had always had certain reservations about opera as a genre, and saw his musical ideal realized in symphonic music; he did, however, admire Mozart above all as an opera composer. For him, too, *Don Juan* was an incomparable masterpiece, but he critically distanced himself from any excessively Romantic interpretation of the opera. When looking back in 1829 he believed he had detected an intrusive, false development at work: 'I leave musical experts to examine and determine whether or not we have recently, to a certain extent, lost the path which Mozart had shown us by wishing to overdo that miraculous element which Mozart, in *Don Juan*, so beautifully pushed to its extreme limit.' He demanded as a counterbalance a marked return to comic opera: 'And it is this unending richness of humour, wit, sentiment and sweetest love and most fervent passion which characterizes and makes unique all the works of our great Mozart, even his Belmont: this richness acts as example and model, and shows the genius manifold ways and vistas.' In Tieck's understanding of music it is this ideal of the 'unending richness' which serves as the *tertium comparationis* between symphonic music and opera.

In his praise of *Die Entführung* Tieck was apparently concerned to hold life and art, genius and normality, together; with E.T.A. Hoffmann this ideal is viewed from a most un-idealistic angle. In his dialogue *Der Dichter und der Komponist (The Poet and the Composer)*, Hoffmann refers to Mozart's *Così fan*

76

tutte and characterizes *opera buffa* as a combination of the 'fantastic' and the 'comical' with the 'intrusion of the improbable into everyday life'. So, a generation after Mozart, what kind of challenge did this 'comic Romantic' provide for the artists of the day? They hesitated between two solutions – either admiring the genial naïvety of Mozart's music and letting it shine through in their own works or stressing the deviation of their own compositions and forcing this divergence into something bizarre, sarcastic, parodistic.

Tieck demanded that a good opera librettist or composer should produce something which 'Mozart has already done unconsciously through his genius, and his poets through their innocence, which makes their poems something akin to natural phenomena'. In a similar fashion Carl Maria von Weber admired *Die Entführung* in 1818:

For me as an artist this serene creation, blazing with the fullest, richest youthful exuberance and yet virginally delicate in its sensation, is an especially lovely work. I think I can see in this opera a feeling of what those happy youthful years must be to all of us, that blossom-time which we can never experience in such a fashion again, and whose irretrievable charms are lost when its blemishes are removed.

The later writer Eichendorff, who tended very much to be a critic of his times, loved *Figaro* above all and thus prepared the way for the adulation for this opera by the conservative Mozart enthusiasts in the second half of the century.

The name of E.T.A. Hoffmann arises when we consider the other reaction, the one that leads to distortion. We see that there is a tension existing between the two halves of his psyche when a Romantic poet like Hoffmann adopts Mozart's Christian name – Amadeus – and, going beyond this, makes this ambivalence into an artistic means of representing his own exaggerated autobiography in the imaginary figure of Johannes Kreisler. The '*Kapellmeister* and demented musician *par excellence*', with his 'overwrought temperament', his 'imagination which flares up into a consuming flame' and his inability to succeed in life, is nothing like a picture of Mozart (perhaps Friedemann Bach served as a model) – but Hoffmann gives Kreisler the same birth date as Mozart. Tieck's path was the reverse: a parodistic alienation preceded his later idealization of Mozart. In his play *Der gestiefelte Kater* (*Puss in Boots*) we have parodies of Papageno's glockenspiel (which makes the Moors start to dance) and of the trial by fire and water. *Das Ungeheuer und der verzauberte Wald* shares with *Die Zauberflöte* a miraculous world, the interaction of three spheres, similar characters (evil queen, noble prince, etc.) and dramatic constellations. To call the work a 'musical fairy-tale' has an ironic tone, for an attack on official life and institutions is inferred. Tieck, in all probability, did not rate Schikaneder's libretto particularly highly: *Die Zauberflöte* served him *pars pro toto* to distance himself from various other writers (Kotzebue and Iffland). We notice that there is a very complex relationship between self-conscious alienation and idealization here.

Joseph von Eichendorff, when looking back in his late essay 'Halle and Heidelberg' on that central tendency of Romanticism 'to relate the mundane to something higher, to relate the secular to the greater Beyond' did so with the following comment on the development of music: 'That same more earnest awareness leads music from the frivolous titillation of the senses towards religion, from the old Italian masters to Sebastian Bach, Gluck and Handel; even in secular music it awakens that mysterious, miraculous melody that slumbers in all things – and Mozart, Beethoven and Carl Maria von Weber are genuine Romantics.' With that 'more earnest awareness', Eichendorff, in passing, establishes a progression from the cultivation of oratorio and *opera seria* in the late eighteenth century to the contemporary discussion concerning the 'purity of music'. He does not mention the development of symphonic music and thereby lets the early Romantic metaphysics of instrumental music look like something derivative. He was concerned here with a Romantic concept of the sublime.

Mozart's *Requiem* was a much more fitting example for any discussion concerning the breakthrough of the supernatural (as a 'Romantic Portrayal of a Mass for the Dead') than the pantheistic naïvety of Haydn's *Die Schöpfung*. This was E.T.A. Hoffman's view, and it was consistent that he should regard a concert performance of the *Requiem* as highly inappropriate. Yet it was in the symphony that we get the clearest example (in early Romanticism's speculation on pure instrumental music) of the way in which the sublime could move from this world to the next. It is surprising that the early Romantics at least saw the sublime incorporated in the symphonies, and only later in the *Requiem* or in serious opera; this is explained by looking at the history of the idea of the sublime.

The point of reference is Kant's philosophy (and not only for the Romantics). For him greatness is a necessary feature of this concept. The feeling of sublimity is evoked by 'dread' and 'melancholy' – 'We are touched by the sublime and charmed by the beautiful.' When Rochlitz speaks of the *Jupiter* symphony as a 'fearful symphony', or when C.M. von Weber calls it 'great, all-powerful and shattering' (and the very nomenclature – *Jupiter* –

78

which is met from 1820 onwards was not accidental), they are both referring to the work's sublimity; there is no idea of any contrast between Classicism and Romanticism. Jean Paul defines sublimity as 'an applied infinity' and talks of 'Mozart's thunderclouds', and so gives another clue for the understanding of sublimity, particularly in the symphonic music.

For Schelling (and he, too, saw the connection between the infinite and the finite as essential here) it is chaos which is the sublime element of nature which, incomprehensible to the senses, becomes a 'symbol of infinity'. Mirrored in art, a detail such as the famous representation of chaos at the beginning of *Die Schöpfung* becomes sublimity itself. This 'infinity' and the 'mingled feeling of sublimity' are most easily developed in symphonic music: the ineffability (constantly stressed) of what purely instrumental music expresses, comes close to that concept of 'infinity' and also to Schelling's attempted reconciliation of the traditional contrast between the beautiful and the sublime.

If this concept (through E.T.A. Hoffmann) finds its adequate musical realization in Beethoven's symphonies then Mozart's last symphonies must also be included. Beethoven's designation *Eroica* for his third symphony is independent of all this, and orientated more towards antiquity; an even more concrete conception, however, was found in Mozart's case. Christian Friedrich Michaelis, for example, finds that 'there is, in many of the great symphonies of Haydn, Mozart, Beethoven and others . . . an arrangement, and a spirit which is similar to the structure and the character of an heroic poem'. In particular, the 'heroic character' of a theme is expressed in such a way that 'it triumphs over many opposing tendencies'. Johann Abraham Peter Schulz had already compared a symphony to a 'Pindaric Ode'. In *Hesperus* Jean Paul speaks of the 'dramatic plan' of a symphony by Stamitz, and Tieck put forward the opinion that 'symphonies can portray a varied, complex, confused and beautifully developed drama such as no writer can achieve'. The specifically heroic is now becoming an untranslatable musical mesh which presumably encouraged critics to speak of the dramatic, rather than the epic.

A few years later, in 1824, Friedrich Rochlitz drew quite openly from Kant and Schiller in defining the 'sublime' as one of the four categories of Mozart's music and, less clearly, as 'the richness of harmony of great, profound ideas'. The examples which Rochlitz chose are more interesting for us: the first movement of the D minor string quartet (K. 421); the *Prague* symphony; the *Requiem* and the first finale of *La Clemenza di Tito*. As regards content, these works form a bridge from instrumental music across religious music to *opera seria*, and here Rochlitz, like Eichendorff, looks back to an earlier connotation. Before 1800 the term 'sublime' was a very common epithet to describe Mozart's *La Clemenza di Tito*; indirectly Rochlitz was taking up again that model of antiquity which Niemetschek had before him when he spoke about the 'simplicity' and the 'tranquil sublimity' of *La Clemenza di Tito* and the dramatic emotiveness and 'heroic sublimity' of *Idomeneo*.

The increasing popularity of *La Clemenza di Tito*, a popularity dating from before 1800, now reached its climax. The monumental Roman pomp and splendour of the Frankfurt production of 1799 moved Goethe's mother 'to tears', and was even successfully emulated in Weimar. This particular style of production represented the Empire's craze for antiquity and Classicism and, in its way, realized the demand for sublimity: antique models and exotic orientalism achieved some remarkable combinations. This constellation is reflected, for example, in such details as Pamina's costume in Schinkel's scenery for *Die Zauberflöte*, which combined an Egyptian-like headpiece with an Empire costume. Giovanni Pedroni's sets for the production at La Scala, Milan (1816) represent the most extreme example of strict Egyptianism, but it was not simply on the history of theatrical production that Mozart's influence was felt: a whole rash of operas followed on the Italian stage around 1800 to which *La Clemenza di Tito* stood as godfather (Simon Mayr's *Ginevra*, Ferdinando Paër's *Achilles*, Nicola Zingarelli's *Romeo and Juliet*). We find this also in the Mozart parodies and quotations and probably also in the genesis of Rossini's *Tancredi*, although this has not yet been researched.

Any further development in German opera was therefore faced with the alternative of understanding sublimity either as something Romantic or as something archaic. And the view of Franz Horn, formulated in 1802, proves that there could be a third answer: he believed that Metastasio had no inkling what 'Romanticism' meant and that his music did not reach 'sublimity' but rather an 'ideal tenderness', that 'nameless enchantment which floats in a gentle breath of blossom across the frontier from "that land where the lemons grow"'; Horn now compares Mozart's *La Clemenza di Tito* with Goethe's *Torquato Tasso*. This would be an interpretation in the sense of Weimar Classicism – as seen by a Romantic.

The success of *La Clemenza di Tito* contradicts the banal conclusion that *opera seria* had become anachronistic with the French Revolution and of no interest to the bourgeoisie. But another contradiction is not resolved, namely, that Mozart's music dramaturgy had placed him squarely in a tradition of serious opera *à la* Gluck. The operatic work of both had prevailed and remained exemplary; German opera had become independent, and Gluck and Mozart represented alternatives with which both artists and critics saw themselves confronted. One example here: Tieck, an admirer of Mozart, found when working with Reichardt that the latter's indebtedness to Gluck was problematic; for his own part, Reichardt disapproved of Mozart's *La Clemenza di Tito* and also his arrangement of the *Messiah*, feeling that Mozart had not achieved sublimity in these works. But after collaborating with Goethe to prepare a performance of *Tito* for the opening of the new theatre in Bad Lauchstädt, and after he had worked as a *Kapellmeister* in Kassel and got to know this and other operas better, Reichardt changed his opinion.

Already in 1806 he had praised *Idomeneo* as 'the greatest work of art that even our great Mozart has ever produced' – it was not, however, that stroke of genius with which Mozart broke, in music and in drama, with the old conception of the *opera seria* which Reichardt praised, but rather 'its great, heroic character, unadulterated by an alien admixture; we detect, amidst the storm of emotions and elements and their most violent and vital expression, an inner tranquillity which defines the truly heroic character in art as well as life.' Reichardt thus remained true to his pragmatic argument but transformed his negative judgement into something positive. His personal contacts with Tieck, Wackenroder and probably also with Novalis would hardly have caused him to choose *Idomeneo* above all as the 'purest' opera; it was probably the mood of the time, the vogue for 'our Mozart' which caused him to revise his opinion. There is a similar situation with Goethe's friend, the musician Carl Friedrich Zelter. Zelter adored J.S. Bach, and Mozart's music was alien to him; later, however, he saw that the two were of equal status, detecting something 'mystical' in Mozart and setting *Don Giovanni* and *Die Zauberflöte* alongside Bach's achievement.

There had always been something precarious about holding Mozart's *opera seria* in such high esteem: such esteem could easily become problematic during the progress of operatic history. And the one who encouraged development in the world of German opera was Gasparo Spontini, who was active in Berlin from 1819 onwards. There is scarcely a musical personality who can represent the *Empire* period so well as Spontini, who took no less a figure than Napoleon as his personal model; at the same time he represented a successor to Gluck and to the tradition of serious French opera. Now Mozart's status was questioned here: in 1811 the Mannheim lawyer Gottfried Weber, a musician from Carl Maria von Weber's 'Harmonischer Verein', called *Idomeneo* a 'Classical work' and placed it in the same class as Cherubini's *Medea*, Méhul's *Jakob und seine Söhne* (*Jacob and his Sons*) and Spontini's *La Vestale*. In 1810 an anonymous writer in the journal *Der Sammler* brought the name of Gluck into the discussion, a composer whom he played off against Mozart. After a delicate polemic against *Idomeneo* and *La Clemenza di Tito*, two works which, ostensibly, had been composed in rather a hurry, our critic posited a 'purely heroic opera', a 'new tragic *Singspiel*' which he set up in opposition to the old *opera seria*, and here he had in mind the operas of Spontini, operas which he saw as true successors to Gluck, whereas Mozart gave no clue at all for an assessment of Spontini's *oeuvre*.

E.T.A. Hoffmann drew up a detailed account of a third possible developmental model. In his review of Gluck's *Iphigenie en Aulide*, which also appeared in 1810, and in the dialogue *Der Dichter und der Komponist* (*The Poet and the Composer*) Hoffmann took up a position as regards *opera seria* which is diametrically opposed to his Romantic interpretation of symphonic music and which is comparable to his ideal of church music. He seeks in the past, he tells us, for the 'true *opera seria*' in all its unadorned sublimity and finds it in 'the truly tragic pathos' of the 'giant Gluck'. Mozart's *La Clemenza di Tito*, in comparison, is scarcely worth a mention and even the 'exuberantly overflowing Spontini' cannot stand the test. Hoffmann's aversion to French opera to which Spontini was indebted probably played a part here; a nationalistic German prejudice is very much in evidence, a prejudice which, even today, has led to the importance of French opera for its German counterpart in the early nineteenth century to be underestimated.

After thoroughly studying the score of *La Vestale* – and perhaps under the influence of the success that Spontini was having in Germany – Hoffmann changed his opinion; with the new positive evaluation of Spontini we have, surprisingly, Mozart before us again. The finale to Spontini's *Olympia*, we are informed, is reminiscent of the finale of the first act of *Don Giovanni*, and the aria 'Ha! Tyrann!' brings Donna Anna's first aria to mind. In *Kater Murr* Hoffmann arrives at a teleological model that seems to anticipate the progressive ideas of the New German School of Berlioz, Liszt and Wagner; we now have Gluck, Mozart, Beethoven and Spontini. With this reconciliation of the opposites Gluck/Mozart (and indirectly also Opera/ Symphonies) Hoffmann had hit upon the right direction – also as far as Spontini was concerned. Perhaps it was more than a courtesy for Spontini, in 1811, to send to Constanze (he was in touch with her about the purchase of a Mozart piano) a coloured lithograph of himself with the dedication: 'To the worthy widow of the immortal Mozart, from his most ardent admirer, Spontini.'

A word *en passant* about Hoffmann's idea of opera; the marked difference between it and Tieck's may well have historical reasons. For Hoffmann in his earlier years it was Beethoven and that 'musical tragedy' of the 1820s

82

(against which Tieck inveighed) which represented points of identification: he may well have anticipated this in his *Don Juan* interpretation of 1813. His interest was, accordingly, concentrated on *Don Giovanni*. He certainly mentioned *Die Zauberflöte* often, but says nothing significant about it, and the other operas, even *La Clemenza di Tito*, are only seldom mentioned. Only once, in the dialogue *Der Dichter und der Komponist*, does he engage in detailed discussion of *opera buffa*, and sees in *Figaro* 'more of a play with vocal parts than a true opera'; he does, however, praise the 'expression of the most delightful irony . . . which rules supreme in Mozart's magnificent opera *Così fan tutte*'. His interpreters may be surprised that Hoffmann should see one feature of the *opera buffa* in the 'intrusion of the fantastic into everyday life'; this may let us assume that 'the most delightful irony' which Hoffmann detected in *Così fan tutte* is not irony in Schlegel's Romantic sense of the word but more like the debunking sarcasm that we find in Heinrich Heine. Here he sets up in opposition to that other interpretation of *Così fan tutte* which an anonymous writer (Tieck?) set out in a *Musikalischer Briefwechsel* on the occasion of Treitschke's successful adaptation in Berlin in 1805; we learn that 'all the characters and situations of real life . . . should be banned from the world of ideas, and from that most ideal art, music . . . above all from the music of Mozart. Thus we preserve his dignity and his powers of characterization . . .' The impression is strengthened here that Hoffmann was the most pragmatic and foresighted of all the Romantics as regards musical matters.

After all this we can safely assume that with this multiplicity of interpretations as regards Mozart's music there is also a similar variety of claims about his personality.

The cult of the hero which was very prevalent in European attitudes of the early nineteenth century fits well into our picture; it was doubtless encouraged by Napoleon's emergence but was certainly not restricted to him nor to his military opponents. Thomas Carlyle believed that world history was determined only by powerful individuals, and this view of his achieved notoriety; he called Goethe the 'hero as man of letters' and saw him alongside Napoleon, thus classifying the hero from different points of view. To speak of the 'art-heroes of our age' was quite common; in 1799 Rochlitz called Haydn and Mozart, as well as Schiller and Goethe, 'heroes and leaders'. It was obvious that there would be comparisons with, and references to, models of antiquity, and also that the new Mozart images used older models from his lifetime. It was easier to bathe his appearance in an antique light than it was his work: we have a steel engraving by Franz Burchard Dörbeck, dating from 1808 and based on a model by David Weiss, where Mozart stands as a Roman, wearing a toga-like costume, manly and forceful. There is a coloured print by John Chapman for the *Encyclopaedia Londonensis* of 1817 which transports him into an *Empire* setting: the weighty backdrop portrays an organ and a purple curtain, and he is characterized by the emblems of laurel-wreath, satyr's mask and lyre as the hero of both comic and tragic art. Two books are also portrayed, and these bear the titles *Don Giovanni* and *La Clemenza di Tito* – this makes us realize what kind of attitude it was that made his *Tito* such a popular opera. If the physiognomy of the Chapman print is drawn according to Posch-Absenker's model, then the 'new', Roman head of Mozart (in its diverse copies) achieves an ugly facial expression, as it does in the steel engraving of the Nuremberg artist Carl Meyer. Posch-Absenker's model, on the other hand, tended towards an opposite stylization: in C. Stadler's lithograph the features are softer and more plump. Another facet appears in Eduard Lehmann's lithograph, based on the model of the unfinished Lange portrait: the slight additions tend to smooth the picture, the hair is tidier, the bottom jaw more handsome and the somewhat protruding eyes of Lange's portrait are concealed, and Mozart's penetrating gaze made softer.

To make heroes of musicians in this way, through visible tokens, was a comparatively new phenomenon. We read in a 'report' in 1800 about 'Monuments of German Musicians' that there were indeed monuments in the Panthéon in Paris and in London's Westminister Abbey, but nothing similar existed in Germany (though there *is* mention of two of C.P.E. Bach and one each of Haydn and Mozart). But the reference to authorities, in an evaluative and an objective sense, is an old custom in musicological writings: linked to the new glorification of the hero it leads to the solemnity of the contemplation of Palestrina, Handel or Bach. The pictorial equation with Apollo or Orpheus (Baerend's Mozart coin of 1796 shows a representation of Orpheus) belongs, rather, to a later period. But the verbal epithet of 'the immortal favourite of Apollo' was used for Haydn and Mozart, and the *Wunderkind* Mozart was frequently compared to Orpheus in panegyric verses. The quotations from the literary experts primarily extend the picture in a different direction: Mozart was seen as a modern 'hero of music', and hence compared with models who were both venerable and actual beyond the confines of music. Two figures who were fascinating for the arts at the time were Raphael and Shakespeare. We might have expected, given the fundamental importance of Raphael for contemporary painters, that there would have been an inevitable 'Raphaelization' of his pictures; this was hardly the case, however. But the references to Raphael and Shakespeare were present in the literary comparison of artists.

Since a new Mozart image began to circulate during the *fin-de-siècle* period, an image meant to oppose that of Wagner, the notion arose that the nineteenth century saw Mozart as a Romantic, Apollonian figure, and that he had been a Raphael-figure for the first five decades. This is a far too summary idea, and a misleading one. Even today the Raphael comparisons will arouse interest, even if most of them rarely go beyond a cliché-ridden genuflexion before a figure of genius. But what is not so easily remembered is the fact that Mozart, in the musicological writings of the early nineteenth century, is more often – and more meaningfully – compared with Shakespeare. Certainly the similarity in the greatness of Raphael and Shakespeare was felt from the beginning to be more essential than the differences in their artistic aims. A brightly occupied Parnassus is frequently extolled, as in Tieck's poem *Der Traum* (*The Dream*) where, towards the end, we read the following: 'And here they are, the great, exalted spirits,/With venerable Homer in the lead,/Then Raphael and with him that glorious Master/Who always, ever, filled my soul with joy:/The bold, intrepid Briton . . .' It was Tieck and Wackenroder who were the writers whose enthusiasm for Raphael had the stronger effect on musical thought (the older reflection of the French Raphael cult, on, for example, the music of Grétry, is scarcely of significance for the reception of Mozart).

The thought of Raphael also brings with it that of the trivialization of Mozart's image, the 'divine youth' of many a belletristic account. But this thought, from the very beginning, was meant quite differently; we can see this from a few quotations by Wackenroder (or Tieck) – 'In all innocence and naïvety Raphael produced the most ingenious works, in which we see Heaven itself spread out before us.' He sees in 'the children in Raphael's pictures' an echo of 'that heavenly sweet innocence . . . we gaze ever more deeply, more seriously, more severely into the reflecting waters'. In his essay 'Die Töne', Wackenroder links their childlike figures to music: 'This seems to me to be the greatest thing of all the arts, but especially music, that their origins are so childish and childlike; to external reason their striving seems almost foolish, and they are ashamed to express it in words – in this bashfulness, in this childlike game the breath of the Highest may be felt, which rules the world of matter: this we can only feel or suspect.' The end of the *Berglinger Novelle*, from which our first quotation is taken, posits the idea that with Raphael or Dürer an ideal is envisaged which is higher than 'the power of the imagination' and contains within it a conquest of 'earthly life': this ideal represents an opposite to Berglinger's modern musician. When this was later applied to Mozart there was a dilemma – one had to fuse his topicality with the remoteness of an ideal, or translate his image into this remoteness, or free Raphael from any attempt at idealization.

A common practice was to illustrate Mozart's artistic achievement and his untimely death with references to Raphael. There are also comparisons with Torquato Tasso (Hormayr), Lord Byron (Goethe) or Alexander the Great (Rellstab). In his *Mozart und Raphael* (1800) Friedrich Rochlitz goes as far as to ascribe to both a 'new period' in their art, and also puts Raphael into a historical dimension. A similar chain of association, reaching from Wackenroder's ideal heights down into musical history, links Rochlitz's formulation that J.S. Bach was the 'patriarch of German music . . . the Albrecht Dürer of German music' to Reichardt's contention that Bach 'found in Mozart a kindred spirit who would know how to introduce his own [Bach's] profound artistic vision into the music of today'. We now approach the concept of the hero who, in Hegel's terms, 'knew what the times were, and what they needed'.

More problematic is Wackenroder's (and also Fichte's) notion of the hero as 'heaven's interpreter'. Even if Wackenroder had, in his *Berglinger Novelle*, listed Guido Reni after Raphael – Reni, 'who led a wild gambler's life', and yet 'was able to create the gentlest and most holy pictures' – then the usual Raphael-Mozart comparisons stressed the harmony of life and work. Rochlitz portrayed a selfless Mozart, with a 'sense of friendship, of general benevolence'; he was following Niemetschek here, who was probably the first to refer to Mozart as 'our Raphael in music'. Both Rochlitz and Niemetschek share the notion that Mozart certainly did have a sense of the beauty of nature and of the other arts, even if he 'as it were, only depicted this beauty in the form of his own art'.

Whereas Schlichtegroll still held to a concept of genius dating from the Enlightenment, Niemetschek and Rochlitz stand between two differing conceptions. Rochlitz regarded art as ideal nature, that is, the contemplation of ideal natural forms: the life of the artist is harmonized by reason. But this older, humanistic concept of the artist is given a modern dimension precisely by the comparison with Raphael – the childlike nature of the artist who does not know why the works he creates 'should take this form and no other' because he belongs to a higher sphere. These mutually exclusive characteristics – level-headedness on the one hand and childishness on the other – remain curiously undecided in both Rochlitz and the authors who followed in his footsteps. Mozart's tragic destiny and the disappointment of his last years are by no means interpreted as an inner necessity, enmeshed within his personality: the comparison with Raphael helps to avoid interpreting Mozart as a Berglinger figure. We notice how strong the influence of the

Zeitgeist (a pressure above and beyond such balancing acts) was, however, when Reichardt apparently converted to Romanticism; we see this in his *Vertraute Briefe aus Paris (Intimate Letters from Paris)* in 1802 and 1803. What he says about Haydn and Mozart supersedes both their and his own spiritual origins and involuntarily ends up in bitter self-criticism: 'Who knows whether or not Haydn and Mozart would have reached that high degree of Romantic art if their youthful education, their way of thinking and living had been different? and whether or not the works of many a rational, thinking artist often lack the magic of genius because this artist thought when he felt, and judged when he imagined?'

The Shakespeare comparisons deserve more interest than they have hitherto enjoyed because through them it is possible to grasp more clearly those peculiarities of Mozart's music that were at first scarcely understood and only later extolled. These characteristics were also durable ones, above all in that basic pattern which Grillparzer uses in his diary thus in 1826: 'Goethe, Shakespeare and Mozart hovered before me, men who knew how to combine the deepest artistic insights and powers with the freshness of lively, happy surroundings.' We find this also with Ernst Bloch, who admired the fusion of serious and *buffa* elements in Mozart's operas – 'this element which, in this sense, makes Mozart's work a Shakespearean work in music'. Niemetschek, in 1808, already points at the difference between the comparisons with Shakespeare and with Raphael when he writes: 'Mozart was a natural genius like Shakespeare, but Mozart is superior in taste and civility.' It was not Shakespeare's genius that Niemetschek disapproved of but his aesthetics, which flouted what Haydn had praised in Mozart, that is, his 'taste and his highest powers of composition'. There is a tacit criticism here against that outmoded *Sturm und Drang* idea that Shakespeare composed his plays in an inspired or brilliant lawlessness.

As early as 1793 Ludwig Tieck, in the introduction to his translation of *The Tempest*, had, unbeknown to the musicologists, stressed the psychological finesse with which Shakespeare had 'registered the finest stirrings of the human soul'; he also averred that, in this particular play, the spectator can never fix his gaze on a particular subject steadily and firmly because the poet constantly distracts our attention and keeps the imagination in a state of flux. But Tieck was scarcely thinking of Mozart here, of *Così fan tutte* or *Die Zauberflöte*, and the musicians were not thinking of Tieck's Shakespeare interpretations (Schikaneder, actually, did play a lot of Shakespeare – did the varieties of structure in *Die Zauberflöte* perhaps have a Shakespearean model?).

Shakespeare's name scarcely appears in writings about music before 1800.

When Christian Friedrich Daniel Schubart referred to the 'sublime, the terrifying, the Shakespearean' in his book *Ideen zu einer Ästhetik der Tonkunst*, then this was an exception, as was the characterization of the churchyard scene in *Don Giovanni* as 'the language of the spirits of Shakespeare' (in the *Dramaturgische Blätter*, Frankfurt, 1789). Rochlitz sees something similar (1798) in the first finale of *La Clemenza di Tito* which he greatly esteemed; he writes of 'Mozart's Shakespearean, powerful ability to portray the great, the splendid, the terrible, the fearful and the moving'. In his essay 'Mozart and Raphael', however, Rochlitz discusses Shakespeare in terms of his Romantic preference for artistic *inventio* over *elaboratio*.

Rochlitz does not shrink from mentioning Raphael's *School of Athens*, the first finale and the 'spirit scene' from *Don Giovanni* and the scenes relating to the king's death in *Macbeth* in one breath as examples of the fusion of inventive 'perfection' and 'happy execution'. In 1801 Triest takes this up critically and sees the following negative common ground: 'a certain indifference against the old artistic rules, for example in Shakespeare against the unities and in Mozart against stylistic purity'; he detected, he tells us, a 'lack of refinement in taste', as well as 'scholarly learning' and a 'frequent transgression of the seemly – in Shakespeare with anachronism and scenes of atrocity, in Mozart with an excessively frequent contrast between the comical and the tragic and with bizarre sequences of notes'. This old-fashioned view can hardly be called Romantic; Triest's standpoint is basically left open, for he did find most adulatory terms especially for *Don Giovanni* and in general for the 'lively portrayal of emotions' in Mozart and in Shakespeare.

The unknown author of the *Musikalischer Briefwechsel*, a source which we have frequently quoted, went a step further in his discussion of *Così fan tutte*. His intellectual starting point may be derived from Tieck's views on Shakespeare and Wackenroder's Raphael-image, the latter in the ideas concerning the childlike quality of genius: 'We see the genuinely childlike attitude in the way in which the earnest, the sombre sides of human destiny are treated with humour and levity, indeed, in which the most terrible gravity of life is not admitted without an inner smile.' There is an insistence, as there is in Tieck, upon the transfiguration of life's commonness. The central idea, the idea of a unity in the mutual mirroring of earnestness and serenity, seems very much intensified when the discussion turns to opera: 'Everything is but a mock, a game, a jest, a dalliance, an irony, things that are more difficult to grasp than the normal uniformity of life.' This observation, that art is a 'mirror of life', stands in opposition to the older conception, namely, that life itself becomes art, and leads to the proposition that, 'The two heroes of this world, the Romantic world, are Shakespeare and Mozart. Therefore we find in both of them that those two opposites are most inextricably joined.'

So here the old stipulation concerning the unity of the emotions is completely abandoned, and the traditional conceptions of form begin to falter. In an essay with the somewhat daunting title 'Veranlassung zur genauen Prüfung eines musikalischen Glaubensartikels' ('On the occasion of an exact examination of a musical article of faith') Rochlitz discusses the question of unity in operatic finales. He is against transposing dramatic conflicts into sequences of recitatives and arias and pleads for an 'uninterruptedly flowing music' as the 'expression of the feelings of the whole of nature, as we grasp it in the aesthetic idea, as it steps before our imagination . . . Such a finale would be a natural scene, a unique, colossal portrayal.' Here also the train of thought leads to the conviction that 'the Genius drove Mozart to this, and beyond, Mozart, like Shakespeare, a phenomenon of nature'. The natural force of genius, and the unity of music beyond the sphere of tangible formal regulations – this 'article of musical faith' has as its conclusion the following statement: 'The system can err, but feelings cannot!' And this is more than just a phrase.

The next stage of reflection – that reached by E.T.A. Hoffmann, and according to which an apparently chaotic surface is joined to an order which lies deeper, whereby the symphony is seen as being the 'drama' of the instruments – directs the Shakespeare comparisons away from Mozart to Beethoven.

I would like to draw particular attention to an author whose detailed Mozart/Shakespeare analogies are appropriate when we lead up to the discussion on that pair of contrasting opposites 'Classical' and 'Romantic', a discussion we have hitherto avoided. I mean Franz Horn who became known as a literary historian but who published the *Musikalische Fragmente* in 1802. These writings represent a very early attempt to use Mozart's operas to establish a Romantic ideal for music. The oldest point of reference is the 'Querelle des Anciens et des Modernes'. Horn prefers the moderns, praises Mozart (along with living composers like Domenico Cimarosa and Peter von Winter), latches on to the idea of natural genius that was current at the time and 'lets the Germans know that even the errors of their earlier Masters emerged from the depths of their feeling . . . that even these errors have been removed from us, and the day of annunciation dawns in a beautiful radiance, a tranquil verity – in a word, Mozart is ours.' This preference for modern authorities links the Romantics with the Classical: it was nothing unusual for the time around 1800 for Horn to see Mozart 'to be one with the modern

89

poets' (that is, Goethe) and find Shakespeare's Romantic art confirmed in Goethe's *Wilhelm Meister*. Friedrich Schlegel was another who saw Goethe, Shakespeare and Cervantes as the greatest exponents of irony in literature.

In his *Fragmente* Horn was concerned on the one hand with the vitality of art and on the other with its religious aspects. Both trains of thought have in common the rejection of the pictorial element in music, which is replaced by an 'invisible painting' which only a genius can achieve. The observations concerning the religious element see music as 'pure incomprehensibility', leading to a 'purely intellectual vision' that could not be learned. No modern poet, Horn informs us, felt this vision as deeply as Shakespeare did: 'How Romantically it suffuses each delicately structured situation in *The Tempest*.' He detects a similar process in *Don Giovanni*, and draws the conclusion that Mozart was the only one 'among the modern artists' who 'could stand comparison with Shakspear [*sic*]'. The language used here reminds us of Friedrich Schlegel's utterance: 'Through all the tones we hear/In the coloured dream of life/A gentle singing note/For him who quietly waits' – a statement that, a generation later, Robert Schumann would use as a motto for his Fantasie for piano Opus 17, implying a formal principle of high import. As the 'unbounded' could only be 'conceived by reason', art, 'by limitation', must make the infinite 'tangible for the imagination' (an idea corresponding to Schelling's notion of the sublime). The acid test for artists is the representation of the spirit world. In contrast to all the other theatrical conventions it was only Mozart and Shakespeare (in *Don Giovanni* and *Hamlet*) who succeeded in 'presenting a spirit in the spectator's mind' in such a way that the spectator is forced to believe in its incomprehensibility. This transition from the finite to the infinite is, in the convincing words of 'a modern religious thinker' (Horn must surely mean Schleiermacher here), a 'defining characteristic of true religiosity'.

Horn also contemplates the 'most blossoming, harmonic life' in Mozart's *Die Zauberflöte*, in *Don Giovanni* and in *La Clemenza di Tito*. Under the concept of 'the vital' he did not simply mean an interweaving of the comic and the tragic but a juxtapositioning of the Romantic with a parody of itself: there is no longer 'any strife between the real and the ideal, the intensive and the extensive'. Horn approaches Schlegel's concept of Romantic irony here, refers to it, puts forward the opinion that Grétry's attempt to 'express irony in music' only ended up as 'persiflage', makes a positive reference to Mozart but names as the only specific example Axur's 'Joy of the proud, aloof Irza!' from the third act of Salieri's *Axur (Tarare)*; he emphasizes in general the function of irony for opera – 'Here in the realm of opera let there be the game of games, life which rejoices in life, whose deepest mysteries only music may express.' This 'transitoriness' which leads on to ever higher unities he sees as the 'finest fruit of the modern spirit', and he extols with emphasis freedom in both opera and music. 'The character of opera must be freedom, freedom in all directions. Let no destiny determine the actions of the hero.' He continues: 'Music can only exist in freedom, not in necessity.' Art, when seem from above, is (for Horn) a breakthrough of the supernatural; when seen from below it represents an ascent towards freedom. He was therefore consistent here in criticizing Körner for having attempted (in the 'Horen' essay from the year 1795) 'to divide up the arts according to extra-essential (material) criteria' and he turned the aesthetics of Körner and Schiller upside down by arguing: 'It seems to me that it should be the task of a composer of operas to blur the distinction between Ethos (that which is fixed and resting) and Pathos (the volatile, the transitory) in his musical creation' and also 'that he should represent life in its highest potentiality, freedom that has become something necessary, *the limitlessly limited'*.

Horn was actually constructing a Romantic conception of music before the fight for or against Romanticism began in the year 1808. We see quite clearly in his case, and, later, in the case of E.T.A. Hoffmann and others, that *our* understanding of Romanticism and Classicism in music is not the same as that of those living at that time. We can explain the apparent discrepancy between the Romantic conception of art and its musical *exemplum classicum* Mozart by pointing out that Romanticism would first have to find its adequate correlative because, at the beginning of the century, there was no Romantic music. This was the view of Horn and Hoffmann: the music of Mozart or Beethoven would be a compensation for what was not at hand. And yet it becomes clear from their writings that it was not a compensation, but a consummation. Hoffmann's own compositions, so very difficult to categorize, show that this consummation has nothing to do with our conception of Classical and Romantic music.

The Mozart reception at the beginning of the century was not completely Romantic, but its literary formulation was increasingly conditioned by the Romantics. There can be no talk of specific counterbalance, of a pointedly Classical musical aesthetic. The continuous use of words like 'Classical' and 'Romantic' does not demonstrate a clarity of insight, rather its opposite. The two terms have much in common: both are modern, they want to prepare the way for something new; both are fashionable, both are *à la mode*.

The custom of calling Romantic all that was of a higher provenance, that was neither stuffy nor Philistine, often leads to empty phrases, and Nestroy was supposed to have amused himself mightily whenever he heard the

91

well-known expression: 'That's a Classic.' More handy is the contrast between the modern concept of the 'Poetic' (and thus of the 'Romantic') and the older ideas of 'character' in music. Here Tieck and Horn are in opposition to Körner and Schiller. It is only about two decades later that we get a clearer opposition between Romantic and Classic in writings about music.

The predominance of the Romantics within aesthetic argumentation lies on the one hand in the new position of honour which music now inhabits within the hierarchy of the arts and, on the other hand, in the view promulgated by Friedrich Schlegel and Novalis that artistic criticism, by adequately mediating the impression that art inspires, could become an art-work itself. The question now arises as to how we should understand these writings about music – as an aesthetic or as theory, as an interpretation of certain works and musicians, or as art-work themselves with their own laws which are not to be confused with the laws of the musical subject itself. Musicology tends to the former, literary history to the latter opinion. What we do know for certain is that this central area of application of Romanticism within Mozart reception occupies an élite position and tends to a subject-matter which is highly charged. Henrici expressed this very drastically in 1806: 'Why should we be interested in the wretched ballads of the streets, the cacophony of the alleys, when Mozart's divine harmonies can make us touch the holy music of the spheres?'

This Romantic notion of an élitism is supported by a desire to transcend all boundaries and to fuse all the arts together. Metaphors expressing intangibility now creep into music-criticism, and a lot of what E.T.A. Hoffmann wrote about music – writings regarded as literature (*Dichtung*) – appeared as reviews in the *Allgemeine Musikalische Zeitung* in Leipzig. In Horn's *Musikalische Fragmente* too the argumentation becomes concentrated in a scarcely rational manner: we have quotations from Shakespeare's dramas, nature descriptions ('a rushing brook is Romantic, a thundering river sublime'), and descriptions of Mozart's 'oscillating emotions' couched in terminology which evokes 'a ruin beneath shrubbery in a charming landscape'. The same kind of imagery is found when Hoffmann, as a critic and a writer, evokes Mozart's E flat major symphony, a work which he loved; in the essay 'Beethovens Instrumental-Musik' we hear the following: 'Love and sadness sound in a sweet chorus of ghostly voices; night rises in a gleaming purple radiance and, in inexplicable longing, we follow those forms which, beckoning us in their friendly ranks, fly in an eternal dance through the heavenly spheres.' And in the *Abenteuer der Silvester-Nacht* (*Adventures of New Year's Eve*) we read: 'Berger sat again at the piano: he played the andante from Mozart's sublime E flat major symphony, and all the love and the joy of my highest, most radiant life, soared upwards on the downy wings of song.' Both pictorial descriptions latch on to the epithet 'Swansong' which contemporaries gave to the E flat major symphony: the function is, of course, different according to the context.

We see how complicated on the whole the relationship between the details can be when we look at the most famous example of Romantic writing dealing with a work of Mozart's – Hoffmann's novella *Don Juan* with its subtitle 'A fabulous incident which befell a travelling enthusiast'. We cannot overlook the fact that an enthusiastic admirer is speaking when we read the following:

The horrors of the fearful, subterranean *regno all pianto* seized me in the andante; I was filled with ghastly premonitions of terror. The exultant fanfare in the seventh bar of the allegro seemed like a triumphant blasphemy: I saw fiery demons stretch their glowing claws from the darkness, desirous of seizing those happy beings who were merrily dancing on a thin crust above a bottomless abyss. I could see, clearly before my mind's eye, the conflict between human nature and the hideous, unseen powers which sought to destroy it. The storm finally abated: the curtain swiftly rose.

We are obviously concerned here with 'the deeper significance of this opera of operas,' to fathom 'this splendid work of the divine master in the depths of its characterization' and to understand 'what the initiate [Mozart] uttered in his inspiration'.

Yet this 'interpretation', reported to the narrator's *alter ego* Theodor, functions as an introduction and a finale to an exalted effusion which runs throughout *Don Juan* or leads to the depths already invoked. And it is the singer of Donna Anna who shows the way here. Just as an Italian performance of the opera 'here in this German setting' promises to bring us closer to Mozart's 'spirit', so it is the exotic quality of the Tuscan woman and her mysterious appearance in the box during the interval (thus stepping out of her stage role) which completely opens up to us 'the miraculous realm of Romanticism'. The singer of Donna Anna and the poetic ego of an opera-composer find themselves in this realm: 'I have understood you – your feelings were expressed to me in song! Yes – I have sung you, as I am your melodies.' And it is no longer Mozart's melodies that are meant here. This happy moment of deepest accord (the woman's death the following night

93

lends an even greater import) is found in the field of his own art which is able to 'realize the magic rapture of love which longs eternally'.

The action, admittedly, determines the image of Mozart's opera: that of a worthy secret love between Donna Anna and Don Juan. Consistently but in contrast to Da Ponte, the importance of sin and punishment is reduced; instead Donna Anna is in vain 'chosen by Heaven, in her love for Don Juan, to make him aware of those immanent springs of divine nature within him'. Don Juan now mirrors the tragedy of the Romantic artist, yearning for the perfect love, yet torn and rent in his emotions, full of 'scorn for those petty people around him' and with 'something of Mephistopheles in his physiognomy'. So a drama which, for Mozart and Da Ponte, is still firmly fixed in the tradition of Baroque allegory is now made into a myth and a theme for a *novella*.

However, we cannot simply state that Hoffmann has romanticized Mozart's opera and ignored the central ideas. Mozart and Da Ponte themselves were the first to enhance the status of Donna Anna (in contrast to the Don Juan operas of Bertati and Gazzaniga), even if the motif of love-hatred is lacking. And in marked contrast to Goldoni and all the other Don Juan plays of his time, Mozart intensified in his music the breakthrough of the supernatural in the figure of the Commendatore. Hoffmann, therefore, emphasizes the untimely elements in Mozart's opera and thus points back across Mozart to the mythical formulations of the theme in the seventeenth century. And gazing chronologically in the other direction we may also claim that Hoffmann's considerable influence on the productions and the writings on *Don Juan* did not stem so much from the story itself as from his interpretation of the work – even though this may have been based on a misunderstanding. This was confirmed by Adolf Bernhard Marx in 1824: 'Through his exemplary depiction of Mozart's masterpieces Hoffmann has paid the most beautiful homage to him, and erected the most magnificent paragon for all those singers who wish to execute the role of Don Juan.' And it was Wilhelmine Schröder-Devrient, in her greatly admired role as Donna Anna, who finally established the definitive persona of Donna Anna, changing her from an emotional girl to a true heroine.

The narrative work of Joseph von Eichendorff shows how rich the palette of Mozart's influence can be. The assumption could be made that the admirer of *Le Nozze di Figaro* had taken over the figure he loved most of all – Cherubino – into his own work: an example would be the novella *Das Marmorbild*. And yet the constellation of Florio and the two women characters in the story (the 'lovely lady' and Bianca) is hardly comparable to that of Cherubino and the Countess, Susanna and the childlike Barbarina.

Can Florio be called a Cherubino figure at all? If he is, then Eichendorff has very eloquently transposed the castle and the gardens of Count Almaviva, which are suffused by a web of feelings and intrigues, into a Romantic world where 'wild terrestrial spirits' are to be tamed, and spirits 'reach out for us from the depths'.

The innocent, impetuous youthfulness of Florio may perhaps be related to that of Cherubino, but those realms of Venus which tempt Florio, those powers which 'exert a seductive power through diabolical deceptions on young and innocent beings' are closer to the world of Wagner's *Tannhäuser* than that of *Figaro* – apart, of course, from that which we can only (and unfortunately) vaguely call the musicality of the text. The situation is reversed, and we may be permitted to assume that Eichendorff appropriated to himself the principles of Mozartian *opera buffa* – musical characterization, conception and execution of ensembles and tableaux in finales. One might also talk about a 'scenic structure of narration' *à la* Mozart, except that Eichendorff has changed those techniques so radically that words like adoption and model are too crude. (The same is true for the paraphrasing of the Don Juan figure in Tieck's *William Lovell* and Roquairol in Jean Paul's *Titan*.)

Music also contributed to the convergence of the arts: quite early on, in 1806, August Apel attempted this with Mozart's late E flat major symphony. Using the title *Musik und Poesie* he went beyond the old idea of 'character depiction' in instrumental music and demanded that the generality of a poetic mood be concretized in particular images. Perhaps it is rather daring of me, but I would argue that the consequences resulting from this are a principal anticipation of Liszt's thinking. Apel sees in the symphony 'the depiction of an idea through the sensuous medium of sound'; the idea, however, is not 'chained to the sound'. He continues: 'To transpose a symphony into a poem means nothing less than grasping its idea and its particular characterization independently of the means of depiction and representing it again through the medium of literature.'

With this idea in mind he composed a poem to which, significantly, he gave the title 'Sinfonie nach Mozart in Es dur': it deals with noble ideals, heroism and finally the all-conquering power of love. We also have Greek mythology and the restless longing of a suffering youth *à la* Werther. The reason why we are tempted to see an analogy with Liszt lies in the dramaticization of the music by the text, whose constant impetus may be called *per aspera ad astra*.

When we look at Mozart's musical succession in the narrower sense the situation is basically similar and by no means easier to assess. There are

95

various reasons for these difficulties; one of the prerequisites (still hardly met) would be a precise formulation of Mozart's personal style so that a clear point of reference could be reached. The question would, however, still remain open – did a composer who followed in his footsteps, or one who deliberately avoided him, grasp the essential nature of his style or not? Was the reference to Mozart simply lip service or did it presuppose a thorough study? What was specifically Mozartian in the succession?

A precise answer was scarcely sought in earlier times, and even today research prefers to concentrate on musical quotations from Mozart or the less obvious similarities in details. Perhaps the outcome is the same as that situation prevailing among composers a hundred and fifty years ago and more: the problem with imitativeness is that it tends to prefer the details rather than that for which they stand. Many quotations bear witness, certainly, to a reverence for Mozart, but not every musical similarity stems from a serious intention. In general we can say that the composers who came after Mozart regarded him in the same way that he regarded his predecessors. Much was simply picked up by him, and many a theme, and many a movement which seems to us to be 'Mozartian' is, in fact, typically traditional. But the fame of Haydn and Mozart made their music into a paradigm in any search for identification (not epigonic, but seen as the climax of the age) and also into the means of communicating a tradition which, through the introduction of new developments, was slowly achieving historical remoteness.

If we go a step further, our dilemma becomes clear because of the fact that art is more than a simple acceptance of models. When referring to the young composer August Fesca, Carl Maria von Weber put it as follows: 'Mozart and Haydn were, in the noblest sense, his models, as is appropriate for every true artist, and there is no progress in art without the external stimulus, the spark.'

So the Mozart veneration in the music of respectable composers like Johann Nepomuk Hummel or Louis Spohr is more difficult to assess than that of imitative composers of lesser status. Hummel's compositional life began – symbolically – in Vienna, and there are aspects of his life which remind us of Mozart: he was a prodigy, then became known and esteemed as a pianist and a composer for the piano. On the title-page of his piano variations Opus 6 (1798) he referred to himself as a disciple of Mozart, Albrechtsberger and Salieri; much later, he also published arrangements of Mozart. The associations in his work may be explained by his biography and the general conditions of his time; his piano music and chamber music were oriented towards Mozart, but his church music more to Haydn, and there are references to Beethoven in his later development, and his piano concertos also reflect the newer virtuoso practices.

It is also axiomatic that Hummel himself was influential on others – we can point to Chopin's piano movements, and Alfred Einstein spoke of a 'Hummelish Schubert' in the scherzo of the *Wanderer* fantasy. But how is it possible to detect the influence of Mozart in all of this? Perhaps it is most obvious in the invention and treatment of themes in the early work, but here we also find the juxtaposition with elements that are not Mozartian – a uniform structure of movements for example or a mannerly periodicity. As soon as Hummel succeeds in composing in a more elastic fashion we can see that many 'influences' are present – it is more correct then (even if it is vaguer) to see Mozartian elements more readily in Hummel's striving for refinement in the construction of movements, a more objective expression and the application of a measured use of musical means.

Louis Spohr, a few years younger, no longer possessed immediate access to Mozart's musical environment but grew up into a world which, as regards ideas and musical history, Hummel was never to reach. In his autobiography Spohr tells us how he experienced 'thrills of bliss' and 'dreamlike delights' when he first heard *Die Zauberflöte* and *Don Giovanni*. When it was pointed out that the overture of his early opera *Alruna* contained echoes of *Die Zauberflöte* he explained: 'Given my veneration for Mozart and the esteem in which I hold this overture it seems that my reproduction was something very natural and laudable.' He continues to describe the next stage in his self-awareness thus: 'And so, made aware of myself, I saw the necessity to free myself [from echoes of Mozart] and believed that I had managed to achieve this completely in my next dramatic work, *Faust*.'

Despite this, both the musical and the dramatic conceptions of *Faust* (1816) and of *Don Giovanni* are very close, and offer one of the early examples of the fusion of these great themes. As a mature artist Spohr would become an esteemed and noble traditionalist during the age of Biedermeier: the individuality of his compositional style shows at once a proximity to, and a distance from, Mozart. The melancholy of Spohr's music may, as Spohr would have wished, call Mozart to mind, but it is also the melancholy of a contemporary of Lord Byron; the balance and transparency of Mozart's music was realized in Spohr as a kind of musical exclusiveness which was not meant to 'excite the common crowd' – but this would unwillingly and severely curtail Mozart's universality, particularly in *Die Zauberflöte*, a work which Spohr loved so much. Yet the generation which succeeded Spohr would look back on him as being 'immediately illuminated by the radiant sun of Mozart': this simplification, formulated by Richard Wagner in his

97

obituary for Spohr, amounts to a friendly distancing from Spohr as well as Mozart.

Of much greater significance is the question concerning the musical relationship between Beethoven and Mozart, a relationship suggested by the concept of Viennese Classicism as well as the utterance of Count Waldstein about 'Mozart's spirit from the hands of Haydn'. Throughout his life Beethoven let his veneration for Mozart be publicly known and found many fine words for *Die Zauberflöte* and also the *Requiem*. And yet for the musical amateur of then as of now, regardless of any schematic division between Classicism and Romanticism, the music of Mozart and of Beethoven are characteristic of two very different worlds of expression. And even the experts are not quite certain about the similarity between the two: stylistic studies have shown that it was Haydn, rather, who was a source for Beethoven, so that Waldstein's comment, when reversed ('The spirit of Haydn from the hands of Mozart') seems almost more meaningful. Yet this retouching only glosses over the 'gap between Mozart and Beehoven' which the Mozart scholar Hermann Abert mentions. Abert here by no means ignores the fact that Beethoven learned from Mozart the 'multiformity and opposition of themes': the 'gap' is covered, rather, by those similarities of motifs and analogous details avidly sought by both experts and amateurs.

Because Beethoven wrote variations on themes by Mozart or more or less quoted him, it does not necessarily mean that there was an affinity between the two. Here too the context of tradition made appear as a quotation what was really part and parcel of the current types and models; we find this above all in the light-hearted compositions, in the music of Beethoven's where the old spirit of the divertimento could still be found. But when we get an affinity, say, between the last movement of the B flat major symphony (K. 319) and that of the Eighth Symphony, in a work of Beethoven's, that is, which is generally known as a 'music-making on musical models'; or when, say, themes from *Die Zauberflöte* (a work that we know Beethoven particularly admired) are to be heard in the Second Symphony and also in the *Prometheus* music (no. 16) – then we have a mixture of both a sympathetic *and* an alienating attitude on the composer's part.

It is also, on the other hand, difficult to prove the distance between Beethoven and Mozart by enumerating details. Studies such as Hans Gal's on the style of early Beethoven are convincing, although they also tend to generalize: Gal differentiates between Mozart's 'style of retardation' and Beethoven's 'absolute melody' (by this Gal means 'purely diatonic melody, a melody which forgoes retardation, or the progression to an accentuated bar').

Individual examples are more succinct, although they do not prove anything: I would like to give just one example here. I was once listening to the andante from Mozart's *Prague* symphony and, quite by chance, was reminded of Beethoven, particularly the tercet no. 13 'Euch werde Lohn in bessren Welten' ('Thou shalt be rewarded in a better world') from the second act of *Fidelio*. It was not the course of the movement, but two particular themes which triggered off the association: it was, then, the usual hunt for reminiscences that was the starting point. The character of the first theme reminded me of the beginning of the tercet, but also of the passage 'In des Lebens Frühlingstagen' ('In the Early Spring of Life') from Florestan's aria and also of the second theme of the 'Allegretto' of the Seventh Symphony. It was less a particular melody, a sequence of notes, that led to a feeling of similarity but rather a kind of movement, a quiet *legato melos* in parallels of sixths and thirds, over a resting bass within a complete cadence with emphasis on the subdominant. On the one hand this structure amounts to an old type of pastoral; on the other hand, to use the technical jargon, it may be regarded as a Classical 'tone of humanity'. The second association was triggered by a rising melody, more lengthy, played in unison by oboe and bassoon (bars 45ff. and 132ff.). We have something similar in Florestan's tercet 'O dass ich euch nicht lohnen kann' ('O, that I cannot reward you'), also accompanied by unison flute and clarinet.

On looking through the scores I noticed that both the initial themes, one similar to the other, took up a dominant position in the following sections, while the second theme, in Mozart and in Beethoven, had the function in both composers of introducing the final passage. It was the relative conspicuousness of the common ground that led us more easily to recognize the differences in the way in which both composers used their material. With Beethoven the rising *unisono* theme is the goal of a process of intensification and, as such, is executed in broader sweep; with Mozart it appears by chance, as it were, and yet as a varied inversion of a melody placed immediately before it, without great import for the movement as a whole and yet pointing towards its finale. The pastoral mode is a musical pendant to the picture of an arcadian idyll. Beethoven introduces it as an independent unit, Mozart modifies it repeatedly, particularly in the middle of the movement, when he releases it from the tonic reference point and darkens it in the minor key. But perhaps the contrast is already exaggerated here.

In the Allegretto of the Seventh Symphony, Beethoven contrasts the legato pastoral melody with the dactylic staccato repetition of the first theme. Within this movement the contrasting types of expression frequently relieve each other: it was obviously not Beethoven's intention that they should interpenetrate. His Allegretto movement is far more block-like than Mozart's Andante, which is finely differentiated down to the last detail, with each detail finding a new impetus. This obviously says nothing about the quality, but something about the expressive intent. Mozart likewise contrasts the legato pastoral melody with a staccato motif; after a few bars, however, the initial character of the music is dissolved (bar 8ff.) and within that same phrase returns to the legato mode as at the beginning. Nevertheless, Mozart repeats the rhythm of the staccato theme ($\mathbf{\frac{6}{8}}$ ♪ ♪ ♪ ♫♩ | ♩) repeatedly during the movement (also as a response to the rising unison theme in bar 47), yet he does not hold on to it obstinately, as does Beethoven, but lets it emerge as though by accident, so that a red thread, if you like, runs through the weave of the movement. Taken as a principle, and applied as such to the pastoral theme, a releasing, liberating function is given to the chromatic semiquaver passage of the first violin which begins in the third bar, a sequence which loosens what went before – a function which Mozart actually does take up and exploits above all in the movement's central section in order to tempt the listener on to the 'unsafe' paths of musical imagination.

Why we need such a description, a hermetic sounding account, is easily explained: it is for my own personal feeling; for the depiction, which is difficult to formulate, of the ambiguity of expression in Mozart's music, which found a cipher in the Mozart-Shakespeare comparisons already discussed (whereby an apparently spontaneous feeling was unmasked as the result of an historical awareness) – finally as a symptom of the difference between Mozart and Beethoven.

The search for what Schubert had in common with Mozart, and what separated them, is hardly less difficult. It does not lead to a succinct illustration of the conceptual contrast between Classicism and Romanticism, for Schubert is the composer who is one of the most difficult to classify among all the great musicians. Once again we have similarity in detail, attitudes to tradition and sometimes even of intentions. What do we make of the melodic similarity between Schubert's *Heidenröslein* (composed in 1815) and 'If only every worthy man' from *Die Zauberflöte?* We cannot know whether Schubert wanted to document his special liking for *Die Zauberflöte* or whether or not the two examples are linked 'simply' by being examples of popular airs. The reference (now somewhat of a stereotype) to a shimmering interweaving of near and far is also valid for Schubert's instrumental music. In the Andante to the Second Symphony (1815) he gives us a theme which is related to Don Ottavio's aria 'Il mio tesoro' from *Don*

100

Giovanni and develops a sequence of variations from it. The Andante for piano from the year 1812 may be understood as a series of fantasies on a theme from *Figaro*. But the intention is not to copy Mozart's variation technique but to seek out new ways leading from a familar focus.

Schubert certainly adopted some of Mozart's techniques and pre-dilections: Walter Vetter described the instrumentation of the B flat major symphony as a 'homage to Mozart's late G minor symphony'. That Schubert's technique of transition and of mood-change would have been unthinkable without Mozart stands to reason both biographically and historically; to maintain that there is 'spiritually something completely new in Schubert' is meaningful and would be confirmed by anyone who has ears to hear. Yet it still remains unsatisfactory as it cannot be taken literally, but only pursued into endless differentiations. To talk about new wine in old bottles is to aim into the void, as content and form are here indistinguishable.

The critic's dilemma is less intrusive in those works in which Schubert – especially in the year 1816 – aimed his attention specifically at Mozart for reasons which we can recognize. One year before he had achieved the breakthrough as a composer of *Lieder* with the song 'Gretchen am Spinnrade'; he felt personally much freer after he had given up working in his father's school; the relationship between him and his teacher Salieri progressed in a positive manner. It was in these hopeful days that Schubert wrote his famous Mozart credo in his diary (see page 71), using the images of 'the darkness of this life' and the 'beneficient impressions of a lighter, higher existence'; it was the 'wondrous sounds of Mozart's music which 'left the stamp of beauty in his soul'. Mozart's music represented hope: in words it remained the reflection of a 'beautiful remoteness' which Schubert, however, sought to realize in his own music.

The B flat major symphony and the string quartet in E major – both of them works which refer to Mozart's G minor symphony – date from this time, as do the three sonatas for piano and violin. The latter are seen to have much in common with Mozart: they are misunderstood as being pretty but trivial pieces 'for young musicians'. Schubert, however, intended them to be sentimental rather than naïve; the first two works mentioned are not so much of interest because of echoes of particular themes, or the taking over of an orchestral sound, imitation of formal structure, and so on, but rather because of the striking fact that the G minor model is taken by Schubert and transposed into the brightest possible ethereal light. We may assume that Schubert, also in other compositions dating from that year (1816), wished to create a 'music of the angels' with Mozart as the inspiration. (We might claim the same for the octet in F major and the A minor string quartet of the

101

year 1824.) The finale of the A minor sonata, that ethereal transparency touched by a light melancholy, is all the more important here with its reminiscences of Pamina's aria 'Ach, ich fühl's', although earlier in this movement there was a clear parallel to the untroubled final movement of the E flat major sonata (K. 380).

The situation is basically the same with the third great composer of the early nineteenth century – Carl Maria von Weber. Mozart's music is the prerequisite for the early piano music, for the songs and the operas, but it is not the only factor; even for *Der Freischütz* the models may be found in Gluck and the *Singspiel* tradition from Peter von Winter to E.T.A. Hoffmann. What is far more important, of course, is the intrinsic value of Weber's music which cannot be reduced to these models; it is quite another matter when Weber, as a self-assured artist, showed a commitment to Mozart's music. He demonstrated this frequently as a conductor of opera, and there were patriotic motives here, a deliberate gesture in the face of the fashionable Italian opera. The fitting words (already quoted) which Weber found for Mozart's music and his noticeable reserve – despite due deference – felt towards Beethoven give an indirect but unmistakable confession of his own aesthetic origins.

Without wishing to impose upon the public a *Diktat* concerning taste, both Weber and Schubert – the one with his Romantic operas, and the other with his songs – took certain groups of Mozart's works, added a distinctive characteristic, and altered them for the ears of their contemporaries. The question of the relationship between Mozart and Beethoven is more problematic if only because it was Beethoven who became the most influential composer of the nineteenth century. Before it was the formula 'Haydn and Mozart' which stood for quality – and also modernity. It was an event such as the 'Grand Concert' in the Viennese Freihaustheater on 27 October 1798, where the twenty-eight-year-old Beethoven played his First Piano Concerto after the Overture to *Die Zauberflöte* and arias by Mozart, with Haydn's *Drumroll* symphony given as a finale, which seemed to represent the consummation of Classical unity and which, with hindsight, took on a symbolic significance: yet only a few years later the music of Beethoven would represent a challenge to the established 'Haydn-Mozart' duality. The awareness of what was modern would be dislocated by Beethoven and also by operatic developments in Paris, although to begin with the assessments would by no means be uniform.

In 1804 the young composer Georg Abraham Schneider wrote the following in the Leipzig *Allgemeine Musikalische Zeitung* about a concert which included Beethoven's Second Symphony: 'In general, this symphony

102

did not cause the kind of sensation that a symphony by Haydn or Mozart might.' A Viennese correspondent of the *Berlinische Musikalische Zeitung* found (in 1805) the *Eroica* symphony to be 'garish and confused' but admitted that there were many people in Vienna 'who idolize the shortcomings and the talents of this composer with the same amount of ardour which touches at times upon the ludicrous'. Perhaps we are already seeing here the beginnings of that later battle between Mozartians and admirers of Beethoven, a battle which, especially in Vienna, would rage *con brio*. In 1805 Christian Friedrich Michaelis, in the same journal, pronounced the three (Mozart, Haydn and Beethoven) to have equal status: but the grouping is completely different in an obituary for Luigi Boccherini which appeared in 1806. Here the 'original and naïve' works of Haydn and Boccherini are contrasted with 'the difficult, artistic quartets' of Mozart, Romberg and Beethoven. In 1807 Reichardt, until then a despiser of Mozart, extolled the latter's 'magnificent artistic skill' in the symphonies and played them off against Beethoven.

But the tendency to see Mozart as a rock of tradition and Beethoven as a guarantor of innovation grew apace. Tieck, who was an admirer of Mozart, wrote in 1816 in his *Phantasus* that the symphonies of Beethoven (whom Tieck had got to know personally in 1813) were the music of a 'madman'. In his essay 'Beethovens Instrumental-Musik' (1810) Hoffmann implied an idealising distance from Mozart which was lacking in the case of Beethoven: 'Beethoven's music pulls the levers of dread, of fear, of horror, of pain, and awakens that eternal longing which is the essence of Romanticism.' Earlier we read the following about Mozart: 'Mozart leads us into the depths of the spirit world: fear surrounds us, but without torment; it is more of a premonition of the infinite.' Hoffmann, even earlier, had said friendly things about Haydn, and thereby had grouped the Classical trinity together in a graduated model which was at least hinted at long before such things became common under Hegel's influence on writings on music (the exception being Reichardt, who expressed something similar in 1810 when discussing the development of the string quartet).

It was only in the 1820s that the hierarchy became clarified. An essay written in 1824 by Adolf Bernhard Marx, 'Etwas über Beethovens Symphonien' elucidated the feeling of somehow being at the goal of a developmental process. Marx was a biographer of Beethoven whose thought had been conditioned by Hegel; he was also the dominant music-theorist in Berlin at that time. He writes:

It is precisely those who set the tone in matters of music who were educated in the Mozartian period, and not a few of them remained on this level ... They applauded Beethoven as long as he followed Mozart: when his later originality began to show itself at this time it was regarded as an aberration, a youthful dissipation, and the hope was expressed that he would find his way back to Mozart's path. These opinions may well persist, but art does not remain static, Beethoven does not remain static, Beethoven, in whose work the greatest advances in music after Mozart are visible, above all in his sonatas and his symphonies.

At the end of the same year, 1824, Marx provided as an epilogue to the first year of his *Berliner Allgemeine Musikalische Zeitung* a markedly programmatic article on the 'Andeutung des Standpunkts der Zeitung' ('Elucidation of the Standpoint of the Journal'). In was his aim, politely, to dispatch a musical epoch – together with its lodestar, Mozart – into the dim and distant past. What was new above all was

the depth of idea in Beethoven's compositions, the new richness of sound in the tone-combinations of his symphonies, his bold, new, expanded modulations, the magnificent sense of wholeness, the passion unheard of since Spontini's operas and the garland of ingenious insights *à la* Weber, his bold and elaborate striving for a characteristic quality hitherto inaccessible, even the voluptuous sensuality of Rossini, and the wit of the French.

Marx gives us a vivid picture of the standpoint and the optimism of the progressive party. It seemed as though the eighteenth-century French habit of indulging in partisan battles over matters of taste was now being resurrected in the German cultural centres of Vienna and Berlin. Marx describes the battles between supporters of Weber and adherents of Spontini and their united onslaught against Rossini, and continues: 'How even the admirers of Mozart and Beethoven, in mutual misapprehension and misinterpretation, retreat from one another!'

His intention, an intention portrayed with a professional sense of superiority, is to alleviate the situation: Rochlitz had already suggested an answer in an obituary for Hoffmann which appeared in 1822. When faced with the question whether or not Mozart's *Figaro*, Salieri's *Axur* or Cimarosa's *Matrimonio Segreto* were antiquated, Rochlitz asked another, that is, whether a work 'that had been preferred in the theatre yesterday' could be new. The answer is clear and unambiguous: 'The truly natural, that is, the spirit that is always original, can never become antiquated.'

104

Franz Stoepel, with his *Grundzüge der Geschichte der modernen Musik* (Berlin, 1821), emphatically held the same viewpoint. It was certainly provocative to begin a survey by claiming that Homer was the first 'hero in the cultural history of mankind' and to end it by citing Mozart as a 'hero in musical history'; what Stoepel writes about Mozart should be seen as a credo of the traditionalists who were now closing ranks:

He is the greatest of the masters, for in his works are found all the conditions of that which is truly beautiful – truth, sublimity and grace, joined in a mysterious manner. No artist has ever worked his material in such a free, and at the same time such an ordered manner, with a controlling spirit that never imposes itself as cold reflection but which forms his works into an organic whole, a whole from which all that is individual necessarily develops, and by which the whole is, again, necessarily conditioned.

We then get a few swipes at the 'janglings of the Italians and the French' and the 'clip-clopping of the present age'. In Vienna the discussions were certainly no less agitated: we also get a report by Vesque von Püttlingen, in the 1820s, that his opponent in an argument tried to floor him with the ingenious remark that 'as a Beethoven-fanatic he was unable to appreciate a Mozart quartet'.

But it would be erroneous to look at this polarization from the point of view of literary history, that is, as a battle (somewhat delayed) between the supporters of Classicism and Romanticism. The state of affairs is confusing because on the one hand there was, in the 1820s, a definition put forward by Amadeus Wendt of a musical Classicism represented by 'the clover-leaf: Haydn/Mozart/Beethoven' and, on the other hand, an emphatic defoliation of this clover. Developmental models with Beethoven as an aim offered a solution to the conflict. If I myself may be provocative – the concept of a trinity of Viennese Classics seems to me a misrepresentation glossed over in a Hegelian manner: there was actually an ever-deepening contrast. If he and his solution are already present in E.T.A. Hoffmann, then Marx and his supporters are actually to be understood far better as precursors of Wagner and the New German School, those then representing the climax of the Romantic philosophy of music.

We can also determine the way in which the positions clarified when we look at certain individuals. Rochlitz, for example, never really exemplified a Romantic theory of music. In his Mozart anecdotes he had taken a lot – and not only biographical information – from his predecessors; he was benevolently critical towards Tieck's *Phantasien über die Kunst* (1799). Yet it was only in the challenges of the early 1820s that he adopted an unambiguously Classicist position. The position from which Niemetschek, in 1808, inveighed against the 'chaotic entanglements', the 'dense obfuscation' and the 'confusions of our latest composers', contrasting them with the 'tranquil sublimity, the clear, simple songs of our favourite', is taken up more intensely than ever.

Musical life, even in Prague, showed that a lot had changed in the meanwhile. In the early nineteenth century the Mozart cult continued unabated. A vigorous representative was the Czech composer Wenzel Johann Tomaschek, who expressed the same views as Niemetschek, seeing Beethoven particularly as being gifted, but mistaken. Carl Maria von Weber, who was *Kapellmeister* in Prague from 1813 to 1816, got to know this Mozart cult well; he found it was all very well, but antiquated and narrow-minded. Already earlier, under Wenzel Müller, the situation had begun to change: a regular Beethoven cult had emerged and ousted the cultivation of tradition.

In musical practice, however, the progressive party was on the up and up, and the traditionalists were slipping more and more into a less hopeful defence position. When we read the reports of the correspondents in the musical journals we increasingly become aware of a waning of interest in Mozart's music and a fall in the number of performances of his works. The printing of his scores and their sales reflect a similar decline. When the publishers Breitkopf & Härtel (a firm so important for Mozart's work) made an inventory in 1823 they listed as their main stock the holdings of Mozart, Haydn, Clementi and Dussek. The selection was very varied indeed, although the chamber music outweighed the orchestral music by far. The scale of arrangements for the instruments fashionable at the time (violin, flute, guitar, then, secondly, for harp and mandolin) is very wide; piano works and arrangements for voice and piano were very popular. But about the time of Beethoven's death there was an 'almost radical break', scarcely noticeable in concert programmes, but certainly in the demand for music for the home – and Beethoven was included in this negative trend. The interest of the music-buying public shifted from the Viennese classics to a more modern, more international circle of composers, many of whom were associated with Paris: we may name Thalberg, Kalkbrenner, Chopin, Pleyel, Cherubini, Bellini, Berlioz, Bertini, Meyerbeer, Rossini, also Weber and Mendelssohn.

There was in the reception of Mozart a moment of tender retrospection: already at this time his music seemed to represent a kind of recuperation from the exertions that the newer music demanded. A reviewer in the *Haude-und Spenersche Zeitung*, describing a concert on 17 March 1827 featuring Beethoven's string quartet Opus 127, wrote the following: 'It was very soothing and agreeable, after the exertions, to hear the tasteful quintet in D major of our noble master Mozart. What a uniform work this is, what a wealth of ideas and what a flow of melody, and yet so well ordered with nothing misplaced, nothing too much, nothing too little!' Even the piano concertos – an undisputed domain since Mozart's lifetime – were pushed to one side. At a Mozart memorial concert given in Berlin in 1830 the D minor piano concerto (K. 466) was performed, a concerto more appropriate to the new taste of the times; we read the following in the above-mentioned paper: 'It was highly interesting to hear at last one of Mozart's pianoforte concertos again, which are remote from our modern virtuosi because there is not enough passage work in them.' Criticisms are even raised against *Don Giovanni*, which had become Mozart's most popular opera: we hear it called 'an antiquated' piece, and in reviews from Munich, Dresden, Vienna and even Prague we occasionally hear that the audience's reaction was 'cold'.

But a lot that was new was able to establish itself independently of the literary feuds, and Vienna was a striking example here. Rossini was not legitimized by any aesthetic programme, but his opera *Tancredi* had a triumphant success in 1816. During Domenico Barbaja's tenure the Viennese Court Opera put on no fewer than eighteen different works of Rossini between 1822 and 1828. In 1822 the enthusiasm for Rossini reached its culmination all over Europe, including the city where Mozart had once held sway; personalities such as Metternich announced that Rossini was their favourite composer. On the opposing side we have the 'German' party, which supported the tradition of Gluck, and its adherents Salieri, Cherubini, many of the French and, with reservations, Spontini. Mozart's operas took up a special position in this German–Italian conflict, as they had during his lifetime: they were respected, they were always being performed, yet they somehow lay outside the main centres of interest. G.L.P. Sievers, a fervent admirer of Mozart, made a prophecy in 1821 which, however, bore little fruit: 'Rossini is only the composer of Today & Tomorrow; he will, even in Italy, enjoy only a short span of popularity.' In the decade between 1818 and 1828 the craze for opera in Europe was at an all-time high.

These changes in musical evaluation make it tempting for the historian to look at the reception of Mozart's work in the first third of the nineteenth century not from a positive viewpoint, that is, not as a continuance of what had been hitherto achieved, but rather from a negative angle, as a continuous rescue attempt in an environment that was constantly changing.

A few thoughts here: it was in music-theatre that the new made its most sensational impact. Classicism in opera is a phenomenon of L'Empire, and its triumphal march began in Paris with the works of Grétry, Méhul and so on. The spirit of the *opera seria La Clemenza di Tito*, this musically 'humanized' adaptation of another Classicism, namely that of Metastasio, is remote from the brash, monumental elements which began to become fashionable on stage – and which at the same time made possible the lasting success of precisely this *Tito* and perhaps even of *Die Zauberflöte*; *Idomeneo* would scarcely have been performed again if it were not for these developments taking place independently of Mozart.

E.T.A. Hoffmann's *Don Juan* interpretation is certainly no rescue attempt, rather a Romantic piece of art. The mythicizing stage interpretations which followed it (and also preceded it) were, however, well suited to bringing *Don Giovanni* into line with the new concepts of musical tragedy, concepts which were unthinkable without the influence of French opera. Wilhelmine Schröder-Devrient (who made her début as Pamina in Vienna in 1821) was surely not the first singer to understand Donna Anna as a tragic heroine. It was certainly without thinking of Hoffmann's *Novelle* – but certainly in the manner of the opera of L'Empire – that Francesca Festa Maffei interpreted the role in Milan in 1816 and in such a way that Stendhal could admire 'qual energia di passione – per dar verità ed effetto a qual sublimo pezzo: Fuggi, crudele, fuggi'.

But the frequent references to the 'eternal youth' of *Don Giovanni* and its wide popularity which we meet in reports of performances do indeed sound as though an attempt were being made to convince the public of something. And the mawkishness, popular above all in Vienna, exceeded itself, and surely not without reason. (Listen to the following: 'How often has Mozart's genius not lifted the breast of his contemporaries, and of posterity, and how often will the immanently divine not radiate a magical power on all feeling hearts! Even today the wondrous tones murmur around us like familiar spirit voices, and all feelings and hearts are opened.') Perhaps those reports – and they are by no means infrequent – that the audience remained 'cold' did in fact mean something, and it was very probable that the lack of Mozart productions lamented by Marx was caused by the actors who were demanding something new.

There were many changes in performance habits at this time, and these had a profound effect on the conception of Mozart operas. Since the beginning of the century there had been a growing fascination with the individuality of certain singers in German opera. The audience was willing to make concessions; they accepted permissiveness and the liberal condoning

108

of excisions, additions or the practice, say, of handing over the *coloratura* phrases in the arias of the Queen of the Night to a flautist. Some roles were even adapted to suit the tessitura of a popular singer: the famous Anna Milder-Hauptmann, for example, appeared as Tamino – for our contemporary tastes a somewhat scurrilous conception of the function of a breeches part.

We can deduce from the polemics of the one side what the other side was up to. Already in 1798 Rochlitz was criticizing the choice of excessively quick tempi; this recurs constantly. During a Mozart celebration in Berlin in 1828 we get a complaint that the overture to *Die Zauberflöte* was churned out 'in the wildest tempo'. Tempo is, of course, something very tricky but also something very important; for Mozart it was 'the most important thing in music'. This points to the fact that correctness is here something determined by the situation. The tendency to take quick tempi even quicker and slow ones even slower has something to do with the general craving for sensation. Even in 1805 we meet the opinion that, 'In olden times, what would have been called lack of an ability to keep time is now fashionable under the description *tempo rubato*, or *rallentando*, etc. The uniform flow of emotion is interrupted in the most objectionable manner.' At the same time, the far-reaching effects of this 'false and fashionable taste' were recognized: 'The very nature of a work of art is one and the same thing as the clarity of its musical style and execution, in so far as one understands its character in its expression.'

Another practice which we find confirmed in an excerpt from a review from the year 1820 points in a similar direction: 'Would even Mozart have worked for such a mass of instruments as we have in today's performances? By no means! It may be appropriate for Gluck, or for the grand operas of the new French school, which tend more to a *recitativo*, declamatory lyric style – but Mozart's opera is ill-served by such a setting.' Extreme tempi, an intensified emotionalism emanating from one or another detail, the massive blocks of sound, the interest of the audience for the solo prima donna or instrumentalist – all this led to the fear that 'the fine, ethereal spirit would dissolve in the face of such unnatural fire'.

In all these quotations we detect a conservatism on the part of the critic and his judgement of artistic matters: I leave it open whether or not this attitude was in all points closer to Mozart than the practices deplored. The difficulty lay and indeed lies in the fact that the structure of Mozart's music and the conventions of his time already began to conflict with each other; particularly the richness and the mobility of the musical characters (so should we talk of emotions? even the terminology is uncertain) and the strict

109

demand for a *tempo giusto* leave scope for differing interpretations. This variety in expression, tempo, harmonics and dynamics could be seen from a modern point of view as being forward-looking, and preparing the way for Rossini; F.R. de Toreinx, in his *Histoire du romanticism* (1829), acknowledged this diversity as being a progressive achievement of the composers Mozart, Paisiello and Cimarosa. On which side do we place the metronome-marking of *Don Giovanni* by the Prague Mozart fanatic Tomaschek? He claimed that it was authentic, but it probably reflected the custom of the 1820s. Tomaschek's attempts at a solution (which leaves the musician and the historian of today helpless) had at least something good about them: he asked the question whether or not topicality or authenticity, whether or not a distorting attempt at rescue, or a hardening anachronism were to be preferred.

We now approach the nadir of Mozart reception, and I would like to look back again at the time around 1800 and examine the dissemination of Mozart's *oeuvre* outside the German-speaking countries. When we talk about the crisis around 1830, the international success from 1800 onwards and the gaps in reception outside Germany before this, we are referring primarily to his operas; in the other genres the story of his impact (both positive and negative) is less dynamic. That is why the emphasis will, in what follows, be on opera.

France, for many reasons which only partly have to do with Mozart, is the most significant factor here. Paris, the city which was, in the nineteenth century, extolled as the capital of Europe, had exerted a particular magnetism on the musical world since the beginning of the century. The high standards of orchestral playing, and the level of training at the Conservatoire, were exemplary. In both the emotiveness of musical tragedy and in the colourful *opéra comique* contemporaries experienced a freshness and a topicality which both Italian and German opera emulated. There arose here, as there had in the field of Beethoven's instrumental music, a progressive novelty which inwardly distanced itself from the music of Haydn and Mozart and distracted from it externally.

The influence of French opera in Germany seems paradoxical when we consider the political background but is part of a thickening web of cultural interrelationships. On the French side it had been Mme de Staël who, with her essay 'De l'Allemagne' of 1810, had made the first breach in the 'Chinese wall of prejudice' (to use a metaphor of Goethe's). She also mentioned Mozart here, partly positively, in that she singled out the composer of *Don Giovanni* as being the most talented music-dramatist able to combine words and music, and partly negatively (she claimed that our enjoyment of his

110

music derives from 'reflection'). But the wall, from the point of view of the history of music, was long since no longer standing; serious French opera of the age was unthinkable without Gluck, and the high-class orchestras around 1800 were adequately provided for by the symphonies of Joseph Haydn. Mozart's non-operatic works only very slowly emerged from the shadow thrown by 'le grand Haydn'; the first great Mozart occasion in the prestigious Parisian Conservatoire was the *Requiem* performance under Cherubini on 21 December 1804 in St Germain-l'Auxerrois; this was an ill omen of sorts as the work was planned as a funeral ceremony for Haydn who was actually still alive. A correspondent from Berlin spoke of the 'unfortunate impression . . . which the Romantic depiction of the *Requiem* made, as well as the imagination of our Mozart, who had departed this life too soon'. In Paris they must certainly have expected quite another sort of musical sublimity.

An example here are the *Mémoires au Essais sur la Musique* by André-Ernest-Modeste Grétry. In his second *Figaro* finale Mozart had shown his reverence for Grétry; Grétry never mentions Mozart once in his memoirs. In spite of this the intellectual interrelationships are highly significant. Grétry advocates an Enlightenment understanding of music, speaks of nature as a divine Mother and admires Raphael (his opera *Aspasie* was determined by Raphael's *School of Athens*); Grétry thus brings Raphael into a musical context before Niemetschek and the German Romantics had taken up the painter and brought him into a discussion of Mozart. The older Grétry stood in spirit much closer to Classicism than to the ideas of Wackenroder, Tieck and so on, and at the end of his memoirs he utters a musical prophecy: 'I have the vision of a charming creature who, endowed with a melodious instinct, and whose head – and soul above all – is full of musical ideas, will not dare to infringe the dramatic rules which are known today by all musicians; I see him combined with a beautiful character and party to the harmonic plenitude of our young athletes.' Every Mozart admirer will concur with Romain Rolland that the only thing that this character study of the longed-for liberator lacked was the name of Mozart. But Grétry had earlier placed his hopes for progress in Gluck's succession, and the only Raphael-figure he detected in musical history was Pergolesi.

It was difficult to mount successful performances of Mozart's operas on the Parisian stage; when they were finally put on they were already, in fact, 'old hat'. There were, consequently, two obstacles which had to be overcome in the audiences. Mozart finally did become known through the lasting successes of two arrangements: one of *Die Zauberflöte* as *Les Mystères d'Isis* (1801) by Etienne Morel de Chédeville and the Prague horn player

111

Ludwig Wenzel Lachnith, and the second of *Don Juan* (1805) by the brigadier-general and occasional poet Henri-Joseph Thuring de Ryss, the librarian and dramatist Denis Baillot and the pianist Christian Kalkbrenner.

It would be easy enough to join in the chorus of scathing condemnation about the mutilation of classical masterpieces. We detect here – and as late as Richard Wagner – an undertone of prejudice against the frivolous and superficial tastes of the French. But Chédeville and Lachnith were by no means only concerned to be fair to Mozart – they were, rather, trying to make him comprehensible to Parisian audiences and aligning him with the traditions and expectations which prevailed in the city. And they succeeded here. Opinions may differ as to how they did it, aesthetically and practically. From a distance we can see that the practice of making arrangements which we find everywhere in the late eighteenth and early nineteenth centuries – in opera and in the theatre – was an attempt to render something topical: we find a similar concern, *mutatis mutandis*, in theatrical productions of our time. And arrangements are, historically, extremely informative.

The aim of the arrangers was to latch on to something familiar: the themes of *Le Nozze di Figaro* and of *Don Giovanni* were already known to the public. In 1793 Figaro was the first opera to be performed in the Paris Opéra, an Opéra which had lost its funding of *privilège* as a result of the revolution. The *recitativo secco*, considered somewhat tedious, had been replaced by spoken dialogue from Beaumarchais's comedy; in a similar manner the dialogues in *Don Giovanni* would be replaced by dialogues from Molière's *Dom Juan*. With *Die Zauberflöte* there was no comparable work to hand, and no French genre that could correspond to Viennese magic opera. So there only remained the violation (also found with *Don Giovanni*) to force *Die Zauberflöte* to become a Classical tragedy (or a *tragédie lyrique*) and to orient it entirely towards the world of Sarastro. In this form, and as *Les Mystères d'Isis*, the work was topical, in part because a fashion for all things Egyptian had resulted from Napoleon's Egyptian campaign.

The predilection for ballet scenes helped, and the arrangers used these to make a piece which was perhaps difficult to sell more palatable to an audience. To make room for these the action was made more taut and also to some extent more logical, which even the Salzburg musician Sigismund von Neukomm had to acknowledge in 1816, a man who was usually a most scornful critic. And French operatic taste of the early nineteenth century also demanded musical retouching: new, more pompous instrumentation was known to be added and, what is probable (although cannot be proven), the method of performance was adapted, with intensified excitement in the

112

tempi, agogics and phrasing. All in all it should not be seen as curious but rather as a resonance of French preferences that Stendhal, in his *Lettres écrites de Vienne* of 1814 and the *Vies de Haydn, de Mozart et de Métastase* of 1817, should occupy himelf almost exclusively with the operas of Mozart, praising *Figaro* above all, then *Idomeneo, La Clemenza di Tito* and *Don Giovanni*, and calling Mozart the Corneille amongst the composers.

What separates Stendhal's admiration for *Figaro* from that of the German Romantics is his melancholy conception of the opera: 'Nothing in the world can compare with *Le Nozze di Figaro* as a masterpiece of pure tenderness and of melancholy, a work utterly free from any admixture of majesty or tragedy.' In many comparisons with Cimarosa, Rossini, Michelangelo, etc., Stendhal constantly emphasizes Mozart's ability to express melancholy, tenderness, sadness and also terror: 'It is the fusion of these two qualities – the terrible, and the tenderly voluptuous – that makes Mozart unique among artists. Michelangelo is only terrible; Correggio is only tender.' Like many a German Romantic, Stendhal made his pilgrimage to the city of Haydn and Mozart; what Stendhal (actually Marie-Henri Beyle) wrote about Mozart in the *Vies* (using another pseudonym, Césare Bombet) is quite frankly a plagiarism of Schlichtegroll's 1801 obituary, translated by Théophile Frédéric Winckler. More informative are the other allusions which are scattered throughout his work. Even though Stendhal was guided by concepts derived from classical French tragedy he preferred (as, later, Georges Bizet would) German and Italian music as against French opera. The epitaph which he composed for himself on his tombstone in Montmartre reminds us of the German comparisons made between Mozart and Shakespeare: 'Errico Beyle Milanese, Visse, Scrisse, Amò, Quest'Anima Adorava Cimarosa, Mozart e Shakespeare'.

In Stendhal's work, music awakens far-reaching chains of association with which the writer tracks down the 'sounds of the soul', the primary union of sound and colour in the music of nature: this sublimation of musical impressions leads, however, in a direction different from that to purely instrumental music. What Stendhal has in common with the plagiarized Schlichtegroll is an interest in the mysterious quality of superior beings; he does not, however, simply observe these *êtres supérieurs* from outside, but seeks to identify with them, and especially with Mozart. We find veiled hints of this already with E.T.A. Hoffmann, but with Stendhal the traces are different and much stronger.

According to his own confession the visionary power of Mozart's music, which conjured up the infinite, caused him suddenly to be seized by the most profound melancholy in which he became completely lost. And in his *Histoire*

113

de la peinture en Italie (1817) he projects the following picture of his own ego:

When one is happy one prefers Cimarosa; but when melancholy ensnares us, in late autumn, say, in the park of an old castle, in an avenue of high birch trees, when the surrounding silence is only broken by the rustle of a falling leaf – it is then that one turns to the genius of Mozart. One longs to hear one of his songs, from afar, deep in the red deciduous forest, played upon the horn. Mozart's gentle thoughts, and his shy happiness, precisely share the atmosphere of this autumnal day, where a gentle vapour clothes the charms of the countryside in sadness, and where the sun itself appears to shine in the woe of parting.

It is difficult to determine whether such introspection should be seen against the background of *Werther* or Lord Byron (in *De l'amour* Stendhal compares *Werther* with *Don Juan*) or as an anticipation of the sceptical decadence of the *fin de siècle*; what is noteworthy is the egocentric linking of Mozart with melancholy, autumn and departure. Nowhere else at this time does this aspect of Romantic yearning receive such powerful expression. But Stendhal does not only lose himself in Mozart's music: he finds in it as well a deep human knowledge and is fascinated, in *Figaro* above all, by the subtle richness of erotic feelings, something which was an encouragement for his own artistry and led immediately to his own major work, *De l'amour*.

Alphonse Lamartine's gentle, tender poetry, and his enthusiasm for Mozart lead us to expect a similar attitude to Stendhal: his musical contributions to the *Cours familier de littérature* (1858ff.) place Mozart alongside Cimarosa and Rossini. Like Stendhal, Lamartine prefers Italian music (meaning also Mozart); *Don Juan* is singled out for special praise (with E.T.A. Hoffman quotations), as is *Figaro*, but there is little personal involvement behind his effusive images.

With his depth of feeling, Stendhal is only partly representative of the French Mozart reception; he should be seen, rather, as a somewhat eccentric special case within a broad spectrum. The positive switch in Mozart's favour did not only concern the operas (*Figaro* was first put on in Paris in Italian in 1807; the French version by F.H.J. Castil-Blaze was famous from 1818 onwards throughout France and Belgium; *Don Giovanni* was put on in Italian in 1811 under Spontini; *Così fan tutte* was put on in Italian in 1809, and in Chédeville's French version in 1813; there were even German-language performances of *Die Entführung aus dem Serail* in 1801, *Die Zauberflöte* in 1829 and *Don Giovanni* in 1831). From about 1810 onwards the symphonies crop up

114

more and more in concert programmes. There were even concerts devoted purely to Mozart's music at the end of the 1820s (such as those offered by François Antoine Habeneck at the 'Concerts de la Société du Conservatoire'). Mozart's chamber music was constantly in the repertoire of Pierre Baillot's concerts, and the church music was a prominent feature of musical life in the 1820s with surprisingly frequent performances of *Davidde penitente*. And yet the operas remained the dominant feature and became very popular through Castil-Blaze who arranged them and brought them into line with French opera. So in contrast to Germany there was an upsurge of interest around 1830. *Don Giovanni* achieved enormous success at this time and in this the literary popularity of E.T.A. Hoffmann may well have played a part. And Berlioz's observation (incomprehensible from a German angle) that it was only the Grand Opera of Meyerbeer and Rossini (*Guillaume Tell*) that made the success of *Don Giovanni* possible did correctly identify the underlying trend. At the same time Fétis was probably right to surmise that composers such as Cherubini, Méhul, Boïeldieu and Spontini had continued their musical education 'according to Mozart's system'. But the specifics of the French reception had already begun with the kind of arrangements such as *Les Mystères d'Isis* which Berlioz, too, had criticized.

The approval of Mozart increased in the writings also and went hand in hand with a process of purification. The views of François-Joseph Fétis were extremely influential – even up to the time of Charles Gounod: Fétis considered Mozart to have been the most important composer of the last one hundred years and honoured him in many an article in the *Revue musicale*. Like Castil-Blaze before him, he rejected alterations in Mozart's instrumentation and was always very critical *vis-à-vis* the practice of arrangements. The growing appreciation of Mozart's work obviously brought with it a sense of its sacrosanct nature which, however, was not completely without compromise. Fétis too called *Don Juan* a revolutionary work and admired its melancholy depths, but he stands further from French Romanticism than from the intellectual traditions of Classicism.

We see how little sense it makes to label the new understanding of Mozart 'Romantic' when we take Jérome-Joseph de Momigny as an example. There may be some 'spiritual yearning for transcendence' in his musical thinking; what does seem Romantic is his procedure, when he analyses the Allegro moderato of the D minor string quartet K. 421/417b, of adding a text underlay throughout. The dramatic scene between Dido and Aeneas is not supposed to represent some hidden programme but rather to disclose the speech-like character of the music. Apart from being interested in the formal aspects and also techniques of composition Momigny sought what

115

the German Romantics termed 'the poetic'. Using an image from another artistic realm as a mirror, the essence of a musical utterance and an atmospheric mutuality (which normally would be concealed beneath the score and the text) are made manifest. Yet Momigny also thinks in a very traditional manner: as a man of the Enlightenment he strictly rejected the growing cult of Mozart, seeing both him and Haydn as the heirs of Handel and Bach. He was completely at a loss when confronted by the music of Beethoven and always preferred Haydn's; his writings on Mozart were an attempt to understand that composer's different qualities.

In contrast to Paris, London's cultivation of Mozart began to wane early in the nineteenth century: there was a lack of great personalities and reforming zealots. A lot of the development in the Mozart reception reminds us of Paris or Amsterdam – the slowly increasing popularity of the instrumental music, for example, or above all the various features of the impact made by the operas – an impact which took a surprisingly long time to be felt. Da Ponte had tried in vain during his stay in London in 1794 to get a production of *Don Giovanni* off the ground: it finally appeared in 1817.

It was probably the English tradition of oratorio which was responsible for the fact that the first substantial work to be performed during Lent 1801 was Mozart's *Requiem*. But his music did not appeal to the public and Ashley's performance was, apparently, a bad one. The critic of the *Morning Post* wrote the following disappointed comment: 'The talents which have celebrated the name of Mozart can scarcely be justly appreciated by such a composition as the *Requiem*.'

The first operatic performances were put on as benefits for famous singers: in 1806 the Prince of Wales ordered a production of *La Clemenza di Tito* in the King's Theatre for Mrs Billington (without success); *Così fan tutte* (1811), for Bertinotti Radicati, was more of a winner, however. In contrast to Paris, we can sense that the breakthrough came not in arrangements and versions in English but as a symptom of the popularity of Italian *opera buffa*. Even *Die Zauberflöte* was put on in the following year as the *Flauto magico*; *La Clemenza di Tito* also followed in 1812 and – especially successfully – *Figaro*.

In these performances the plots were considerably modified and simplified and, as in Paris, Mozart's instrumentation was made more pompous by the introduction of trombones and other brass. From the statistics concerning the sequence of performances we can detect the degree of popularity ranging from *Don Giovanni* through *Figaro, Tito, Così fan tutte* to the *Flauto magico*. We can also detect the change to a more positive reception of Mozart in the fact that the London publisher Richard Birchall printed piano excerpts from Mozart's last six operas in the years between 1809 and 1815.

116

The journalists were also becoming more enthusiastic: William Gardiner, in the *Monthly Magazine* (1811), praised Mozart's operas as being 'the highest of all intellectual pleasures' and regretted that 'a great nation, like England, has not talent, or ability, sufficient to represent and perform any of the works of this great master'. Both the Italian qualities of the *buffa* operas, and the elements of antiquity (inspired by the French) associated with *La Clemenza di Tito* and *Die Zauberflöte* had, we may safely assume, a particularly Anglo-Saxon atmosphere about them which we only begin to detect in the dates and the reports concerning the English versions of the 1820s; James Hopwood's charming vignettes of the two ladies from *Così fan tutte* give us a flavour.

Mozart operas had reached canonical status in the London of the 1820s, and even the craze for Rossini failed to erode it. Lord Mount Edgcumbe made pronouncements similar to Stendhal and Rossini in 1823, claiming that Rossini would be forgotten, whereas Mozart, Haydn and Handel 'will live for ever'. Somewhat later the same degree of immortality was bestowed on Mozart's instrumental music: the personal commitment of two friends – Thomas Attwood (a pupil of Mozart's) and Vincent Novello – was a decisive contributory factor. Novello was one of the founders of the Philharmonic Society of London (1813) whose exemplary concerts performed works by Mozart alongside Haydn, Beethoven, Cherubini and Boccherini. Novello's intermediary role as organist and publisher was important, and his friendship with great poets such as Samuel Taylor Coleridge, John Keats and Percy Bysshe Shelley also played a part. Each of these three was an admirer of Mozart's music even if this admiration varied in intensity; Coleridge, whose views on music closely approximated to those of the German Romantics, actually preferred Beethoven. In his poetic works Keats sometimes found wonderful things to say about Mozart, as in the following couplet from the Epistle to Charles Cowden Clarke: 'But many days have passed since last my heart/Was warm'd luxuriously by divine Mozart.' Mozart was, finally, the acknowledged favourite of Shelley, and it was *Figaro* above all that he loved. For Shelley, as for other poets, we feel that the musicality of the language is somehow a metamorphosis of musical impression. The supposedly musical structures in *Prometheus Unbound* have been commented upon, but it would be impossible to distil any particular drop of Mozart's music from the poetry.

One would have thought that the phenomenon known as Mozart would have been better understood in Italy than France or England. The fact that Mozart had absorbed an Italian tradition and, even more, the fact that his operas began to dispute the Italian claim to musical hegemony in Europe may have given rise to envy. Stendhal tried to explain the resistance felt towards Mozart's music by talking of 'the patriotism of the antechamber, the great moral sickness of the Italians, which had awoken in all its fury'. Nascent nationalism may also have encouraged a feeling of reserve towards Mozart the Austrian. The reservations – expressed elsewhere too – concerning the lack of *cantabile* and an excessively complicated style in Mozart are typical reflections of Italian musical taste. The Roman correspondent of the Leipzig *Allgemeine Musikalische Zeitung* expressed quite openly that Mozart's operas 'were not suitable for his country's taste' because 'so many pieces just come to an end, and we know not how'. And an opera like *Die Zauberflöte* had no basis in Italy, no grass roots which could help it to become a success – let alone a sensation as it had in Germany.

After Napoleon had established his power in Italy and Mozart's operas appeared again in the theatres, French opera become a provocation for the Italians, until Verdi was able to bring about a synthesis. The first production of *La Clemenza di Tito* (1809) in Naples and the comparatively favourable reception of *Don Giovanni* (1811 in Rome and Bergamo, 1812 in Naples, then Milan, Turin, Florence, Bologna, Parma and Genoa) can be understood as successes from the point of view of French tragic opera. Mozart's *buffa* operas (*Le Nozze di Figaro* – 1811 and 1826 in Turin, 1814 in Naples, then Milan and Florence – and *Così fan tutte* – 1797 in Trieste, 1805 in Varese and 1807 in Milan, then Turin and Naples) had some success. But the Italian ethos of these works had little effect, since *opera buffa*, in the land of its origin, rapidly became of little interest.

On the German side too there were feelings of national resentment. We find this above all quite clearly in Niemetschek when (in 1798) he triumphantly claimed – doubtlessly using a report of Peter von Winter's – 'In Florence they had to cancel a rehearsal of the first act of *Don Giovanni* after nine attempts, arguing that it was unplayable!' And after the Congress of Vienna had recognized that Austria had new – and old – claims to Italian territory the political mood became such that the cultivation of Mozart, encouraged by Austria, bore little fruit. But Milan, a Habsburg city, encouraged all sorts of new impulses. In his *Cenni biografici intorno al celebre Maestro Wolfgango Amadeo Mozart* (1816) Pietro Lichtenthal quite rightly spoke of Milan as a metropolis 'la quale coltiva la musica de' celebri maestri tedeschi, piu di qualunque altra citta d'Italia, e che tien in gran pregio il nome di Mozart'. If Lichtenthal goes on to praise the 'gran teatro alla Scala' because of its Mozart productions, then this reminds us of the powerful influence of Italian opera on the Viennese court theatre – an inter-relationship, then, that would lead, some twenty years later, to a union between the opera houses in Vienna and Milan under Bartolomeo Merelli. How far the unusual resonance in Milan (1807 *Così fan tutte* with thirty-nine further performances, and a new production in 1814; 1814 *Don Giovanni*; 1815 and 1825 *Figaro*; 1816 *Die Zauberflöte* – with very limited success; 1817 *La Clemenza di Tito* – to popular acclaim) relied on personal commitment and the contact of certain individuals is seen in the case of Lichtenthal. This man, who was born in Bratislava and gained his doctorate of medicine in Vienna, who was personally known to Mozart's family and was himself an active amateur composer, became a civil servant in the Kingdom of Lombardy and Venice and, together with Mozart's son Carl, was actively engaged in promoting the music of his idol. In his *Vie de Rossini*, in the description of 'Mozart en Italie', Stendhal observed the situation in Milan closely; he also reported that Italian amateurs of music in Napoleon's entourage had experienced productions of Mozart operas in Munich.

As well as the cult of Mozart in Milan we also have the Mozart craze in Trentino, a craze with visible manifestations. Giuseppe Antonio Bridi (a rich businessman, musician and close acquaintance of Mozart's who sang Idomeneo in Vienna in 1789) erected in his park outside Rovereto a 'temple of harmony' in which stood the statues of the following: Antonio Sacchini, Handel, Gluck, Jommelli, Haydn, Palestrina and Mozart. As well as the predominance of German composers, the old-fashioned selection of Italians is also a source of surprise; Mozart is singled out by the following inscription: '. . . qui a sola natura/musicae doctus/musicae et artes princeps'. In a brochure which appeared in 1827, entitled *Brevi notizie intorno ad alcuni più celebri compositori di musica*, Bridi's son Giovanni confirmed this judgement with a quotation from Cimarosa: 'In una parola io ad altri non saprei paragonan il Mozart, se non che al gran Raffaello.' We recognize the unrealistic aspects of this cult of Mozart with reference to the prevailing musical tastes when we scrutinize Bridi's characterization of Mozart's music: he uses such terms as 'sublimity, naturalness, novelty, *bel canto*, richness of ideas, candour, a noble, sublime and judicious instrumental accompaniment'. In the rest of Italy Mozart's music was scarcely greeted with such terminology. But Bridi was not an isolated case in Trentino: we also have the composer Gotifredo Jacopo Ferrari, who was also a committed Mozart enthusiast.

Another example in any discussion of German-Italian cultural contact is provided by Johann Konrad Friedrich of Frankfurt who, as an officer in Napoleon's army, wandered throughout Italy with Schiller's *Don Carlos* and *Fiesko* and Mozart's *Don Giovanni* in his knapsack: from Genoa in the north to Naples in the south he encouraged the performance of Mozart. As King

119

Murat's captain of the guard he succeeded in putting *Don Giovanni* on in the Teatro del Fondo in Naples; the opera remained in the repertoire for nine months and reached over seventy performances. The famous impresario Barbaja was inspired by this success, and he encouraged further performances (in 1814 there was *Figaro* with forty repeat performances, then *Così* in 1815 and *Don Giovanni* again in 1816). The Viennese Robert Wenzel Graf von Gallenberg had already prepared the way for the reception of Mozart's music in Naples.

Louis Spohr reported that Mozart was played by dilettanti in many Italian cities, but public concerts were rare. We get similar accounts – and some very disparaging comments about standards of performances – from travel descriptions by Stendhal, Moscheles and the correspondents of German music journals. One curiosity here is the arrogance of Nicola Zingarelli, to whom Spohr had recommended Mozart's music: Zingarelli was of the opinion that Mozart was undoubtedly talented and he might perhaps have written something good if only he had studied another ten years. We know, on the other hand, that important Italian composers like Cherubini, Spontini and Bellini had studied Mozart's works (and some of Haydn) and esteemed him highly. This was particularly true of Gioacchino Rossini: in his childhood he had got to know the music of Haydn and Mozart and studied them with such enthusiasm that he was known as 'il tedeschino'. Later, however, he could hardly be called a successor to Mozart, neither in his serious operas, nor in the *Barber of Seville*: his melodies, in contrast to Mozart's, are built from a sequence of almost rudimentary motifs. He was also very conscious of the difference between German and Italian music, and yet in his ensembles and his instrumentation he must have profited a lot from Mozart. As an old man he spoke most warmly of him. It is difficult to know what is discrepancy and what is dialectical in this relationship, but it certainly preserves Rossini's aesthetic position *in nucleo*.

Mozart was far better received by the public in the north of Europe than in the Mediterranean countries: Denmark and Sweden especially (and Copenhagen and Stockholm above all) devoted themselves quite early on to the cultivation of Mozart's music. We have already spoken (pages 30–1) of the preference for his instrumental music in Sweden; the operatic works were only able to assert themselves against their French rivals comparatively late. It was not *Die Zauberflöte* (1812) but *Don Giovanni*, in the following year, that became a unanimous success; after this came *Die Entführung aus dem Serail* (1814), *Figaro* (1821), *La Clemenza di Tito* (1823) and *Così fan tutte* (not until 1830). Only *Die Zauberflöte*, *Don Giovanni* and *Figaro* were able to establish themselves as permanent successes; all of Mozart's operas were performed in Swedish. In contrast to today's ideas of authenticity, the habit of translating operas into the mother tongue was regarded then as a serious attempt at understanding and appreciating the work: the foreign touring companies who mostly offered Italian or German performances were regarded as having an exotic cachet.

We can say the same about the Danish productions in Copenhagen (*Così fan tutte* in 1798, *Don Giovanni* in 1807, *Die Entführung* in 1813, *Die Zauberflöte* in 1816, *Figaro* in 1821 and *La Clemenza di Tito* in 1823). The temporal proximity of the performances in Copenhagen and Stockholm can probably be traced back to the fact that, in both countries, the German *Singspiel* first, and the fascination exerted by Rossini later (with *Figaro* and *La Clemenza di Tito*), were considerable stimulants; later, it was the popularity of Weber's operas which encouraged an interest in Mozart. In Copenhagen there was also the Nissen couple, husband and wife, who were very active in the Mozart cause. One curiosity in the Nordic Mozart cult are the three jagged rocks with the names Gluck, Mozart and Haydn (runestones, if you like) which the Danish dancing-master Claus Nielsen Schall (who had known Mozart personally) erected in his garden near Copenhagen.

We can safely assume that Amsterdam, a traditional centre for music-printing, was keenly aware of Mozart's instrumental achievements. There was also a long-established interest in his operas: we know that they were performed in the eighteenth century, and that *La Clemenza di Tito* followed in 1809. The styles of production were very varied; translations into Dutch only came later, and with *Figaro*, first performed in 1794, there was not a Dutch version until 1825. In 1794 *Don Giovanni* was sung in German; it was performed in Kalkbrenner's French version in 1803, done in Dutch in 1804 and in Italian in 1809. The same can be said for the reception of *Figaro* and *La Clemenza di Tito*. Holland's cosmopolitan atmosphere is also seen – in a more limited fashion – in the theatrical practices of Rotterdam and The Hague.

In a whole series of countries Mozart's music was cultivated in the home in a manner we can hardly quantify but which must have been significant; there were also the smaller concerts and, in the larger cities, a small number of representative, prestigious productions. In Dublin *Figaro* was performed in English in 1821, and *Don Giovanni* in Italian in 1828; in Bucharest *Die Zauberflöte* was performed in German in 1818; the first Spanish version of a Mozart opera in Madrid was *Figaro* in 1802; in 1827 *Don Giovanni* was performed in Buenos Aires, also in Spanish. Lisbon saw its first Mozart opera in an Italian version of *La Clemenza di Tito* in 1806, and Sigismund Neukomm describes a performance of the *Requiem* in Rio de Janeiro thus: '. . . all the different talents strove one against the other to make themselves worthy of receiving the genius of Mozart in this New World'. As regards the United States of America, we hear of an English version of *Figaro* first appearing in New York in 1824 and an Italian version of *Don Giovanni* in 1826 (in Philadelphia in 1827). A colonial curiosity was the Calcutta production of *Don Giovanni* in 1833.

It becomes apparent that the reversal in the reception of Mozart was related to the prevailing stage of development in each particular case. One event which had nothing to do with art was the cholera epidemic of those years, something which severely curtailed interest in opera. When it was possible to put operas and concerts back on their feet again it was new works which were preferred, to Mozart's disadvantage.

The basic criticisms levelled against Mozart – and these were particularly pointed in Germany – demonstrated that firmness of judgement had begun to vacillate. Usually it was the old non-sellers that were only now being aired, such as Giuseppe Sarti's criticism (and the opera-composer had made it almost forty years previously) concerning the extended introduction to the Dissonant Quartet. Actually these criticisms had been long obsolete as Gottfried Weber had painstakingly analysed the harmonies of the problematic passages according to all the rules of composition and agreed to let each individual listener pronounce his own aesthetic judgement. And Hans Georg Nägeli's critique also came a generation too late. But it did achieve considerable attention as Nägeli, a Swiss inspired by Pestalozzi, looked to the future as regards popular music culture and the fostering of choral singing.

His judgement of Mozart seems, correspondingly, to be extremely reactionary: 'Notwithstanding his undisputed genius . . . Mozart is the most style-less of all the great composers.' Yet Nägeli does at least try to prove this apparent stylistic mischief from an analytic point of view: he complained about missing bars and illogical cadences in the balance between rhythm and metre. The mixing of genres, of *cantabile* vocal music with the instrumental music (here given the very old-fashioned description of 'free tone-play'), is usually found, Nägeli claims, in the 'exaggerated, boundless habit of contrasting'. Yet Nägeli, in his turn, defended Haydn and Mozart against Anton Friedrich Justus Thibaut in the dispute about 'real church music': neither, apparently, was inspired by the spiritual texts they were setting, and Thibaut sharply criticized the 'glittering and booming choral singing', thereby introducing the later hostility which would be directed against both by the Cäcilian choral tradition; Mozart, however, would come off better than Haydn, the more famous composer of masses.

III

1830–1900

It is only in the time around 1900 that we find a radically new awareness in the reception of Mozart: this does not exclude the possibility that, individually and subliminally, many new interpretations were in existence that were, however, not representative of the image of Mozart that is generally found in the second half of the nineteenth century. The change that occurred around 1830 did not affect the assessment of Mozart himself as much as the background in which this assessment became apparent. External developments called forth a reaction, and the aesthetic reference to Mozart, as well as the artistic achievement associated with it, were forced into a defensive position in which they long remained.

The concept of the beautiful changed above all. Whereas Mozart confessed to a type of music in which, when expressing the terrible, the ear was not offended, we find in Grand Opera the significance of the subject matter intensified to such an extent that the composer was driven to provide characterization which demanded a *'musique terrible'*. And no genre is so much the expression of the cultural consciousness of the epoch following the July Revolution than Grand Opera.

We get a sense of the new direction in this and other musical institutions when we look at an example of average literary quality – Wolfgang Robert Griepenkerl's *Das Musikfest oder die Beethovener*, a novella which appeared in Brunswick in 1838. The book is dedicated to the Master of Grand Opera, Giacomo Meyerbeer, 'in true devotion': Meyerbeer reciprocated in the second edition (1841) with the setting of a tendentious text. In his 'Introduction' to the novella, Griepenkerl challenges art to meet the new ideas thrown up by the growth of science, in philosophy and as an aftermath of the July Revolution. He sees in art a 'secure anchor against the endless diffusion, the excessive dissipation into the measureless and the limitless, the plunge into unadulterated untruthfulness': it is difficult not to hear an attack against Romanticism here, above all against Jean Paul. Griepenkerl waxed enthusiastic about 'works of high artistic consecration: the dramatic opera, the oratorio and the symphony find their worthy representatives, the first the worthiest of all. Here is a spirit full of the most powerful intentions, the creator of a work which pulses through world-history' – and Meyerbeer is probably his name. Griepenkerl was obviously speaking of a vision which was only in its initial stages: he thundered against 'the most particular form of one-sidedness' and painted a harsh but pertinent picture of tiresome reality:

> What do we get served up? Songs full of subjectivity, great masses of them, so that the shops of the music dealers scarcely have the space to pile up the waste-paper. On top of this we have dances full of the most wretched commonplaces, acrobatic antics of a travelling virtuoso bedewed with the sweat of a decade's socage – nowhere the eternal dew of an idea. One external proof of this flood breaking in upon us is the fact that everything we purchase is wrapped in a tissue of musical notation.

Where is Mozart in all of this? He fits neither into the grand visions, nor into the current fashions: 'Mozartian' dance-music, the fascination of the virtuosos and the 'songs full of subjectivity' are a very long way from what Mozart had in mind with his dances, concertos and songs. He would probably be found above all in that 'waste-paper', those masses of notes – arrangements above all – that Griepenkerl most harshly criticized. But the idea that the point of art was to emphasize some particular idea is diametrically opposed to what Mozart had in mind: this would be the concern, rather, of the New German School, conditioned by the ethical needs of the middle classes after 1871.

In Griepenkerl's novella we have a count who represents the new, Adalbert, a man inspired by music and poetry 'because of the progress in which these arts are made manifest'. Note well – it is not progress which is manifest in the arts, but the arts that manifest themselves in progress: the essence of art, then, lies in its historical sequence and goal. In this view of art, a view determined by Hegel's philosophy of history, Mozart's status is devalued. Beethoven's Ninth, for Adalbert, is the *opus classicum*, 'the truest mirror of our age: since Beethoven it has been possible for music to attain a world-historical significance on a different path from that which leads through the Church. You talk about Haydn, about Mozart! These were only the precursors of the true Messiah.' Beethoven was also great because 'he despised flirtation with form'.

126

Although this sounds a negative portrayal it does, in fact, attribute to Mozart a significant historical position; the mixture of reverence and reserve conditions the metaphors that were circulating since E.T.A. Hoffmann and which illuminate the historical grading of the three Classics. Griepenkerl uses the image of the triad: 'Haydn . . . is the creator, the root; Mozart is the beautiful third, beautiful in the middle; Beethoven is the fifth, streaming powerfully through every region.' The dilemma here is that Beethoven stands, as it were, at the beginning of musical modernity and yet, at the same time, is part of the Classics; this is not altered by giving Mozart instead of Beethoven a positive accentuation. In the 1830s Amadeus Wendt, professor of history, gave a distinctly Hegelian stamp to the concept of Classicism by claiming that Haydn represented the Symbolic, Mozart the Classical and Beethoven the Romantic spheres of art. Even if Wendt used the harmonious image of a 'clover leaf' he cannot help, when referring to the subject matter, talking about the complete interpenetration of form and content in Mozart's music – and not in Beethoven's.

Griepenkerl is also very fond of talking about the 'world-historical significance' of contemporary music: this concept is occasionally – and not without a certain degree of awkwardness – applied to Mozart in order to stress his topical relevance. The Silesian man of letters and friend of Schumann, Karl-August Kahlert, saw in Mozart a dialectical mediation between Germanic and Italian musical elements; a leading theoretician of the New German School, Franz Brendel, granted Mozart the status of 'world composer' who was able to 'break down the barriers of nationalism and lead the peoples closer to one another'. Such a view, however, differs sharply from Griepenkerl's vision of the future: 'The *daimon* of our century, whether it be good or evil . . . demands from the composer the symphony and the dramatic opera as, from the poet, the epic and the tragic.' Here we have a partial anticipation of Richard Wagner's concept; Griepenkerl, actually, imagined a synthesis of Beethoven and Spontini.

That a man of letters of the 1830s should at one and the same time refer to Hegel and also to Hoffmann demonstrates the drive towards grand syntheses which was a characteristic of the age. The 'crazy' end of the novella draws particularly on the example of *Kapellmeister* Kreisler, and I would like to claim further that Hoffmann's covert references to Mozart occur again in Griepenkerl.

In his novella the overwrought artistic enthusiasms of Adalbert and his circle (they are making preparations for a music festival with a performance of Beethoven's Ninth Symphony) lead to clashes with the philistinism of their contemporaries and finally to a situation where the real fuses with the unreal. The insane double-bass player finally physically assaults his gentle, sensitive son Amadeus: ' "Only those who meet a violent end will be resurrected as the Lord. Out of your corner, you marmot! . . ." And with the words "Down with you into the lower depths!" he flung his son to the floor.' Is it possible that Griepenkerl, in a confused reversal of things, was trying to free himself by personifying the double-bass recitative from the last movement of the Ninth Symphony from his precursor (Mozart? Hoffmann?) in order that he should rise again as the son? It is certainly not an exaggerated interpretation to see a Don Juan figure à la Hoffmann in Adalbert, who finally also goes insane: 'Look, wretch, for the whole of my life I was looking for the highest, the most noble – yet I have only reaped misery and, as you see, caused misery . . . I yearn to hurl myself into the maelstrom of life, there where the current is most violent! I shall not shrink from naked sin . . .' To this confession the curate replies: 'There are elements here which could persuade a Faust to join them. Give me a foretaste, an instalment, Lord Don Juan!'

Even in this distortion we see the world-historical significance of the unity of the Don Juan and the Faust themes: there is an allusion here to Christian Dietrich Grabbe's tragedy (1829) as if in pointed reference to Hoffmann's Don Juan who did, in fact, approximate to a Faust figure. Incidentally, the combination had already been anticipated by Nicolaus Vogt (1809) in his play *Der Färberhof oder die Buchdruckerei in Maynz* (*The Dyer's Yard or the Printing Works in Mainz*) where he has Faust, Don Juan and the printer Johann Fust come together in a sort of quodlibet of music by Mozart and Haydn. And another peripheral observation in cultural history is, indirectly, Goethe's resigned comment that Mozart should have composed *Faust*; Anton Heinrich Prince Radziwill, in the overture to his *Composition zu Goethes Faust* (a work which Zelter praised, and which was printed in Berlin in 1835) paraphrased Mozart's Adagio and Fugue in C minor K. 546.

The megalomania of such syntheses as those proposed by Griepenkerl leads us away from Romanticism. His novella believed in progress, but ended in *bizarrerie*, and this is, perhaps, surprising, but its ending does represent one of the basic ideas concerning the deeply dislocated relationship between artist and society – this is an inheritance of Romanticism and runs throughout the whole of the nineteenth century. In succession to Hoffmann (there are direct references in Grabbe, Gautier, Dumas, Pushkin and Zorilla) Don Juan assumes the mythical proportions of an exceptional being: he personifies a vital principle, the need, unconditionally, to dare that which was most extreme. In his *Don Juan* (1844) Nikolaus Lenau gives us a completely secularized hero, one who is driven to satiety and finally, out of *accidie* and disgust with life, to seeking death in a duel; there are, however, echoes of Mozart's opera even here.

It was Gustav Kühne, a writer close to the Young Germany group, who projected a radical consequence of this attitude in his novel *Eine Quarantäne im Irrenhaus* (*A Quarantine in a Madhouse*) (1835): he refers specifically to *Don Juan* when claiming that Mozart 'had so richly endowed this sinner that there can be no doubt that he was not able to celebrate the life-principle, the personified vital urge, in any other way; he led life's representative to the very limit, to that point where this very principle became an incarnate demon.'

The principle, however, is incorporated in Sören Kierkegaard's *Either/Or* (1843) rather than in Mozart. It is no longer the world-weariness of Lenau but a 'genius of sensuality' which is the goal that Don Juan achieves, and he achieves it in such purity of form that this sensuality becomes 'the most abstract idea that may be conceived'. The intensification of the concept goes so far until – and this also is a radicalization of a Romantic idea – it transcends itself, as it were, and becomes music. For music's immediacy stands above linguistic speculation: we see here what a thorough reading of *Either/Or* makes clear, namely, that Kierkegaard is not concerned with interpreting a work but rather in illustrating, with examples, the need for a choice between the aesthetic, the ethical and the religious forms of life. Mozart's operas *Le Nozze di Figaro*, *Die Zauberflöte* and *Don Giovanni* represent three stages of aesthetic existence: the statements concerning the first two operas are as factually disappointing as they are intentionally fragmentary. Cherubino personifies 'dreamy desire', his sensuality is 'melancholy' and ill-defined; Papageno's desire is, already, 'searching'. As a by-product of the discussion of this second stage we find a negative criticism of *Die Zauberflöte* in its entirety – it is consistent as, according to Kierkegaard, Tamino's process of development, based upon reflection, is an 'entirely unmusical idea'. But this criticism, indirectly, means much more: the subject of *Die Zauberflöte*, unsuitable as an opera, contains an ethos which is directed against a musical aestheticism. It is only Don Juan that Kierkegaard – the aesthete – discusses in detail. He, Don Juan, is nothing more than 'desire which desires', he is not an individual character but represents 'essential life' and the 'infinity of passion' – this goes far beyond any conflicts with society. Don Juan is a demon. That Mozart had illustrated him with incomparable music is ambiguous praise, depending on which side of the *Either/Or* dichotomy one stands. It is, however, typical of the Romantic tradition that Kierkegaard should have chosen not to relate his Don Juan example to Mozart's person as a genius of musical sensuality; it is not as a contextual parallel but as a contemporary statement that we should understand the

129

utterance of the aged Goethe, who remarked that 'the demonic spirit of his genius had . . . the composer of *Don Giovanni* in its power, so that he had to carry out what it demanded'.

Kierkegaard's meditations concerning the sensuous immediacy of music and his reference to Mozart's *Don Giovanni* inadvertently point to something else. That opera of Mozart's which was esteemed above all others in the nineteenth century prevented for a long time the appearance of any other memorable Don Juan musical settings – these found, and still do find, literary manifestations instead. We see a great many strenuous literary attempts after Mozart to dissociate the theme from a musical setting: narrative (Hoffmann), tragedy (Grabbe), dramatic poem (Lenau), drama (Rittner) and comedy (Frisch).

After Alexander S. Dargomizhsky's Pushkin-opera *The Stone Guest* it was only Richard Strauss who succeeded in dealing with the Don Juan material in a carefree manner – this time as a symphonic poem. It was easier to overcome inhibitions concerning a qualitative comparison with Mozart, as well as the historical distance from him, in the realm of ideas than in the same genre. The dilemma becomes particularly apparent when we look at the well-intentioned attempts to bring Mozart's operas closer to the spirit of the times, and the arrangements by Anton Wilhelm Florentin von Zuccalmaglio provide a graphic example. This already traditional practice covered a wide range, reaching from simple translations on the one side to far-reaching alterations on the other.

The much-discussed paradox of our theatres today, namely, the insistence on a radically topical treatment of the action and a refusal to alter one note of the music is not such a modern phenomenon as a contemporary analysis of ancient works would have us believe: the paradox looks back, rather, to the example of Zuccalmaglio. We remember him as a collector of folk-songs from the Heidelberg circle of Romantics around Thibaut, but to his contemporaries he would be better known as 'Sexton Fly-swat', who, in fine Teutonic fury, submitted the Philistines to a verbal barrage. He set forth his intentions quite clearly in the preface to his *Idomeneo* arrangement of 1835: 'It was my intention to bring the figures closer to us and to banish the old mechanical gods.' He had no understanding whatever of the conventions of *opera seria* and finds, for example, 'the appearance of the storm and the divine miracles . . . highly ludicrous'. He saw 'the main reason for the neglect of an art-work' not so much in 'the indifference of the mob and its desire for something new' but rather in the work itself and its antique subject-matter.

Just like the first Mozart arrangers Zuccalmaglio justified his actions by criticizing the plot 'over which Mozart poured the wealth of his music' and sought to make – also in a moralizing sense – German opera out of the Italian ones. His *Idomeneo*, under the title *Der Hof in Melun*, takes place during the time of the Hundred Years' War and has as its theme the love between Agnes Sorel and Charles VII. German history, Frankish honour and the battle for Lombardy are the themes in the *Tito* opera (1837), which was now called *Karl in Pavia*. Zuccalmaglio also believed that Enlightenment, Freemasonry and oriental mysticism were quite out of place in *Die Zauberflöte*, and so he called the work (1834) *Der Kederich* and transposed the action to that realm of knights and elves made so popular by Albert Lortzing. In his arrangement of *Die Entführung aus dem Serail* he did, in fact, keep the Turkish milieu which had long ceased to be fashionable, but he historicized it and let a poet of world renown appear – he turned Belmonte into Miguel de Cervantes Saavedra who, after the battle of Lepanto (1571), ended up among pirates and was finally brought to Algiers as a prisoner of the Turks.

Despite all their patriotism, Zuccalmaglio's arrangements are unthinkable without the model of Grand Opera. Hyper-Germanness, world-historical significance and a personal enthusiasm for Mozart are too disparate to allow for the emergence of a homogenous whole. Zuccalmaglio's actual coup was to change the different plots completely without going too far (apart from substituting dialogues for the recitatives), as he explained in the preface to *Idomeneo*: 'So no bar has been transposed, no note has been altered.' Yet he wrongly calculated the chance of making Mozart's operas more interesting: his arrangements met with no success; indeed, we do not even know whether or not they were performed. Zuccalmaglio suffered the same fate as the conservative composer Johann Peter Lyser with his one-act operetta *Winzer und Sänger*: Lyser cobbled together a *Singspiel* in which Mozart makes an appearance to save a loving couple in distress, and blended in with his own music various numbers from *Così fan tutte* and *Idomeneo*. The apparent insouciance with which such arrangements disregard the essential qualities of well-known masterpieces arouses our scorn – yet unjustly, because it is not so much a matter of ignorance but of a genuine desire to make Mozart and his work popular and topical. The futility of these enterprises has something placatory about it – even for purists.

The situation was principally the same in concert life. Griepenkerl enthused about 'national festivals' as an appropriately topical form of communal artistic experience: he may well have been thinking of the examples of the Swiss choral festivals, or the patriotic self-portrayals of the male choirs whose popularity was spreading, or above all of a musical

131

festival with Beethoven's Ninth Symphony. We get echoes here of the artistic utopias of Richard Wagner and the cultivation of art in musical societies which flourished in the second half of the nineteenth century.

The male choir movement had little idea of Mozart's music: the theatrical festivals which were emerging already in the 1830s (the Düsseldorf 'Model Stage' of Karl Immermann, for example, and the 'Gesamtgastspiele' of Franz von Dingelstedt of 1854) found no counterpart in the opera world before Wagner. There had, of course, been a tradition of music festivals since the late eighteenth century: it was simply a matter of taking up their noble ideals and using them correspondingly. But we see in the programmes of the famous Music Festivals of the Lower Rhine from 1818 onwards that Mozart was not felt to be suitable, and that lesser works were a better choice. Even in the second festival, at Elberfeld in 1819, the name of Mozart only appears as the arranger of Handel's *Messiah*: the Handel arrangements make up the major part of the Mozart performances (*Messiah* in 1819, 1839, 1853, 1857 and 1866; *Alexander's Feast* in 1825, 1846 and 1856; the *Ode to St Cecilia* in 1863). The *Davidde penitente* was the first original Mozart work to be performed (in 1836 under Mendelssohn), followed by the *Dies irae* in 1830 and, in 1845, the complete *Requiem* under Julius Rietz.

If this seems very late for a performance of the *Requiem* then it is even more surprising to find the first Mozart symphony (the *Jupiter*) was only played in 1834 (in 1844 and 1861 we find the D major symphony, and in 1846 the G minor). And Berlin concert life, extremely prestigious, showed that the Lower Rhine festivals did not represent an exception in the reception of Mozart; in the year 1848, for example, we have fifty-three Beethoven symphonies, thirty-six Haydn symphonies and only twenty Mozart symphonies in the programmes. In the same year Moritz Hauptmann, Robert Franz and the young Hans von Bülow were unanimous in finding Cherubini's *Requiem* 'much more sublime' than Mozart's.

We should not assume that the decline in Mozart's popularity meant that his works were scarcely ever played: the late operas and the symphonies continued to remain in the repertoire. Yet the piano works did not: previously a major factor in Mozart's popularity they now – according to a report (only slightly exaggerated) in the journal *Cäcilia* of 1832 – had disappeared from the concert programme. And it was true that the cult of the virtuoso and the concomitant new techniques in playing had ousted Mozart's concertos. It would be none other than Franz Liszt who would later try to heal this dereliction by emphasizing, in his memorial address in 1856, Mozart's significance for the development of virtuosity.

One inconspicuous, but perhaps the most important, reason for the recession could be the fact that Mozart's works had become part of everyone's cultural baggage. Retouching during productions had hardly any success in counteracting this. It was Meyerbeer who, in 1845 in Berlin, provided *Don Giovanni* with a string quartet accompaniment in the recitative passages and started a long-lasting tradition against which Otto Nicolai vehemently fought as early as 1847. (Yet Karl Böhm could still remember the Munich Opera substituting a string quartet in the recitatives, also inserting diminished seventh chords.) A further attempt to make Mozart's music more emotive was Friedrich Schneider's habit (dating from 1830) of strengthening the instrumentation of the G minor symphony by using timpani. Johann Nepomuk Hummel did the same when he arranged Mozart's piano concertos 'in the newest mode'.

The principal futility of all the attempts to reconcile opposites must inevitably lead to an intensification of that particular situation where it is ideologies which determine the verdict. Among the prominent representatives of the Young German school it was Heinrich Laube who enjoyed the closest contacts with musicians and yet – he disregarded the music of Weber and Mozart. In his influential (and artistically revolutionary) *Ästhetische Feldzüge* (1834), Ludolf Wienbarg took no notice of Mozart. After Beethoven's death (1827), the growing polemics concerning his later music became crystallized in the progressive party, but a conservative opposition also closed its ranks, an opposition represented by François Joseph Fétis in France, Gottfried Wilhelm Fink of the *Allgemeine Musikalische Zeitung* in Leipzig (who rejected all those who followed Beethoven by calling them lost souls) and Ludwig Rellstab of the Berlin journal *Iris*. The opposition was most noticeable in southern Germany and in Austria, above all in Vienna. And a significant about-turn in the reception is connected with this. Since Mozart's death it had been Saxony and Prussia which had encouraged the new impulses for both the practical and the theoretical interpretation of his work. Spontini and Meyerbeer, Schumann and Mendelssohn, and later Wagner, all achieved success in central and northern Germany. There was, as regards progressiveness, a conspicuous difference which persisted; it was the musical models which changed, to the disadvantage of Haydn and Mozart. Their work was, so to speak, free for new relationships and offered itself as a resounding symbol for an Austrian, patriotic opposition to an external, progressive threat.

The local, Viennese attitude to Mozart, an attitude long established, now came into its own in no uncertain manner. This was obviously connected with an ideology which supported the state and with old political resentments, but it also had to do with the preservation of a particular image

133

of the spirit, and of man. But let us look first at the official activities. They were not as Austrian as one liked to pretend but in their manifestation they followed the familiar monumentalization of noble ideals. This was particularly true in the case of Salzburg's Mozart memorial: it was mostly non-Salzburgers who were involved in the planning. The ideas put forward were partly curious ones; Ludwig Schwanthaler, who designed the casting mould, put forward during discussions the view that, 'In Stuttgart they gave Schiller an eagle on an orb; our good Mozart was also an eagle of his kind, so it seems to me that we mustn't lag behind.'

The extent to which Mozart was regarded as the spiritual possession of all the Germans is documented by the willingness to give financial support to the erection of the monument: among the patrons we find not only the Emperor Ferdinand I but also the kings of Prussia and Bavaria, dukes, middle-class music societies and prominent musicians. A great many musicians, some better known than others, participated in a 'Mozart album . . . for the support of the Mozart memorial' which was brought out by the Brunswick publisher Johann Peter Spehr.

We cannot quite compare the enthusiasm for Mozart's cause with that of the Bach craze which was instigated by Mendelssohn's revival of the *St Matthew Passion* in 1829, but Salzburg took the opportunity to draw attention firmly to its status. Whereas the Mozart festivals in 1836 in Koschirsch (a small town in Bohemia) and then, 1837, in Darmstadt and Elberfeld had had more of an intimate character, the tendency now was for a more official manifestation. Such was the creation of the 'Mozart Foundation' in Frankfurt am Main in 1838 which took up the education of impoverished young musicians (Carl Gollmick, a man of letters, urged the large cities like Vienna, Berlin, Leipzig and Hamburg to follow suit); in 1841 there followed the opening of an educational establishment (the 'Mozarteum') in Salzburg, and plans began to circulate in Prague and Vienna for a statue of Mozart. One of the first Mozart libraries, with all the printed scores, was opened in Prague in 1837. In the Charles Church in Vienna a memorial was to be erected in memory of the trio Gluck-Haydn-Mozart (not Beethoven!); the Salzburgers, however, forestalled this. Nevertheless, the first Viennese Mozart Festival was organized in 1841 (others followed in 1856, 1879 and 1891) – but this was outstripped by the Salzburgers with their four-day Mozart celebrations culminating in the unveiling of the memorial on 14 September 1842.

In the centre of this patriotic, popular festivity we find the performance of a cantata, 'In honour of the unveiling of the Mozart memorial in Salzburg, compounded of compositions by the celebrant, and garnished with a suitable text by the son of Wolfgang Amadeus Mozart': this doubtless fitted in well with Schwanthaler's Classical view of Mozart. The festival was in the artistic hands of the Salzburger Sigismund Neukomm, Franz Lachner from Munich and August Pott from Oldenburg. This symbiosis, this fusion of being rooted-in-the-soil and also cosmopolitan in its hero worship seems to be an anticipation of the later idea for the Salzburg Festivals, but also had as a consequence a scurrilous provincialism as we can see from the programmes of the 1852 celebrations: the overture to *Die Zauberflöte*, 'Mozart and Schikaneder' (a patched-up arrangement of *Der Schauspieldirektor* by Louis Schneider) and 'Ju-Schroa' (a rustic extravaganza with music by Ignaz Lachner). Mozart, actually, even after 1842, played hardly a part in the musical life of Salzburg and was scarcely understood there. The memorial committee hoped that 'the number of strangers pouring into Salzburg, as well as the influx of the citizens, would be greatly increased' – this only happened much later. Travellers who visited the city in the middle of the century, such as the Mozart biographer Otto Jahn, gave devastating comments. When Grillparzer visited Salzburg with his friend Bogner in 1847 the latter called it 'a truly awful hole . . . centuries behind the times'.

But also for Mozart there began, in 1841, a never-ending series of commemoration days. Whether or not these festivals then – or now – brought a new understanding of the work or not depends more on the particular circumstances rather than the date: they certainly all have a popularizing effect. The next jubilee that loomed, the centenary of Mozart's birth in 1856, could build on the success of 1841 and the ever-growing cult of the hero. Not so favourable, however, was the temporal coincidence of the rise of Wagner, Liszt, Offenbach, and so on, and the gap between public acclaim and insufficient inner appreciation yawned ever wider. And yet it is only half-true to see only empty façades in the commemorative festivals. A lot may be incomprehensible to us now – the emotional pathos, the ceremonies (the erection and crowning of a bust during a festival concert), the variety and the hyperbole of the concert performances, the speeches and the panegyric effusions and the closing tableaux, where Mozart was frequently portrayed in the centre of a group of divers persons from his operas. But some things preserved a lasting validity: Eduard Mörike's novella *Mozart auf der Reise nach Prag*, for example, and Otto Jahn's monumental monograph, both of which are connected with the year 1856.

A *Musikalisches Gedenkbuch*, edited by Carl Santner, documents the extent which the secular festivities reached: he lists and describes the celebrations of each city in a most ordered and thorough manner. Within the boundaries of the imperial territories there were celebrations in Salzburg, Vienna,

Graz, Prague, Budweis, Brno, Pest, Cracow and Trieste; Santner also lists the following foreign cities: 'Berlin, Bonn, Bremen, Breslau, Carlsruhe, Chemnitz, Cologne, Danzig, Darmstadt, Dessau, Dresden, Düsseldorf, Frankfurt am Main, Glogau, Gotha, Hamburg, Hanover, Kassel, Königsberg, Leipzig, London, Lübeck, Magdeburg, Meiningen, Munich, Nuremberg, St Petersburg, Potsdam, Stein-Schonau, Stettin, Stuttgart, Weimar, Wiesbaden, Würzburg, Züllichau and Zurich'.

This list was probably more or less complete only as regards the German-speaking lands: we also get occasional references to the presentation of tableaux vivants, Mozart busts, the picture of Mozart's life ('Mozart') by Leonhard Wohlmuth, and to lectures (by the municipal school-inspector Albert, for example, on 'Mozart and Raphael' in Stettin). Usually the best-known Mozart operas were performed in whole or in part – very often, surprisingly, *Idomeneo* and *La Clemenza di Tito*, sometimes even *Il re pastore* and the oratorio *Davidde penitente*. We find the same conservatism in musical taste as we do in Santner's commentaries. Santner inveighed against the 'standard bearer of the so-called Music of the Future' – Franz Liszt – in his capacity as a Mozart conductor in Vienna, and noted that Richard Wagner was to have directed the memorial concert in Zurich, but had refused.

During the commemorative year, 1856, the essentially Austrian elements did not achieve the prominence that they did later, when the newly built Vienna Court Opera was opened on 25 May 1869 with a performance of *Don Giovanni*. The cultural and political aims of this new institution precisely illuminated the official attitude to Mozart; a new opera house belonged to those magnanimous visions of civic expansion with which the imperial house wished to gain prestige after the crises of the year 1848 had been overcome. The gaze was directed backwards towards the 'heroic age of Austria' under Charles VI and especially towards the Viennese tradition of Italian opera of which many of the stylistic elements in the new opera house were reminiscent – the clear definition of the loggia, for example. Particularly interesting are the iconographic motifs for the decoration of the building and its various rooms for which Eduard Hanslick and Friedrich von Hentl, ministerial adviser for the arts, were mainly responsible. Pictorial images relating to the power of music (*Die Zauberflöte* and Gluck's *Orpheus und Eurydike*) and to the history of opera itself were tastefully interwoven with praise of the imperial dynasty.

Mozart served as an intermediary and had a particular historical function – he was the link between the Baroque and the nineteenth century, between Italian and German opera; there was also his early connection with the Habsburgs. A veil of transfiguration lies over much of this. The imperial room is decorated with a devotional scene in tribute to *Figaro* (by Eduard von Engerth) and the central cameo of the loggia ceiling represents the boy Mozart on the lap of Maria Theresia, 'the darling child of Austria, as it were', as Minister Hentl formulated it in the documents. Above the hearth in the empress's room we have a picture of an idyllic view of Hohensalzburg from a wooded ravine – and Mozart's name is scratched upon a rock. The choice of fourteen modelled representations of composers is deliberately such as to distance them from the topical (which would have included Wagner and Verdi) to the time before 1848. The heroes of Austrian music alone are celebrated twice, as statues in the loggia and as busts in the foyer: Mozart, Beethoven, Haydn, Schubert and Gluck. Reliefs on the mantelpiece in the foyer show how the Habsburgs had promoted and encouraged opera – rightly as in the case of Leopold I, and incorrectly in the case of Maria Theresia: her involvement is only justified by the picture with the boy Mozart, and these two representations mutually support each other despite being very dubious historically.

One of the idylls has Mozart as a hero (as Joseph von Hormayr had already envisaged him in his *Österreichischer Plutarch* of 1807-14); all of the representations (also Moritz von Schwind's sketch for the Mozart lunette in the foyer) follow this tendency. Here the transfiguration of music overlaps with its trivialization – and the décor now becomes a political factor. The tension in the relationship between the spirit of the age, the traditional idea of the state, and the religion of art, lies now in an aesthetic-patriotic ideal, for opera could no longer fulfil the courtly role allotted to it in the time of the baroque, and sought to remain aloof from everyday reality. So we have a 'realm which is profane and sacred' as Adorno described it, in which the rather banausic Emperor Franz Joseph, in contrast to his baroque ancestors, found himself somewhat displaced.

What the spirit of all these endeavours meant, despite all their contradictions, is convincingly seen in a writer like Franz Grillparzer whose patriotism was not opportunistically cultivated, but something, rather, under which he suffered. One of his poems, meant for the Salzburg Festival of 1842 but completed too late, is called 'Zu Mozarts Feier' (On Mozart's Celebration), and we read the following:

[line 52]
With Raphael, the painter of Madonnas,
He therefore stands, a cherub in the throng,
Expressing and protecting truthful art
In which the heaven married is to earth.

137

[line 62]
We call him great? Great was he through his limits.
The things he did, the things he did not do,
Weigh equal in the balance of his fame.

[line 69]
The realm of art is like a second world,
Essential and as actual as the first,
And all things real obey the measure's law.
Think then of this; let this day teach the time
That great things seeks, and only reaches small.

Grillparzer's view of Mozart – indeed his view of art as a whole – is concentrated in these verses. There is not so much a flight from the world here, but rather a criticism of the times. Grillparzer confessed in a letter to Franz Lorenz (2 April 1853) that 'he did not see, in everything that had been achieved in music since Mozart's death – including even the splendid Beethoven – any kind of advance, or increase in excellence'.

It was not only in old age that he praised 'Mozart's unsurpassability'; as early as 1809 a diary entry associated Beethoven with 'chaos' and Mozart with 'humanity'. While criticizing 'something bizarre' in Beethoven (although the latter's talent he placed on an equal footing with that of Mozart and Haydn), a tendency deriving from that composer's 'desire for originality' and his 'mournful circumstances, which are known to all', Grillparzer saw Mozart as being in harmony with himself. In his opinion there was a moderation in Mozart resulting from the unity (also described in the poem) between Mozart's art and the landscape around Salzburg; Grillparzer also paraphrases this basic thought with the traditional artistic comparisons. Music, he writes, arises from feeling and reaches the spirit; in poetry it is reversed. 'Thus Shakespeare may go to the most hideous lengths: beauty was Mozart's limit'; Grillparzer also stresses again the old Raphael comparison. And yet, in the poem quoted, he calls Mozart 'an alien figure of greatness'. In his toast for the Vienna Mozart festival of 6 December 1841 he even praises the fact that Mozart's grave is unknown, in that his immortality could be experienced even more powerfully. For Grillparzer, however, a world does not separate into beautiful ideal or bare reality: the 'second world' of art is just as 'real as the first', and 'all things obey the measure's law'.

Many were concerned to preserve this world and set it against another one: we can trace this in music to Johannes Brahms and Johann Strauss the

Younger. A feeling of security in a world handed down from a previous age was expressed in many a thought and image reminiscent of Grillparzer. Raphael Georg Kiesewetter came to the conclusion that 'the epoch of Mozart and Haydn – with all due respect for the best of the new – will, for my contemporaries at least, be a time which, by common consent, may be described as "the golden age" '.

This attitude was nowhere more prevalent than in Vienna: that which was Classical in Mozart was formulated in a theoretically more precise manner elsewhere. Wendt observes in Mozart the identity which has already been mentioned between form and content, he notices the 'most beautiful marriage between vocal and instrumental music', the idealizaton of 'nature', the 'profound exploration of human feelings, the unity of richness and comprehensibility in the musical language', a unity attained by 'a thoroughness of style'. There is no conceptual expression here of a dichotomy between Classicism and Romanticism: this conservative view of Mozart is essentially, and in its details, indebted to what was current before and around 1800. The Stettin musician Karl Kossmaly, for example, calls Mozart 'the most objective of all the composers', yet indulges in apologia for him with – of all people – Novalis quotations concerning infinite interpretability as a token for quality and also that simplicity which needs greater intellect to understand it than does the artificial.

Images and comparisons from antiquity were willingly conjured up to defend an argument: the novelist Adalbert Stifter, for example, in his book *Nachsommer* recognized the unattainable model of the Greeks most readily in the 'simplicity and greatness' of the music of Mozart, Haydn, Bach and Handel and explained: 'The men who produced this had a picture of life that was simple and antique.' What we see most clearly in contemporary music criticism was an attack against false progressiveness, that 'daubing materialism' with which Robert Schumann reproached the 'French neo-Romantics', and not against the art of German Romanticism prior to 1830. One of the most bitter opponents of progress was Alfred von Wolzogen, father of the prominent Wagnerian Hans von Wolzogen. In his *Die musikalischen Leiden der Gegenwart* (Musical Sufferings of the Present) (1857) he speaks of a 'Catechism of Music' based upon the era from Palestrina to Mozart, calls Mendelssohn the last composer and sees in the music of the New German School nothing but 'chaos' and 'degeneration'.

Yet people were not blind to the difficulties of holding up to the present some ideal of 'a golden age'. Grillparzer could thus praise Hummel as 'the last untarnished disciple of Mozart' with the reservation, however, that 'there was something workmanlike in his mentality'. Kahlert looked at

Mozart's imitators and noticed that they emulated his simplicity and nothing else, and so were writing music that was correct, light-footed yet empty. Through their one-sidedness epigones were contravening the demand for measure and balance. The efforts to achieve a delicate weighing certainly could not break the ideological barriers, nor dissolve them. That which would prove unconquerable for decades had already been summed up by Adoph Bernhard Marx in 1825 in his lapidary, provocative question: 'But supposing the New Musicians were not striving for the simplicity, fullness, clarity, tranquillity, balance, etc., of their precursors? Supposing they wanted something quite different from these, and that their ideas and aims could neither continue to tolerate nor admit those qualities?'

So it was quite consistent for Richard Wagner to seek to immortalize the most prominent critic of progress in the second half of the century – Eduard Hanslick – as the ossified marker in his *Die Meistersinger von Nürnberg*. What we now call typically '*Beckmesserian*' – a well-known concept – thus nearly had another name. Yet Hanslick was by no means a formalist. In his criticism of Mozart's *Così fan tutte* he called the opera 'an inane work' whose bad libretto had 'even lamed Mozart's creative imagination and had led him astray to an effeminate formalism': it did not incite 'sympathy' amongst the audience. *Don Giovanni*, on the other hand, receives the highest praise of all the operas because of its 'unheard-of combination of highest musical beauty and dramatic genius'. In contrast to uniformity, which leaves us cold, Hanslick posits his central idea of 'imagination' (whose modelled representations in the Court Opera and the Musikverein building he may well have suggested). For him, beauty is vitality of the spirit. In his much quoted phrase about 'moving, resounding forms' the emphasis lies not only on the 'forms' but equally on 'moving'. And the word 'resounding' is directed against the overloading of music with external ideas.

Hanslick's views, then, are very close to those of Grillparzer, about whom Hanslick wrote one of his finest essays. It is possible that Hanslick's views are closer to a Hegelian 'sensuous apparition of an idea' than Grillparzer's, but when he aimed at 'living sympathy' he meant something similar to Grillparzer who saw a basis for musical efficacy in 'states of mind'. As well as an intellectual tradition, both have the ideal of Mozart in common; this is hardly surprising as Hanslick came from Prague and had Tomaschek, a Mozart-enthusiast, as his teacher. After passing through a phase of neo-Romantic enthusiasms (especially for Wagner's *Tannhäuser*) he acknowledged his true roots in 'Vom Musikalisch-Schönen' ('Concerning that which is Beautiful in Music') and strove to create a musical aesthetic based on the models of Viennese Classicism. He qualified as a university lecturer with this dissertation at the University of Vienna in – of all years – the Mozart year of 1856. Theoretically it is an inconsistency perhaps, but it also speaks for the vitality and the honesty of his musical thinking that Hanslick gave up his programmatic goal of a systematic musical aesthetic in favour of history, and regarded as urgent a thorough and conscientious attitude *vis-à-vis* the present.

As well as the irreconcilable, ideological conflict on a high intellectual level we also find, particularly in the Vienna of the 1840s, a kind of party game – for or against Mozart. Adalbert Stifter describes this in his *Feldblumen* (Wild Flowers) of 1841 and speaks of 'female Mozartians' (this implying to the reader that Mozart's music appealed particularly to the ladies), but also reconciles the differences between Mozart and Beethoven: this corresponds to his own view of music. One of the main characters of *Feldblumen* formulates the difference thus: 'With a friendly countenance Mozart distributes priceless gems, giving something to each of us; Beethoven however, explodes over us like a cloud-burst of jewels . . .'

Crazes – something like those for pop stars of today – provided rich material for trivial narration: it is worthwhile giving a brief résumé of Friedrich Dornau's 'Mozart und Beethoven' which appeared in 1843 in the *Wiener Zeitschrift für Kunst, Literatur, Theater und Mode*. Two couples are discussing a music festival in support of the memorial for the Classical composers in the Charles Church. Emanuel enthuses for the 'Titan' Beethoven, Ernst for Mozart; Eveline tends to the former opinion, while Marie finds Mozart to be 'an ideal'. A conflict is in the offing between Marie and Emanuel – the reader suspects that this is a sign of secret love. Marie praises feeling and passion in Mozart's music, and when she finally sings one of his songs Emanuel renounces Beethoven, asks Marie for her hand and thanks 'Mozart from the depths of his heart for being a miracle-worker'. The sort of cultural and political substance that was concealed by this literary icing became clear to Schumann in Vienna in 1838; there was a movement afoot against the male choir – 'this poison from Germany' in Metternich's words – which manifested itself in a crass and distorted manner in the fanatical Beethoven supporter Alfred Julius Becher who was one of the ringleaders of the uprising in Vienna in October 1848 and who met his death in front of the rifles of a firing squad. Grillparzer wrote this epigram about his music: 'Your quartet sounded as if someone were hacking mightily with an axe, and like three women who were sawing and chopping up a load of wood.'

After the century had reached its halfway mark there were – also in Vienna – certain concessions towards the middle-class idea of progress:

musical innovations were increasingly tolerated. Yet the old contrasts were still found in the idea that future developments would make it necessary to group the musical models differently and to give up personalizing the Mozart versus Beethoven notion. The organist and publicist Selmar Bagge differentiated three parties in Vienna's musical life in the 1860s: the 'Progressists' (who put their hopes above all in Liszt), the 'Reactionaries' (who looked back to Bach, Haydn, Mozart, Beethoven and Mendelssohn) and the 'Liberals'.

Leaving aside the cultural-political background and its evaluations, the inner life of Mozart's image remained essentially stable in the second half of the century – I might even claim that, despite all the craving for status of this age, the overtly Biedermeier aspects still remained. We can argue that during the activities of 1856 something was extrapolated from a long, progressive development, and that, emblematically, something valid was achieved – but that a truly productive, intellectual phase was realized before, rather than after, this date. And by 'Biedermeier' I mean to describe the kind of way a subject was treated, rather than the subject itself. We get an undeniable tendency to trivialize, a loving cultivation of that which was familiar. Yet we need not necessarily interpret the will to harmony as being Biedermeier; none the less, the intimacy of Biedermeier, and the ethos of the Gründerzeit are the quiet and the loud sides of the same thing, with Mozart being claimed by both.

To get a clearer picture let us look again at the tendencies to idealize and historicize Mozart: this has nothing to do with any particular epoch and its ideas. The innumerable pictures and statues may be embarrassing in their dubious solemnity or their triviality – this is a matter of intellectual taste and standards. An example of the former is given by the technically accomplished memorial picture by 'the Austrian Menzel', the Salzburger Peter Johann Nepomuk Geiger, in 1856: we see a depersonalized Mozart, as it were, in flowing robes, sitting at the organ and surrounded by the emblems of his art; he gazes upwards, where angels play music before the *Agnus Dei*. An example of a sweetly pretty idyll is, in contrast, the watercolour depicting *Mozart as a child with his father and sister in Robinighof* by the many-sided Lyser. Of a much higher artistic quality are Rudolf von Alt's *Mozart on the Kahlenberg* and the idealistic Mozart apotheosis of Anton Romako (in which the model of the plain Lange portrait appeared richly adorned as never before). Mörike firmly rejected the idealization popular at the time; none the less, Mozart was an ideal for him, albeit in a complex way.

The evaluation of the idealization – a somewhat one-sided idealization – of painters of the status of Jean Auguste Ingres or Moritz von Schwind is a little more problematic. Ingres compared Mozart with Raphael, called him a 'god of music' and *Don Giovanni* a 'masterpiece of the human spirit'. For him Mozart was a model of perfection, tenderness and precision, a confirmation of his own artistic aims. Schwind, who is known in musicology through his friendly (although episodic) contacts with Schubert, was a Mozart enthusiast who showed the same reservations as Ingres about Beethoven. Do we not detect in Schwind's art a superficiality 'walled in by culture'? In his early *Reisebilder* Schwind also chose *Le Nozze di Figaro* as his subject. The final picture, that of the happy couple Cherubino and Barbarina, is a quintessentially lyrical idyll: in the manner of Eichendorff and other Romantics Schwind called the page 'the basic motif of the opera'. Later, when he was working for the Vienna Court Opera he was more concerned with *Die Zauberflöte* ('an apotheosis of music, according to its subject matter') and above all with Tamino and Pamina ('the most ideal, the most solemn of all loving couples'). His *Don Giovanni* drawings (1870–1) are startling in their unsentimental representation of a manly, determined hero. But it was the charming, gaily coloured idealism of his early work which appealed to Grillparzer and Mörike – pictures which, however, did not do justice to their views on Mozart. Perhaps Schwind's Mozart depictions meant as little to them as Beethoven did to Schwind for his picture *Die Symphonie* and, to express it unsubtly, they were satisfied with a confirmation of the idealism of their ideal Mozart.

There are reasons why, in the field of literature, there is nothing (apart from Mörike) of comparable stature to the pictures of Schwind. Aesthetic judgements were also discriminating after 1830; the vivid representation of the person of Mozart within the artist-novella only really got underway with the Biedermeier period and sought to link the edifying with the entertaining – the '*delectare prodesse*' of Horace was, however, considerably trivialized. The stories of Johann Peter Lyser (gathered as a *Mozart Album* in 1856), Carl Gollmick, Heribert Rau, etc., were meant to be an apologia for Mozart and a demonstration against the decline in the number of performances of certain of his works – an extended arm, if you like, of that process of popularization which earlier had been effected by domestic playing and which now sought, using anecdote and biography, to encourage a true-to-life identification. What is characteristic of the situation is the blending of popularization and historicizing which was regarded as axiomatic; basically, however, popularization sought to bring Mozart closer, and to historicize him meant to alienate him. This contradiction was, however, avoided by the illusion that one could curry favour with Mozart's transfigured inscrutability.

The loving details found in descriptions of Mozart's person and his circumstances are historically true and also talk the reader into believing something that he generally knew anyway. And where it was a matter of music, and thus a matter of a distance between Mozart and the present, the difference remains an illusion and is less concerned with historical consciousness than with the rejection of progress. When Tomaschek 'remembered' Mozart's original tempi, or when Ignaz Franz von Mosel (1843) held up the Italian singers of fifty years previously as a model for the virtuosi of his day (they were better actors, 'in *cantabile*, in the expression of different feelings and passions, in the way they project themselves: they were far better than the best of our time'), then the aim of this report is clear, even though its content is historically uncertain. Even a sceptical sobriety (such as, say, Otto Jahn possessed and which he turned against the anecdotes of Rochlitz) was not able to deter such stories in the style of 'true happenings from Mozart's life' which were published by actual or ostensible acquaintances of Mozart.

Many of these reports are in stereotyped clichés. Even the much respected *Denkwürdigkeiten aus meinem Leben* (Memorable Events from My Life) of Caroline Pichler (Vienna 1844) lacks depth of characterization: her statement that Mozart and Haydn 'had no kind of intellectual education' continues to exert a fascination even today because of its incomprehensibility. We shall not discuss trivial literature in tedious detail, especially as it offers only a particular tendency rather than a thorough illumination. One example will suffice of the way in which many writers outdid each other in praising their object; Carl Gollmick defended his hero's childishness in his *Rückblick auf Mozarts geistige Wirksamkeit* (On Remembering Mozart's Spiritual Efficacy) of 1846 with the following words: '. . . and yet it was this childlike quality of his personality which shines through all his works; it was this unpretentiousness and naïvety, this remoteness from all excessive pomp and speculation which gained him candidature for heaven'. As Niemetschek before him, Gollmick insisted that Mozart's spiritual essence was expressed in his music: the description of Mozart's universality reaches excessive proportions. Gollmick calls Mozart a 'psychologist' ('He poured truth and beauty upon the whole of nature'), a 'friend of humanity' and a 'poet' ('His blossoming imagination was Schillerian, his penetrating depth of perception was Goethean, his strength and his bubbling sense of humour was Shakespearean'), a 'mathematician', an 'architect', a 'philologist', a 'philosopher', a 'theologian', a 'victorious general' and, finally, even a 'necromancer'.

It would be a mistake to claim that, with this enumeration, Gollmick was

144

inveighing against Caroline Pichler: both, rather, were concerned with the same thing, that is, to illustrate something enigmatic – in particular the childlike quality and the subconscious creativity of a man like Mozart. Adolph Bernhard Marx unintentionally confirmed what the majority of Mozart's apologists were writing in his Beethoven monograph when he proposed that Beethoven had 'left behind him the time of Haydn and Mozart with its modest complacency and concentration on private interests and feelings'. The general validity of Marx's opinion is seen in the fact that both Mozart and Haydn were trivialized in anecdotes, stories, novels, *Singspiele* and portraits; Beethoven scarcely ever was. Mozart was the topic of over fifty plays in the nineteenth century (for example, by Wenzel Müller and Carl Meisl, 1818; Grillparzer, 1826; Pushkin, 1830; Lortzing, 1832; Franz von Suppé, 1854; Lyser, 1856; Franz Pocci, 1877; Rudolph Genée, 1896).

Historical research into the figure of Mozart was well under way, but for a long time there was a fixation with the mysterious nimbus which surrounded him. How else do we explain the violent reaction, in both essays and letters, to Gottfried Weber's 'Über die Echtheit des Mozartschen Requiems' (Concerning the Genuineness of Mozart's *Requiem*) of 1825? This explosion of scholarly activity (which, all the same, did bring about André's critical edition of the score) had, in fact, other, hidden, causes: they are manifest in, say, Alexander Pushkin's play *Mozart and Salieri* which gave the poisoning theory its poetic radiance. In 1829 Vincent and Mary Novello went on their 'Mozart Pilgrimage' to Vienna and visited Mozart's sister and widow in Salzburg. In this description of the journey we get again much discussion about the *Requiem* problems and even the poisoning theory (very readable are the impressions of the 'musical scene in Europe in 1829'). This secularization of the idea of a pilgrimage would become an artistic-religious catharsis, and probably began with the devotional visits of young musicians to the aged Haydn in Gumpendorf near Vienna.

We find a similar motivation in the hobby of collecting autographs and portraits, a hobby indulged in by such famous composers as Mendelssohn and Sigismund Thalberg. On the one hand this led to the veneration of devotional objects which were frequently fakes, but also on the other, to an internationally recognized expertise. The Viennese collector Aloys Fuchs was one of these. The Mozart biography by Georg Nikolaus Nissen, which Constanze published posthumously in 1829, is also sustained by this collecting spirit. This book has frequently been blamed for not being a biography as such, but an uncritical juxtaposition of material – and yet we should be grateful to Nissen for his diligence and his piety: there was nobody in Haydn's circle who would have built up a similar collection for posterity.

The concerts which stand out most clearly from the amateurish hobby-like activities of this kind are those 'Historical Concerts' which Mendelssohn organized in Leipzig and Kiesewetter in Vienna. In contrast to works like Spohr's 'Historical Symphony in the Style and Taste of Four Different Periods' (1839) they are not intended to criticize the present, but refer to a musical development and approximate to the concept of historicism.

The three most important Mozart depictions of the nineteenth century stem from three *nobili dilettanti* in musical matters – the Russian aristocrat and amateur Alexander D. Ulibischeff, the Swabian poet Eduard Mörike and the North German classical philologist and archaeologist Otto Jahn. The distance from music as a profession and from close contact with Mozart's immediate surroundings may have intensified the tendency to idealization and that belief in the unity of art and life which despite all the differences is common to their writing. Their conservative attitudes are seen in their rejection of musical progress: Ulibischeff even heard 'an ugly miaowing' in Beethoven's music. The other side, represented by Liszt, Hans von Bülow and the Russian music critics Wilhelm Lenz and Alexander Serov, consequently launched a vigorous attack against the ostensible musical ignorance of the dilettante Ulibischeff; the Wagnerian Serov, however, wrote in a surprisingly positive manner about Jahn's book.

Ulibischeff, educated in Germany, was first of all impressed by the *Requiem* discussions (he later wrote some hundred pages on them); in 1830 he read Nissen's book and decided to order the material and form it into a biography – this would take him ten years. The three-volume work appeared in French in 1843 and in German four years later with the title *Mozarts Leben, nebst einer Uebersicht der allgemeinen Geschichte der Musik und einer Analyse der Hauptwerke Mozarts* (Mozart's Life, Together with a Survey of the General History of Music with an Analysis of Mozart's Major Works). It was the thought concerning the harmony between art and life which gave the inner impetus for the writing of the book: 'As I began my task . . . I noticed to my great surprise the same mutual relationships between many of Mozart's works and the concomitant biographical circumstances as we find in the history of the *Requiem*, relationships which impress and astound us.'

Ulibischeff does not, however, see this harmony in some kind of Biedermeier idyll but in the exceptional character of genius. 'The primary, and the true events in the life of an artist are his works.' He continues:

We wish to explain the artist through the moral individual, and this latter through the artist; we wish to prove their complete interdependence or, rather, their complete identity. We shall let musical analysis go hand in

146

hand with the psychological and, indeed, in such a way that both, in context, mutually support each other; we shall finally give a brief mention of where there may be an apparent influence of circumstances upon the work.

Ulibischeff goes so far as to see, in the central masterpiece, the figure of Don Giovanni as a self-portrayal of Mozart's moral personality and the Commendatore as the 'shadow of his father'. He also makes no attempt to excuse Mozart's 'considerable shortcomings': he admits of deficient human understanding, irresponsibility with money and 'verbal lack of restraint', but turns these faults in character round to an attack against an image of the artist current during the Biedermeier period. If Mozart had been different he would have left his family a fortune, he would have 'held a respectable position and had another thirty years to live . . . who can doubt it? But then we would have been unable to demand a *Don Giovanni* from this bourgeois paragon, from such an admirable paterfamilias as he would have been.'
Another of Ulibischeff's trains of thought attempts to explain Mozart's predetermination by means of long music-historical explications and, as an apologia, reduces it to the following quintessential apophthegm: 'Mozart's mission was to establish the rules of art, an art which had hitherto been incomplete.' Ulibischeff's stimulating book is scarcely known today, but was much praised by his contemporaries, and in the *Allgemeine Musikalische Zeitung* of Leipzig we even read 'that no musician has such a splendid biography as Mozart has through this document'. This is why Mörike intended to use this quotation of Ulibischeff about Mozart's personality as a motto in the first instalment, in 1855, of his novella *Mozart auf der Reise nach Prag* in the *Morgenblatt für gebildete Leser*. There is to be no trivialization here – yet there are quite a few Biedermeier elements in the story: the literary form itself (Mörike is concerned to give us a 'character study' rather than a story of action), the delight in detail, the portrayal of Constanze as a good-humoured, rather garrulous little housewife, the narrator's fussy, rather twee condescension (Mozart is our 'Master', our 'friend' or 'our dear little golden man'), and the way in which trifles are given great attention. Yet all this does not simply give a conventional framework for a well-grounded report: Mörike succeeds, rather, in skilfully using this framework for the report itself. The mixture of earnestness and lightheartedness, of the conventional and the extraordinary is a mirror-image of that image of Mozart that we have already met with in Grillparzer, Hanslick and so on. Mörike seeks to express essential things without emotive effusion. He shows us a Mozart who plays with life and who throws himself

147

into life, who unexpectedly turns away from what he had hitherto been pursuing, and who, in a mood of relaxation, suddenly reveals something which is deadly earnest; Mörike sees that these traits are closely bound up with Mozart's music. His novella, then, hunts down the very creative process itself.

Mörike scholarship seeks to explain this process, but its results occasionally encumber the subtle correlations in the story itself. One example: Mozart's memory of the Neapolitan water games which he tells to the assembled company in Count Schinzberg's palace can be seen as a significant coding of principles of musical form. Even more so as Eugénie makes the enthusiastic comment after hearing the description that she has heard 'a painted symphony', 'a perfect symbol of Mozart's spirit', 'all the charm of *Figaro*'. Yet Mozart is already speaking, and tries to interpret his little story: today, he says, 'that lovely evening in Naples seventeen years ago had arisen before him with unprecedented clarity'. He heard that merry music again, and 'then suddenly a completely new dance tune emerged, in six-eight time' – that long awaited duet of Zerlina and Masetto with the chorus 'Giovanette che fate all' amore' from the first act of *Don Giovanni*.

The apparently chance nature of this memory is given a particular meaning in the novella by the object which triggered it off, the orange tree from which Mozart absent-mindedly plucked a fruit. And now our researchers are given a further impetus to investigate the symbolism of fruit, gold, tree, paradise, and so on. But how oscillating is, say, Mörike's use of the word gold! That he should apply it to Mozart, and call his music a 'heap of gold', or the fact that he associates this colour with brightness and serenity does not mean very much. On the first couple of pages we get a description of the covered buttons on Mozart's overcoat; we are told that 'a layer of gold foil shimmered through their star-like fabric'. We also hear of Constanze's annoyance at Mozart's clumsiness at having spilt a bottle of real Rosée d'Aurore: 'I saved it like gold.' From these passing references to gold we later get a mention of the golden-yellow orange which Mozart, in his letter of apology to the countess, compares to Adam's apple in paradise. We have oranges, golden balls and finally a 'golden fish' in the Neapolitan water games. Later, Franziska alludes to Mozart when describing 'a scene from the golden age of the world' in a copperplate engraving, and she expresses the hope that 'Apollo will recognize himself in this situation'. And when Apollo is referred to as 'the god whose golden locks/dip into the Castalian spring' – and there are frequent quotations from Horace in this company of gentlefolk who are eager to improve their minds – then Mozart dents the halo somewhat, begs a kiss from Eugénie and, at the same time, placates her fiancé by saying that there is no danger as long as the god 'does not lend him his long fair hair'. And so this part of the story, the one which illuminates the creative process, flows into that mood of *leggiero di testa* which is evoked in that duet of Zerlina and Masetto, now happily found.

Mörike almost completely abjures discussions on the technicalities of music, yet finds a subtle and compact linguistic picture for the music which Mozart plays upon the piano before the aristocratic company:

It was one of those radiant pieces in which pure beauty, as if by caprice, placed itself voluntarily in the service of elegance, but in such a way that, only concealed, as it were, in these more arbitrarily playing forms, and behind a cluster of dazzling lights, it nevertheless betrayed its deepest nobility in every moment and poured forth its fervour in abundance.

More important still is the description, towards the end of the novella, of the fearful chorale 'Thy laughter will die before the dawn!' from *Don Giovanni*: 'As if they came from remotest galaxies the tones of the silver trombones fall through the azure night, icy-cold, transfixing body and soul.' Here there is a hint of the connection between art and death, a connection that is meant to clarify the mystery of Mozart's genius. It is extremely problematic to see in the Mozart of the novella a self-portrayal of Mörike, but the novella does portray something which affected the latter deeply, for Mörike admitted that he had 'never written anything with more love and more care'. Mörike's *Don Giovanni* experience is strangely bound up with the death of his brother August; in a letter he confesses that he was always afraid before any *Don Giovanni* performance 'because it contains too many subjective elements for me and pushes over me . . . the old flood of perfume, pain and beauty'.

Mörike's image of Mozart is fundamentally different from that of his old friends from the early days in Tübingen. Ernst Friedrich Kauffmann, one of the dedicatees of the novella, had once played Mörike a great deal of Mozart. After he had been mixed up in the Koseritz conspiracy of 1838 he was sentenced to confinement in the fortress of Hohenasperg; his wife accompanied him to his cell and suddenly he had a vision of that music from *Die Zauberflöte* which goes: 'We wander helped by music's spell.' In contrast to Mörike's *Don Giovanni* experience this story, told to David Friedrich Strauss, sounds forced and melodramatic; the enthusiasm for Mozart of Strauss, another friend of Mörike and a critic of theology, is overtly conventional. Strauss visited Salzburg in 1848 and sent Kauffmann the following quatrain: 'How near in this holy place/Of Mozart's cradle are you, friend,/Who let the cornucopia of his notes/Pour over me from the piano at our home.' When we read his *Die Zauberflöte* and his *Figaro* sonnets we detect a naïve reverence. But in *his* sonnet, 'Seltsamer Traum' (Strange Dream), dedicated to his friends in 1828, Mörike portrays *Figaro* in a most Romantic manner: from 'velvety ground of spring', full of cherubs, masks, flowers and ribbons there arise 'melodic powers . . . as sober shadows'; but at the end we read: 'And *I* sang, as a clown, on flowery meads'. In his novella, too, Mörike was concerned with this 'gentle transformation' in those pictures which seemed to be painting themselves.

The judgement of the publisher, Cotta, probably has lasting validity: he described it as being 'like an old jewel . . . from the best of times, and charming and fine for all times'. An official letter of King Maximilian II of Bavaria confirms the extent to which Mörike appealed to the conservatives: the king speaks of 'the grace', 'divine proportion' and a 'beneficient appearance'. Maximilian's father, Ludwig I, had also written a poem 'To Mozart' in 1856 in which he praised Olympia and eternal youth, and finished with the words: 'Long may the ideal of beauty live/In the magic of your fantasy.'

Otto Jahn's monumental Mozart biography, which appeared in three volumes in Leipzig between the years 1856 and 1859 (second revised edition 1867) was to provide the foundation for all Mozart scholarship. Its far-reaching influence was such that it provoked the English scholar Alexander Hyatt King to suggest, in 1956, that it was time, at last, to strike out in a new direction. But the question as to how far Jahn's Mozart image rested upon his own personal viewpoint remains unanswered. He first intended to write a biography of Beethoven, but then completely turned away from progressive tendencies in music, publishing an attack on Wagner and Berlioz at the beginning of the 1850s, and became a fervent admirer of Mozart. His picture of Mozart is correspondingly Classicistic, which is not surprising for a scholar who wrote about antiquity and also Goethe and Winckelmann.

The picture drawn by Ulibischeff and Mörike has far more Romantic elements than Jahn's. The proximity of art and death, the subconscious activity of genius beyond the sphere of convention – these are themes that Jahn sought to smooth into a harmonious whole, and Ulibischeff would have considered this to be very bourgeois. Jahn believed (as did his friend the great ancient historian Theodor Mommsen) that, as well as being a historian, he was also a 'moralist': Mozart is ennobled and transformed into an edifying paragon. We see this ethos in one of his letters from Salzburg, written when he was studying the Mozart sources there: 'What brings me

150

great joy is the fact that Mozart's image is not only becoming clearer, but also more beautiful and more pure than the normal picture.' That a scholar, above all, should idealize Mozart in such a pronounced manner is surely surprising: it may have to do with Jahn's feelings of reservation about the political developments after 1848, but also with something in his private life, where Jahn was much in need of some compensating force to counterbalance misfortune and feelings of personal guilt. He was just as unfair towards the psychological subtlety of Mörike as towards Hanslick's aesthetic demands. The success of his study (a success also outside the bounds of scholarship, where a *Kleiner Mozart* [Miniature Mozart] was planned for use as a reader amongst the general public) is probably explained by the similarity of content between Jahn's description of Mozart's person and what was prevalent in belletristic writings of the times.

There is an epistemological difficulty in the way in which Jahn was convinced that his ideal was the result of objective scholarship: 'Its final goal is the truth, and I have only sought to find and to depict the truth.' The great achievement of the work, and one which was indeed forward-looking, was without doubt its consistent use of historical sources, a discipline which had been developed in the historical school of jurisprudence during the early part of the nineteenth century. Jahn was a classical philologist, and the methodology of this discipline had been long established: he was therefore better prepared for the task than any musical theorist.

The second father of Mozart scholarship, Ludwig Ritter von Köchel (whose *Chronologisch-thematisches Verzeichnis sämtlicher Tonwerke W.A. Mozarts* [Chronological and Thematic Register of All the Works of W.A. Mozart], which appeared in Leipzig in 1862, is known to all music lovers at least by name), was also, like Jahn, a private scholar of the late Biedermeier period. Both were versatile and cultured men who sought to exert an influence upon the public and who were also active artistically: Jahn wrote music and Köchel's first publications on Mozart were canzonas written for the centenary celebrations. Jahn worked as a professor in Leipzig (vice-chancellor in 1858); Köchel was a tutor to the sons of the Archduke Charles, an inspector of schools, botanist and mineralogist of repute, who became a hereditary peer, vice-president of the Viennese Society for the Friends of Music and also of the Imperial and Royal Zoological and Botanical Society. Both men project an image diametrically opposed to Romanticism.

Further developments in Mozart scholarship led to an increase in specialization: Jahn, for instance, appended to the first edition of his book a list of works, ordered according to groups. As Jahn and Köchel got to know each other they attempted to work in close harness, with the result that Jahn

151

gave up the idea of completing the work register and handed this over to Köchel. Jahn kept the other appendices, such as letters and documents, as he considered that Ludwig Nohl's edition of Mozart's letters was unsatisfactory (the first more or less complete edition, by Ludwig Schiedermair, appeared only in 1914). The advances brought by the critical method are apparent most of all in the later improvements made in Jahn's work, partly by himself and partly by Hermann Deiters, and also in Köchel's 'chronological-thematic register' which was supplemented partly by himself and partly by the revision of Paul Graf von Waldersee in 1905. The appearance of Gustav Martin Nottebohm's *Mozartiana* in 1880 marked another step forward in the advancement of new source research, and we should not forget Johann Evangelist Engl, one of the founder members of the Mozarteum and one of its first Mozart scholars.

Despite Jahn, Köchel and others it was the belletristic Mozart work which dominated, writers for whom the aims of scholarship were alien and who were unable anyway to reach a particular literary standard that would have been appropriate. The trivial Raphael-figure drawn by the musicologist Ludwig Nohl in many of his writings on Mozart from 1863 onwards hardly did justice to the demands of scholarship but enjoyed – probably because of this – a great and lasting success. It was the old *Mozart Gesamtausgabe* (Complete Edition of Mozart) which represented the most important practical contribution to Mozart studies, an edition which owes much to the initiative of the Salzburg Mozart Foundation and to Köchel. When we consider that, around 1870, about a third of Mozart's works were unpublished, and that the works that were known were often only in the form of arrangements made from some very corrupt scores, then the importance of this edition becomes clear, even if it remained unheeded for a long time. Its slender impact (despite the commitment of such great names as Johannes Brahms and Joseph Joachim) is seen in the small number of subscribers – only ninety-three in the year 1883, although large parts of the work were ready and the retail price could be kept remarkably low.

The starting point was the critical analysis of details, and the intention was to remove, step by step, those prejudices and myths of which some of the researchers themselves may have been guilty. Jahn's criticism, for example, was directed against the view which is still prevalent today, namely, that Mozart composed without sketches or studies, and that he never reworked his material. But protests against the voice of scholarship soon became apparent: the *Lieder*-composer Robert Franz wrote a letter to Mörike (26 August 1856) in which he explained that he had felt liberated by reading Mörike's novella after he had 'struggled' through Jahn's opus. 'The fruitless mass of antiquarian, pedagogic hair splitting, the manifold indiscretions –

152

doubtless committed in the name of thoroughness – had darkened the Master's image and impressed upon it a repellent, philistine veneer.'

Friedrich Nietzsche, in his 'untimely observation' entitled 'Vom Nutzen und Nachteil der Historie für das Leben' ('On the Use and Drawbacks of History for Life') of 1874, was much sharper and surprisingly direct (he probably knew Jahn in the context of classical philology) when discussing research into Mozart and Beethoven:

There are some people in Germany who look for a healing-power both radical and reforming to arise from German music: they are angered and consider it unjust that a blow has been dealt to the living quick of our culture when such composers as Mozart and Beethoven are swamped by this huge heap of learned biographical material and tormented by the torture-chamber of historical criticism into giving answers to a thousand importunate questions. Is our creative spirit, which has at least potentially much more to give, not prematurely dismissed or lamed by this excessive curiosity, which is directed against countless micrologies in both life and work, so that all sorts of cognitive problems are sought where, instead, we should learn to live and forget the difficulties?

We see here, in its most vehement form, the conflict between historical knowledge and living reality (and in Nietzsche it is a far more drastic confrontation than that between a humanistic way of thinking and the thirst for life of a decadent) – a conflict, at any rate, that still exists today in many different shadings.

Behind the tendency of the age to idealize Mozart there were other conflicts and discrepancies. The two thinkers whose philosophies had the greatest influence on musical theory and practice were Hegel and Schopenhauer. The ideology of the New German School was profoundly formed by Hegel: a work such as Richard Wagner's *Ring des Nibelungen* owes him much. But better known is the importance of Schopenhauer for Wagner's music dramas. We are not concerned here with the question of how such disparate philosophers could be synthesized in Wagner – what is more interesting is to see what these arch-rivals had in common: both rejected progressive music and remained great admirers of Mozart. When it was pointed out to Schopenhauer in a conversation that he shared with Hegel a love of *Die Zauberflöte* he commented sarcastically: 'Well, it is quite a shock to hear that one is of the same opinion as Hegel somewhere.' In the end this *bon mot* contains a discrepancy between musical philosophy and musical taste which does carry weight in Schopenhauer, a philosopher who, in his

Die Welt als Wille und Vorstellung, concedes to music a privileged status and who also, in the explanatory *Analogien*, gives his own personal view of music. The fact that such a radical advocate of absolute music should admire Mozart's operas above all has to do with those old habits of reception which have already been discussed. But for a philosopher who emphatically demanded a scrutinizing openness *vis-à-vis* the art-work to confess that 'I, Schopenhauer, remain true to Rossini and Mozart', two composers whom he held up as talismans against the progressives, *does* deserve an explanation. The enthusiasm for Rossini (which he also shared with Hegel) is only admitted in writing in 1830. Schopenhauer knew Mozart's music from boyhood (he had been able to experience *Die Zauberflöte* under Schikaneder in Vienna only ten years after its première, and also Goethe's *Zauberflöte* production in Weimar); it must have given the impulse for the relevant concepts in Schopenhauer's major works. However much Schopenhauer may have been inspired by Rossini's music, the personality of that musician always remained faint: the sole meeting with Rossini, which did not lead to a conversation, gave Schopenhauer the opportunity to confirm the lack of any visible connection between work and personality, a connection frequently absent among musicians.

Mozart, however, who was not in a position to disappoint him personally, seemed more appropriate to Schopenhauer's idea of genius. In his major works he defends the claim (which had long since become a platitude) that Mozart's mentality was such that he never became a man. Schopenhauer sees in his childlike condition a token of 'objective interest' and the 'remoteness' of the genius from the world, and was certainly thinking of Mozart when he talks thus of the artist: 'That pure, true and profound knowledge of the world's essence is now the only absolute goal for him; he remains committed to this.' Mozart provides him with an extreme example of intuitive dominance for his conception of genius. Without repeating the parallels with his other contemporaries we can assert that Schopenhauer is the most pronounced of the philosophical representatives of Mozart conservatism in the nineteenth century. For decades he clung to the same repertoire with his daily flute-playing, and we can perhaps find the explanation in the fact that Mozart (as well as Rossini and Pleyel) gave him musical confirmation and solace in his philosophy and in his sweeping social criticism.

Neither Mozart nor music in general played such an important role in Hegel; Hegel's importance for the progressive musical ideology had less to do with his aesthetics of music than with the triumph of his thought in general. It is noticeable that the historicizing of music that Hegel inspired,

154

the notion that Mozart represents the Classical, and that Beethoven, as a Romantic, succeeded in breaking through the restraints of form, surprisingly disregards Hegel's concept of the loss of substance characterizing modern art, and also his own musical taste. Hegel's specific references to Mozart in his *Aesthetics* tell us little that is new. The concept of 'the transitory' in music (a concept which makes it possible 'even to proceed to the ugly', because it 'does not remain there' – Hegel singles out Donna Anna's first recitative in *Don Giovanni* as an example) has already occurred in Horn. Still older is the idea of the 'drama' of the instruments in the symphony – and Hegel specifically analyses Mozart's *Jupiter* symphony as an example, and goes on to talk of the 'internalization of dramatic action' (as a sublimation of opera within the symphony)—this reminds us of Hanslick—'This objectless internality regarding the content, and also the mode of expression, creates the formal aspect of music.'

However momentous and conflict-ridden the battles were between progress and tradition, programme music and absolute music – the great composers were able to transcend them in their works. Looking at it more clearly, we see that most of the creative musicians who counted were able to act as intermediaries between the two fronts. Geniuses wish to project themselves and prefer to tangle with each other rather than become involved in aesthetic disputes. This is also reflected in their far less partisan relationship with Mozart. Clever observers, for example, saw something very different behind the imposing externality of Meyerbeer's operas: Heine, for instance, claimed that 'the actual religion of Meyerbeer is the religion of Mozart, Gluck and Beethoven – it is music'. And a very different contemporary, Grillparzer, noticed in 1833 when talking of *Robert le diable* that this opera 'distances itself from the New German programme which seeks and finds the task of opera as being the barren amusical instrumentation of text.'

The three great composers of the time immediately before and around the middle of the century, Felix Mendelssohn Bartholdy, Robert Schumann and Frédéric Chopin had a very original view of Mozart. Hector Berlioz, on the other hand, had for a long time little interest in Mozart until he also, with age, began to idealize him. Schumann said the following about Mendelssohn in 1840: 'He is the Mozart of the nineteenth century, the brightest musician who most clearly sees through the contradictions of the age and is the first to reconcile them.' It was only Mendelssohn who enjoyed direct contact with Mozart's world and times: his parental home encouraged this and, quite naturally, as a child prodigy himself he had been hailed by his contemporaries as a Mozart *redivivus*. In the travel letters that

155

he wrote to his family the young Mendelssohn also tended somewhat to act the part of Mozart. He took as a model the aged Goethe's spirit of Serenity – which also embraced the music of Mozart – and he remained true to this, however much it might appear to be out of fashion; this makes him, to a certain extent, also a spiritual disciple of Mozart. But he, too, was unable to reach in his music either the universality of Mozart or his 'internalization of dramatic action', although he did find his way towards a certain Classicism.

Like many others he started by imitating Mozart, but then became a despiser of epigonal imitativeness and unimaginative superficiality in instrumental composition which was supposed to have a bearing on Mozart. He once confessed to Carl Friedrich Zelter: 'I really cannot stand the disparagement of Haydn and Mozart – it makes me furious.' Mendelssohn's conflicting position is closely linked to the peculiarity of his own compositional method: he shares in common with the Mozart epigones a unity of form and topic and a regularity in the structure of musical periods and proportions, yet it was only he who was able to achieve (but not without effort) a certain quality and clarity which cannot be mistaken for Mozart. In his string quartet Opus 44/2 he introduced into his major theme notes from the last theme of Mozart's G minor symphony, but all in all the piece is a 'paradigm of differences rather than analogies'. The same is true of his genuflexion before the D major Violin Concerto K. 218 in the *Italian* Symphony. As a Romantic he had elevated to musical reality what a generation before him had felt and experienced in Shakespeare's *The Tempest* and *A Midsummer Night's Dream*, also in Mozart's lighter operas; if one refers his view of art in general to those ideals which shaped the reception of Mozart around 1800, then the apparent discrepancy between Mendelssohn the Classic and Mendelssohn the Romantic is resolved.

Chopin, a musician who was refined and shy of appearing in public, carried his melancholy – and that of his age – into his music. In the battle between Classicism and Romanticism Franz Liszt saw Chopin as belonging to the former camp, but also claimed that 'he condescended far less frequently than anyone else to overstep the line which separates refinement from vulgarity. It was this that he loved in Mozart.' For Chopin it was Mozart – and Bach – who provided a counterweight to the present, an example of self-discipline and naturally a source of musical variation as well.

We can get closer to his attitude to Mozart in a roundabout way when we look at his discussion on art with his friend the painter Eugène Delacroix. Delacroix, who had wanted to be a musician in his youth, was, together

156

with Ingres (who hated his painting), the most important Mozart admirer among the French painters of the nineteenth century. For him Mozart represented tradition, education and self-discipline, all counter-poles to his own elemental expressiveness. In his theoretical writings on art (the *Journal* and sketches for the *Dictionnaire des Beaux-Arts* of 1857–60) Mozart is referred to under various headings – 'proportion', 'sublime', 'execution' – and as an artist who knew how to preserve balance and avoid 'fearful music'. Meyerbeer and Verdi are denigrated correspondingly. Beethoven's music is, for Delacroix, 'a long cry of pain'. In a conversation about Beethoven's *Eroica* in 1849 Chopin characterized his music as dark through lack of unity: Beethoven, he claimed, had, in contrast to Mozart, transgressed eternal principles. Delacroix does not see Mozart as simply a conciliatory Classicist, but admires his unity of expressive depth and elegant serenity – his own artistic ideal, in fact, and one which he believed he had achieved in the painting *Jacob Wrestling with the Angel*. Chopin's music, in his opinion, did not correspond to this ideal. He saw quite clearly the hopeless historical distance which separated his friend from Mozart, and which ruled out any comparison with Mozart's perfection. We do not know whether or not Chopin felt the same about Delacroix's position.

Schumann's pronouncement concerning the 'Hellenic hovering grace' of Mozart's G minor symphony is well known; it is, however, incomprehensible why he should single out this particular symphony in a minor key and invest it with an analogy from antiquity reminiscent of Winckelmann, and doubly so as he otherwise said little about Mozart or about particular works (he did praise *Die Zauberflöte*, and the first act of *Figaro*). We find another pronouncement in the *Kritische Bücher der Davidsbündler* (Critical Books of the League of David) which runs: 'Serenity, calm and grace – the characteristics of the art-works of antiquity, are also those of Mozart's school.' Schumann sees Beethoven and Jean Paul as being without doubt far more significant for his own work; he gives Mozart preference only from a pedagogical viewpoint. 'Don't let the young get their hands on Beethoven too early, but nourish and strengthen them with the freshness and vitality of Mozart!' – a doubtful compliment when we remember the topos about the piano composer for young people.

Mozart's position becomes clearer when we look at Schumann's differentiated views on contemporary partisanship. He categorically rejected 'French neo-Romanticism' but also the conservative rule-mongers and the imitators of Classicism. He sees the 'original Classicism of the Hadyn/Mozart period' in a very positive light. But above all he was seeking a music beyond the strife of conflict, advocating a 'new poetic age', and

157

shows himself to be a late-born representative of the German Romantics of the beginning of the century. His Mozart image too lives from the veneration for Jean Paul and E.T.A. Hoffmann – with the difference that Mozart is still further removed for him, and hence has become a high, but diffuse and a somewhat pale, antique ideal. It is certainly anything but disparaging when Schumann confesses the following: 'There are many things in the world about which we can say nothing, for example, about Mozart's C major symphony, much of Shakespeare, some things of Beethoven.'

Schumann's wife Clara had a more well-defined, pragmatic and practical approach to individual works by Mozart. She played certain of the piano concertos and esteemed them highly; she communicated her enthusiasm to Johannes Brahms in 1861. It is difficult to grasp Brahms's Mozart image because Brahms was disinclined to make striking confessions; the trains of thought and the fine words of those conservative circles in Vienna who had taken him up (and, in Hanslick's words, saw him as a 'redeemer') are not to be found in Brahms. Brahms had a particularly close relationship with Mozart's chamber-music. When we look at the late works, which are characterized by profundity and melancholy, we notice one piece which stands out by its taut, concise form and by the cheerfulness of its mood – the string quintet in G major, Opus 111 from the year 1890. Brahms hints in a letter to his friend the violinist Joseph Joachim that this work has, albeit in a coded fashion, Mozart as its model: if Joachim did not like the second string quintet then he should 'console himself with the first (Opus 88), and with Mozart's he should get over both of them.'

When he decided to write a clarinet quintet Brahms must certainly have thought of Mozart. We can, in fact, trace a direct link between that composition and Mozart: Brahms's teacher Eduard Marxsen had studied in Vienna with Ignaz von Seyfried who had, in turn, been a piano pupil of Mozart. But Brahms's intensive, and also comprehensive, preoccupation with tradition prevents a precise attribution of a Mozartian influence.

Brahms lent his support to Mozart's work in all sorts of ways: as the artistic director of the Society for the Friends of Music he performed Mozart's little known choral works – for example, in 1874, the oratorio *Davidde penitente* which had been very popular in the first half of the century. Mozart's *Requiem*, edited by Brahms, appeared in the *Collected Works* in 1877. Brahms deviated in a remarkable manner from the current ideas about Mozart: he demanded that his piano pupils play Mozart 'not simply with charm and ease' but 'with the expression of sublime emotion'.

In a conversation with Richard Heuberger in 1896 he showed a subtle awareness of a change which was underway: he, Brahms, had never tried to play Mozart off against Beethoven and showed an historical understanding of the preference for Beethoven's symphonies during the first half of the century. Nevertheless he put forward the following opinion: 'The last three Mozart symphonies are much greater! People are beginning to realize this in different places!' And this comment was not just an arbitrary one. Already before Nietzsche the painter Anton Romako asseverated that from Mozart 'fire could be fanned as from a glowing coal'; in the same year, 1877, the poet Emanuel Geibel prophesied that the world would begin to look backwards again '. . . to the holy peaks/Crowned with true laurels/And it will hear again/Goethe's songs, and Mozart's tones'.

Franz Liszt, a very refined and sensitive musician, demonstrated by his speculations on music that querulous partisan attitudes could be transcended. We see this in his contribution to the Viennese Mozart Centenary celebrations, whose concerts he directed. He did not simply admire, but found perceptive words which would have been an honour for any conservative; he particularly stressed the 'most wonderful elasticity' and the 'most splendid union' of musical opposites. Mozart the artist was characterized by 'his quick psychological perception, his constant objectivity, his divinatory grasp of the choice and manipulation of means': from Mozart radiates 'a new age . . . of sensuous concord and pleasure'. We find Mozart's works in Liszt in the form of transcriptions. The *Don Juan* fantasy (1841) is a masterpiece for piano, in which Liszt emphasizes the demonic quality of the opera in the choice of themes. Characteristic for Liszt's compositional development is the later version for two pianos (1877) which, in reducing the emotiveness and clarifying the structure, comes closer to the Mozart original.

But more and more the interest moved from Liszt to Wagner. Wagner is not only the focus of progressive musical thought: his life and his opinions became, through his triumph, the impulse and the epitome of the musical age in which he lived. And a history of Mozart's activity and influence cannot get round this fact. I would like to go into Wagner in particular detail, not simply to filter out a particular picture of Mozart but rather, from Wagner's angle, to look at the challenge which Mozart posed for him. It is an attempt, then, to grasp a particular development from the two extremes – and we shall see that Wagner is not to be confused with the Wagnerians, whose judgements on Mozart were less respectful.

Mozart was not a major concern of his, and Wagner also avoided trying to profile his own artistic activity as a sharp contrast to that of Mozart. He did not, as a conductor, promote Mozart particularly vigorously and had little

159

luck with his Mozart performances. The listener will hardly be spontaneously aware of any Mozartian echoes in his operas and music-dramas. And yet – when Wagner was musical director in Magdeburg in 1834 he successfully opened the summer season in Lauchstädt and the autumn season in Magdeburg with a German version of Mozart's *Don Juan*. After that, his interest in Mozart seemed to have receded. The reasons probably lie in Wagner's turning to the Young German School and in his enthusiasm for Meyerbeer.

The far-reaching crisis which overtook Wagner in Paris at the beginning of the 1840s brought about a significant change. With his story *Ein Ende in Paris* he produced a somewhat outmoded piece but one which may nevertheless be understood as a product of Wagner's Parisian Hoffmann craze, a piece of Romantic writing in which he confronts himself with a macabre self-portrait. A young musician perishes in Paris, destroyed by the banausic prose of life, and finally loses himself in labyrinthine visions which lead to the dying man's ultimate credo: 'I believe in God, Mozart and Beethoven, likewise in their disciples and apostles . . . and in the truth of the one and indivisible Art . . . I believe that all men are blessed through Art . . . I believe that in my life on earth I was a dissonant chord which death will resolve in glorious purity . . .' A radiant heaven for musicians appears in a Pythagorean harmony of the spheres. Two things are apparent in all this: firstly, the fact that Wagner emphatically includes Mozart in the inner circle of his ideals and, secondly, that he portrayed this credo through the medium of poetry while, at the same time, removing it into a remote impalpable vision. In a word: perhaps the most positive utterance Wagner made about Mozart was placed, by him, in the mouth of an *alter ego*.

Wagner was present at the funeral ceremony for Napoleon in Les Invalides on 15 December 1840, at which Mozart's *Requiem* was played; he vividly portrayed the public's helplessness *vis-à-vis* such a work, and understood this as a symptom of the superficiality of the Parisian upper classes. It was logical for him that the veneration of Mozart should mean respect for a German musician. 'This German, this greatest, most divine genius was Mozart' – this he wrote in his essay 'Über deutsches Musikwesen' (Concerning German Musical Activity). Wagner insists that *Die Zauberflöte* is 'the first great German opera' and praises the 'universality of the German genius' which it makes manifest.

The emphasis of Germanness is to be understood as a reaction to the misery of the years in Paris. Wagner's description of Mozart's development and character culminates in the definition of a particular characteristic which corresponds to the topos of Mozart's 'otherness', a characteristic which Wagner sees as being typically German. He refers to Mozart's modesty and continues: 'He performs the most remarkable things in a selfless manner; he bequeathed to posterity the most priceless treasures, not realizing that he was doing anything except following his own artistic urges. No other artistic history can show a more touching, a more edifying phenomenon.'

This thesis concerning Mozart's insouciance is something that Wagner shares with the traditionalists of his age, yet he avoids playing off Beethoven against Mozart. Waxing poetic, he wrote, under the title 'Ein glücklicher Abend' (A Happy Evening), a dialogue concerning the essence of music: the impetus is a fictional open-air concert with Mozart's great E flat major and Beethoven's A major symphonies. The narrator senses 'a wondrous relationship between the two compositions', a beautiful synthesis between 'a clear, human consciousness of an existence which is dedicated to joyful pleasure . . . with an awareness of something higher, something super-natural', albeit with the difference that 'in Mozart's music the language of the heart forms itself into a lovely longing, whereas in Beethoven's view longing itself, in a bolder wilfulness, grasps the infinite'. There are further discussions concerning absolute music and the contrast between the élite and the popular. The dialogue, spoken on an evening in spring, also ends in an artistic, theoretical harmony: 'That which is expressed by music is eternal, infinite and ideal; it does not express the passion, the love, the yearning of this or that individual in this or that situation, but passion, love, yearning itself, in endlessly manifold motivations which lie in the exclusive character of music itself.' Here Wagner is falling back (in words which are astonishingly like Schopenhauer's) on the musical thinking prevalent in Romantic poetry.

The article 'Der Virtuos und der Künstler' (The Virtuoso and the Artist), an essay which was critically aware of contemporary problems, shows again how Wagner, around the year 1840, stylized and idealized both Mozart and Beethoven together: the two composers are described in a style which could have stemmed from a Romantic *Märchen*. A 'wondrous jewel' – that is the genius of music – lies buried in a mountain. A 'poor miner from Salzburg' feels 'his heart beat with a voluptuous sensation: through a crack he sees the jewel gleaming; with one gaze he sees the whole labyrinth . . . he penetrates the darkest chasm, and reaches the divine talisman itself'. No one ever sees him again. Then there came 'A miner from Bonn', seized with 'divine vertigo' he plunges forward, 'the shafts burst . . . a dreadful uproar resounded, like the end of the world'. He also is never seen again. Those who dug to find them only found gold; the wondrous jewel, and the two miners, were forgotten.

The remarkable conclusion of his essay 'Über die Ouvertüre' (Concerning the Overture) of 1841 shows that Wagner, in these speculations, was basically searching for new directions. 'In that starry trinity Gluck, Mozart and Beethoven, we possess the lodestar whose pure radiance will always brightly guide us on even the most confusing paths of art: whoever wishes to choose only one of them for an exclusive, guiding star must needs go astray, into the labyrinth from which only One ever emerged triumphant, namely the One Inimitable.' What is Wagner trusting in – the lodestar of the trinity? Or would he rather not become that 'Inimitable One', who dared only follow one of the three? His plans for a monumental Beethoven biography at this time, and the novella that he actually *did* complete, *Eine Pilgerfahrt zu Beethoven* (A Pilgrimage to Beethoven), lead us to suspect that Wagner had already set his sights on Beethoven as a guiding star for the future without wishing to make a clear admission.

Wagner had little success as a Mozart conductor at the Dresden Court Opera. The reasons are unclear. In *Mein Leben* his reply to the friends who argued that he did not think a lot of Mozart was that the everyday life of a *Kapellmeister* was limited in opportunities. Whichever was the truth – the consequence was a reticence on his part when it came to Mozart performances. When Wagner saw a *Don Giovanni* in December 1845 in Berlin, with Jenny Lind in the part of Donna Anna, he wrote to his wife of his bitter disappointment, expressed his preference (as we might expect) for Schröder-Devrient and put forward the resigned opinion: 'In general everything was dry as dust, as we expect everything to be in *Don Giovanni*.' And in 1851, in the 'Mitteilung an meine Freunde' (Announcement to my Friends), Wagner expressed the disillusioned view that today 'there is no true understanding any more of *Don Giovanni*'.

In his reformist publications of the 1850s three main factors interrelate: firstly, Wagner did not wish to give up heedlessly the idealization of Mozart that had been propagated a decade earlier; secondly, the disappointments he had experienced as a Mozart conductor had left their mark; thirdly it was important to support his vision of 'Das Kunstwerk der Zukunft' (The Art-work of the Future) by cogent argument. Wagner's determination to reflect on his own position as opera-composer necessarily meant a distancing from Mozart; Wagner also stressed the necessity for tragedy in the same essay and rejected the composition of light-hearted operas (such as Mozart uninhibitedly created during his time). There was to be a deeply felt earnestness and an awareness of the social and political problems of the day.

In his essay 'Das Kunstwerk der Zukunft' (1849) Wagner takes up again

162

the traditional model of the Viennese Classical trinity. Haydn's music, he writes, is full of serenity and tranquil, inner contentment; Mozart contributed 'a depth of yearning from the depths of his heart'; Beethoven, finally achieves the expression of 'a primitive, powerful urging and longing'. The aim of this historical sequence is to show that Beethoven is the decisive musical link for Wagner.

In *Oper und Drama* (1851) Wagner gives a critical discussion of the history of opera, and sees himself compelled to denigrate Mozart's historical significance even further; it is Gluck and his followers, Cherubini, Méhul and Spontini, who seem far more important for him. Wagner makes good this demotion by calling Mozart 'the most absolute of all musicians', placing him decisively higher than the composer Gluck. In a parallel – and again an unconscious one – to Schopenhauer, Wagner admires Mozart less for his instrumental writing than for his operas, written 'in the veracity of dramatic expression': this shows Wagner to be an adherent of an old traditional view and in surprising conformity with the opposing conservative party. Wagner sees this 'truth' confirmed in Mozart's 'artistic nature' which consists of 'the undisturbed, immaculate clarity of a clear sheet of water'; this surface, however, is in its turn 'only the surface of a deep, infinite sea of longing, of yearning, which reaches from the immeasurable richness of his being to the surface, as the expression of its content, to gain shape, form and beauty from the tender greeting of a lovely apparition as she bends down to him, desirous of knowledge of her own being.' (See Wackenroder's Raphael image!)

Wagner's much quoted reproach that Mozart 'wrote his works with a careless lack of discrimination' is praise at the same time: for Wagner finds it 'good that Mozart was not able to write a music like *Don Giovanni* for *La Clemenza di Tito*, or like *Figaro* for *Così fan tutte*'. Wagner explains the successes of Mozart's musical-dramatic solution by drawing our attention to the crucial function of poetry for the inspiration of Mozart the musician: 'The more we gaze through the glowing clouds of Mozart's music to the foundations, the more surely we recognize the sure, clear, pen-and-ink drawing of the poet which first, through its strokes and lines, determined the colours that the musician would use and without which the miracle of that music would be absolutely impossible.' In 'Mozart's masterpiece, *Don Giovanni*' we find 'a surprisingly happy relationship between poet and composer'.

The resolution of the dialectical tension emerges at the end of the first part of *Oper und Drama*, when Wagner returns yet again to *Don Giovanni* and finally establishes the happy coincidence of music and poetry with the emphatic exclamation: 'Where else has music achieved such infinitely rich individuality, where else has it been able to characterize in such a richly exuberant plenitude as here, where the musician, according to the nature of his art, is nothing less than a woman whose love is unconditional?' Wagner also speaks at the end of the second part about 'music as a woman, splendid in her love': Mozart, apparently, stands for the feminine, the devoted, the emotional, the naïvely unconscious, and for the musical as such. And Wagner here conforms to traditional views – and also those of light fiction. The question he next asks in his essay, however: 'Who should be the man whom this woman should so utterly love?' very much leads away from an ideal image of Mozart to a new concept of drama.

Wagner was unable to resolve the other paradox, namely, that it was precisely the work that he admired most, *Don Giovanni*, that was the one for which there was 'no understanding any more'. It was about this same time, the end of 1850, that Wagner, as a conductor, concerned himself once more with *Don Giovanni*. He had thoroughly prepared the Zurich production with Hans von Bülow, he had translated the Italian recitative passages into German himself and also carried out some scenic changes and simplifications. But this attempt brought no satisfactory solution for him; indeed, it intensified the *Don Giovanni* problem in the long term.

Almost three decades later, in his essay 'Das Publikum in Zeit und Raum' (The Audience in Time and Space) of 1878 Wagner spoke about *Don Giovanni* in such a way that we detect a ruthless criticism of his own attempts to make the opera topical in Zurich:

Almost every operatic producer feels the need to do a *Don Juan* in the spirit of the times, whereas, however, anyone with any understanding should realize that he cannot make this work correspond to our times; we should, however, change ourselves to make ourselves suit the times of *Don Juan* in order to understand Mozart's creation. In referring to the unsuitability of making any attempt at repeating the old productions of this work (and precisely *this* work) I am not talking about our means of portrayal, which are totally inadequate for this purpose: I disregard the distorting effects of translations done for the public of the Italian text into German, as well as the impossibility of replacing the so-called Italian *parlando*-recitative. I shall assume that it might be possible to train a troupe of Italian singers for a correct performance of *Don Juan*: but in this latter case we would – looking back from the performance to the audience – have to realize that we are in completely the wrong place. Our imagination, however, will be spared this embarrassment, because we cannot imagine such a performance, a performance ideal for our times.

Wagner also speaks, in his 'Bericht über eine in München zu errichtende deutsche Musikschule' (A Report about a Music School to be Founded in Munich) of 1865 about 'the complete lack of life and colour in performances precisely of Gluck and Mozart'. He repeatedly pushes the blame for the 'disgraceful dryness' of Mozart productions on to the conservatories, which regarded themselves as centres of tradition. It is indeed a bitter résumé of the history of performance in the nineteenth century to claim that Mozart's works were unrealizable. And Wagner is not isolated in his criticism. Complaints had been made ever since the 1820s (by Marx, by Mosel, etc.): Lyser was of the opinion in 1856 that, for an appropriate peformance of *Così fan tutte*, 'neither our German, nor our Italian singers, who know nothing about *opera buffa* any more, will suffice'.

The assessment of Mozart reaches its nadir in the essay 'Zukunftsmusik' (The Music of the Future) of 1860 and consistently at that point where Wagner, linking on to *Oper und Drama*, extends still further his teleological speculations on the history of opera and symphony. Mozart is even more guilty than Haydn of

falling back frequently – or even as a matter of course – into a banal formation of phrases which makes his symphonic movements look like something akin to so-called table-music: a music which as well as allowing the recital of charming melodies also offers pleasant noise for conversation. When I hear those half-cadences of Mozart's symphonies which return in such a stable fashion and noisily make themselves apparent it seems that I have before me, translated into music, the sound of courses being served and carried away from some princely table.

This is not an especially Wagnerian bit of malice: Wilhelm von Lenz, for example, in his book *Beethoven. Eine Kunststudie* (1855–60), constantly and sneeringly refers to the 'Haydn-Mozart template'.

In later years Wagner grew increasingly more receptive to Mozart's individuality. In *Mein Leben* he talks about an argument he had with the famous architect Gottfried Semper in the year 1857. Semper rebuked Wagner for taking everything far too seriously, claiming that it did one good 'to break the mould of seriousness and to find pleasure in that which moved one most deeply'; Semper particularly liked the fact that, in Mozart's *Don Giovanni*, 'one meets the tragic types only as in a masquerade, the domino being preferable to the characteristic mask'. Wagner was evasive, claiming that it would certainly be pleasanter for him if he could take life more seriously and art in a more light-hearted manner. Many years later, in 1878, he came back to this discussion and implied that Semper's objection, meant in a serious manner, deserved a less casual answer. Wagner opened up the topic and gave his own opinion:

> Intelligent people praised the way in which the roughly sketched and incomplete nature of his texts, for example in *Don Juan*, lent itself to a masque, which corresponded so agreeably with his music, a music that reflected the most passionate aspects of the human situation in a charmingly delightful game.

> If this opinion could be easily misunderstood, and could even be disparaging and harmful, well, it was meant seriously and contained within itself the generally current opinion of our aesthetic experts regarding the proper activity of music, against which it is difficult to fight, even today. But I believe that Mozart completely exhausted this form of art, a form which, in a very deep sense, may be open to the charge of frivolity; he exhausted it by elevating it to an aesthetic principle of beauty. It was his own, and anything that could be considered his successor was botched and boring.

Wagner reaches here an ironic understanding of Mozart, so to speak, which is deeper than that of the majority of his apologists and may be seen as related to Mörike's in as far as both dip into the well of Romanticism (see Horn, Hoffmann, etc.)

Wagner's attitude to Mozart's 'otherness' led to differing, and significant, reactions in the last years of his life. We can, for example, glean from Cosima's diaries that Wagner played a lot of Mozart during his work on *Parsifal* and liked to talk about him. Was Mozart a kind of cathartic counterweight to his own work? Occasionally Wagner knew how to bridge what separated them in a remarkable manner: he lamented to Cosima how little the 'feeling of beauty, in which I call myself Mozart's successor, has been regarded, for example in *Die Walküre*, where Brünnhilde is talking to Wotan about Siegmund':

Der die- se Lie - - - - be mir in's Herz ge - haucht,

'You who this love . . . . in my heart inspired.'

What does Wagner mean by this? It must be the 'infinitely free melody' which he admired in Mozart. Cosima accounted for the public's disregard of such contexts by reference to the suggestive power of Wagner's music dramas. But this suggestive power is no simple adornment concealing a

Mozartian 'feeling for beauty', but is diametrically opposed to it; or, to use Nietzsche's words – Mozart's music is not the kind of music whose images leap out at you. The reference anyway has something unreal about it and reminds us of the curious parallelism whereby Wagner felt himself to be 'the last Mozartian' as Rossini had claimed to be 'the last Classic' – and Wagner also found friendlier words for *him* in later life.

Wagner himself was not so certain of his proximity to Mozart, for he sometimes reacted to his music in completely different ways. When thinking of the beauties of *Figaro* he exclaimed: 'Ah, a dead world.' The ostensible strangeness of this music (music, on the other hand, which was known to him since his childhood) was for a long time no longer simply a means for him to create a distinctly personal image for himself. He sought the ideals of his youth with a greater intensity; in old age he liked to read his Parisian writings. At the very end he was working on an essay entitled 'Über das Weibliche im Menschlichen' (Concerning the Female Principle in Humanity) – did the female element of Mozart's music appear before Wagner, undisguised? Perhaps it did, when we remember the thoughts expressed at the ending of the first part of *Oper und Drama*. Is Mozart, the 'most absolute of musicians', a constantly clouded ideal, a reflection of Wagner's own yearning for absolute music? Nietzsche believed that he had seen through this longing. There is one thing, and perhaps it is the most essential, that binds the later Wagner with Nietzsche, a man who had become his passionate adversary: Mozart was for both an inexplicable phenomenon from a different world from that of the late nineteenth century, the anti-decadent *par excellence*, or, as Wagner said, 'a wholesome temperament'. Something else separates the two: throughout the whole of his life Wagner was far more unsettled by Mozart than Nietzsche was.

I would like to go as far as to maintain that Wagner's conflicting attitude to Mozart, an attitude made manifest in extreme judgements, is a symbol for the vulnerability felt by the nineteenth century *vis-à-vis* tradition. We can trace in Wagner what Karl Jaspers called, in Nietzsche, the existential movement of thought. In Nietzsche's case it leads, via a criticism of Wagner's *oeuvre*, to a vision of something new in music, a vision which, in a way, anticipates the change to a new topicality in Mozart at the beginning of our century. At first Nietzsche took over almost word for word the picture of Mozart adumbrated in the historical survey in *Oper und Drama*, a picture that was not entirely favourable.

Before he openly turned against Wagner, Nietzsche began to evaluate Mozart. In *Menschliches, Allzumenschliches (Human, All Too Human)* (1875–9) he finally holds up against Wagner (who lacked 'bright, liquid fire') the ideal of the 'Mediterranean': Mozart's music, apparently, is inspired by 'a vision of life, of the liveliest Southern life'. In opposition to the intensely expressive Bayreuth style of performance (a style that was felt to be the *dernier cri* at that time, and which led to constant changes in tempo), and also in opposition to a one-sided *Don Giovanni* reception, Nietzsche raised the question of whether or not a musical style of 'high relief . . . were not in fact a sin against the Holy Ghost, against the bright, sunny, tenderly light-hearted spirit of Mozart, whose earnestness is benevolent and not terrible, whose images do not leap out at us to terrify us and force us to flee. Or do you think that Mozart's music is the "music of the guest of stone"?' Nietzsche's Mozart image, in contrast to that of his praise for Bizet's *Carmen*, is always idealistic and abstract; he never deals in detail with any particular work. And finally he becomes absurd when he claims that an opera by the superficial 'Allegro Musician' Peter Gast is 'the most beautiful music since Mozart, and yet a music that Mozart would not be able to write'.

Nietzsche's own compositions stand completely under the shadow of *Tristan* and nowhere betray a 'Mediterranean' quality. Nevertheless, Nietzsche saw quite clearly what was needed as a counterweight to both Wagner and himself – and Wagner knew it too. Nietzsche brilliantly formulates his vision thus:

> Concerning the artists of the future, I see here a musician who speaks the language of Rossini and Mozart as his own, that tender, crazy vernacular, sometimes too gentle, sometimes too loud, with its roguish indulgence of everything, even the 'base'; a musician who lets slip a smile, a smile of the discriminating, the sophisticated, of one born late, a musician who constantly makes fun, from the depths of his heart, of the good olde times and their very good, very olde, very old-fashioned music – but it is a smile full of love, full of poignancy itself . . .

And here he expresses that yearning for the *homo novus* in music who, in the *fin-de-siècle* period, was readily linked with the figure of Parsifal; even Hanslick alludes to this when he desired for opera 'a new pure Fool . . . a naïve composer of natural, powerful genius, perhaps a kind of Mozart'.

Who could fit Nietzsche's vision? It demands too much, and no musician could quite fit the bill: perhaps there are individual works that are more suitable – *Ariadne auf Naxos*, say, by Strauss and Hofmannsthal – but perhaps this is already too far from Nietzsche's horizon. The image corresponds surprisingly to *Falstaff*, this *opera buffa rediviva* from the year 1893, whose composition gave the aged Verdi such sublime enjoyment. Now we cannot argue that *Falstaff* was a work written in Mozart's image. But Mozart was without doubt an important link in the tradition of *buffa* for Verdi, even though he only spoke politely about him and even disparagingly.

As a young man in Milan, Verdi had got to know that Mozart cult of which we have already spoken, or at least its after-effects, and, at a decisive point in his life, 1836, he received a lasting impression of a *Don Giovanni* performance – a bad one, in fact. In his first *opera buffa* (and last before *Falstaff*), *Un giorno di regno*, he quotes the minuet from *Don Giovanni* in the trio of the second act. Bearing in mind the contemporary conception of this opera as a tragedy, the ensembles at least must have provided a model for Verdi's serious operas. The finale of the first act shows obvious similarities with the first scene of *Rigoletto*: the dramatic situation of a feast at a libertine's residence which ends in uproar, the three orchestral groupings (placed one after the other by Verdi) and the narrative continuity provided by the onstage music are hardly arbitrary parallels. Mozart's model is, then, manifest in precisely that work with which Verdi in 1851 broke through to an undeniably personal style.

But nothing can alter the fact that both Wagner and Verdi pursued different paths from those followed by Mozart. Even in Italy Wagner made more of an impact than Mozart, according to the motto, 'If German at all, then totally German.' The anti-Wagnerian Hanslick saw that young musicians were in an unenviable position – they either had to write like Wagner, in which case they were lost, or *not* like Wagner, in which case they were well and truly lost.

We find a classic example of this true-to-life dilemma in the poet and composer Peter Cornelius. His youthful ideals were Mozart and Goethe, his favourite work was *Figaro*. Although he preferred not to leave this circle, and tells us of 'evil forces', he did none the less come into contact with the New Germans, suddenly prefers Gluck to Mozart, wishes to become an opera composer like Wagner (only 'more melodic, more piquant, freer and more humorous') and sees himself heading in the direction of becoming 'a second Lortzing, only with a more distinct style of writing'. In order to free himself from his model, Mozart, he chose Berlioz as a guide. His *Barbier von Bagdad* is a respectable attempt to continue the tradition of light German opera. Cornelius consequently tried to keep his distance from Wagner, who esteemed him highly, yet the *Barbier* remained an episode, and the goal was a grand, serious opera. To follow Mozart, that is, to write a work that was serene and 'with a noble structure', remained an empty promise in German-speaking countries – perhaps the exception was Johann Strauss who, with his dances and his operettas, was able to achieve that right and distinguished

169

balance between effective brio and tender melancholy which met the demands of the traditionalists.

It was easier to come to terms with the other legacy, Mozart's serious side. *Don Giovanni* was narrowed down more than ever to an example of musical tragedy, and, at the same time, became by far his most popular work. On 29 October 1887 the five hundredth performance took place in the Berlin Court Opera. From the statistics gathered together by Rudolf von Freisauff on the occasion of the work's centenary we find that Berlin was beaten by Prague with its 350 German, 153 Italian and 90 Czech performances. Within this space of time *Don Giovanni* was put on some 4,500 times in Germany, and about 2,000 times in Austria. And it was in the face of this popularity that Wagner made his pronouncement about the work's unperformability.

There lies concealed behind this contradiction a deep-seated conflict in the work's esteem; this comes to light symptomatically in the wretched state of the translations. The general directorship of Royal Prussian Court Theatre (which administered the theatres not only in Berlin, but in Hanover, Wiesbaden and Kassel) still clung, in 1896, to Rochlitz's version of the year 1801. But new versions started to challenge the old-established order (by G.H. Sever in 1854; W. Viol, 1858; L. Bischoff, 1860; A. von Wolzogen, 1860; C.H. Bitter, 1866 and 1871; B. Gugler, using Wolzogen's version, 1869; Th. Epstein, 1870; J. Rietz, 1871; F. Grandaur, 1871, 1874 and 1882; K.F. Niese in the *Collected Edition*; M. Kalbeck 1886 and 1887). The director of the Munich Court and National Theater, Baron Karl von Perfall, encouraged a committee in 1883 to create a uniform *Don Giovanni* version for all German stages; the initial enthusiasm of the participants, however, did not last long. Freisauff's suggestion to compile all that was usable from the current translations would have resulted in a curious pastiche, but, surely, no standard solution to the problem.

In both the practical as well as the theoretical interpretations the orientation was effortlessly moving away from E.T.A. Hoffmann to the music-dramas of Richard Wagner. To justify this disregard of original intentions there was a constant invoking of Mozart's subconscious genius. As early as 1838, Gottfried Weber had denied neither the variety of structure in *Don Giovanni* nor the intention of Da Ponte and Mozart to write a 'comic *Singspiel*', but he then asseverated that Mozart, by his music, had involuntarily made the work into a tragedy. In 1880 the prominent Viennese critic Ludwig Speidel speaks – as though it were the most natural thing in the world – of that 'vital tragic feeling' which enabled Mozart 'to create *Don Juan*, the only musical tragedy that we possess'. The *Don Giovanni* translator – and Prussian finance minister – Carl Heinrich Bitter sought to establish the

170

tragedy firmly upon the basis of a moral order, and stressed its cathartic effect. Don Giovanni becomes a timeless figure whose destruction bears witness to that very morality which is incorporated in the Commendatore and Donna Anna.

These speculations found suitable expression in the productions; these were also well suited to the manic desire for significant meaning which permeated all spheres of life in the late nineteenth century. A piece full of tension between good and evil, morality and sensuality, was fitted out in such a way as though *Don Giovanni* were taking part in one of Makart's fancy-dress balls. (Incidentally, the common veneration of the two Salzburgers – Mozart and Makart – that was even expressed on picture postcards is, as regards content, absurd, but historically telling.) As fashion demanded that individual rooms should be furnished in different styles, so we have Don Giovanni's castle decorated in a lavish oriental fashion, whereas the sphere of the Commendatore and of Donna Anna are characterized by Gothic starkness.

Carlo Brioschi's sketches for the opening of the Vienna Court Opera on 25 May 1869 are typical here. For our tastes today, meaningfulness equals delight in inauthenticity, as, in the Munich production of 1879 Donna Anna sings her aria before the second finale, 'Non mi dir, bell'idol mio', within a cemetery chapel with altar, prayer-stool and sanctuary lamp, or when Don Giovanni, at his descent into hell, flings his arms heavenwards, whereupon the spirits of his dead mistresses appear, and his castle disintegrates as though it were Valhalla at the end of *Götterdämmerung*.

These are all modes of resolution which, indeed, have not entirely vanished from our stages today. Sometimes the echoes of Wagner's concept of redemption are blatantly obvious. Even after decades had passed Lilli Lehmann still remembered the Prague production of 1866 with a final tableau that looked as though it had come from *Der fliegende Holländer*: 'The Commendatore, hovering on high, blesses Anna and Octavio.' The music critic Max Kalbeck gives a delightful description in 1898 of all the ideas which had been tried to make the ending more sensational: 'In various German towns we have observed, one after the other, the following variations: The ghost sinks through Don Juan. The latter is either speared by devils with tridents, or else the devils seize him and hurl him into a fiery abyss. The ghost sinks with Don Juan. The devils perform a triumphant dance, then they themselves leap into the abyss. Don Juan stabs himself after the ghost has disappeared, or falls down dead. The backcloth opens and we see the stone monument, but without a rider . . .' The awkward closing sextet is, of course, always cut. Even Charles Gounod thought it was dramaturgically superfluous, a convention from the time of Mozart and only

171

of purely musical interest. In 1891 George Bernard Shaw was one of the first to insist that the original ending be kept and thundered against vulgar sensation-hunting with tongues of fire, ghostly apparitions and Don Giovanni's plunge into the depths.

We see how far the staging of this opera had already moved away from the Romanticism of Hoffmann when we consider the following: the overloading with 'significance' began when the Don Juan theme was linked with that of Faust. Yet the comparison with Goethe's *Faust* (which David Friedrich Strauss, too, entertains in *Der alte und der neue Glaube* [The Old and the New Faith]) from now on takes up a conservative position which is counter to that held by the predominant conception of tragedy. Joseph Schlüter, in his *Geschichte der Musik* (History of Music), Leipzig 1863, admired precisely that vital interplay between tragedy and comedy as being something incomparable, characterizing above all 'these greatest masterpieces, although both . . . were too loosely placed together and seemed to lack a deeper dramatic connection'.

After Wagner it was Gounod (between the years 1882 and 1890) who criticized performances, now more from a practical point of view. He looked very closely at questions of detail, turned against all forms of musical sensationalism and against the 'modern vice' of not keeping time; he advocated far greater nuances in breathing, pronunciation and phrasing – in short, he was seeking to break away from the Bayreuth style of performance. How much of this style was applied to Mozart is an open question; the relevant analyses of tempi in the decades around 1900 produce a bewilderingly varied picture.

Despite his criticism, Gounod sees *Don Giovanni* as a completely topical work and describes the music, bar by bar, with illustrative thoroughness. And finally all his pernickety discussions take an extreme idealization as their starting point: this opera, misunderstood by his contemporaries, remained a revelation to him throughout the whole of his life, the purest incorporation of 'dramatic and musical sinlessness'. Basically, then, Gounod is close to Wagner's viewpoint. The numerous declarations inscribed by many celebrities in the 'Mozart-Album' of the Salzburg Mozart Foundation since 1874 demonstrate what was typical of the times. High emotionalism, intensified feeling of self, and currying favour in dialect poems – all this seems tasteless today, and yet Mozart's 'incomprehensibility' was taken seriously by the Styrian poet Peter Rosegger who wrote the following laconic entry in 1881: 'I only measure great artists with my feelings, that is why I cannot find words to express my love and veneration for Mozart.'

There was another way in which Gounod precisely summed up the mood of the times. He sees Mozart's art as being as perfect as that of a Phidias or a Molière, and considers that it is no longer possible to exceed Mozart in the creation of new works. Shaw added the names of Praxiteles, Raphael and Shakespeare to the list and quite openly states that Mozart was not the founder of a new direction in art, but stood at the culmination of a development. But, Shaw argues, he was by no means reducing Mozart's status here: anybody could make a beginning, but it was the highest thing of all to mark an end. The *fin de siècle* of the nineteenth century thus recognized itself in that of the eighteenth century – this explains the preference for *Figaro* at that time. This opera was not regarded as being topical in its criticism, but as a picture of the Rococo world. Much comes together here: the transfiguration of the past and of transience and the hope for something new, in the youthful innocence of Cherubino and Barbarina (looking back at the same time to the Romantic reception of *Figaro*) and also in the lightness and serenity of *opera buffa* (pointing forward to the Mozart reception of the turn of the century).

Shaw's ideas had been anticipated by Wagner in old age, and above all by Nietzsche with his aphorism that all music of note was a swan-song. Another idea preferred and propagated among Wagner's followers was that Mozart was a typically German musician. *Die Zauberflöte* was always quoted as the starting point for any discussion concerning German Romantic opera: it was the 'most ideal', the 'most significant' work, as Heinrich Adolf Köstlin formulated it in his *Geschichte der Musik*, where he none the less sees Mozart as well as Haydn and Beethoven primarily as 'Classical composers of instrumental music'.

The hyper-Germanness of these critics also took delight in an anti-clerical attitude: Mozart was observed in the battle against 'nocturnal spiritual menace and dark zealotry' and was idolized, together with Freemasonry and the reforming zeal of Emperor Joseph II. We find this in Köstlin and also in the writings on Classicism of Adolf Gelbcke (1881). The old conflict in the appreciation of either Mozart or Beethoven, a conflict which seemed to have been resolved, grew more intense again towards the end of the century with the growth of a Beethoven cult – this did not lead to a disparagement of Mozart, but rather to a much more intense idealization. The association of 'the Classical' with the smooth paleness of marble is exemplified nowhere better than in Gelbcke. Mozart's music, for him, is equivalent to an ideal balance of idea and expression, with freedom of spirit and a serene philosophy; small wonder that Gelbcke saw the time of Joseph II as a (historically incorrect) time of peace, security and tranquil progress.

So Mozart, at the end of the century, is still enmeshed in the ideological conflict between conservatives and liberal-progressives. But after the Franco-Prussian War (1870–1) the old idea of preserving the European spirit had become unreal. Hence the forced, exaggerated yearning for the world of the Rococo which becomes noticeable in many of the utterances on Mozart that have been quoted. A prominent Germanist of our day, for example, calls Mörike's Mozart novella a 'German final salute to the Old Europe'. The great cultural historian from Basel, Jakob Burckhardt, recognized immediately the threat contained in the change towards imperialism and the egoism of national awareness. In his *Weltgeschichtliche Betrachtungen* (World-historical Observations), posthumously published, he consequently comes to speak about Mozart in an entirely different manner. He characterized the fashion of portraying the lives of artists (and here he will encourage Nietzsche to do the same) as 'being derived from a very unhealthy source'; he strictly rejected biographies which strove to harmonize and to ignore the dangers an artist is exposed to, and he also turned against the legend of Mozart's ostensible childlike qualities, stressing as a contrast Mozart's great strength of will. Burckhardt also expressed the fear that a future generation would be as alienated from the music of Mozart and Beethoven as we are from the Greeks.

Friedrich von Hausegger, in his 1901 posthumously published book *Unsere deutsche Musik. Bach, Mozart, Beethoven, Wagner* drew on Burckhardt's criticism and related it to music. Hausegger must surely be one of the most intelligent and sophisticated of all the Wagnerians, and behind all the Germanness, and the teleological view of history, we find some very subtle observations on Mozart.

With many a side-swipe at the formalists Hausegger insists that music is essentially an art which is able to express the most manifold stirrings of the soul without the mediation of reason. He deviates, however, from Wagner's view that Mozart's musical achievements may be explained by his self-abandonment to the text; Hausegger only considered the libretti to be of importance in that through them the possibility was preserved of letting the personality of the musician develop freely. He sees the artist as being the result of a prehistory, a development and an environment; Johann Gustav Droysen had already objected to this in his *Historik*, claiming that Mozart's gifts had been unpredictable and not the results of any demonstrable causes.

Droysen's belief (which was indebted to Hegel's concept of nature) that a talent represents itself in all that it expresses and achieves, and thus grows increasingly conscious of its own character and giftedness, is also present in Hausegger. He refers this to the problem of absolute music and puts forward the following view: 'It is not the absolute sound which achieves mastery in instrumental music, but the absolute ego.' Absolute music, then, was 'purest lyricism', and here Hausegger falls back on the views of the early Romantics, as he does in the following examples. When discussing the G minor symphony he refuses to hear either 'forms that are merely sounding' or 'the character of passion'; he explains: 'Before the stirrings of feeling grow to passion they are dissolved into sounds and bring us knowledge of the power that lies beneath passion, but not of its struggle.'

This mediating position comes close to E.T.A. Hoffmann's view of Mozart, and Hausegger begins his discussion of *Don Giovanni* with a quote from Jean Paul about humour, a spirit 'which suffuses all, and invisibly animates it'. He goes on to consider it erroneous to measure this opera by the standards of tragedy (and thus necessarily runs counter to the current ideas that were prevalent), for the simple reason that the catastrophe is not motivated by the hero's essential being, for Don Giovanni is not an ideal hero but a man moved by the whim of the moment. The demonic greatness to which he soars towers up above comedy but does not make a tragedy. With this interpretation Hausegger reaches back across Hoffmann to the early Shakespeare-Mozart comparisons.

Hausegger also found a radical solution to another essential problem. A conflict had arisen between the older Mozart idealization which prevailed in the first third of the century and the view of the progressives, who saw that the historical position of Haydn and Mozart has been superseded; the more recent transfiguration of the Rococo world during the *fin-de-siècle* period remained too abstract to be able to refute the charges of conventionalism which were raised against Mozart's music. And neither Nietzsche nor Wagner had actually managed to bring the ideal and history together. Hausegger saw the essence of Rococo in its playfulness. Every great art, he believed, lived from the 'nakedness' of the artist who, in the 'pure mirror of his soul' reflects the world around him and, at the same time, stamps his individual character upon it. Of course, Hausegger experienced and assessed everything in a most positive manner: Adorno's view that in art and music we also find expressed the duality of an historical situation is just as alien to him as the view of the Naturalists who were very close to him in time and who believed that an artist should be a true mirror of existence, expressing the good and the bad. There seems to be more of the time's Impressionism in Hausegger's solution: it unites the far-ranging artistic vision of Romanticism with the naked perception of reality in a positivistic sense. Obviously nobody hit upon the explanation which, morally, would have been much more modest – Mozart lovingly and impartially registered

175

cunning as well as goodness and all the other fluctuating emotions. But then one would have had to recognize Wilhelm Busch as a Mozart of the present.

It was not only conceptually that the ideal and history were difficult to fuse: most musicians were unable to translate their love of Mozart into music. To use Nietzsche's words – their decadence stood in the way or, to put it differently, they were too deeply concerned with the importance of what they were writing, and their longing for Mozart was too great. This was not only the case with German musicians, although the burden of inheritance lay upon them particularly onerously. The most talented among the composers were the melancholy ones. Edvard Grieg, for example, was a fervent admirer of Mozart, and not simply in words. But when he appended 'the freely added accompaniment of a second piano' to some of Mozart's piano sonatas (1876–9), then the musical genuflections have something pompous about them that does not in any way correspond to Mozart. The same is true of Charles Gounod's arrangement of the quintet from *Così fan tutte* for piano, cello and organ, also of Wendelin Weissheimer who, emulating Gounod's 'Meditation on a Prelude of Bach', wrote an obbligato violin part for all the preludes from Bach's *Well-Tempered Clavier* and also used Mozart's *Ave verum* to make the music more solemn.

Russian composers loved Mozart as defined by the emotional feelings of their great poet Pushkin: Pushkin's short plays *The Stone Guest* and *Mozart and Salieri* were set to music even though they were not intended for this. The former was composed by Alexander S. Dargomyzhsky in a music of realistic character-portrayal using an unmelodic, terse *Sprechgesang* – quite un-Mozartian, that is. Nikolai Rimsky-Korsakov, who completed this opera, set *Mozart and Salieri* to music in 1897. But he went about things completely differently from Dargomyzhsky and tried to get closer to the title figures by inserting many musical quotations. And yet the character of this duologue remains melancholy, as is the text itself: Mozart, playful and insouciant, gains knowledge through his premonitions of death.

The greatest admirer of Mozart among all the Russian composers was Peter I. Tchaikovsky. He idolized Mozart, to whom he was grateful for helping him find his way to music, as he confessed to his friend Nadezhda von Meck of all people, who did not like Mozart. His views, most certainly, were conventional: Mozart was, for him, the artist *par excellence*, and he loved *Don Giovanni*, *Figaro* and the *Jupiter* symphony above all, music which represented a vision of a golden age. It seems doubly reasonable to see this simply as the yearning of a decadent for that which is alien to him, partly because Tchaikovsky did call himself morally sick and called Mozart an

176

artist untouched by reflection, and partly because Adorno, fifty years later, denounced him as a composer of 'beautiful appearances', of 'grand sentimental gestures'.

Yet Tchaikovsky did succeed in counteracting the emotive pathos of his music with something delicate and miniature – something modern, that is. And it was not just lip-service. The opera *The Queen of Spades* (1890), again based on Pushkin, brings an echo of Mozart in the form of theatre within theatre: in the second act an intermezzo is performed to the guests at a masked ball. The innocent play of *Daphnis and Chloe* does not only contain musical quotations, but is also an atmospheric picture of Mozart's world as many imagined it at this time – as an arcadian idyll. This view had already been expressed in the *Mozartiana* (Opus 63) of 1887: the form of the suite, the gigue, the minuet, etc., suggests an association with the Rococo world. What is new in this piece is Tchaikovsky's intentional aim to draw the attention to small, and generally little known works of Mozart (K.574, K.355, the *Ave verum* in Liszt's transcription and K.455).

Whenever we seek comments on Mozart from famous musicians of this time we always come across the same, uniform idealization. Yet there were three composers who especially admired *Figaro*, and who attempted to realize anew Mozart's old-fashioned interplay between seriousness and gaiety in music full of vitality and colour. Georges Bizet's *Carmen* is perhaps the only piece of French lyrical theatre which succeeded here. The same might be said for Friedrich Smetana's Czech national opera *The Bartered Bride*, which initially met with little success. Just as Bizet felt more at home in the German and the Italian tradition than in the French, so Smetana was well acquainted with the history of light German opera from Mozart via Lortzing to Cornelius. Smetana's method of composition looks back to *Figaro* in making the ensembles carriers of comic effects (a link between Mozart and Smetana is Lortzing with the billiard-scene in *Der Wildschütz*). Antonin Dvořák, inspired by Smetana, also left the generation of Wagner devotees and moved closer to Mozart: his *Cunning Peasant* is a variation on the *Figaro* theme. In any case, the *Figaro* reception of these three composers contradicts the conception put forward in a conversation between Wagner and Nietzsche in 1870 which saw Beaumarchais's cunning actors transposed into 'transfigured beings, suffering and lamenting'.

The reality of Mozart's cultivation very rarely overlapped with the attested admiration for the music; the reality consisted, rather, of a very limited knowledge of his work, of memorial concerts (1887 and 1891) and attempts at Mozart festivals. The same pieces were played over and over again (*Don Giovanni, Figaro, Die Zauberflöte*, the *Requiem*, the late symphonies and string quartets, the D minor piano concerto, piano sonatas for learning or for practice). This was still quite a lot in comparison to what Haydn's sesquicentenary (in 1882) and Rossini's centenary (1892) put on offer.

The quality of performances had indeed scarcely improved since Wagner's devastating criticism: it was Shaw who described the state of affairs exactly when he said that the reason why Mozart's music was so difficult to play was that everything was so clear in it; that was why it was so little played, and when one *did* get to hear it its reputation was more likely harmed. At the commemoration of the centenary of his death the *Jupiter* symphony and the *Requiem* were the works which were preferred, and Shaw mockingly observed that this choice exactly corresponded to the spirit of pious melancholy that characterized such festivals. Shaw was referring to the 'Mozart Centenary' at the Royal Albert Hall at which a poem by Joseph Bennett was read out: Mozart's music, he tells us, rose to that of the angels, 'so shall thy genius hover o'er/E'en Heaven with strains of godlike power.'

It had always been the aim of heroic cults to inspire high and profound feelings in the face of the Great: they are less concerned with the distinctive quality of the one who is being venerated. An example here is provided by the discussions concerning a Mozart memorial which took place in Berlin at the beginning of the 1890s. Voices were raised against the idea; it was demanded that a Beethoven monument be erected first as the latter was of greater importance in musical history. There was a compromise: a Haydn-Mozart-Beethoven monument was proposed as a topic for a sculpture competition, and everyone was pleased. The fact that the preceding controversies had lost all sense disturbed nobody.

It was probably the theatrical tradition of 'model performances', and the example of Bayreuth which inspired the Kassel theatre-manager Freiherr von Gilsa to put on a 'Mozart cycle' which performed, in chronological sequence, all the operas from *Idomeneo* to *La Clemenza di Tito*: the success was considerable. Similar cycles were put on in Vienna (under Jauner), Hamburg (under Pollini), in Frankfurt, Leipzig and other cities. They usually finished with a commemoration and a scenic epilogue (perhaps in the form of tableaux vivants like, say, J. Weilens's 'Salzburg's grösster Sohn').

The activities in and around Salzburg provide the best examples of the increasing institutionalization of Mozart worship. After the opening of the Mozarteum and the unveiling of the statue we may note the following: the Memorial (1852); the Centennial Concert (1856); the provisional formulation of the International Mozart Foundation by Karl Freiherr von Sterneck (1870); the Viennese World Exhibition Festival Concert (1873); the first – and in the following year the second – Mozart Festival at Covent Garden

(1874); the first (1877, that is, one year after the Bayreuth Festival) and then the second (1878) Salzburg Music Festivals; the definitive opening of the International Mozarteum Foundation (1880); the *Don Giovanni* centenary (1887). In 1890 plans were drawn up for the building of a *Festspielhaus* on the 'Festival meadow' on the Mönchsberg; the theatre was meant to be visible from afar – as in Bayreuth. The statutes for a 'Society for the Patronage of a Mozart Festival Theatre at Salzburg' were printed; a director for the festivals was, ostensibly, also ready at hand. The centenary of Mozart's death was celebrated by a performance of the *Requiem* under Joseph Hummel, in the cathedral; there was a speech by Robert Hirschfeld, concerts by the Vienna Philharmonic under Wilhelm Jahn and by the Hellmesberger Quartet as well as a performance of *Don Giovanni* in the municipal theatre. Finally the town had risen from provinciality to international renown.

The cultivation of Mozart in other countries began increasingly to resemble that in Germany and Austria. Despite the political rivalries and the attempts to promote national musical languages there arose, slowly but surely, through civilised progress that cultural exchange and flow of information that we know today. The well-attested preference for particular works however, remained everywhere: *Don Giovanni* was just as well known in Melbourne as it was in Santiago de Chile. On 4 November 1872 it was heard for the hundredth time in Paris. Some odd facts are worth singling out from a rich plenitude: *Die Entführung aus dem Serail* did not go down at all well in Italy, but was often given (in Italian) in London; *Don Giovanni*, after 1864, was given in Paris with ballet-interludes which François Auber arranged from Mozart's music; in 1873, in Paris again, *Così fan tutte*, under the title of *Peines d'amour perdues*, was given a new libretto based on Shakespeare's *Love's Labour's Lost*; in Victorian England that delightful Mass, the so-called Twelfth, was the most favourite church music of Mozart – except that it was not by him. While in more distant lands Mozart performances increased up to and after the turn of the century, we find a drop in France, England, Italy and also Poland, similar to the one that there had been in Germany. This was particularly noticeable in Italy. In 1871 *Don Giovanni* was still successfully performed in Milan, the next production, in 1881, was a failure, and afterwards the opera was not played at La Scala for nearly fifty years. But here, as elsewhere, the *Requiem* was often played on suitable occasions.

IV

From 1900 Onwards

If we were confronted by the question: what characterizes the reception of Mozart today? then the optimists, at least, would point to three features. Mozart is known throughout the world and appreciated as never before: to avoid him would give all those concerned with cultural matters a bad conscience. The trend towards 'authentic performances' is no longer simply a matter for experts: halfhearted compromises are being abandoned and methods of performance are being challenged. Psychological probing also allows Mozart's personality to appear in a very different light. It was only eighty years ago that Rudolf Genée wished to burn the so-called 'Bäsle letters' for reasons of discretion and respect for Mozart's genius: now they are available on the market as a paperback, in a scholarly format edited by a prominent writer. The quest for a new image of Mozart is fascinating: it began around the year 1900. Perhaps the different initiatives which have emerged during the course of the century have now reached a point at which they can supersede old habits and ideas, forcing the music market to take a truly appropriate stance – but perhaps we are entering the realm of prophecy here.

But it would be very one-sided indeed to use the phrase 'a new upturn' to describe the reception of Mozart in the two decades before the First World War. Here as well as in other areas it is impossible to separate clearly the modern from the *fin de siècle*. But what we can call indisputably modern phenomena are the slogans used to define Mozart in relation to what followed Wagner, and also those new productions of Mozart's operas which were meant to cleanse the original concept of any disfigurement. What is new here is the emphasis with which these phenomena were championed. Let us explore all this more closely.

When Hermann Levi and Ernst Possart chose, of all works, *Don Giovanni* for a completely new production in Munich in 1896 they were certain of the public's interest. And they chose the original title, not *Don Juan*, as a confession of faith and a challenge. Innovative endeavours like to look back to origins: the special thing about the Munich production was that, from the very beginning, the work was given both a philological and a historical scrutiny. Possart wrote a brochure to accompany the production and, in terms redolent of Enlightenment emotionalism, expressed his intention 'of allowing *Don Giovanni* to arise, after one hundred years, in all its original purity and authenticity'.

But we cannot claim that there were no compromises: the element of theatricality was emphasized anew. The Prague première of October 1797 was regarded as authoritative, and the orchestral strengths, as well as the three-dimensionality of the sets, were made to match those of this production. It was fashionable to stage operas in spaces more suitable for a circus, but Possart rightly objected to this, and his choice of the old Cuvilliés Theatre could not have been better. He used modern stage techniques in production and sets (Karl Lautenschläger's revolving stage was highly praised), but Possart also discussed the possibility of a Shakespeare-style stage which would have been completely opposed to the techniques of the Meiningen Court Theatre which dominated at that time with their cluttered stage scenery. In insisting on the original text the producers wished to expunge excrescences and cuts and to revise the German translation: it still seemed inconceivable to perform it in Italian. Levi reworked the text using Grandaur's translation and removed the choral insertions from the score as well as the use of trombones in the cemetery scene, etc.; to make up for this, however, he put the concluding sextet back in. Hence the earlier philological conclusions (L. von Sonnleitner and B. Gugler, 1867) were put into practice on stage.

Criticism was inevitable. Heinrich Bulthaupt, in the second edition of his *Dramaturgie der Oper* (a standard work of the times), saw himself forced to defend Mozart against the Munich Opera which saw itself, ostensibly, only accountable to Da Ponte. Bulthaupt had 'no understanding' of a production within a small framework and with the idea of *Don Giovanni* as an *opera buffa*; he was certainly dumbstruck by the happy ending. The new production of *Figaro* by Levi and Possart, with sketches for the stage decorations by Christian Jank and Angelo Quaglio, had shown the way in 1895; in 1897 there followed *Così fan tutte (So machen's Alle)* in Levi's translation (after E. Devrient and Niese), in Possart's production and with Richard Strauss conducting (he had stepped in after Levi had become seriously ill) – an opera that for years was little appreciated. It was exactly with this *opera buffa* that the new stylistic elements were felt to be most obtrusive; Carl Hagemann equated Munich with *Così fan tutte* in 1905. It was also

184

symptomatic for the emerging trend that Max Slevogt's plan (encouraged by Richard Strauss but which never came to fruition) was to design, for the *La Clemenza di Tito* figurines, not the usual costumes of antiquity, but those of the Rococo.

There is a great deal that is conspicuous in these new stimuli, not least the strange relationships with the cultural inheritance of Richard Wagner. The Bayreuth model had already been implict in the Salzburg Mozart Festivals twenty years earlier. Out of Possart's special Mozart performances there developed the Munich Opera Festivals which, however, were first dedicated to the work of Wagner; they were extended in 1904 to cover Mozart, who was performed in the Cuvilliés Theatre (except for *Die Zauberflöte*, which was performed in the National Theatre). Hermann Levi was a faithful follower of Wagner, and had, indeed, been the first conductor of *Parsifal*; Richard Strauss, at the time of the Munich Mozart renaissance, was also a Wagner enthusiast. It would, then, be over-simplified to talk of an emerging change of course, away from an epigonic Wagner imitation.

Already before Levi's death, in 1900, Richard Strauss had taken the new ideas and techniques to cities other than Munich (Berlin in 1899). That which had already emerged much earlier now became more apparent – innovative elements in the cultivation of Mozart's work were associated above all with southern Germany, whereas Berlin, above all, stuck to the old traditions. Gustav Mahler's activities in Vienna must be seen in a positive light. He celebrated a triumphant début on 11 May 1897 with Wagner's *Lohengrin* which was followed, much to the audience's surprise, with an equally successful *Die Zauberflöte* a little later. Mahler had taken over into the repertoire *Don Giovanni*, *Die Zauberflöte* and *Figaro* from his predecessor Wilhelm Jahn. Inspired by Richard Strauss's success he performed *Così fan tutte* in Vienna in 1900, a work which had not been played there for a long time. He also used the revolving stage and was able to capture an intimacy which was entirely appropriate to the piece; he also sought to present the spirit of *buffa* in the music. But statistics show that the audience's interest in this opera was slight (fifteen performances in contrast to sixty-two of *Figaro* and forty-eight of *Don Giovanni*). In 1902 the young Bruno Walter conducted *Zaide*; it was, however, Mahler's Mozart cycle of 1905/6 which long remained in the memory.

Mahler did not have a consistent aesthetic as they did in Munich: his *Così* performance differed essentially from the later *Don Giovanni*, particularly in its visual aspects. The concept of authenticity was also more relevant to the Munich productions than to the Viennese. In both cities a battle was waged against careless inefficiency. But Mahler was too much a sovereign artist in

185

his own right to feel bound to stick too closely to a text or even to Mozart's manuscript. In *Figaro*, for example, he inserted a recitative into the third scene of Act One and a whole scene of Beaumarchais into Act Three, which he himself set to music, in order to make the background and the development of Figaro's obligation to marry Marcellina more understandable.

Mahler avoided the 'empty scene-changes' during which the audience grew restless and lost concentration, and consequently inserted interval music, repeating bits of the overture or using pieces of Mozart's instrumental music which had nothing to do with the opera. He also interfered with the instrumentation, inserting as well as omitting passages; he was also concerned to emphasize the dramatic flow, to smooth transitions and to build up the climaxes more effectively. This extensive touching-up also included varying Mozart's dynamics; such interventions as these were derived from a very ancient theatrical practice which, as it so happens, was not much used in Mozart's own time but which became very prevalent in the nineteenth century. And in his high-handed treatment of the works of other composers Mahler shows himself to be very much an heir to Wagner. He engaged singers with dramatic voices for Mozart roles (singers such as Anna Mildenburg, Hilgermann, Leo Slezak, Richard Mayr, etc.) and quite uninhibitedly transposed whole arias into another key. But he rejected other current adoptions from Bayreuth – exaggerated liberty in the choice of tempo, for example, or the use of *rubato* and similar habits; he also refused to follow the older practice of inserting embellishments and cadences. Under Mahler Mozart's operas must have sounded precise and subtle, as well as vital and dramatic. Whether or not a new Mozart style was born remains open, as there was not an old Mozart style. The decisive factor was that Mahler took Mozart seriously and committed himself to achieving polished, uniform performances.

Mahler had a keen sense for the changes which were occurring then in theatrical productions (A.Apia, Gordon Craig). He made lots of experiments, not arbitrarily, but alert to the old forms and genres. *Don Giovanni* was always a tragedy for him, and *Die Zauberflöte* a German mystery-opera; *Figaro* and *Così fan tutte*, however, received new life as that lasting enthusiasm for the Rococo, which was seen as an antidote to modern life, achieved artistic realization.

The musical side of *opera buffa* performances also stood out from the normal opera practices by having an orchestration akin to chamber music or through the use once more (in Munich) of the harpsichord, an instrument long frowned upon. The audience's desire for self-identification with an

186

operatic hero was disappointed. Mahler chose his singers with a view to ensemble effects and preferred a production which concentrated upon the interplay of persons in changing configurations. And here he conformed to the Munich renaissance, but his famous *Don Giovanni* production of 1906 diverged strongly from this model. Yet we cannot call it an old-fashioned production – his collaboration with Alfred Roller alone would prevent this, Roller being a famous artist of the Viennese Secession.

The problem which arose with all the new Mozart productions was that a more mobile form of staging presupposed a newer, more sparsely furnished stage with fewer props; there were practical reasons for this, but the audience's attention was also meant to be deflected from customary ways of seeing and feeling. The ambience in which the singers enacted their roles was, with Roller, not one of ethereal lightness but of rich, gleaming colours in striking contours. Through the use of practical, tower-like sculptures, which he used from first to last in varying positions on the stage, Roller was able to achieve an impression of unity and weightiness.

But we see more clearly how difficult it was, particularly with *Don Giovanni*, to break away from conventional patterns when we look at the events organized by the Salzburg Music Festival in 1906. Mahler brought his *Figaro* production across from Vienna without altering it, a performance full of lightness and sparkling vitality in the finely balanced ensembles; Paul Hirsch, however, when describing *Don Giovanni* in his memoirs, talks of excellent singers but little awareness of how to do ensembles. Lilli Lehmann, who sang Donna Anna, was in charge of the artistic direction; a second-rate *Kapellmeister* conducted. The star of the performance was the most famous Don Giovanni of the time, the Portuguese Francesco d'Andrade. He impressed not so much by the power of his voice as by his stage presence and his fascinating acting; Max Slevogt caught his presence and his elegance, his lust for life and his demonic qualities splendidly in his pictures of the 'white', 'red' and 'black' d'Andrade (1902–12). D'Andrade's Don Giovanni was manifestly that hero of the moment whom Hausegger had envisaged.

But we also see at the Salzburg Mozart Festivals the depths to which Mozart's instrumental music had sunk; there was little awareness of any renaissance in the concert halls. It must surely amount to a disrespect for Mozart's music that it was not even permitted to represent its creator in a worthy fashion. How else are we to understand it when Felix Mottl finished his concert, in which the seventy-year-old Camille Saint-Saëns played the E flat major piano concerto (K. 482), with a performance of Beethoven's C minor symphony, or when to conclude his concert, Richard Strauss conducted Bruckner's ninth symphony? We should, meanwhile, not forget

187

that Saint-Saëns, after Carl Reinecke's essay 'Zur Wiederbelebung der Mozart'schen Clavier Concerte' (On the Revivification of Mozart's Piano Concertos), had actually done a great deal for the cause of Mozart.

In practice there may have been much variety, but at least the motto, 'Vorwärts zu Mozart!' (Forward to Mozart!) was uncompromisingly clear. Felix von Weingartner thought it up: he was Mahler's successor as conductor at the Viennese Court Opera, and dedicated himself energetically to the interpretation of Classical music, although as a composer he remained in Wagner's thrall. He was, therefore, not fully convinced of his own slogan, although he saw the rightness of 'working with modern methods in the spirit of Mozart'. This watchword was, in fact, exemplified quite early, in 1903, by Ermanno Wolf-Ferrari in his light-hearted opera *Susanna's Secret* with its gay conversational style inspired by *Così fan tutte* and *Falstaff*. Wolf-Ferrari considered Mozart to be a completely unselfconscious genius, one of those 'true artists' who are differentiated from those 'inauthentic', reflective kinds: he anticipates Hildesheimer here. The famous piano teacher Rudolf Maria Breithaupt propagated the same slogan, albeit somewhat diluted, in his 'Mehr Mozart'. But he expected nothing from modernism, and everything from that 'healthy naïvety' whose present absence Edvard Grieg was lamenting at the same time.

Things are different with Ferruccio Busoni. Like Weingartner, he also hoped for a more modern Mozart reception and, like Weingartner again, he had a teacher who, in Busoni's words, sought above all to impress Mozart's music upon his pupils – Wilhelm Mayer. He had been born in Prague, was a schoolfriend of Ambros and Hanslick and, as a musician, had taken on the name of W.A. Rémy (note Mozart's initials). We find, nevertheless, the following statement in Busoni's 'Mozart-Aphorismen zum 150. Geburtstag des Meisters' (Mozart Aphorisms for the Sesquicentenary of the Master): 'Mozart is a completed, round number, a summation, an end and no beginning.' Nietzsche's yearning for the musical South, found its first Italian, or at least German-Italian composer, in Busoni – yet for Busoni, as for Nietzsche, Mozart represents musical perfection *per se*, untroubled, perfectly formed beauty, a beauty which is therefore inconceivable, 'almost extra-human'.

Busoni also takes up the metaphor that Wagner's music leaps, as it were, out of the wall, whereas Mozart's remains within a set framework. And, like many before him, he leaves Mozart in harmony with the world around him and transfigures this remote world of the eighteenth century. For decades his favourite work remained *Figaro*, and, basically, Busoni continued to hold those views which he had put forward during the *Don Giovanni* jubilee.

188

These views represent a conservative position, they turn against everything demonic and supernatural in Mozart's art and, as regards content, take up the old Shakespeare comparisons (the fusing of seriousness and gaiety, of reality and idealism) and also Schopenhauer's extreme preference for absolute music. Curiously enough it is *Don Giovanni* which remains the exception, a work which Busoni, furthermore, took to be a tragedy. With his concept of genius (the genius brings forth perfection, the man of talent something new) he expressly looks back to Max Nordau and Lemcke: his ideas on Mozart, then, are by no means modern.

It was in the same year that Alfred Heuss stressed the demonic element in Mozart's music in unwitting contrast to Busoni. This learned study attacked above all the popular trivialization of Mozart which sought sweetness and harmony and advocated his 'demonic artistic temperament'; it had very little rapport with the Mozart renaissance and the interest in *opera buffa*. Heuss had not discovered anything new as the Romantic (and particularly late Romantic) interpretation of *Don Giovanni* had also aimed at the work's demonic elements. But Heuss decidedly goes beyond the bounds of Mozart research set by Jahn by heightening our awareness of fine nuances in Mozart; his intention was to detect Mozart's demonic qualities in those passionately agitated passages which suddenly erupt, 'in those places where, by their very nature, they should not occur'. He took into account Mozart's juvenilia here, also the instrumental music. Heuss laid particular emphasis on the difference between Mozart's sudden outbursts and the extensive passages of deliberate and architectonic emotionalism in Beethoven, passages which, because they *are* deliberate, do not unsettle the listener. But already before Heuss the conductor Siegmund von Hausegger had referred to those 'stepchildren' in Mozart programmes, drawing particular attention to the expressive intensity of Mozart's little G minor symphony (K. 183).

But the sesquicentenary of Mozart's birth was stamped with events of quite a different order. A flood of Mozart publications swamped the market; even such Verismo composers as Mascagni and Leoncavallo praised Mozart as being 'the genius of music itself'. There was an enormous number of celebrations, festival concerts, gala performances and unveiling of statues; there were masses of picture-postcards with portraits of Mozart, of his birthplace or of his snuff boxes. When we consider the continuity in developments from then to the present day it seems symbolic that, at this time, the plan was hatched in Salzburg to erect that Mozarteum building (the foundation stone was laid in 1906) which today is a centre of world-wide activity in all matters to do with Mozart, and that in Japan, a country which has become dominant in the execution of music and its propagation,

189

the first notes of Mozart were heard in a concert. But the number of performances do not demonstrate a sudden turning point in Mozart's favour. In Graz, for example, a very Wagner-oriented town with an operatic stage of average quality, we have, between 1854 and 1899, 581 performances of Verdi, 483 of Wagner and 281 of Mozart; in the first twenty-five years of this century we have Verdi played 687 times, Wagner 397 and Mozart only 152. But I would now like to use some very disparate contemporary statements to illustrate what the year 1906 brought in the way of actual effects and attitudes.

With the very title of his book, *Mozart Heuchelei* (Mozart Hypocrisy), Paul Zschorlich launched himself into an attack against the rising wave of hero-worship; fury, threatening anonymous letters and popularity were the (foreseeable) results. But Zschorlich's essay is more than just a pamphlet: it also contains, in a distorting mirror, a criticism of culture which expresses more than the author intended. He denounced the mendacity of that 'calendar enthusiasm' which 'celebrates away' the sins of omission.

We would all agree with this very relevant critique, particularly when Zschorlich reminds us that smaller towns often have a sincere and honest dedication to Mozart's music. In the centres of musical culture, however, he detects the poses struck by society people, those 'whose lives are led in the conventionality of lies'. He is particularly hard towards those conservatories which felt themselves to be guardians of the Grail, of a tradition in which the teachers no longer believed. And the following question of his is surely justified: what has this stilted solemnity got to do with the speed of life, the strains and stresses of the business world, and the artistic fragmentation of the present? But despite all the irritation, Zschorlich knows suspiciously well what is relevant and what is not: Mozart's art is not, but that of Wagner certainly is. And his book culminates in a way of thinking well known to the Wagner societies and the 'Bayreuther Blätter': Mozart is for the backward, Wagner for the intelligentsia. Mozart is a Classic, Zschorlich writes, but the idea of Classicism is only book-learning. The most important thing is a structure for the future – and this has been provided by Wagner.

Zschorlich's sortie against the slogan 'Back to Mozart!', which he sees as a 'sin against Wagner' and a 'historical perversity' seems to indicate that the Wagnerians were beginning to feel that the banner of progress might be torn from their hands. Eighty years later Zschorlich himself would appear reactionary, mainly because he had not seen the complicated amalgamation of both Wagner and Mozart as models for the artistic endeavours of his own time, although, to a certain extent, this amalgamation goes back to Wagner himself.

Hermann von der Pfordten also criticized that popularization of Mozart (which Zschorlich had called mendacious) in his small book which appeared in 1908, but he reached a more positive viewpoint. If we look at the concert programmes of the times we see that Mozart was certainly a much-praised master, but that his works, in glaring contrast to Beethoven's, were hardly known. The jubilee year, von der Pfordten tells us, had only resulted in a very few new findings or new performances. Pfordten is particularly suspicious of the aesthetics involved in any praise of Mozart. Such phrases about the 'beauty' of his music have, as an aftertaste, a sense of limitation, a limitation concerning that which is beautiful only; that which is smooth, charming and childlishly naïve could also be easily misunderstood as something superficial, dainty and old-fashioned.

Pfordten then brings to light the incompatibility of that ethereal translation of Mozart to a higher realm with his contemporaneous classification as a Rococo composer: how on earth could a man of the Rococo, a man exemplifying the heights of elegant frivolity, be at the same time an innocent, dallying child? Pfordten's reply, a reply that is both disconcerting and topical, familiar and yet prophetic, looking forward to the next sesquicentenary year – 1941 – is that Mozart is 'a truly German man and artist': this is a drastic solution.

His other visions of the future are more interesting. The times of 'Mozart versus Wagner' are, he claims, *passé*, but a one-sided 'Beethoven mania' was still to be overcome. The only sensible way forward was the performance of Mozart in good, innovative concert programmes, and 'specialists' had already committed themselves to these. Pfordten found it particularly annoying that the papers were full of sensational accounts concerning Albert Kopfermann's ostensible unearthing, in 1907, of Mozart's Violin Concerto K. 271: this pursuit of a phantom elegantly disregarded our ignorance of the other six.

The Wagner centenary year of 1913 showed how little the times of 'Wagner versus Mozart' were in fact *passé*. Mozart's music was increasingly regarded as an antidote to the heavy, sultry creations of Wagner: Emil Ludwig formulated it in this drastic fashion in his book *Wagner oder Die Entzauberten* (Wagner or The Disenchanted). In the same year Oskar Bie, a former Wagnerian, admitted in his well-regarded book *Die Oper* that he saw in the future of this genre a promising reunion of Mozart and Verdi. The German Youth Movement also brought something new into musical life, a rejection of Wagner, Beethoven and the nineteenth century as a whole – but Mozart did not suit its tastes either. August Halm, one of its committed – although not uncontroversial – representatives, turned against pseudo-

191

drama and false emotionalism and argued that, 'We do not seldom find that Mozart's intentions did not match his abilities' – an astonishing judgement considering Halm's reputation as an intellectual musicologist.

It is in the commemorative speeches that the official view is promulgated, and the pronouncements of Richard Beer-Hofmann, a dramatist friendly with Schnitzler and Hofmannsthal, have become famous. Using the tone of the elevated fairy-tale he tells of an Orpheus living in close harmony with nature who, remote from all suffering, has given mankind an immaculate music. In words of beguiling beauty Beer-Hofmann paints that picture of Mozart which others had already begun to attack:

> Our soul will not always remain with thee, Wolfgang Amade Mozart! We have been taught too much to burrow in the deepest shafts of our being, and we know of too much sorrow . . . But when in spring, or in the days of fortune, when we step into our garden in the early morning, enjoying, with limbs still loose with sleep, the moist air of the early year and the scent of the earth as a great happiness, and high above us a bird, released from the encumberances of earth, hurls itself heavenwards, streaming the very joy of its existence into song – then we greet thee, Wolfgang Amade Mozart!

As Mozart shared the same birthday as Kaiser Wilhelm II – 27 January – a great deal of sublimity was to be expected in the speech before the Berlin Academy given by the music-historian Carl Krebs in 1906 on this dual celebration. Beginning with hackneyed phrases of devotion, and ending with three cheers for the emperor, the speech does, in fact, contain surprisingly modern ideas about Mozart. Krebs quickly distances himself from the notion of a transfigured genius, consummately perfect in itself; he puts the same questions as the other two critics as to Mozart's vitality and puts forward the view that much in Mozart can only be appreciated by a twentieth-century audience, above all his 'infinitely fine awareness of the life of form and his powerful art of characterization'.

Krebs is seeking to overcome the picture which was valid in the late nineteenth century. He sets up, in opposition to the playful elements of Rococo, the *Sturm und Drang* movement, a movement which, although running parallel to the Rococo, exemplifies the 'dark passions' of much of Mozart's instrumental music. Krebs attacks the trivialization of Mozart in his interpretation of the song *Das Veilchen* (The Violet) seeing it as an expressive, dramatic scene; he also rejects the ostensible lightness of Mozart's work and its apparent naïvety. He also criticized the idea of

192

causality which had entered Mozart scholarship: Mozart had not necessarily evolved from a process of development but was 'something quite accidental'. Contrary to the official optimism Krebs speaks of the transience of culture (as had the classical philologist Ulrich von Wilamowitz-Moellendorff nine years before in his speech on the Kaiser's birthday); but in order, perhaps, to overcome the 'sickness' of the present age he expressed the hope that modern music might learn, in a suitably topical reinterpretation, much from Mozart's example.

What, then, did become of the activities which emerged during the commemorative year? How far did the modern composers and, in a different manner, the modern scholars succeed in realizing the call for a new interpretation? A look first at the latter: in the preface to his monumental Mozart monograph of 1919, Hermann Abert considers the change that had occurred since the time of Otto Jahn. He claimed that Mozart's art was heard and experienced in an essentially different way from that of the past. Abert the scholar is primarily interested in the reasons why, he believed, it was necessary to write Mozart's biography anew. What he objected to was that Jahn had portrayed Mozart in a manner that was far too decent, far too *bürgerlich*; he had regarded Mozart's music as a model of perfected equipoise; he had, in short, idealized him too much. These objections boil down to a demand for a historical view (a demand that Jahn himself supported) and which Abert now intensifies. Abert quite consistently sees the deeper justification for his project in the fact that, since Jahn and Köchel, many new sources had been discovered and the methods for evaluating them had grown much stricter and far more subtle.

The scholarly advances taken up by Abert had some striking features. Paul Graf von Waldersee published his much improved and amplified new edition of Köchel's index in 1905; Ludwig Schiedermair, with his collected edition of *Briefe W.A. Mozarts und seiner Familie* (The Letters of W.A. Mozart and his Family), Munich and Leipzig, 1914, created a much more important basis for understanding Mozart's personality than the old familiar anecdotes and legends. An iconography is appended which (after someone else's preparatory work) gave a definite encouragement to seeking precise source research in this field as well, instead of haphazard guessing: it is indeed significant that, for example, the contributors to the Salzburg Mozart Festivals of 1906 were given a commemorative document with a portrait of Mozart that had been forged.

There was something abstract about the attempt made by Ulibischeff and Jahn to see Mozart's artistic consummation as the result of an historical process because, at the time in which they were living, there had been far

193

too little historical research by music scholars into pre-Classicism. Meanwhile, great steps forward had been made both here and into Mozart's juvenilia. Friedrich Chrysander made it quite clear in his essays on Mozart's youthful opera *Mitridate* that Mozart was not always, and certainly not in everything, superior to the musical world which surrounded him: Oskar Fleischer drew attention to the significance of Johann Christian Bach as a precursor, and Hugo Riemann pointed to Johann Schobert. In 1902 Riemann published the first volume of the music of the 'Mannheim Symphonies' and, at the same time, the music of Viennese pre-Classicism was researched by Guido Adler and his pupils, who edited a great deal that had been unknown. The significance of Italian music for Mozart and for German pre-Classicism and Classicism *per se* only emerged later. In all of this the main interest concerned the instrumental composition. This was as axiomatic as was the evaluation of Mozart's early works and was more especially directed against traditional habits of reception.

The lavish, five-volume stylistic examination by Théodore de Wyzewa and Georges de Saint-Foix, *W.A. Mozart. Sa vie musicale et son oeuvre, de l'enfance à la pleine maturité* (Paris, 1912, 1936, 1939, 1946), showed, however, how the old methods still prevailed. Both of our authors concentrated on Mozart's work up to 1777, which they divided up into no fewer than twenty-four periods (out of a total of thirty-six). Their procedure rested on the old and well-loved hunt for reminiscences which was elevated, with astounding meticulousness, as a basic principle. The analysis of concrete details was modern, as was the increased reliability of the findings, achieved by coping with enormous masses of material.

At the same time, however, the radical nature of the procedure leads to a point where the study of art threatens to tip over into an abstract existence of its own. The thesis that art is the result of an historical development is taken by Wyzewa and Saint-Foix so literally that every single compositional detail appears to be justified by influences, and the sum of these elements becomes a closed system which detaches itself not only from the work as a whole and from the intentions and the individuality of the artist, but also from the influences, which may have come from outside the musical sphere itself. Wyzewa, correspondingly, denies the importance of biographical details for Mozart's art.

The explosive potential in this work only really comes into its own in Arthur Schurig's Mozart monograph, published in Leipzig in 1913. Schurig, who called himself a 'vassal' of Wyzewa and Saint-Foix, was the first to turn away from the tradition established by Jahn. He breaks with the old hero-worship and, instead of an ideal figure, presents an everyday Mozart;

the father, Leopold, is not a man who wisely directs his son, but a narrow-minded philistine. His scepticism *vis-à-vis* trivial anecdotes and mytho-logizing was as justified as it was necessary; the problematic nature of Schurig's position today is the same as that of Hildesheimer, whom we shall deal with later.

But in the long term it was Abert's image of Mozart which remained dominant: there are probably many reasons for this. One must be the clear and balanced structure and its multifaceted core of information. We get a portrayal of life and work, of important contemporaries, the history of individual genres, of centres of musical activity, and of theatrical and concert practice. Another reason for the book's success is its mediating function. The book has practical advantages for the reader who is looking for a synopsis because Abert does not separate life from work, but continues to divide the material up into periods.

His book has content and direction; those who know it, and then read the preface, will be surprised by the far-ranging and objective criticism of Jahn and the earlier Mozart scholarship; Abert obviously agrees with the views of Alfred Heuss. But in spite of this he kept his subtitle: *Eine neuarbeitete und erweiterte Ausgabe von Otto Jahns* Mozart (A revised and extended version of Otto Jahn's *Mozart*) – there was piety here, but also a willingness to compromise. Abert's sympathetic and far-reaching tolerance became, in the case of Jahn (whose individuality, Abert claimed, was characterized by 'a beautiful fusion of level-headedness and enthusiasm'), a personal affir-mation. Abert (who was also a classical philologist) remained closely attached to his precursor, more than he cared to admit in his preface; we see the legacy in the unity between life and work which Abert insisted on, together with the developmental, historical model, the ideal of balance which Abert took for himself and his subject and, above all, the loving diction. It was inevitable that difficulties would arise, at some time or another, from this continuity.

The modern composers themselves also faced a dilemma – how to find a middle course between idealizing Mozart and submitting his music to a detailed and penetrating analysis. And they had from the beginning as many difficulties in tackling Mozart as had their immediate precursors. We see their own historical position in the way in which they set about writing their own music. Mahler's modernity, we argue today, lies in his awareness of the fragility of tradition: his music distances itself from Mozart's yet yearns for it at the same time – it is said that Mahler died with the name 'Mozartl' (i.e. 'dear little Mozart') on his lips.

In a letter of November 1914 Max Reger wrote the sentence: 'We need

Mozart, as much Mozart as possible!' He had just finished his Mozart Variations, opus 132, hardly to his entire satisfaction for otherwise he would not have expressed himself so emphatically. This lovely work, uniform in its own way, is successful as a translation of Mozart's music into an orchestral language of late Romanticism, though not successful as a return to a Mozart from whom the composer expected a kind of catharsis. Reger chose a particularly plain theme, the beginning of the A major piano sonata. For his part, Mozart had written a series of variations on this theme, a movement which, despite the variety in style and expression, remained within an established framework, so that the two movements which followed joined quite naturally on to the simple, relaxed atmosphere of the beginning of the sonata. With Reger it is quite different: with him Mozart's theme is tender, successively illuminated by various tonal colours, and, as it were, transfigured, with Mozart's simplicity touched from the start by an aura of melancholy. The melody spins out a mesh of lines and colours, till Reger leads it to that region of 'knowledge of far too much suffering' of which Beer-Hofmann had spoken. The path finally leads into a powerful fugal architecture, and Mozart's theme now resounds in the bombastic fortissimo of the full orchestra.

Reger's composition shows us quite clearly what, according to the understanding of the times, Mozart's music was lacking or, if you like, what yearning added to it, and why the music of Beethoven or Bruckner was played at Mozart festivals. With his Mozart variations Reger reached, in principle, a similar statement as Brahms in his Haydn variations – both works are suffused with veneration of the classics. Reger got closer to Mozart in his chamber music: in the piano sonatinas opus 89, the string trios and the flute serenades opus 77 and 141, as well as in the late clarinet quintet, Mozart's example helps to bring clarity and to shift the attention from the large to the small. There were good reasons why Reger should see chamber music as his own domain: here, and in many other places in musical history, we see the new characterized by a reduction in the use of the forces at hand. Reger here works hand in hand with the boldest musical reformer of the age – Arnold Schoenberg.

The American composer George Gershwin once spoke to Arnold Schoenberg of his plans and added that he wished to write something simple, something like a string quartet by Mozart. Schoenberg, infuriated, retorted that Mozart was by no means simple. This reaction hints at the reason why, in his essay of 1933 on 'Brahms, der Fortschrittliche' ('Brahms the Progressive'), he should call Brahms 'a pupil of Mozart'. In an essay written the year before, entitled 'National Music', Schoenberg professed his indebtedness to his most important teachers, Bach and Mozart, and precisely formulated what he had learned from Mozart: the 'prose-like' irregularities in thematic construction and length of phrase, the thematic combination of varying elements, the art of transition and the formulation of secondary motives. Mozart's ideal had thus become a very concrete example for Schoenberg, and he was aware of this more than any other.

The analyses in *Die formbildenden Tendenzen der Harmonie* (The Form-building Tendencies of Harmony) also prove how stimulating Mozart was for Schoenberg in the details of compositional techniques. It was exactly those areas in Mozart's art (which Wagner, for example, had charged with conventionality in phrasing) which served Schoenberg as a confirmation of his own 'musical prose'. The idea of naïve, blissful melodiousness is thus forgotten – whether or not the opposing assumption is valid, namely, that Mozart anticipated the technique of serialism, is questionable; looked at differently, the assumption is not perhaps entirely without sense as there must have been something there for Schoenberg to refer to, and refer to in a very fundamental manner. This could be claimed – with another question mark – for Karlheinz Stockhausen's Mozart interpretation; parameter-thinking he applied on a large scale to Mozart.

When we listen to Schoenberg's music hardly anyone would think of Mozart; the worlds expressed are completely different. Yet a composer who was utterly remote from Schoenberg, Claude Debussy, wrote a form of music which seems to stand much closer to Mozart. Debussy esteemed Mozart most highly, but hardly ever referred to him. But he did possess something that we can more readily call a kind of elective affinity with Mozart which, indeed, only came about obliquely. Those French virtues which he valued so highly – 'clarity of expression; precision; compact formal density' – are also Mozart's virtues, or the virtues of the eighteenth century. A former concept which was central to aesthetics – taste – comes into its own in Debussy once more. Debussy professed an allegiance to this concept when placing Mozart in opposition to the Gluck-Beethoven-Wagner line-up, seeing in Mozart a genius of taste and in Beethoven a sombre, tasteless genius.

The music of Busoni, an apologist for Mozart, is of particular interest. The comments on transitions in Bach and Mozart which he made in his *Entwurf einer neuen Ästhetik der Tonkunst* (Design for a New Musical Aesthetic) lead us to assume that his reception of Mozart would be the same as Schoenberg's; the same intensity, however, is lacking. Busoni's hopes were firmly placed on music-theatre, and his attitude towards Mozart faithfully reflected this. And it was more natural to concentrate on this rather than on instrumental music, given the preference for Mozart's operas.

For Busoni the future of opera lay in the possibility of deliberately portraying what could not be found in real life, that is, the creation of an illusory world 'which reflects life either in a magic, or in a distorting mirror'. So Mozart himself was less an example than the Mozart seen through the eyes of Romantic irony – and, in fact, Busoni's utopias do owe much to early Romanticism. But Busoni's demand for the intellectual independence of the music within opera refers immediately to Mozart: a textual tautology via music was repellent to him. In addition he found in Mozart that clear division of operatic numbers which could be opposed to Wagner's legacy.

Die Zauberflöte suited his vision better, actually, than his favourite opera Figaro, particularly when we think of the way he realized it in Doktor Faust; he did, however, compare his own Arlecchino with Die Zauberflöte. He referred to Shaw here who is supposed to have said to him that he had learned from Mozart how to say significant things in an entertaining manner. Admittedly, Arlecchino did not offer much entertainment, it only allowed, rather, a 'painful laugh'. Busoni wanted the content of this opera, an opera which was aimed at human egoism, to be understood as a personal affirmation. He defended himself against the charge that the opera was scornful and misanthropic and claimed that, after Die Zauberflöte, Arlecchino was 'the most moral opera'. Busoni also signalled his veneration for Mozart by taking his leave from the concert platform by playing nine Mozart piano concertos on three separate evenings.

Busoni's belief that the operatic public should remain incredulous and hence unimpeded in their intellectual reception of the work gives advance notice of epic theatre, that theatrical form which his pupil Kurt Weill, together with Bertolt Brecht, would later realize on the operatic stage. And Mozart's work turns up here also, anticipating the new. Figaro itself had been an opera 'dealing with the times'; in Die Zauberflöte we get frequent interruptions of the action and the insertion of moralizing aphorisms, and it is at least worth considering whether or not the arias of the Queen of the Night and the priestly duet 'Bewahret euch vor Weibertücken' do not have something in them that nowadays would be called alienation.

Weill saw Mozart's operas as ideal music-theatre, and it is a pity that he never spoke about them in detail; we can, however, see from certain comments how he envisaged this ideal. Like Busoni, he took over the structure provided by operatic numbers, and he highly regarded the ethos of Die Zauberflöte. And Weill concentrated further on musical drama in nuce, on the 'gestic character of music'. He was convinced that music must, in its very nature, be 'theatre-music in the sense of Mozart' in order to free itself

198

from the stage's insistence on making up our minds for us. Mozart's music, he argued, was always felt dramatically, even outside the operas, and was unambiguous in its expression; Weill here sees the rhythmical setting of the text as the basis of what he called the gestic. Like Schoenberg, Weill fixed his attention on details, although less on the subtleties of transition and variation than on smaller units which were definite and self-explanatory.

Perhaps the greatest event in the operatic history of our century was the collaboration between Richard Strauss and Hugo von Hofmannsthal. Nietzsche's vision of the future lived on in this collaboration, a vision which had undergone several attempts at realization since Verdi's *Falstaff*. That 'reconstruction of tradition' which had looked at antique drama from the beginnings of operatic history through Gluck, Wagner and finally *Elektra* now turned its attention to the opera of the Rococo age and – especially with Strauss and Hofmannsthal – particularly to Mozart. It is well known that *Der Rosenkavalier* was meant to be a modern *Figaro*, and *Die Frau ohne Schatten* a new *Die Zauberflöte*. And as these works have still lost none of their vitality it would seem reasonable to look at their authors' attitude to Mozart in some detail.

Strauss and Hofmannsthal were very different personalities, but they agreed in their love for Mozart. From his earliest years Mozart was a high ideal for Strauss, an ideal, however, which remained without consequence for his own work: it is remarkable how this ideal was compatible with a love for Wagner, Liszt and Berlioz which did clearly find expression in his music. Later, Strauss became a supporter of the Mozart renaissance which radiated from Munich. But Strauss's arrangement of *Idomeneo* (1930) shows how remote Mozart was from the musician Strauss, even after his collaboration with Hofmannsthal; his version was sharply criticized for being sacrilegious, a criticism which was exaggerated, even though not without basis. Strauss indirectly admitted Mozart's remoteness in a conversation with Willy Schuh in 1944 when he talked about 'platonic ideas and archetypes' when referring to Mozart's melodic idiom. He was only able to translate Mozart's example into actual music in old age, at best, probably, in the oboe concerto which he wrote when he was eighty-two. When Strauss insisted (with reference to Goethe) that the aim of artistic maturity was the achievement of the right balance, we can detect the influence of Hofmannsthal in the musician's remark.

As Rudolph Pannwitz recognized as early as 1919, Hofmannsthal had achieved a deeper understanding of Mozart via Goethe; from the beginning however, he had adopted that image of Mozart which was prevalent at the end of the nineteenth century. In his early essay, written to commemorate the centenary of Mozart's death in 1891 he gave Mozart the status of a distant ideal: 'It is just as impossible to return to Mozart as it is to the Greeks.' Later too, like Strauss, he did not renounce this idealization and when he gave the Beethoven address in Zurich in 1920 he talked of Mozart's work as 'a second antiquity, as beautiful and as comprehensible as the first, but more innocent than the first, more purified, as it were, a Christian antiquity'. It was Mozart's form which he admired above all, a form which he compared to that of Goethe and Shakespeare.

This intensely abstract conception of Mozart must needs lead to difficulties where concrete practice was concerned, and we see this above all with the opera *Die Frau ohne Schatten*. In 1919 Hofmannsthal looked back at the work in his essay on its genesis and referred to *Die Zauberflöte* as its only model. Yet the context in which he now places this work deviates from his original intention. In his letter of 20 March 1911, where he first informs Strauss of his plans for *Die Frau ohne Schatten*, he mentions a 'certain analogy' with *Die Zauberflöte*, a 'varied and powerful action, in which the textual detail is less important'; he talks about a 'magic fairy-tale'; about the 'magical naïvety of many scenes of *Die Zauberflöte*' and about a content that would be 'much brighter and happier' than others. The further working out of the opera gave the lie – in more ways than one – to this statement in both libretto and music. The alteration was, on the one hand, caused by the fact that, despite all Hofmannsthal's exhortations, Strauss did not overcome Wagner's 'musical armour plating' and, on the other, by the poet's own change of mind.

Hofmannsthal's starting point was Goethe's continuation of *Die Zauberflöte* (about which he wrote an essay); he began by denigrating Schikaneder's libretto and sought, in preference, to find ethical values in Mozart's music. In 1919, then, he dissociated himself in retrospect from all the plans concerning a popular play and described in the following manner the way in which he and Strauss became aware of analogies with *Die Zauberflöte*: 'The musical nature of the motif of suffering and purification, and the relationships with the basic motif of *Die Zauberflöte*, struck us both, and we then decided that both groups of figures [the dyers, and the imperial couple] were to be treated in the same way, in elevated language.'

In a word, Hofmannsthal's analogy concentrated first of all on the scene with the two men in armour, and the journey through fire and water: quite consistently, then, the central scene in *Die Frau ohne Schatten* was the scene where the Empress stands in the temple before the petrified Emperor. But it is exactly the decisive passage – where the Empress, through her pity, redeems the dyers – that led to serious differences between Hofmannsthal and Strauss and can, quite honestly, be regarded as a failure (on the stage it is radically cut). Strauss ignored the art of hinting, of silence, which is found in Hofmannsthal and instead demanded 'sufficient space for lyrical effusion'. Hofmannsthal would not admit that his digression from the multi-layered structure of *Die Zauberflöte*, a digression which eliminated all humour and gaiety for the sake of an ethical concentration of action, must necessarily have consequences for the choice of musical style. In his opinion the piece, after the Emperor's redemption, should begin its final scene with a totally new musical texture – a much lighter texture – which was an impossibility for Strauss, a man well versed in the practices of opera. Strauss recognized that *Die Frau ohne Schatten* had succeeded as 'the last Romantic opera'; Hofmannsthal remained dissatisfied and was very pleased to receive a letter from Rudolph Pannwitz (2 November 1919) in which the latter wrote the following about *Die Frau ohne Schatten*: 'The affinity with Mozart (also with the spirit of the text of *Die Zauberflöte*) is very great. It is indeed a tragedy that you and Mozart were not contemporaries.' This statement (historically meaningless) illustrates best of all perhaps the status of Mozart in the Hofmannsthal-Strauss collaboration.

The hopes and fears in the artistic and communal enterprise leading to the Salzburg Festivals – an enterprise moulded by Hofmannsthal and Strauss, the producer Max Reinhardt, the writer Herman Bahr, the conductors Franz Schalk and Bruno Walter, the stage-designer Alfred Roller and many others – were of a different order. It was primarily Hofmannsthal, Reinhardt and Bahr who had the spirit and the courage to fuel this utopia – and the word utopia is entirely justified here. The spirit of the Salzburg Festivals is one of a living tradition. Something very old was to be preserved, some cultural ethos that had been defended a century before with the help of memories of Mozart and that, as a political reality, had become increasingly endangered throughout the course of the nineteenth century.

When Hofmannsthal in his *Aufruf* (Appeal) of 1919 spoke of the European spirit, and Reinhardt (1917) talked of an eminent work of peace, and Bahr, earlier, described Salzburg as the capital of Europe, it all sounded like an insubstantial illusion. There was nothing to justify the hope for a new European order and for a similar institution to the Congress of Vienna which met after the Napoleonic Wars. The patriotic Austrian idea had lost its basis. Yet nevertheless, between the wars, an 'Austrian cultural idea' was propagated here and there; in 1918 the first book appeared which sought to detect what was specifically Austrian in music. Both here and in the plans for the Salzburg Festivals the possibility was mooted of forgetting the miseries of the present and of creating a positive, ideal world as a contrast and of bestowing upon it at least an artistic and spiritual reality. Salzburg as a place of great tradition, as an idyll, a harmonious cultural landscape, as Mozart's birthplace, as an image of the Baroque love of art, as a city standing where the North meets the South – this city seemed most suitable, most ready to give that utopian ideal a palpable form. However the resulting reality may be judged, the fact remains that Salzburg *did* become the emotive and prestigious centre of a world-wide cultivation of Mozart's art.

The Salzburg Festivals of the time before the Second World War are transfigured in retrospect, but they were not spared the political and economic problems facing Austria at that time. The history of the institution, with its happier and more negative aspects, began long before the opening of the first festival year. Since the unveiling of the monument in 1842, both the patriotic and the cosmopolitan elements, together with the activities of those from Salzburg and those from outside, strove to form a unity; they complemented each other but they also led to rivalry and intrigue.

After earlier attempts had come to nothing the Viennese Heinrich Damisch and the Salzburger Friedrich Gehmacher founded a 'Society for the Promotion of the Festspielhaus in Salzburg' which met in Vienna and set itself up in opposition to Lilli Lehmann and the Mozarteum. From Vienna it was possible to get Reinhardt's interest and involvement; he was also meant to be the director of those 'Festivals in Salzburg which are linked to the Court Theatres', which the Emperor Charles permitted shortly before the end of the monarchy.

The Festivals opened, despite serious difficulties, in 1920 with Hofmannsthal's *Jedermann* (Everyman) in Reinhardt's production. The lack of unity between the organizational committee and the artistic advisers, and the rivalry between Festival and Mozarteum led to unnecessary tensions; in 1921 the Festival was devoted purely to Mozart. The Mozarteum organized a series of orchestral concerts and chamber concerts, a concert in the cathedral and the first serenade in the Residenz; Bernhard Paumgartner conducted nearly all of them. Richard Strauss reacted very violently to this development: he considered it quite unsuitable that he had been put on the same level as Paumgartner and feared that the whole idea of the Festival had been discredited. This thrust on his part did not go without success: in the future the planning was in his hands, and in those of Schalk, and an operatic culture was promulgated which was equal to that of spoken theatre. But that was not yet the end of the crises: in 1924 the Festival did not take place at all. It was only after the rebuilding of the Festspielhaus in 1926 and the gradual consolidation of the enterprise's finances that a basis was established for future developments.

The Festival's glory was derived from the presence of many exceptionally gifted singers and conductors who eclipsed other shortcomings: Mozart's *oeuvre* was in evidence, from his operas to his church music. The Mozarteum and other Salzburg organizations concerned themselves with lesser known works from his early years; the driving force, till 1938, was Paumgartner, whose serenades with the Mozarteum orchestra (and partly with the Vienna Philharmonic) achieved a kind of life of their own. In the Philharmonic concerts Mozart was usually played in mixed concerts under the baton of Clemens Krauss, Robert Heger, Franz Schalk, Bruno Walter, Fritz Busch, Felix von Weingartner and others; there were also concerts with soloists like Rudolf Serkin and chamber-music recitals with the Rosé and Busch quartets.

The productions of the five famous Mozart operas were as a rule the responsibility of the Vienna State Opera. Under the conductors already named the following singers were heard: Felicie Hüni-Mihacsek, Elisabeth Rethberg, Selma Kurz, Viorica Ursuleac, Richard Tauber, Helga Roswaenge, Franz Völker, Richard Mayr, Josef von Manowarda and Ezio Pinza, the great Don Giovanni. Alfred Roller's stage sets were also seen in Salzburg, together with those of Oskar Strnad and Ludwig Sievert. Lothar Wallerstein and Herbert Graf were prestigious Mozart directors. Of historical interest is the fact that when Bruno Walter did *Don Giovanni* in 1934 and *Le Nozze di Figaro* in 1937 he went over to using the original Italian text, something that Lilli Lehmann had already encouraged decades before and which was now made possible by d'Andrade's appearance on the German stage. The only Mozart opera that Arturo Toscanini conducted in Salzburg was not an Italian one, but *Die Zauberflöte*.

It is difficult to assess the musical standard of the concerts and the particular nature of the performances but we get some idea from the gramophone recordings of the 1930s and 1940s. But even if we did have more of them, and the sound quality were better, an evaluation would still be a pretty precarious business. When we compare the Mozart interpretations of Walter, Toscanini, Busch or Beecham we get a far from uniform impression. The aims of the Mozart renaissance were meant to demonstrate – in the practicalities of performance – a departure from earlier habits; but they only seemed to be partly realized.

Bruno Walter was regarded as a great Mozart conductor of the time, whose noble personality and humanity (expressed also in his writing) won everyone over. And yet I must admit that I do not like his recording of his

Salzburg *Don Giovanni*. Hectic tempi (the scene in the cemetery!), a constant wavering between urging and restraint and forced tonal effects – all this tends to produce a somewhat superficial theatricality.

My judgement is, naturally, inconsequential, and yet it does concern those performance practices which prevailed at the time. Those fast Mozart tempi which Wagner had demanded in his time seemed to have become the accepted norm; even Toscanini's Salzburg *Die Zauberflöte* seems on records to be agitated. Richard Strauss proposed 'ten golden rules' for a young *Kapellmeister*, and the ninth goes as follows: 'When you think you've reached the most extreme tempo, take it just as quickly again' – but he did revise this much later: 'If I wanted to change anything today [1948], then I'd say – Take the tempo half as quickly (for the attention of Mozart conductors!)' Wilhelm Furtwängler adopted very broadly spaced tempi with his Mozart operas. We cannot, unfortunately, answer the question whether Bruno Walter (who had, as a young man, conducted Mozart under Mahler) interpreted *Don Giovanni* as Mahler had during his time in Vienna. But his successor at the Munich Opera, Felix Mottl, did not remain free of Bayreuth influences.

A generation later it was Fritz Busch (as we hear him on recordings) who best fulfils the requirements proclaimed by the Munich reformers. At this point our attention is drawn to the British practice, a practice which now experienced a great revival. In Britain as elsewhere it was *Figaro*, *Don Giovanni* and certain orchestral works which were part of the standard repertoire, but *Die Entführung aus dem Serail* and *La Clemenza di Tito* had not been performed since 1882 and 1840 respectively, and *Die Zauberflöte* was still, as always, only known with Italian singers as the *Flauto magico* (apparently many English musicians did not realize that the work was based upon an original German text). Between the wars very little Mozart was played at Covent Garden, although Hans Richter had had great successes in 1904 with *Don Giovanni* and *Figaro*. It was Sir Thomas Beecham's devoted commitment to Mozart that brought several new initiatives into musical life after 1910: there were several attempts – attempts which were amateurish in the best sense of the term – to produce Mozart operas on smaller stages with the Munich model in mind. *Idomeneo* was performed that way in Glasgow in English (1934). But above all, there emerged in the same year from this heady atmosphere of experimentation the Glyndebourne Festival, which rapidly became known to *cognoscenti*.

This new festival enterprise was born from the initiative of the soprano Audrey Mildmay and her husband John Christie; it had its own opera house which opened on 28 May 1934 with a performance of *Figaro*. Christie, a Wagnerian, originally had other ideas, but Busch convinced him that Mozart would be ideal for the available setting. Busch had left Germany in 1933 and now sought, together with the Berliner Carl Ebert, to continue the work that they had both started in Salzburg with *Die Entführung aus dem Serail*. Rudolf Bing and Alberto Erede, both of whom would become known later, were responsible for scenery and music; members of the London Symphony Orchestra played, but there were no stars among the singers. Busch was particularly concerned to encourage a good ensemble spirit and a willingness to work hard in the ensemble scenes, at the expense of the arias. Mrs Mildmay sang Susanna, Willi Domgraf-Fassbänder was Figaro (Mariano Stabile in 1938), Aulikki Rautawaara was the Countess, Roy Henderson the Count Almaviva and Luise Helletsgruber was Cherubino.

The gramophone recordings by His Master's Voice confirmed what was always praised in the Glyndebourne performances: unforced naturalness, humour and intelligence in characterization resulting from a homogenous and detailed musical and dramatic preparation. Such polished and lively performances were to be found neither in Salzburg, Vienna, Munich, Covent Garden nor in the New York Metropolitan Opera. The five famous Mozart operas were produced before 1939: aside from *Figaro*, it was *Così fan tutte* which became the Glyndebourne opera *par excellence*, marking an actual change in both performance and understanding of Mozart.

But Glyndebourne is in no way representative for the reception as a whole. And the burden of inheritance is most clearly felt with a work like *Don Giovanni*: the *dramma giocoso* could not make its way as such. Mahler's interpretative 'relapse' was no exception. After Hermann Levi's Munich version and d'Andrade's success with the original Italian text the need was still felt, and strongly felt, to preserve the German *Don Juan* tradition: this meant that Ernst Heinemann wrote a new translation of the opera in 1904, that Felix von Weingartner followed Wagner's forgotten arrangement in a new production in Boston in 1912, that the German Stage Society awarded Karl Scheidemantel, Wagner baritone and music-teacher, a prize for his translation, and that Rainer Simons, when preparing the work for the Vienna 'Volksoper' should go back to Rochlitz's text, whereas the Court Opera still kept on using Kalbeck's translation. But Arthur Bodanzky's arrangement for Mannheim, 1914, does correspond to a modern treatment: he sought to enliven the recitatives (and his successor, Wilhelm Furt-wängler, continued this process).

In the years before and around 1920 the problems of production were much discussed and critical voices were raised against Mahler's 'rape' of this opera. From this clash of opinions only one possible common view can emerge, a view which Eugen Kilian formulated in 1917 to the effect that 'absolute piety is only necessary *vis-à-vis* the music', but 'in all textual, dramaturgical and decorative questions the great differences in the times must be considered'. To play off the spirit of Mozart's art against the older manifestations is a practice sufficiently known, and has become a tradition, but it now achieved a rigidity which would be strengthened on the one hand by Mozart philology, and on the other by theatrical production. The imminent incompatibility of the two strands of development invited solutions which would take place in a new type of scenic musicalization. The Hamburger Hans Loewenberg thus suggested portraying the actions in the usual manner but moving the arias to a place which was no longer a place, a *topos atopos*, and to have them sung as concert arias before a coloured backdrop, without gestures.

It was expressionistic interpretations above all that were regarded as modern. The slogan 'Expressionism' which seems wayward, eccentric, when applied to Mozart refers to aspects of a production which have a Romantic orientation and which attempt to exaggerate Don Giovanni's demonic qualities in an extreme manner. Ernst Lert, who also wrote a book *Mozart auf dem Theater* (Mozart and the Theatre), specifically looks back to Kierkegaard in his 1917 Leipzig production. This was no accident, considering the growing influence of the Danish thinker, but the findings might just as well have been applied to Lenau's *Don Juan*; Don Giovanni's sensuality was emphasized, a sensuality which burst forth in a sexually driven vitalism. The earlier, meaningful discussions concerning Don Giovanni's demonic nature now lose all their pathos; all that remains is wildness and tumult.

The symbols of sensual excitement become visibly real in the stage sets of Rochus Giese (1921), Oskar Strnad (1923) and Max Slevogt (1924): they are all characterized by a vibrant restlessness. According to Strnad the scene should not attempt to suggest a pictorially enclosed space, but space itself should, as such, become active: in opposition to Nietzsche's view it is now Mozart's images that leap out from the wall. This style reaches its most extreme formulation in the Berlin production of 1923 under Franz Ludwig Hörth and with sets by the architect Hans Poelzig. Here architecture and vegetation are meant to be one with the intention of 'grasping trees as ornamental contours and spraying-out architecture, allowing movement within the lines of Mozart's music'.

This kind of free treatment was meant to cover the tragedy with irony and sarcasm and to let the demonic nature of that painful laughter, of which Busoni spoke, be glaringly apparent. This may be one-sided, but it was at least a consequence of the interpretations of the nineteenth century. But what can follow this grinning demonic mask, this exaggeration of the *dramma* as well as the *giocoso*? There is only the possibility of turning back and once more loosening the extremes of tension. They had tried to reach a relaxed naturalness in Munich a generation before, hence there would be nothing new here. Apart from this, certain conceptions had been offered, so to speak, which had no historical logic but which found their justification in the peculiarities of a particular interpreter or the traditions of a particular house. The cold, clear images of the Berlin production of 1928 in the Kroll Opera House have a lot to do with the sober, modern lines of this building. It is my opinion that Mozart reception finally reaches it present form in this situation, a situation characterized by the juxtaposition of interpretations such as those at Glyndebourne and in Berlin.

Loewenberg's suggestion, which we have already mentioned, shares with Poelzig's concept (a concept which otherwise is so different), the desire principally to fuse together by a visible musicalization of drama those elements which were striving to separate. For many musicians, painters and writers of modernism the convergence with a parallel art became a support to assist the journey into virgin artistic territory. We have a famous example in the contacts between Schoenberg and Kandinsky and their mutual interest in each other's art. It was the painters above all who frequently felt drawn to music. Someone who is closely involved here is Max Slevogt who possessed a dual talent of no mean proportions and who for a long time played with the thought of being an operatic singer; his desire to find a bridge clearly stemmed from a deeply felt need.

Slevogt was first an enthusiastic Wagnerian, but later, inspired by a performance of *Don Giovanni* with d'Andrade in Munich (1894), he spontaneously found his way to Mozart. It became clear to him that Mozart 'in his inexhaustibility only gives each thing and being just as much power as it needs according to where he places it: everything, then, is nerve, race, individualization, character – everything that a painter needs for his creations'. Here Slevogt himself is enumerating those things that stimulated him in Mozart and confirmed him in his own activity. For decades he was preoccupied with both *Don Giovanni* and *Die Zauberflöte*, and it is very seldom in history that art and music have come so close to each other as in Slevogt's drawings in the margins of *Die Zauberflöte*.

There is nothing new in combining pictures with musical incipits – this is a common custom with dedications and entries into visitors' books, etc., but with Slevogt the collage-like qualities disappear in favour of a fusion of drawing and musical notation: he feels his way into Mozart's delicate, clear notation. The autograph excerpts that have been copied out have different functions in the new pictorial compositions: they can, as content, form a centre which is framed, they can also, as a surface, be part of some architectural design or, as it were, stand as a motto-panel or a banner in an open landscape.

On the page 'In diesen heil'gen Hallen' (In these sacred halls) Mozart's notation represents a grating before the entrance to his world of wisdom, reason and nature; in front of the picture Tamino is kneeling before Sarastro – this is surely based upon the iconographical representation of the prodigal son before his father. The pictorial references (biblical and mythological) on the page 'Bewahret euch vor Weibertücken' have a quite different meaning. The couples that surround the autograph from all sides – Adam and Eve, Hercules and Omphalos, Paris and Helen, Joseph and Potiphar's wife, Samson and Delilah, Judith and Holofernes show in a burlesque and drastic manner the dangers which women bring to men. And in 1924 Slevogt's wish to bring his art into contact with opera was granted in the most immediate manner: he designed the stage-sets and costumes for a new production of *Don Giovanni* in the Dresden State Opera and followed in the footsteps of Strnad and others by letting the stage area become an embodiment of an 'exuberant Baroque'.

The range from the sublime harmony in Slevogt's *Die Zauberflöte* drawings to the explosive expressiveness of Poelzig's *Don Giovanni* scenery is excessively wide. Contemporaries also felt that something much more general was being reflected in the situation that the Mozart reception found itself in. What this situation was, and how Mozart could be better understood beyond the conventional level, were questions that were being asked, with a probing urgency, by many a writer and philosopher.

A poem by Karl Kraus entitled 'Beim Anblick eines sonderbaren Plakats' (On Seeing a Remarkable Poster), which was published in October 1915, had the effect of a powerful signal for the idealization of Mozart which had been going on for decades and which the Mozart renaissance had perhaps reduced to human levels, even if it had not quite expunged it. The announcement of a performance of Mozart's *Requiem* for charitable purposes called forth Kraus's biting criticism. Kraus believed that he saw mortars everywhere on the Mozart poster – in chocolate boxes, hats, collecting boxes and also in the representation of a church window. The misery of the war, Kraus explained, distorted the 'divine music' of Mozart, brought it to an inner silence and an outward instrument of propaganda. In the requiem for Europe he saw 'the deception of God' and the cunning of the devil, and this requiem had no longer anything to do with Mozart's. And Kraus, too, does not give up the transfiguration of Mozart: he intensifies it, rather, destroying any contact between the real and ideal, and accuses this reality of blasphemy.

The spiritual disruption caused by the catastrophes of the First World War, which Kraus portrays here, demanded an assessment or stock-taking, some coming to terms with reality in which, obviously, an artistic phenomenon like Mozart and the history of his influence could not be ignored. In 1918 and 1923 the philosopher Ernst Bloch posited a 'utopian spirit' as an antidote to the prevailing desperation and emptiness; the 'philosophy of music' was of great significance here.

What Bloch says about Mozart is a summary of older ideas, but it also points beyond itself. At a first glance he seems to be sketching one of the usual models, greatly reminiscent of Wagner, even though the names and concepts are rather unusual. The first stage consists of 'an endless singing to oneself' (dance and chamber music), followed by 'the closed song, Mozart and the play-opera' and then, finally, we have 'the event-form', the 'open song, the action-opera' (Beethoven and Wagner). Mozart, according to Bloch, represents 'the (still small) secular "I" of Lucifer' and Bach 'the (also still small) spiritual Christian "I" '. Both are a sort of preliminary stage; Bloch talks about the 'still inauthentic Mozartian sonatas which have not yet come into their own'.

Die Zauberflöte, however, as a magic opera, has reached 'the first tapestry of the ontological' which, in Wagner's *Tristan* and *Parsifal*, becomes 'a gain-fulfilment'. Bloch describes Mozart's individuality with a Hoffmann paraphrase: 'Night rises, and sublime shapes draw us into their ranks', but it was 'not yet that night in which there was transformation'. Mozart, with Nietzsche, remains the 'master of Southern music': 'here and there, Rococo-like, akin to the Beyond, but otherwise of mother-of-pearl, only illuminating from without'.

Like Schumann, but more frequently, Bloch bestows on Mozart the epithet 'Grecian': he is 'the Attic counterpoint, the heathen joy, the soul conscious of itself, the emotional soul, the playful stage of the I'. The utopia does, indeed, not lie in this developmental model but rather in Bloch's method of interpreting this development as a path to the authentic, the inner, and detaches us from that which is merely chronological; it lies above all in his intention of leaving the concept of temporal, progressive observation, whereby the difference between Bach and Mozart seems to be very great, and moving across to 'a new wholeness of improved perspective', to the spatial, in which the 'senseless turbulence of progressiveness' is transcended. The impact of an historical component has necessary musical consequences, seen in the operatic world after Wagner, in symphonic music after Mahler, after the modernist experiments of the pre-war years and in the multifarious simultaneities which comes to light in the modern interpretation of Mozart operas. The apparent hopelessness of the situation is countered by Bloch who translates 'straight-line thinking' into another, different form, that of a 'parabolism of forms, which tends to an open system'. And here we have a utopia which has much in common with the motivation of Hermann Hesse's *Das Glasperlenspiel* (The Glass Bead Game) and the 'imaginary museum' of André Malraux – however different the personalities and the ideologies of the authors might be.

Before reaching a utopia in *Das Glasperlenspiel* Hesse presents the crisis in *Steppenwolf* (1927), and presents it with the urgency of an affirmation. In scarcely any other narrative work of quality does the music and the personality of Mozart occupy such a central position, and I shall therefore look at this work in some detail. The 'wolf of the steppes', Harry Haller, is no normal man, but he is one of thousands who, like Nietzsche in his age, despaired of the contemporary cultural malaise, of a world where Christ and Socrates, Mozart and Haydn, Dante and Goethe were simply 'obscure names upon rusty tin plaques surrounded by embarrassed and hypocritical mourners'.

The irrational attitude to music was in his eyes fatal for the German intellectual tradition, for it encouraged men of the spirit to dream of a language without words instead of demanding a *logos*. Haller sees himself as a 'chaos of forms, stages and conditions', as a being split in several directions where 'wolf' and 'man' stand opposite each other, the free, dangerous and strong on the one hand and the desire for goodness, tenderness, the music of Mozart, the poetry of Goethe and the ideals of humanity on the other. He feels that his life is a process of suffering without sense or goal, were it not for the momentary 'precious bubble of happiness'. There was 'a third realm' which stood open, and yet unreachable . . . 'an imaginary world, but a supreme one – the world of humour', a life of superiority, yet also understanding of the world.

Mozart inhabits a realm beyond the divisions that Haller suffers, but he is also part of Haller's human longing. He appears, consequently, in a light which is frequently changing. Put roughly, Hesse's story returns at the end to the situation at the beginning; the 'steppenwolf', meanwhile, has passed through a purgatory which has brought him to the brink of suicide. On the first pages of his 'notes' Haller speaks of how occasionally, when listening to old music, it seemed as if a door had opened into a transcendental realm, and at this moment he did not turn against anything, but praised it rather, giving his heart to everything: through music, that is, he became one with life and the world. When drinking wine in an inn he even saw Giotto's angelic hosts, and recognized in Mozart's music the golden path into the eternal.

Haller's predicament consists in an extreme alternative: either he cuts off all contact with the world of normal, middle-class attitudes by committing suicide, or he heightens, intensifies his innermost being in 'the magic theatre'. His inner world unfurls in radiant colours. Mozart is present in his impressions of childhood when he remembers Rosa, a childhood friend, and Mozart is part of the culturally zealous 'man' in Haller, part of his cultural ideal. But the 'steppenwolf' realizes the extent to which this Mozart is seen through the eyes of the bourgeois and, in his *Tractatus*, he posits an anti-bourgeois Mozart, a Mozart full of greatness in his devotion and his willingness to suffer, and an artist who knows the 'isolation in the garden of Gethsemane'. It is Haller's love for the barmaid Hermine which overcomes this self-stylization of the 'steppenwolf' in Mozart's picture; Haller feels that she sees through him completely and he admires the way in which she plays with life, living from moment to moment. And yet, on the other hand, he once more submits to the need to overload his affair with deeply serious speculations on the context of love and death. He is completely at a loss to understand the musician Pablo and treats him in an intellectually snobbish fashion; Pablo is one of Hermine's lovers, and is ready to play Mozart with the same dedication as he would the latest foxtrot. In Pablo's 'magic theatre' Haller comes face to face with his deepest desires, reflected in heightened reality, and imagines that he has killed Hermine.

There are echoes of Hoffmann's *Don Juan* novella here: over the dead body he hears, coming from the empty rooms in the depths of the theatre, the music of the approach of the 'Stone Guest' as 'though it came from the Beyond, from Infinity'. Then Mozart enters the box and disturbs Haller with his 'bright, ice-cold laughter'. This Olympian then, in conversation with Haller, ruthlessly damns the ponderous instrumentation and the waste of material in Brahms and Wagner, mocks, laughs and 'trills with his legs'. Haller seizes Mozart's pigtail, but Mozart flies away, the pigtail becomes a comet's tail and, clinging to it, Haller feels that he is being whirled through space, until he loses consciousness. When he awakens he again sees Mozart who is now dressed in modern clothes and tinkers with a wireless set, listening to a dreadful transmission of a *concerto grosso* by Handel. He explains to the infuriated Haller that there was a divine spark in this distorted manifestation; he blames Haller for being so earnest in his emotionalism, and so prepared, so ready to suffer, and he condemns him to listen to the 'accursed radio music of life' and to learn to laugh about all the fuss and

211

bother. The 'magic theatre' evaporates and turns into the 'sweet, heavy smoke' of Pablo's cigarette. Haller returns to a willingness to begin the game of life once more and in the hope of learning laughter, the naïve laughter of Pablo, and the frightening, transcendental laughter of Mozart. The 'steppenwolf' also carries across those doubts which he had entertained about the meaning of culture and the sense of his own being into his picture of Mozart, a picture stemming from conventional idealization.

In the purgatory of the 'magic theatre' we get, in a kaleidoscopic confusion and a surreal intensification, the Don Juan fantasies of Hoffmann, Mörike's image of the sounds of Mozart's music 'which fall downwards through the azure night, icy cold, transfixing both body and soul', the conservatives' ideal of Mozart's serenity, reigning supreme over the earth, and also the *fin-de-siècle* Rococo enthusiasms. But in a sober analysis it finally becomes clear that Harry Haller *did* remain true to the deepest aspects of his Mozart veneration, despite all the doubts, and to his search for something absolute. This is the end result of a plot which, apparently, simply went round in circles.

But new trials were about to confront the real world: Karl Kraus's sombre vision of a Mozart used as a propaganda tool, and of the discrepancy between the music and the conditions in which it was heard, would once more, in World War II, become reality. The sesquicentenary of Mozart's death, 1941, was celebrated in a grandiose manner in the Third Reich under the patronage of the Reich Ministry for People's Education and Propaganda. Mozart's spirit was evoked as 'an action relating to soliders in combat'; in his inaugural address for the Viennese festivals Joseph Goebbels spoke of Mozart as a 'uniter of all the nations and the peoples' and added: 'The future of our people, and of Europe as a whole, stands beneath the sign of this great German composer, in whose memory the Mozart Festivals in Vienna contemplate a symbol of those human values that are eternally valid.' The notion of Mozart's world-historical significance had already been voiced a hundred years earlier, without the point having been made, however, that the unification of the world should follow beneath a Germanic hegemony. The even older endeavour to see Mozart as a specifically German artist was now fatally discredited by Goebbels's utterance.

There were, at the beginning of the century, serious advocates who championed Mozart's Germanness, advocates such as the two philosophers Wilhelm Dilthey and the neo-Kantian Hermann Cohen who had nothing in common with the National Socialism that was about to emerge. Cohen had published his book *Die dramatische Idee in Mozarts Operntexten* (The Dramatic Idea in Mozart's Libretti) in 1915 where, in a neo-Romantic fashion, he looked back on the views prevalent at the beginning of the nineteenth century; he also uses a comparison with Shakespeare to emphasize the 'truly dramatic unity of style' (meaning a fusion of sublimity and humour). He goes on to compare *Così fan tutte* with *A Midsummer Night's Dream*, sees Mozart's greatness in a dialectical tension with the poor libretti of *Così* and *Figaro* and, as a consequence, gives his last chapter the title of 'Mozart as Man and as German'. He addresses Mozart as a 'normative, healthy genius' and as an 'original, moral personality' and admires *Die Zauberflöte* above all as it moved away from the aesthetic to the ethical (Kierkegaard, for this very reason, regarded it as a failure) and glorified 'the brotherhood of man'. Dilthey's book *Von deutscher Dichtung und Musik* (On German Music and Poetry), published posthumously in 1933, found a wide resonance; he, too, looked back to earlier concepts. For Dilthey, Mozart belonged to a type of Romantic artist, completely wrapped up in his art and remote from the world but, like Shakespeare, open to life. The formulation of the 'absolute musical genius' reminds us of Wagner, that of the 'naïvely objective genius' of Hausegger. Dilthey understands the dramatist as being the man who can, musically, join the characters together and thus can form a 'context of inwardness, portraying temperament, disposition and emotional tone'.

Many of the leading German Mozart scholars contributed to the Vienna Commemorative Album in 1941. In his preface, the poem 'To Mozart', Josef Weinheber praised 'meaningful goodness in aimless beauty'. There is, on the other hand, a frivolous sentence in Werner Egk's panegyric whose second part could have derived from Karl Barth: 'If the *Reichsmusikkammer* could turn its attention to pondering which music would be played in heaven, then it seems to me that neither Beethoven nor Wagner is the right man, nor even the pious Bruckner; the great Johann Sebastian might do for special occasions, but I think that for the normal earthly day we could only agree on Mozart.' But against whom was Egk aiming his arrows here – at religion, or the arrogance of a musical institution, or against the Wagnerian Hitler? Or perhaps against a pseudo-religious sublimity which attempted to see Mozart as an incorporation of higher powers, for example, in the case of Richard Benz, a critic greatly esteemed in those times, who maintained that '. . . an incomprehensible, demonically extra-terrestrial power is here [in Mozart] embodied and, for the eternal felicitation of all, is trapped in our fleshly being'. Finally Egk divests himself of his sovereign, sarcastic humour, compares Mozart with a little box hedge in a windy garden and dares to proclaim: 'So blossom, Mozart, in this world of ice and iron, for ever.'

Mozart as a refuge. Many must have looked upon Mozart performances in this way during the war, performances which were meant to be a digression and a self-glorification of the dictators. The Salzburg Festivals continued unabated up to and including the year 1943. With *Don Giovanni* and *Figaro* (still using Roller's sets) there was a return, after 1940, from the original Italian text to the German. Ezio Pinza (Don Giovanni) was relieved by Paul Schöffler and Mariano Stabile (Almaviva) gave way to Mathieu Ahlers-meyer and Hans Hotter. Karl Böhm and Clemens Krauss became the preferred Mozart conductors.

Far away from Europe, and on the other ideological side, Serge Koussvitsky had, since the beginning of the 1930s, been organizing in the small town of Tanglewood in Massachusetts a series of festivals which, in 1944, were exclusively dedicated to Mozart and, in 1945, to Mozart and Beethoven; these concerts became a model for others elsewhere in the USA.

Two of the most beautiful, and the most brilliant, books on Mozart written during our century were also a refuge and an affirmation: both were written by German *émigrés* – one by the writer Annette Kolb (in French in 1937 and 1938, with a preface by Jean Giraudoux) and the other by the musicologist Alfred Einstein (1947; the preface is dated 9 May 1945). In order to understand the deeper meaning of its playful earnestness we should remember the external conditions under which Einstein wrote the last sentence of his *Mozart*: 'It seemed as if the world-spirit had wished to express the fact that there was pure sound, ordered into a weightless cosmos, spirit of its own spirit, conquering all chaotic earthliness.'

To use the musical world of Mozart as a prop to surmount a sombre present is an old motif, which can have something heroic about it as a resistance to an historical process which is seen as being negative. But there is also a tradition of sweet triviality, the cultivation of homely illusions which stems more from resignation. When the writer Hans Rudolf Bartsch (who, as we know, made Schubert a 'little mushroom') published stories with the titles 'Die Schauer in *Don Giovanni*' (Terror in *Don Giovanni*), 'Die kleine Blanchefleure' and 'Mozart's Faschingsoper', we get nothing new – a belletristic nineteenth-century escapism whose store of information concedes all the more readily to a 'fair exterior'.

It is a different matter with Heinz Thies's play *Mozart* (1926) whose subtitle is 'His life, portrayed after a strict perusal of the historical sources'. We get just as little of a documentary drama with Thies as we get a scholarly illumination in the trivial writing of famous musicologists (A. Schurig, H.J. Moser, P. Nettl, E. Decsey) of the 1920s. But there were other, more suggestive forms of trivialization. The first talking film about Mozart, *Wolfgang Amadeus Mozarts Leben und Lieben*, was made in 1930 by Karl Freiherr von Bienerth and Friedrich Graf von Beck-Rzikowsky. In 1931 the

214

first radio play of this kind was broadcast in Vienna, Bernhard Paum-gartner's *Aus Mozarts letzten Tagen* (From Mozart's Last Days). Mozart was also the theme in von Bienerth's and von Beck-Rzikowsky's *Ariane* (1930, with Elisabeth Bergner), a feature film whose plot is loosely based on E.T.A. Hoffmann: a performance of *Don Giovanni* in the Kroll Opera House is entangled with the personal life of the woman protagonist.

The year 1945 brought neither a fundamental change in the trivial, nor in the discriminating, conceptions of Mozart; problems concerning the truthfulness of any kind of reference to him were also unresolved. But from a quantitative point of view we may claim that the upward trend in Mozart's reception, up to and beyond the year 1956, has been enormous, indeed immeasurable. The 1981–2 season in the Federal Republic saw the following new productions: *Bastien und Bastienne* (Gelsenkirchen); *Così fan tutte* (Augsburg, Bonn, Coburg, Dortmund, Gelsenkirchen, Kassel, Mönchen-gladbach); *Don Giovanni* (Hildesheim, Krefeld, Wiesbaden); *Die Entführung aus dem Serail* (Bremen, Darmstadt, Frankfurt, Heidelberg, Ulm); *La finta giardiniera* (Essen); *Idomeneo* (Berlin, Pforzheim); *Figaro* (Kaiserslautern, Kiel, Lübeck, Osnabruck, Saarbrücken); *Il sogno di Scipione* (Bayreuth); *Die Zauberflöte* (Aachen, Düsseldorf, Eutin, Hamburg, Mainz, Münster, Nürn-berg, Oberhausen, Rheydt). Between 1955 and 1965 over 18,000 Mozart operas were performed on German stages, and something like 4,000 of these were of *Die Zauberflöte*.

There is no better indication of the determination to preserve what was light and gay in the world of art than the programme for the reopening of the Salzburg Festivals on 12 August 1945. A Mozart serenade was heard first, followed by music by Johann Strauss and Franz Lehár. The opera performances of the post-war years, in Vienna and Salzburg, were distinguished by the playing of that famous Viennese Mozart Ensemble whose passing is mourned today as something irretrievable. Many of its members (Schöffler, Kunz, Cebotari, Hann, Patzak, Cunitz, Dermota) had already been known in Mozart roles before the war; the main difference was, however, that in Salzburg this Ensemble sang in Italian again and that its chief conductor was Josef Krips (in 1948 Karajan conducted *Figaro*, Furtwängler did *Die Zauberflöte* in 1949 and *Don Giovanni* in 1950, and Böhm did *Così fan tutte* in 1953). The new version of *La Clemenza di Tito* (Paumgartner and H. Curjel) had no success in 1949.

Apart from the operas we should not forget the evenings when Edwin Fischer played the piano concertos and, naturally, the return of Paumgartner to Salzburg. One novelty which was not greatly appreciated was a Paumgartner concert with the Vienna Philharmonic in 1946 where the obbligato piano part in the aria K. 505 was played on a 'Walter grand piano from the time of Mozart'. The idea of the 'whole' Mozart, of faithfulness to the original, was even beginning to dawn at this, the biggest Mozart festival. But, as always, it was the opera which had the greatest international resonance. The Vienna Mozart Ensemble, for example (the members now included Schwarzkopf, Güden, Seefried and Jurinac), achieved great acclaim during their guest performances at Covent Garden in 1947. In 1950 Glyndebourne reopened after a gap of eleven years. As regards the other new productions – and there were many of them – the following were especially noteworthy: *Don Giovanni* in Berlin, with stage sets by J. Fenneker (1946); *Figaro* in Düsseldorf, with stage sets by R. Pudlich (1947); *Don Giovanni* in Munich, under Solti and R. Hartmann, with sets by H. Jürgens (1949); *Die Zauberflöte* at La Scala, Milan, and *Così fan tutte*, Weimar (1950); Hans Gal's new version of *Idomeneo* in Glyndebourne, under Busch (1951); and also *Die Zauberflöte* in East Berlin in 1954, in Felsenstein's production.

The activities associated with the bicentenary of Mozart's birth in 1956 demonstrate the extent to which the cultivation of Mozart had grown within the decade which had elapsed since the war ended. Every country which regarded itself as a cultured nation felt obliged as a matter of honour to hold official celebrations. But despite the plenitude of events we can recognize a certain amount of evaluation. Inevitably the 'Mozart Jubilee' was celebrated in Austria with great magnificence, especially in Vienna and Salzburg, by every conceivable musical institution and in every conceivable manner, from the 'Seventh Salzburg Mozart Festival' to the Viennese Mozart Congress; genuine devotion was here bound up with cultural politics in this 'Country of Music'.

Interest in all the German-speaking countries (and in German-speaking areas such as South Tyrol and parts of Holland) was scarcely less than in Austria: a chronicle published by the Mozarteum, *Mozart in aller Welt*, listed no fewer than eighty-four places in the Federal Republic where events had been organized. In Czechoslovakia (instrumental music above all), France (Paris, of course, but also the Aix-en-Provence Festival) and England (concerts by the leading London orchestras under Krips, Klemperer and Sargent) the intensity of dedication to Mozart was a natural historical development; the same was true in Belgium, Luxemburg and the Scandinavian countries. Mozart was especially remembered in Rome, Milan, Naples and Verona, towns where he had appeared as a child.

Outside Europe it was the USA which organized the most in the way of Mozart events; there were also many in Central and South America. We should also list events in Egypt, Morocco, Israel, Lebanon, South Africa,

India, Vietnam, Japan (in connection with the Mozart Society which had been founded in Tokyo in 1955) and in the People's Republic of China (there was a 'Memorial Concert for W.A. Mozart, the Genius of World Culture' in the newly built State Opera House in Peking). The Mozart Societies, spread throughout the world, were the driving force behind much of this.

During a conference in 1984 in Salzburg the academics, producers, literary managers and singers who were present were asked the question: Why do we play and hear so much Mozart nowadays? Most of them were surprised by this, and responded: Because he's there. There is a tradition of loving his work, and of regarding his mastery as undisputed – but history also teaches us that this was not always the case. It would, then, be worthwhile to think about why we are experiencing a high point in Mozart admiration and in the cultivation of his work. The chronicle for the year 1991 will doubtless be much thicker than it was in 1956. The quantity, as well as the temporal proximity, hinders us from gaining an overall perspective of the Mozart reception of the last three decades; the dilemma which provoked decisions half a century ago has not been proved redundant, but simply overwhelmed by the great flood of enthusiasm for Mozart and the resulting commercialism.

The growth of knowledge about Mozart's work, noticeable since the beginning of the century, has also brought with it a shift of evaluation of the content. The reassessment of *Così fan tutte* is symbolic here: the productions at Glyndebourne demonstrated this, as did the Böhm-Schuh production of 1953 and the Böhm-Rennert version in Salzburg from 1961 onwards. The growth of interest in the juvenilia, particularly as regards instrumental music, brought about something similar. This may look like a one-sided judgement, but it seems to me that the demonic element which Alfred Heuss claimed to have discovered, and which was exaggerated by the Expression-istic production of *Don Giovanni*, was matched – and even eclipsed – by the need, particularly in times of darkness, to find a new, a gayer world. The anti-Romantic stance of the young, and the neo-Classicism of the time before World War II certainly played a part.

For decades the driving force behind the investigation into Mozart's instrumental music was the anti-star conductor Paumgartner who combined a personal charisma with a method of leading the orchestra which was both spirited and awkward (like Paul Hindemith). His matinées (from 1949 onwards) breathed the fresh air of a light-hearted musicality which had been elevated to the concert platform. The ideal (which seemed at first esoteric) of having Mozart as a whole, with his complete *oeuvre* before one, became an institution in the Salzburg 'Mozart Week' which has been organized by the

International Mozarteum Foundation in the last week of January every year since 1956.

Throughout the years it has not only been the concert music in the strictest sense of the term (and even including off-beat works such as the Handel arrangements) which has been on offer: a series of concert performances of all the youthful operas was completed, works which since have all been available on record. Some of these were independently presented on stage during the Salzburg Festivals (in 1960 *La finta semplice*, in 1965 *La finta giardiniera*, in 1967 *Ascanio in Alba*, in 1969 *Bastien und Bastienne* and, in 1970, *Mitridate*). A most recent phenomenon – a reaction, perhaps, in favour of sublimity? – is a revaluation of Mozart's *opera seria*, something which has developed out of the endlessly unfortunate attempts at arrangements for *Idomeneo*. Since 1973 *Idomeneo* and *La Clemenza di Tito* have each been performed sixty-five times. *Mitridate* was done in Schwetzingen, Zurich and Aix-en-Provence, and *Lucio Silla* was put on in Zurich, La Scala, Milan and finally under Patrice Chéreau in Brussels.

All these efforts have brought us closer to an unfamilar Mozart; the distance between Mozart and his contemporaries has also become more understandable to us even though we cannot simply reduce it to a personal development from imitativeness to qualitative superiority. The genius of early Mozart, a genius which has nothing to do with conventionality, makes his separateness seem all the more emphatic. But despite this gain the attempt to encourage the cultivation of the whole of Mozart has not remained unchallenged. Doubts were expressed that such a picture might unfavourably distort the reception of his masterpieces, thereby even damaging Mozart's reputation; the best works of his contemporaries, works which are scarcely ever peformed, might also be disadvantaged. Such objections should give us pause, for they have not been invalidated in practice; the task of future 'Mozart Weeks' might be to provide a more dynamic picture than heretofore.

It is both remarkable, and at the same time enlightening, to see that the most vigorous attempts at interpreting Mozart have been confined over the last few decades – as they were around 1800 – to the same works: *Die Zauberflöte* and *Don Giovanni*. We should not see this as a capitulation to old habits – on the contrary, the long tradition of interpretation, and its inability to satisfy the demands of the present, is, apparently, more able to provide a challenge than the 'unknown' or a 'lighthearted' Mozart.

There is an unambiguous preference for *Die Zauberflöte*, particularly in German-speaking countries but also elsewhere (Toscanini's conscious commitment to this opera in Italy, where it had always been an alien work, is symptomatic). The admiration for *Don Giovanni* did not decrease, but its interpretation – apart from the conventional ones – became frequently extravagant, a situation which seems inevitable given the extreme positions which had already been taken up in the 1920s. This extravagance usually consisted of a one-sided over-emphasis on a particular aspect of interpretation.

This tendency – still fairly moderate – was apparent in the new production during the Salzburg Festival of 1953: in the 'Felsenreitschule' Clemens Holzmeister built a 'Don Giovanni city' (as he had built a 'Faust city' in 1933 for Max Reinhardt). *Don Giovanni* emerged from Salzburg's dreams of the Baroque as a mystery-play (in Herbert Graf's production, supported by Furtwängler's tempi, which were broad and solemn) – a restriction of the piece, but one which received more lively features in compensation due to the stage presence of Cesare Siepi and Elisabeth Schwarzkopf.

Walter Felsenstein's Berlin production of 1966 took a completely different direction. Felsenstein took up, after forty years, the old Expressionist interpretation again and cleansed it of all traces of Romanticism and Italianism: the hero was for him no longer a demon or an exceptional man but an insatiable muscle-man, entirely worthy of his social surroundings.

The word 'extravagance' used to describe these tendencies is even more valid for the psychoanalytical components than for the social aspects: already in 1922 Otto Rank had discovered an Oedipus complex in Don Giovanni, and regarded Leporello as a *Doppelgänger* representing his master's fear and conscience. In 1964 Brigid Brophy took up Freud's idea that the characters on the stage are projections from the subconscious of their creator; she also used the old Mozart-Shakespeare parallel to interpret *Don Giovanni* – very freely, after *Hamlet* – as a work which, appearing shortly after the death of Mozart's father, resulted from feelings of guilt, feelings which prevented Mozart from unambiguously punishing Don Giovanni for the sin of patricide.

From this angle, however, Da Ponte and his predecessors who handled the Don Juan material should also have suffered comparable feelings of guilt. Complexes and guilt feelings are difficult to portray on a stage in an immediate and effective manner; the impulses of many a production to uncover and analyse stems unmistakably from psychoanalysis, and its results betray without doubt a new kind of emotionalism.

This also emerges in experiments which, originally, had a completely different motivation. For his Spoleto Festival ('The Festival of Two

219

Worlds') Gian-Carlo Menotti gained the services of the great English sculptor and designer Henry Moore to do the sets for *Don Giovanni*; Menotti became completely won over to Moore's desire to produce an impression of extreme oppression. One critic complained that 'Mozart was not present in this piece'.

It is often the case that the producer is ogling contemporary trends which have nothing to do with Mozart: he does this on the one hand to try to bring Mozart up to date or, on the other hand, to give momentum to a contemporary event by adding Mozart to it. The Theater Carré of Amsterdam put on a piece called *Reconstructie* in 1969, a musical composition by young Dutch musicians which showed Don Giovanni as the tool of American imperialism in South America; his sexual athletics became a stupid symbol of political power. Peter P. Pachl called his Kassel production (1981) a 'cerebral game in an abstract model of a human brain' and offered blatant science-fiction associations.

The feminists triumphed (or satirized themselves) in a *Donna Giovanna* which seven emancipated Mexican actresses took on a successful world tour; a report on the ladies ('who emasculated Mozart's *Don Giovanni*') in the weekend newspaper *Die Zeit* bears the headline: 'What would Wolfi have said?' The oppressive effect of a didactic intention (underlined by a raised index finger) is also found in those productions which eschew magic both old and new: when August Everding, in his Paris production in 1975, leaves out the Stone Guest in the second finale we are left with the question as to what the music that Mozart composed for the character is supposed to mean. It is, of course, different with Max Frisch's *Don Juan oder die Liebe zur Geometrie* (1953), for without the music the idea of letting Don Juan organize his own collapse for the benefit of society, as that frivolous jest which it is meant to be, *does* work.

Die Zauberflöte also entered the field of the modernists, but in a way which had not yet been subjected to quite such a variety of interpretative adventures. But the plenitude of possibilities, paired with a similar range between *seria* and *buffa*, fascinated both theoreticians and practitioners. It was only a case of repressing the Egyptian-style architecture, the over-heavy decorations and the hyper-Germanness of *Die Zauberflöte* (which was intangible anyway) to allow space for new interpretations. Surprisingly enough, it was not the *comedia*-elements that were accentuated (although the revival of *opera buffa* might have been relevant here), but it was as a fairy-tale (*Märchen*) or mystery-play that *Die Zauberflöte* received its wealth of interpretation.

The reason for this was not so much some unwelcome inheritance in the history of its reception as a concrete example of the influence of Richard Wagner. Arthur Drews, in 1906, had pointed out the points of similarity between *Die Zauberflöte* and Wagner's *Parsifal*; Ludwig Sievert's Mannheim production in 1916 applied this comparison. Its conception took as a starting point the belief that *Die Zauberflöte* was 'neither a philosophically nor an historically tendentious play', that it 'had very little to do with Freemasonry and absolutely nothing to do with Egypt' but was, by contrast, 'a Fairy-tale Mystery'. Sievert tried to produce a symbolic world by his use of colour (bluish violet for the Queen of the Night, yellowish-white for Sarastro, and bright colours for Papageno).

In the wake of this type of production the stage itself became increasingly significant, and decoration was banished. Ewald Dülberg used abstract constructions in the Kroll Opera House in 1930. In Munich (1970) Josef Svoboda dissolved the boundaries between time and space by using modern technology and creating a 'fourth stage-dimension'. The trial by fire and water became a play of light which he produced by the reflection of laser beams on to glass structures. A neutral space, intensified use of lighting and a clear, constant symbolism confirm a direction similar to that taken by Wieland Wagner in his production of *Parsifal*. It is not so much the psychoanalysis of Freud as C. G. Jung's doctrine of archetypes which provides the points of reference here.

It is frequently the fairy-tale element which is emphasized rather than the mystery-play: Jürgen Rose's stage sets for the 1978 Munich production provided an extremely successful ambience. Ingmar Bergman combined fantasy and naïve directness, dream and nightmare, the timeless and the historical, to produce a tender fairy-tale. Mozart had certainly not envisaged a psychoanalytical interpretation of dreams, but Bergman, through the medium of film, dissolves this 'misinterpretation' into a world of images which touches everyone with the familiar atmosphere of childhood memories.

It is probable that similar intimate depths of the soul in Marc Chagall (New York 1967), Oskar Kokoschka (Salzburg 1955 and Geneva 1964), Ernst Fuchs (Hamburg 1977) and – why not? – David Hockney (Glyndebourne 1978), inspired the wish to decorate *Die Zauberflöte* with oversized panels; these interpretations seem to be megalomaniac in their desire to enfold Mozart's music like the cloak of the Madonna and to project it as a part of their own being – they must, surely, be erroneous. But he who has a feeling for Chagall's colours and ciphers will also be able to appreciate his dream-vision of *Die Zauberflöte* and to understand the truth of his confession that, for the whole of his life, he had sought to paint his feelings about nature and to

221

'hear' this nature 'out of' Mozart's music. Chagall's Mozart is a different Mozart from Kokoschka's, as the expressive colour values of their painting are different.

Beyond this, Ernst Fuchs achieved distance from himself by functionalizing his own fantastic realism, assigning it to the sensuous sphere in *Die Zauberflöte* and using elemental, abstract forms for the spiritual world of the priests as a counterpoint. Reciprocal reflections were elevated to a principle in the stage sets of the pop artist David Hockney who made the history of the work's interpretation into a puzzle consisting of the best-known *Die Zauberflöte* pictures; these were illuminated, skilfully mounted and given new frames. Hockney expressly had the music of Mozart in mind when he created his sets with such freshness and clarity; who would deny that his idea was a right one?

When we are listing all these examples, the question arises as to the point of all these different interpretations: I would like to press this further. The history of the productions of *Die Zauberflöte* in the Salzburg Festivals gives adequate material. It became the practice there for the new productions of those Mozart operas which were played time and time again to take a stance *vis-à-vis* their predecessors, both from a scenic as well as a musical point of view.

Böhm and Krauss, who succeeded Toscanini in 1937, were themselves followed in 1949 by Furtwängler, a conductor who had a completely different concept. Herbert Graf was the musical director in 1937 and also in 1955, when he collaborated with Georg Solti and Oskar Kokoschka. After Günther Rennert (in 1959 with Szell) and Otto Schenk (in 1963 with Kertesz), Oskar Fritz Schuh attempted (after his production in 1949) to try something quite different in 1967 with Sawallisch. Schuh quite explicitly stated his opinion that the tendency to look back to the Raimund era, to mystery-plays and fairy-tales, was no longer a viable possibility: a sense of surfeit would soon become apparent. Schuh, together with Teo Otto, his stage designer, wanted to create 'a panorama of life', but their interpretation focused on the somewhat manneristic notion of the labyrinth.

The 'theatre-magic' of machines made visible also occurs in 1974 with Giorgio Strehler and Karajan, but under different circumstances. Strehler wished to create an 'original fairy-tale, an eternal childhood' again; his successor, however, found that the 'fairy-tale is not sufficiently interesting', although many producers (including Götz Friedrich in Hamburg in 1978) showed they had been influenced by Adorno's statement that many of the 'most authentic operas' (and he included *Die Zauberflöte*) had their 'true right of abode in the awareness of childhood'. Jean-Pierre Ponnelle's concept of

222

an 'unencoded parable' probably owes its great success since 1978 to its unpretentious appearance; he worked together with Levine. The stage is not animated by tendentious profundities, nor by their stilted parodies, but by human beings of flesh and blood; even the Queen of the Night speaks to Tamino in Act One with both feet firmly on the ground. But what could follow this unusual naturalness? In 1978 August Everding too, in his Munich production, put Papageno into the middle of the action, but more so than Ponnelle; he played up the element of the old Viennese popular comedy. Ruth Berghaus, in her Frankfurt production of 1980, sought to cut the magic out of *Die Zauberflöte*, whereas Achim Freyer (in 1982 in Hamburg) transported it smoothly into a fantastic world of interlocking images. Berghaus portrayed a battle of the sexes which permits of no apotheosis; with Freyer the whole thing is Tamino's dream in which the Queen of the Night and Sarastro appear as bogeymen. Peter Mussbacher (in 1982 in Kassel) makes everything cryptic, odd and humourless (Papageno becomes an elderly little man).

It was Karl Schumann who gave the most priceless formulation of the confusion of quid pro quos surrounding Mozart productions (and not only *Die Zauberflöte*):

A lavish production of *Don Giovanni* on a simultaneous stage, before scenery belonging to an open-air theatre, with and without the G major finale of the second act; *Le Nozze di Figaro* with the social characteristics of the individual actors developed according to a thorough examination of Beaumarchais's text and reinterpreted as a blatant farce of sexual urges and desires, then sublimated into a comedy of emotional responses linked to the Comedia dell'arte with its types and its *coups de théâtre*; *Die Entführung* done as a puppet show, a childish, jokey story about cheated Turks, or else enriched with sentimental *Werther* quotations; *Così fan tutte* as a piece of threadbare frivolity, as a primitive farce of mistaken identity or as an ironic play on the dubiousness of human feelings; *Die Zauberflöte* done as an extravagant and uncontrolled spectacle with reminiscences of popular Viennese drama, also as a deeply stirring sermon to humanity, and also as a simple fairy-tale; Mozart in the peep show, in temporary accommodation, on prestigious stages, in the open air, in parks and in front of architectural settings, Mozart done in court theatres and experimental theatres in front of black curtains – all these variations . . . have been experienced recently.

Schumann wrote this in 1960, and it is just as valid today; both Jean-Pierre

223

Ponnelle in his television production of *Figaro* (1977) and Peter Zadek in his piece of social grotesquerie (1983) continued to play Beaumarchais off against Mozart and Da Ponte. An Augsburg production of 1962 involuntarily caused a further stir. Hans-Ulrich Schmückle the stage designer had used details from some rather suggestive paintings by Boucher, Fragonard, Carracci and Buonascari and displayed them in a very conspicuous manner. A letter to the press was a harmless beginning, but the emotions aroused became so extreme that the public prosecutor became involved and a whole host of Mozart specialists (and opera specialists in general) had to go to Augsburg to visit the scene of the crime, of the obscene *Figaro*, before the proceedings could be dropped. But even this was not a new event if we remember the notorious trial of Schnitzler's *La ronde* in Berlin in 1921. Although everything goes round in circles every interpreter is convinced that he can come up with just the right thing; this is a law of life.

To find the way out of this circle a producer needs something that transcends what is merely of interest for the moment – and this inevitably has to do with ideology. And if ideology is paired with imagination and precision, as in the case of Walter Felsenstein, then this can be the genesis of a whole school of interpretation. Stephan Stompor, in his essay 'Mozart als Musik-dramatiker heute', gives a summary of its theoretical principles. Stompor argues that, in order to see Mozart's work in the sense of a 'modern musical theatre', we have to presuppose the working out of a basic humanistic nucleus in each of his operas. In Stompor's view, *Die Entführung* is concerned with life and death, freedom and slavery; *Figaro* is a realistic statement which has to take as its starting point Figaro's aria 'Does then the Count dare to dance with me': both here, and in *Don Giovanni*, any kind of 'Rococo gloss' must be rejected. He also refers back to Kierkegaard to explain Don Giovanni's destruction as a consequence of his asocial way of life; with *Così fan tutte* we must have an actual, unvarnished Rococo, and hence an ironic, critical attitude.

However, the hope that it is precisely this kind of Mozart interpretation that would enable music theatre to become 'a truly popular theatre of sublimity, edification and ethical artistic presentation' is countered by that imaginative flair which encourages us to dare to be outrageous. It is not so much in the case of Felsenstein himself as with his successors in the former German Democratic Republic, people like Götz Friedrich, Joachim Herz, Harry Kupfer and Ruth Berghaus, who represent a variety of different interpretative directions which willy nilly lose their bearings and end up in the circle yet again.

During the Salzburg opera discussions in 1984 Ruth Berghaus claimed,

'We have broken with the tradition of operatic performance.' But how could it be broken? In many of its details, and by using many of the Mozartian topoi, it reaches back into the eighteenth century; the superabundance of self-cancelling interpretations, at most, might be a break with the past. The need which Berghaus feels to educate and inform – we see this in her controversial Frankfurt production of *Die Entführung* (1981) where she interpreted Constanze's 'Tortures' aria as a bleak visualization of acts of violence – aims at the specific quality of an unadorned veracity. To achieve this we need an act of emancipation with which, here and now, we may penetrate that riddle of the artistic work, a mystery of which Berghaus has been speaking. In recent years this notion has been anything but uncommon, and corresponds more or less to what Adorno meant when he referred to the 'darkness' of a work of art. But it is questionable whether or not the interpreter is thus actually serving to assist in the unfolding of a Hegelian world spirit or simply spinning in a circle of subjective extravagance.

Admittedly, the word extravagance has too negative a connotation. In my opinion, criticism should rather be directed at that hypocritical tendency of making Mozart's works which have, ostensibly, become incomprehensible, relevant to the present age, the urge, apparently, to establish connections between the eighteenth and the twentieth centuries. At any rate, most of the audiences are not convinced that Mozart's works will be made more accessible by interpretations based on the concept of a 'broken tradition'.

Interest at large is concentrated much more readily on the sensational value of something suspected of being blasphemous. If I said before that the search for new and for old starting points in an interpretation springs from an aversion to what is in existence (an aversion due to satiety), this, too, is only half the truth. I see the positive thing about 'producer's theatre' in a procedure which the interpreters themselves generally deny. Every performance of an opera, a symphony, etc., brings with it the creation of something actual and topical. It is equally understandable that there are reasons why it is the undisputed masterpieces that are interpreted most, and also 'extravagantly'.

The situation is as follows: the topicality of Mozart opera – that is, its vitality – stems from the music. This music has survived, and with it a tradition of performance has arisen, an intimacy with the work as a whole; there has also arisen a certain complacency and a sloppiness, but also the need to change something in the accepted conventions. No one disputes the current need to clear the clutter away from such a masterpiece, both as regards its practical presentation and its inner spirit – an intermediary, however, is unnecessary, as it is brought about anyway by the music, no matter how badly it is played, and particularly in an age where every note-head of a Mozart score is regarded as sacrosanct. It is the legitimate interest of every interpreter to project his artistic message across the footlights. Even in cases where this interpretation is unusual it is neither a disruptive factor nor an illegal commentary on the work – but neither is it an auxiliary nor an intermediary. It becomes more of an 'art about an art'.

A basis is provided by the familiarity with, and the quality of, the music, together with the traditional methods of production (and, as well, the tradition of musical performance itself) with which a sovereign game may be enacted or, in opposition, another level posited. From this tension between what is seen and heard in a performance and what is presupposed as being familar and, as it were, objective, an imaginary act of reciprocal reflection arises – the aesthetic utterance, which presupposes that the audience also has knowlege and imagination. That is, in the midst of these multifarious interpretations it is only the expert who is able to manoeuvre in a meaningful manner, an expert who brings his own guides to orientation. This smacks of *Das Glasperlenspiel* and the 'imaginary museum', also of Bloch's utopia. But it is more than *l'art pour l'art*, for the artistic event can become a breakthrough to the truth, truth understood also from a social-critical point of view. It does not become 'popular theatre', but rather something esoteric. It is precisely the history of Mozart reception which teaches us how much art demands expertise and connoisseurship in order not only that there should be something essentially exclusive, but also that masterpieces should indeed be capable of supporting the most 'extravagant' reinterpretations.

Even though it was the production of operas which reached out to the largest audiences, it was the purely instrumental music which appealed most to self-assured experts. The relationship between producer and conductor should not be one of rivalry, but it cannot be denied that where a theatre is at its most demanding as regards production, even if it is most sensitive to the presence of music, it does tend to draw the audience's attention at the cost of the actual music itself. The conspicuous diminishing of ambitious production ploys (conspicuous, that is, in contrast to other operas) in the history of *Così fan tutte* performances encouraged the awareness of the great musical achievements in ensemble-singing and in conducting, which succeeded in Glyndebourne and in Salzburg time and time again. Karl Böhm, who conducted in Salzburg until 1977, was succeeded (after 1982) by Riccardo Muti who was able, like Böhm himself, to achieve the status of an outstanding Mozart conductor. When Agnes Baltsa, who sang the part of

Dorabella, expressed the view that Muti had brought out the work's 'evil' quality, then this means nothing less than the fact that a musical interpretation could, demonstrably, bring about a reinterpretation, moving away from a light-hearted game towards a psychologizing of the opera. Its balanced and complete realization is a credit to the tasteful production of Michael Hampe.

The image of the spinning circle in which the search for originality revolves is, in principle, also valid for the interpretation of Mozart's instrumental music. Conductors, soloists, orchestras, concert agencies and record companies react to the appropriate competition. The goad to achieve superlative performances is already present, yet, in Mozart's case, the public's expectations are not directed at sensational interpretations. This image does not derive so much from the music as from the history of its interpretation. We are baffled at first by Arthur Honegger's statement (1956) that Mozart is 'a composer who is not particularly appreciated by the audiences at large concerts, and not particularly well known'. Honegger is certainly exaggerating, and a lot has changed since his time, and yet his complaint that it is still always the last three symphonies that are played may be confirmed by looking in the record catalogues. Orchestral practice and the general feeling of the repertoire suggest that Mozart, as a composer, is placed somewhere in front of Beethoven; his music is either seen in approximation to Beethoven to give it weight, or else, on the same basis, diluted to a form of light-hearted introduction.

It is difficult to provide an exact analysis of interpretation practices. The Bielerfeld catalogue, for example, for 1980/1 lists the enormous number of thirty-two different recordings on record of the *Jupiter* symphony obtainable on the German market. Böhm and Karajan each have four different versions. The range reaches from a version of Bruno Walter's with the New York Philharmonic to one of the Collegium Aureum. With a large – and often imprecise – orchestral apparatus Walter prefers a heavy-handed playing (the minuet), with tempi which are broad and lavish (the *andante cantabile*). Ferenc Fricsay has the RIAS Berlin Symphony Orchestra play in a taut and very quick tempo (the finale); the contrasts which unexpectedly break in have their model in Fricsay's famous Bartok interpretations. The recording with the highest technical standards as regards playing is that with the Berlin Philharmonic under Böhm: in contrast to Walter, Böhm's version is musically precise and unsentimental. Yet these three very different interpretations begin to resemble one another when compared with the version of the 25-member Collegium Aureum Ensemble, who play old instruments. The slim tone encourages a liveliness with the moderate tempi and an unforced balance between strings and woodwind.

Has the cult of 'the authentic' brought anything new into performance practice? The desire to cleanse Mozart's music of distortions has been an ambition since the beginning of the Mozart renaissance of this century. It has, apparently, got nowhere, even if it does keep bringing novelties in its train. Faithfulness to the original has to seek its way between the letter and the spirit of music, and hence became 'that concept which is most dearly misunderstood', as its advocate Paumgartner explained. Concerts in castles in the summer months, with musicians dressed in livery and wearing wigs, have nothing to do with authenticity; the historical exteriors have a similarly stimulating function to the use of Mozart's music in advertising – it is meant to ennoble something. But the more serious, pragmatic approach has its dangers. The urge to achieve historical veracity in music can lead to a false rigidity – false, because research into the performance practices of Mozart's time show that these practices were going through a period of transition and were by no means strictly uniform. The tension between spirit and letter is, besides, linked to the necessity of obtaining a compromise between a historical difference of quality on the one hand and a commitment to the practices of the present on the other.

The success of Nikolaus Harnoncourt has, in the last analysis, confirmed this interrelationship. What is surprising here is that Harnoncourt took Baroque music as his starting point in his interpretations and did not approach Mozart via the repertoire of the nineteenth and twentieth centuries. And his willingness to collaborate with famous orchestras and with soloists who were not used to playing on old instruments and adhering to the older techniques is also somewhat extraordinary – eventually even with the Vienna Philharmonic and Gidon Kremer. The remarkable thing about this readiness can also, naturally, be seen the other way round, from the point of view of those who have 'made it' in matters Mozartian. Harnoncourt scarcely makes concessions in articulation, dynamics, rhythmics or choice of tempo. He also remains true to the opposite image, that of a four-square desk virtuoso, but his sense of mission, a very convincing one, is in its own way second to none.

Harnoncourt understands music 'as speaking sound'. Even if here he takes Bach and Monteverdi as his starting point his approach – leaving aside historicity in instrumental practice – is not fundamentally new. Weill spoke of a gestic character; Yehudi Menuhin reports that George Enescu impressed upon him in 1932 that Mozart had always been a dramatist in music, 'a musician of syllables and gestures'. Harnoncourt was concerned with shaped, moulded details, details built up in a richly contrasting fashion. He let himself be led by the older concept (pre-Classical above all) that

228

music was primarily an event of performance, of surprise; conductors like Muti, however, tend also (from the other side) to reach a *ciaroscuro*, a Mozart in the guise of 'dialectical composer'. Even Karl Böhm, in old age, rejected both a heroic and a Rococo Mozart and confessed that, increasingly, he learned to recognize 'the image of the revolutionary' in Mozart: 'In contrast to the charming, graceful aspects, he had his fiery, even his Faustian side.' However difficult it may be in practice to realize this polarity it was often encouraged, beginning historically with the Mozart-Shakespeare comparisons. It is a matter of taste as to which interpretation fits best, or most correctly, today; the juxtaposition of varying solutions doubtless has its appeal. At present the Vienna Philharmonic plays Mozart with James Levine (as it did with the late Leonard Bernstein) as well as with Harnoncourt.

Some complain about the highly elaborate (or 'camp') admiration of the interpretation-circus; others praise variety as the enterprise of the workshop. Where should we stand in all this? The question is also valid with the following discrepancy: since the beginning of the record industry Mozart has, worldwide, been at the top of the list of serious music as regards availability, sales, and, probably, application as well. In 1982 Harnoncourt, like others before him, commented on this obvious appreciation of Mozart's work and expressed the following reservation: 'In practice, however, there is very little interest in the greater part of his *oeuvre*, and those works which are preferred have a lesser stature: this is readily admitted.'

The age-old cliché about complaints concerning today's lack of standards has accompanied the reception of Mozart ever since its origins and should not be regarded as the dramatic argument that many a histrionic gesture might suggest. The extreme reactions of the great outsiders in our musical life (we could also call them artists who are suffering from having become establishment figures) continue to bear witness to the fact that Mozart still poses a challenge.

This is particularly true in the case of the pianists. For many of them, Mozart's works remained a beautiful, and a tricky, preface to a great literature; many found a balance (Edwin Fischer, Arthur Schnabel, Wilhelm Backhaus); many concentrated on Mozart (incomparably Clara Haskil). In most recent times the extreme positions have been taken up most clearly by Friedrich Gulda and Glenn Gould. Gulda plays evenings which are pure Mozart, preferably under the title 'Mozart for the people'; in his execution there is faithfulness to the spirit of the work ignoring all the conventions. The escalating arguments between Gulda and the agencies, the critics and the audiences and his struggle for 'up-to-date musical endeavours' (which he himself chooses and evaluates in an unusual manner) are all based on an understanding of Mozart as a phenomenon which Gulda wishes to save from the grasp of 'the paralysed centenarians'. Gulda, certainly, continues to compromise himself – as a Mozart-figure or our age? In any case, Mozart remains for him a symbol for musical presence and novelty.

The Canadian Glenn Gould, a lover of overcast, rainy skies, did not like Mozart, that is, he did not like the radiant Apollonian image. And yet he had the Mozart conductor Josef Krips as a highly esteemed and paternal friend. Gould was often provocative, calling Mozart a mediocre composer who died too late rather than too early: he could not stand the most popular works, the G minor symphony nor *Die Zauberflöte*. This stance is directed against Gulda's 'paralysed centenarians'; Gould became more concrete, however, and gave suggestions as to how the ostensible flaws in the second movement of the E flat major piano concerto K. 482 might be corrected. He attempted to make Mozart's daring compositional feats more accessible and thus joins a tradition of Mozart critics which will soon have lasted some two hundred years. Probably Gould felt the need to hold something dark against the radiance of Mozart's harmonic sequences in order to gain distance from him and thus be able to play – so unusually and so intensively – Bach and Brahms.

There is a difference between the interpretation of opera and that of instrumental music: the latter exclusively has to come to grips with Mozart's sacrosanct musical score (the liberties which Gulda takes in interpolating ornamentation and slight paraphases corresponds to the customs of Mozart's time as well as contradicting our own). Common to both (apart from the topical dilemma concerning objectives) is the support found in Mozart's reputation when attempting to find one's way through a cultural pluralism. The decision about whether or not one should serve Mozart's work or use it for a springboard to something else does not affect this basic position.

Among the many aspects of this position, 'faithfulness to the original work', pursued with the greatest didactic urgency, is, in turn, supported by the work of the musicologists. The great age of Mozart scholarship must, then, have dawned a long time ago. And, indeed, the number and the variety of the topics listed in the *Mozart Bibliography* are enormous. In a discussion at a conference held in 1964 concerning the 'present position of Mozart scholarship' Wolfgang Plath read a much respected paper which argued that a 'complex crisis' existed. It was only twenty years later that a scholarly edition of the complete letters of Mozart, plus commentary, was available, together with a rich collection of documents concerning his life and an iconography. The new Mozart edition nears completion. And yet I doubt whether Plath in the meantime has considered that the crisis has been overcome.

What is it about? German musicology above all, together with its related disciplines, has turned in the first half of our century to a humanities *Geisteswissenschaft à la* Dilthey, an 'empirical science of intellectual phenomena'. After 1945 its idealistic tradition was repressed, and the emphasis shifted to the more concrete values of social sciences and philology. Mozart scholarship in general reflected this development. The discussions of 1964 showed quite plainly that there is no 'one' Mozart scholarship, no monolith, no sodality of experts sworn to protect each other as initiates. And this should certainly be hailed as something positive. What was less encouraging was the diffuse picture of a host of intellectual starting points, some hermeneutic, others more analytical and positivist, which were offered as an amplification of, or a reply to, Plath's provocation.

A crisis, then? Plath had particular doubts about the large-scale studies of Wyzewa and Saint-Foix because it bestowed upon stylistic criticism the appearance of certainty in questions of the dating and the reliability of compositions, a certainty which in actual fact it did not possess. And Alfred Einstein too, in his third edition of Köchel's register, had been led astray here. We can, moreover, reproach both authors for their conviction that they could decipher the concept of genius by means of a causal connection. But, for Plath, the latter was not a pressing problem. It was more the day-to-day difficulties of working on the new Mozart edition which forced him to a comprehensive critique. The edifice of material which had for far too long been accepted as reliable soon appeared to be extremely unsound. A sceptism was called for *vis-à-vis* everything that had been handed down; what was needed was a return to the historical-critical methodology which Jahn and Köchel had introduced into Mozart scholarship. It was necessary for all available hands to devote themselves to the construction of a reliable basis.

Plath distinguishes two tendencies in Mozart scholarship: an 'artistic' one (in Dilthey's sense) and a 'learned, intellectual' one (based on the historical-critical method). In his view the juxtaposition does not correspond to the requirements of the latest developments in research. The efforts with regard to the material is, he believes, the 'prime task'; the understanding of Mozart as an intellectual phenomenon is, as a 'formal goal', the 'most distinguished task' of the researcher. And yet the historical-critical method – even with Jahn's Mozart image – is not able to expunge the prejudices of the author. The goal is, nevertheless, the objectifying abstraction of methodology from the subject of the inquiry with his personal wishes. The reconciliation of

231

strict textual criticisms with interpretation was felt to be possible by many scholars during the discussion. This may not have been pressing in 1964, but it will become so when the new Mozart edition is completed. Plath envisaged how it would look – naturally, 'not as a sum of facts, but as an integral sense-content of the factual'. This has always been the wish of philology, which sees its first task to be the provider of texts which are as authentic as possible but also, none the less, to be a science of textual interpretation.

It is in its consistent application, however, that the historical-critical method avoids that limiting, rashly systematizing definition of Mozart against which Nietzsche had reacted. Seen from this angle it is a matter of moving from certainty in detailed relationships to higher, more embracing degrees of certainty, abstaining from the 'artistic' tendency to make 'an image' of a thing. In the face of all that jumble of grand words and phrases which those of a panegyric bent have piled up in the last two centuries of Mozart reception (under which the factual and the legendary become interchangeable), the reading of sober, scholarly specialist analyses, with their readiness to look at broader contexts, does bring with it a liberating intellectual delight.

We see elsewhere the disadvantages of adhering to 'the prime task'. Nowadays, for example, there is no dispute about the fact that, with questions concerning dating and genuineness, it is a matter of first looking at and evaluating the sources, and not a matter of stylistic criticism. Yet in many instances the source-research does not lead to unambiguous results; we then have to resort to a 'worse' method. It was apparent in all the relevant discussions (they may be consulted in the Mozart *Jahrbücher*) that innumerable arguments were brought together but the criteria for determining what was possible and what was not remained either vague or subjective. The doubts expressed about research into Mozart's life were even more enlightening. The material has been critically sifted and published; many doubtful attributions have been corrected by Otto Erich Deutsch and others. The foundations have been laid, and await the architect; the reference to new insights that might be gained (for example, 'Mozart as pupil and teacher') do not excuse their omission hitherto. There are still, of course, a wealth of Mozart biographies, some traditionally trivial and some of a more cultural-historical bent such as that of Erich Schenk, but there remains a deficit in interpretation.

One thing is very marked: where Mozart scholarship finds difficulty with its basic material, that is, with the work itself, its results – the new Mozart edition and the exploration of performance practices – are slowly beginning to have an effect on musical practice; however, where this insecurity has been overcome, the scholarship has remained practically without effect. It should come as no surprise that outsiders have managed to fill these gaps so effectively, no surprise at all when they are as prominent and as intellectual as Wolfgang Hildesheimer who expressly declared, moreover, that he was not affiliated to the 'brotherhood'. The questions that concerned him were scarcely touched upon during the 1964 discussions about the status of Mozart scholarship. It became all too clear what the insiders were suggesting when they reacted to this outsider according to their different temperaments, or silently passed him by in a rather superior manner. And Hildesheimer's *Mozart* (1977) did without doubt achieve a wide publicity. Mozart's personality is a topic of conversation again, even of gossip.

It is the same with books as it is with practical interpretation – for some reason or other they have to cause a sensation, and the advertising circus gets hold of them to make them available to a wider readership and also to promote serious discussion. This, naturally, says nothing about the quality of the object of the adulation, and yet I must admit that I was annoyed about the announcement that Hildesheimer 'had created the first real portrait of Mozart'. This smacks of the sort of revelations you read about in illustrated magazines. During a reading (Hildesheimer read out the section on *Die Zauberflöte*) I realized that he was trying to protect Mozart from his biographers, to peel away the layers of varnish and, in this act of opposition, to come closer to the Mozart enigma. Strangely enough, the impetus towards educational knowledge and a spirit of criticism links Hildesheimer with Plath; Hildesheimer is also a grateful user of the historical-critical edition of the letters and documents. It is his intention to oppose the image of Mozart found in Jahn, Abert, even Einstein, together with that tendency to idealize and to harmonize which is so widespread and has such a wide cultural and historical application. He uses psychoanalytical methods, methods which had been alien to Mozart research. To apply these to Mozart made sense, for they were popular with modern artist-biographies – although they were seldom used as carefully as Freud used them when writing on Michelangelo or Goethe.

Hildesheimer's Mozart has nothing in common with the Schubert who was ill-treated by other authors. If, with the latter, the question may be asked as to what the insights into Schubert's sexual neuroses actually give us, so Hildesheimer asks his readers (to whom he had already explained Mozart's sexual fantasies and his anal-eroticism verging on coprolalia) whether or not Mozart thus appeared smaller in stature, grubby or despicable. The reasons why Hildesheimer attempts to understand Mozart from this unsavoury – and usually repressed – angle, and why he also dwells on Mozart's eccentric characteristics, none of which suits the image of the hero, are precisely because they do *not* suit this image: they shock and thus provide a deeper insight.

I don't know whether Hildesheimer's Dionysian image is closer to the real Mozart than the Apollonian. Certainly his book demolishes the marble-pale transfiguration of Mozart, also the trivial notion that he was 'a man like you and me'; he points to the strangeness of genius, a strangeness which the earlier biographer Ulibischeff took for granted and which approximates once more to the Romantic concept of the artist we meet in E.T.A. Hoffmann. The decisive factor here is that this typological classification is not Hildesheimer's last word.

The most interesting aspect, rather, is his attempt to think about his own failure when confronting the subject of his book. His desire for conviction was confronted by something that was finally quite inscrutable. The possibility that everything could have worked out quite differently from the way it had been portrayed with such critical fervour corresponds perhaps – as regards atmosphere – to Mozart's own way of thinking; it certainly corresponds to that enlightened urge which, ideally, does not only aim at dogma imposed from without but also at those that it produces itself.

This essential convergence with the object under discussion determines, as I see it, the means of representation. As Hildesheimer himself says, he is trying to reach a kind of 'action writing' or a work report; his book is supposed to bring 'not so much a development of a theme, but rather a variety of views concerning an inexhaustible phenomenon'. This cutting-loose from the pursuit of a goal and the encouragement of a more spacious experience which embraces the reader and invites him to look around has, as a tendency, a fundamental relationship with the general condition (already discussed) of that practical Mozart interpretation prevailing today.

In a lecture which he held subsequently, 'Die Subjektivität des Bio-graphen' (The Subjectivity of the Biographer), Hildesheimer accuses himself of being somewhat naïve in the application of psychology, and thereby legitimizes his stance most clearly. I refer to his hope of being able to be in a position, from knowledge gained from a psychoanalysis which has itself as a subject, to determine the necessary relationship at any one time between distance from and identification with the object; further to be able to exclude emotions, both positive and negative, and, moreover, to be capable as a biographer of applying the knowledge about typical reactions within the psyche, and thereby preserving a distance from the possibility of personal reactions. He now suspects that he has 'gone too far in his faith in psychoanalysis'.

Hildesheimer's scepticism concerning secondary literature is greater than his criticism of historical sources. But to claim that the descriptions by Sophie Haibl and Caroline Pichler of Mozart's eccentric behaviour patterns are completely reliable because these reporters had no imagination is a very self-confident conclusion. The lateness of their contributions also leads us to assume that they wanted to make themselves interesting – and succeeded.

Symptomatic in a negative sense, I believe, is Hildesheimer's exposition of *Die Zauberflöte* (I am exaggerating, for my part, through my choice of this example, as I wish to point out something that lies behind it). He does not like the piece, considering it 'overrated from the beginning'. It was for this reason that he willingly chose the strongest passages from his book for the public reading, and discussed them with others verbally and in print. He uses three arguments to attack *Die Zauberflöte*: first, he criticizes the libretto for being illogical and possessing an inner insincerity – an old reproach about which we can argue endlessly. Secondly, he complains about the masculine atmosphere, the misogynistic elements of the 'initiates', and sees conspicuous parallels with the customs of other opera productions – and not only Mozart's. And thirdly, he combines this with the claim that Mozart lacked – at least in part – an inner sympathy for the composition. He means here the part of the score which is to be sung by the male parts. When he praises Pamina's G minor aria, Hildesheimer – exceptionally – even plays with the thought of autobiographical elements in Pamina's lament. Tamino's compositional construction is never mentioned: the music of the priests is cut down to size. But it's not clear to me why Mozart, when composing, say, the priests' duet 'Bewahret euch vor Weibertücken', should not have been wholeheartedly involved. The merry music for 'Tod und Verzweiflung war sein Lohn' (Death and destruction were his fate) could give rise to all sorts of discussions, for example, about Mozart the joker who was peeping out here; it is hardly an accident that Mozart, in a letter to his wife, makes some very ambivalent comments about just this passage. If Mozart's heart had not been in it he would have written, rather, a conventional duet, quite unambiguous and with an earnest index finger raised on high.

In the case of *Die Zauberflöte* Hildesheimer will simply not listen to what the music is telling him. Instead of this he builds up a negative hero, one who has been haunting the Mozart literature for one hundred and fifty years: Karl Ludwig Giesecke, erstwhile collaborator with Schikaneder and a man who later achieved fame as a natural scientist. As early as 1795 Schikaneder had defended himself against other, ostensible, authors of *Die Zauberflöte*. Because we are not talking with this libretto of an art-work such as the dramas of Goethe and Schiller it is basically a matter of indifference whether Schikaneder wrote every line by himself or whether the 'Schikaneder factory' was involved in its completion. Giesecke was a misogynist (it was 'doubtful whether he even liked ladies') and fits well into Hildesheimer's chain of argument when assessing the ostensible dislike of women in the libretto of *Die Zauberflöte*, something which Mozart attempted musically to change into its opposite. From this viewpoint Schikaneder, who was by no means averse to the female sex, could not indeed have been the author.

We can object that this criticism of details is not fair to Hildesheimer's own assessment of his work. But it helps to classify what Hildesheimer's book wishes to be, and what it wishes not to be: literature and not scholarship. He demands from the biographer a strict division between communication and speculation, and sees the only correct path for himself as one of reaching 'an objective picture via intersubjectivity'. Intimacy with, and distance from, the subject presuppose that the author knows 'the secret quiverings of the soul' and that he himself has also experienced the artist's creative urge. And with this the book's observation comes full circle.

Those non-psychoanalysts and non-artists who are forced to stand outside the door have as a comfort the secret satisfaction of looking through those wish-dreams and prejudices which do not derive from the musicians' guild, but from the Freudians. And if they go a step further they can guess what *Mozart* represented for Hildesheimer's artistic development. After the novels *Tynset* and *Masante*, both of which had autobiographical traits, Hildesheimer, in *Mozart*, freed himself from himself. With Mozart he developed a conception of the genius which 'did not see itself in relation to the world', indeed, did not see itself at all. Characteristic of the pseudo-genius (he names Rilke, for example) is the need for self-reflection, crowing when successful and whining about personal loneliness.

It is for this reason that Hildesheimer insists so forcefully on Mozart's strangeness, an otherness which Annette Kolb some forty years before (and starting from another premiss) similarly proclaimed as the being and end of all wisdom: 'The night never lifts from Mozart. Let him step forward who can make an image of him, of how he walked, how he stood, his glance, his gestures.'

It is impossible to decide whether or not Mozart serves as a model for a particular conception of genius or, going beyond this, whether or not the search for the absolute in life finds in him some form of support. I think the latter is true in Hildesheimer's case. This brings him into fundamental contact not only with that long tradition of Mozart idealization but also with the methods of several of this century's theologians. I know that I'm provoking contradiction here. To repeat it once more: individually, their views are completely different, but in general they share, on the one hand, an insight into Mozart's otherness and, on the other, the irrational belief that they can nevertheless understand him. They also share the opposition, or the polite reserve, of the musical experts. It was the American author Joyce Carol Oates who answered the persistent question as to how one could meaningfully relate to Mozart, and who also threw light on the opposition of the musicians. In her story 'Nightmusic' she gives us a choice of two Happy Endings: one lies in 'the song inside the music' which resists the sensation-hunting of the clueless public; the other is realized in the musical identification with Mozart of a concert pianist, an identification which his professional colleagues distrust, because they can only think of their own Happy End: 'But why resist?'

A theological interpretation of the crystal-clear incomprehensibility (to put it as a paradox) with which Mozart illuminates all contradictions moves in a very delicate area. Mozart could also have intended something quite diabolical with it, a jest, a nihilism behind the appearance of tender understanding, a higher form of amorality. The decisive thing according to Karl Barth's view is that Mozart had no goal, had no message or confession to bring, but stood above the strife in magisterial sovereignty; he did not revolt as a musician but moved with ever greater freedom within fixed parameters. The naïvety of genius (the Raphael comparison) overlaps with the notion of sovereignty over all the contrasts (the Shakespeare comparison) to create an image of freedom in which 'heaviness hovers, and lightness weighs infinitely heavy'.

We are reminded here of the analogy of Mozart with angelic choirs. Barth seeks Mozart's freedom in a Christianized vision of the music of the spheres; he also seeks it in concrete detail and finds it in Mozart's ability to create a 'delicious phrase', something that Mörike was able to represent in his writing and which Thrasybulos Georgiades theoretically investigated in the scores. In his 'Dankbrief an Mozart' (Thank-you letter to Mozart) Barth tells of a delightful dream: he had to examine Mozart in theology, and tried to prevent him from failing – in vain, however, because Mozart knew nothing about dogma and dogmatism.

The two very different Catholic theologians Hans Küng and Hans Urs von Balthasar also take up the problem of freedom. Küng sees Mozart's uniqueness, a uniqueness which transcends historical dependencies and doctrines, in his higher unity, a unity rooted in freedom, in Kant's 'intelligible character' that is. He places 'Mozart himself' in an analogy with the 'differentiating Jesuanic' which is only outshone by the 'differentiating Christian'. Balthasar goes even further and approximates Mozart to the risen Christ in a vision of Mozart 'rising upwards as a transfigured ego with body and soul to the sounds of *Die Zauberflöte*'. This ascension of Mozart to a spiritualized life reminds us of the late antiquity and the philosophy of Plotinus. Balthasar, who wrote a famous *Theological Aesthetics*, goes beyond a philosophical interpretation to the extent that he recognizes in the apparition of Mozart 'the final Revelation of eternal Beauty which transcends all partings, Beauty in a genuine earthly body'.

When we remember the vehement criticism levelled against the conventional Mozart image in Karl Kraus or in Hesse's *Steppenwolf* we will find that the words of the theologians are, in contrast, emollient. But they too are seeking hope and comfort in Mozart's music, just as those writers do who articulate a radical sceptisim about any kind of higher meaning in our world. Mozart becomes an ideal, diametrically opposed to the absurdity of the present. And this stock figure of our Mozart reception loses all the clichés associated with it when the theologian Dietrich Bonhoeffer, a few months before his execution in the concentration camp, in the year 1944, extolled the *hilaritas* of Mozart and Raphael. To take a few other examples: the Provençal Jean Giono, in his *Triomphe de la vie*, takes up the theme of the *fin de siècle* and its enthusiasm for the Rococo. But the admiration for Mozart's harmony with his age has something forced about it: Giono sees in Mozart an ideal leading from the entanglements of hell to freedom. Under the impact of the Second World War Mozart became, for Antoine de Saint-Exupéry, a timeless symbol of human harmony, a symbol lacking today: Mozart, he writes, has been condemned to death.

In the conversation with the devil in *Doktor Faustus*, Thomas Mann refers to Kierkegaard's interpretation of *Don Giovanni*, and in his speech of 1945, 'Deutschland und die Deutschen', he refers to music as 'a demonic realm': he means, here, his own predilection for the music of Wagner and Beethoven. Mann's desire for a sovereign, magisterial view of the world led to a growth of interest in Mozart towards the end of his life (Einstein's book acted as a catalyst here): he was fascinated by the 'celestial', the remoteness from nature, the element of pure musical concentration, the aristocratic qualities in Mozart.

Hesse went a similar path, but one more intensely involved with Mozart, and far more concerned with a flight from reality: already in the poem 'Flötenspiel' (The Music of the Flute) (1940) Mozart represents the expression of eternal significance. Mozart, as a magic cipher, is a guarantor that the world has meaning. For Hesse, but also for Ernst Weiss, this meaning is inspired by the Far East; it is an anti-Faustian harmony.

Eugène Ionesco, in his opening speech at the Salzburg Festival in 1972, formulated the opposing positions in a far more pointed manner. This speech is full of apocalyptic prophecies: Mozart is 'the one who is utterly different', he is full of joy and a 'childlike astonishment', qualities which Ingmar Bergman brings home to us in pictures at the beginning of the film *Die Zauberflöte*. With all these writers music acts as a salvation from horror, just as Mozart had employed it in the trial scene in *Die Zauberflöte*.

Is it impossible to demythologize Mozart? Ingeborg Bachmann made the attempt. In her *Blatt für Mozart* (Page for Mozart) she does not speak of divine music but of a music which is of this world. 'Simply the consummate variation of a theme limited by the world, a theme which has been left to us' – a theme of longing, 'with which men and fallen angels are filled'. The Czech writer Věra Linhartová expresses a similarly unusual idea in her story 'Requiem for W.A. Mozart'. At the centre of this we find the stark insight that Mozart certainly has a consoling function (by the very fact of existence), but he does not bring any justification for hope: his work confronts us to save us from nihilism. Neither the music, nor the study of the sources, brings an approximation to the phenomenon Mozart. The author makes the point that there is nothing to be explained, no enlightenment to be achieved, by having the protagonist, a student writing on Mozart, die a death as senseless and as arbitrary as Mozart's. This, for her, is the beginning of understanding. Linhartová also lets her protagonist have accidental meetings with unknown figures, figures which remind us of 'the shadowy messenger', in order to let him experience the mystery of a thing and also identification with it. It is precisely the bitter-sweet legends surrounding Mozart's final year of life and his death that still maintain something which is tangible, close and familiar, despite all pragmatic matter-of-factness.

What is only a suggestion in Linhartová's little known story threatens to become highlighted in film and drama. And the way in which highlights are treated surely depends upon the quality of the results. The English playwright Peter Shaffer is also concerned with the mystery of enlightenment and identification, and treats it in a very effective manner in his play. *Amadeus* is not simply a drama about Salieri's murder of Mozart; it is a game with the power of suggestion. 'The death of Mozart! Was it me or not?' – with this line Salieri invites the audience to a presentation of his 'last composition', his own battle with death, and dedicates this to posterity, the *ombri del futuro*. The spectator is asked, not forced, to become involved with a past age, a story, a phenomenon. The *venticelli*, the 'little breezes' of rumour, play with all the conceivable arguments, pro and contra: 'Was it he or was it not?' Salieri provides an answer towards the end: 'We have both been poisoned, Amadeus. I by you, you by me.' It is a plausible one when one considers from a more radical point of view what the play is all about.

The critics were of the opinion that the title should really have been 'Salieri'. Salieri is almost always present, as narrator, as one who meditates and one who acts – but he is not present in his music, with one exception, and an exception which is embarrassing for him. As soon as music is heard it becomes apparent what is 'false' and what is 'true'. But the splendid figure of Salieri on the stage makes it difficult for the spectator to dismiss the composer Salieri as a mediocrity and to turn to Mozart. He is made vividly to realize that genius is an act of grace, a gift, in Salieri's eyes, of a merciless God. 'Amadeus', that is, 'love God' – or, rather 'one who is loved by God' – this is a name of enigmatic significance behind which the spectator, guided by the thoughts of Salieri, begins to recognize an adamantine destiny. The tension between understanding, talent, ability and genius becomes, on the stage, one between the sophisticated court *Kapellmeister* and the 'obscene child'. The topos of Mozart's incomprehensibility thus achieves an effectiveness on stage, and Shaffer further intensifies its concreteness by bringing out the old familiar, indomitable images (and thereby suppressing our doubts concerning them): the shadowy messenger, the father as Commendatore, the premonition of death, the grinding poverty and the pauper's grave, the effortless perfection of the compositions which Mozart 'simply wrote down . . . without the smallest correction', and the musician as an 'incarnation' of God.

In Shaffer's play music occupies an unusual and central position, one which words cannot make good. It is not just Mozart's music *per se*, but quite specific passages which exert a peculiar fascination. The beginning of the adagio from the wind serenade K. 361 or the final ensemble from *Figaro* lead to the question: 'How can we grasp a moment with greater reality?' Incidentally, we meet the same in the work of the organ builder Hans Henny Jahnn; in Wiechert's novel *Missa sine nomine*, the larghetto from Mozart's last piano concerto is the 'ultimate', that 'last thing' which the protagonists are capable of grasping; in Giono's *Triomphe de la vie* the 'sixteen notes of the horn call in the *Sinfonia Concertante*' bring about the reconciliation of heaven and earth. Do the writers, then, justify here the desire of the public at large for the 'lovely passages', this desire which the experts treat with scorn? Perhaps Mozart scholarship should look into that which characterizes these flashes of genius or that which – free of all speculation about shape and discontinuity in formal sequence – makes so special the first few bars of any Mozart piano sonata.

Shaffer's play was a theatrical sensation in London in 1979; it became a Broadway hit in 1980 and has been acclaimed on German stages since 1981. It became one of the most successful plays for years. Milos Forman gained the third (and even greater) *coup* after Hildesheimer and Shaffer with his *Amadeus* film. At the end of 1984 there was an 'Amadeus' craze which swept the world from Brazil to Japan, from Los Angeles to Vienna and which, one day, will reach the city in which this film, a film which gained so many Oscars, was largely made.

There will, of course, be much discussion about what this great success made possible and where its significance lies. It is remarkable how much of an impact this film had upon a wide, and a young, audience, an audience which (like Forman) had previously never thought much about a classical composer and which had only felt boredom when his music was played. It was not the sublime yearning for consummate perfection, not simply a crude desire for sensationalism, which made the film so effective. The latter consideration might be true for Slavo Luther's film *Vergesst Mozart* (Forget Mozart), but Forman's film, in contrast, is carefully made by a producer with an unmistakable style. In *Amadeus*, as in his earlier films *One Flew Over The Cuckoo's Nest* or *Ragtime* or in the filming of the musical *Hair*, Forman shows a predilection for neurotic characters, an interplay between reality and illusion. Shaffer's model met this halfway; his tendency, however, towards hyped-up revue, towards the use of multimedia spectacle is primarily cinematic. The medium of film can make suggestion far more compulsive and, at the same time, the action is interrupted less by the speculations of Salieri and is held at a distance.

From a critical viewpoint the suggestive power of the film becomes an inevitable problem: Salieri's question in Shaffer's play 'Was it me or was it not?' is unambiguously answered by Forman, and this does not help the film's allure. Of course, the spectator who knows all about Mozart's biography will quite clearly recognize that the action develops in such a way as to leave reality far behind it. And the magic of the revue goes precisely towards the creation of an historical unreality. But what cinemagoer is there (a cinemagoer more or less free of prejudice) who gets round to thinking about what the artistic imagination is driving at with those overwhelming images before him of Mozart's father, in diverse roles, as an avenging conscience?

What Forman is suggesting to us, however, is a new Mozart figure in the cinema. The myth of the gentle genius, whether it be promulgated by Karl

Hartl in 1942 (*Wen die Götter lieben* [Whom the Gods Love], with Hans Holt) and 1955 (*Reich mir die Hand, mein Leben* [Give Me Your Hand, My Darling] with Oskar Werner) or by Klaus Kirschner in his documentary *Mozart –Aufzeichnungen einer Jugend* (Mozart – Sketches of Youth) is *passé*. The most recent television film, by Marc Dumaine and Marcel Bluval, also demonstrates this. But which Mozart *is* 'Amadeus'? Hildesheimer's Dionysian Mozart for the critical intellectuals? – but he is too unambiguously Dionysian for that. Or Falco's 'Superstar' for the masses? – but the characterization in Forman's film is too sophisticated. Yet Falco's *Rock Me Mozart* did exert a surprisingly wide fascination and hammered home the point that Mozart was Rococo's punk, a 'rock idol': he was 'far out' and 'popular' – this was his 'flair'.

The protest against convention brings about this identification. What was old was regarded as false, and what was up to date seemed new and true, as a correction even. The question was not asked as to how far this kind of protest has itself become a convention. The 'reality' of an object has to do with the level of its acceptance. This kind of opinion seems very cynical when we consider 'Amadeus festivals' or the 'Amadeus outfits' propagated by fashion magnates – waistcoats of velvet or silk brocade. The successful sale of Mozart records is also mixed up here with the 'Amadeus' circus – the original soundtrack got on to the bestseller lists. Is Mozart's music appreciated by his new fans under completely false premises or are countless numbers of people being brought to overcome their prejudices againt classical music in an unsual manner? The history of artistic reception is a collection of curios anyway, a hurdy-gurdy of misunderstandings, some of which are productive – I go along with the optimists.

The 'European Year of Music', 1985, dedicated to the memory of Schütz Bach, Handel, Scarlatti, Berg, etc., and intended to encourage contemporary music and also young musicians became, despite the calendar of memorial anniversaries, a Mozart year. We see this not least in the German book market. In the last three years there have been at least a dozen books on Mozart which have merited attention; some of them have attempted to ride on the back of the successful wave of critical investigations. The claim that one is setting the record straight has achieved topicality once more: what *is* strange is the alliance entered into by enlightenment and advertising.

Books whose contents are so divergent, such as those by Hildesheimer and Kurt Pahlen, are linked by the announcement of a real, true and new Mozart image. Dust-jackets proclaim that the authors 'are cleansing a statue of all the legends which have encrusted it', or that they have 'finally deciphered' Mozart's musical language, which has been 'falsely understood' for two hundred years. What is striking is the preference for Mozart as a person and for his surroundings. Even the 'business dealings of Constanze M.' with the *Requiem* seem worthy of being portrayed in a book.

Books which do deserve a positive recommendation, however, are Volkmar Braunbehrens's thorough and pleasingly sober cultural-historical study *Mozart in Vienna* and Erich Valentin's most recent book *Mozart – Weg und Welt* (Mozart – Way and World) which is supported by an understanding which is cautious and yet represses nothing. But a few interesting books have appeared recently dealing with the work, particularly with the operas. Joachim Kaiser has formulated many witty and stimulating *aperçus* on Mozart's characters from Alfonso to Zerlina; Ivan Nagel's attempts to grasp the basic tension between 'autonomy and grace' in that happy balance in Mozart's operas – these attempts were probably triggered off by the surprising topicality of the *opera seria* – are similarly relaxed in form. Stefan Kunze and Gunthard Born undertake musical analyses. Kunze – similar to Thrasybulos Georgiades – comes out in defence of the 'originality' and 'artistic character' of the music of all Mozart's operas and offers at the same time a compendium of relevant research findings. It is questionable whether Born has found the 'key' to 'Mozart's musical language', but it is also worth discussing. And indeed, the emotional reactions to Born's theses did not come from nowhere. The book's diction is that of a 'forward defence'; the publishers are indulging in aggressive advertisement, and in the conflict between absolute music and programme music (a conflict that apparently rages on) Born's advocacy of the latter should not remain unopposed.

The Mozart circus of the year 1985 brought few changes in the way that the works, musically or dramatically, were interpreted; interest in new developments was even eclipsed in many places. And even a few years before 1991 we were led to suspect that the over-heated 'Amadeus' boom was heading towards recession; *Der Spiegel* brought out an article (under a title which was hardly objective or restrained: 'Amadeus – das Ferkel, das Feuer spie' [Amadeus: The Swine who spewed Fire]) which was full of scorn about the 'multimedia Mozart cult'. Are we experiencing phases of development in an ever-widening commercialization of Mozart which is concerned with things which are nothing to do with art? It is not possible for anyone who is concerned with Mozart, either as artist, scholar or critic, to give an objective judgement here. We are all beneficiaries of his fame, even the Swiss cabaret artist with his cello, Franz Hohler, who, in a song, sarcastically imagines the whole hustle and bustle of Mozart's returning to the present; and also Gisela Mahlmann who gave the title 'Vom Wunderkind

243

zur Mozartkugel – Über die Vermarktung eines Genies' (From Prodigy to Mozartkugel – On the Marketing of a Genius) to a broadcast on television and made mock of the fact that the Mozarteum had demanded a fee for permission to make the film at the memorial sites, an honorarium paid out for restoration and Mozart research.

What has Mozart to do with chocolates, underwear, coffee, trains and hotels – all of which bear his name? Nothing, of course, but the businessmen want to lift their products out of the grey uniformity of what is on offer and make them something special – this is what the critics do with their critical offerings. A lot of this is irritating, indisputably, above all the sensational hocus-pocus about Mozart's death. The eminent English historian Francis Carr, for example, in his book *Mozart and Constanze* (London, 1984) trots out the old rumour about Franz Hofdemel, who is supposed to have murdered Mozart out of jealousy. There was even a mock tribunal in the fashionable seaside resort of Brighton and, after a democratic vote, it was decided that Hofdemel was the most likely murderer of Mozart, followed by Süssmayr and Salieri. In contrast to this, the international agreement signed between Austria and Germany in 1981, whereby only Austria was allowed to export Mozart-Kugeln and only Germany Westphalian ham, seems especially amusing because there was no attempt made to cover it up with a highfalutin' rationale. The world-wide musical and interpretative culti-vation of Mozart is, however, a bigger business concern than that of Mozart-Kugeln, but it is also an artistic manifestation and still serves a noble aim; to use the words of Friedrich Heer, 'Japanese, Chinese, Russians, Africans, Americans and Europeans are today in communion one with another, at least in that heartbeat where they surrender themselves to the works of Mozart.'

The situation is the same with new musical creations and with arrangements. It is easy to reproach the pop version of *Bona nox*, sung by Lonzo, with being false and commercialistic, but this would be a self-righteous attitude. The arrangements that are on offer, ranging as always from pop to exercises for school orchestras, do have a positive thrust, that of bringing art to the people. They can, however, also stem from an empathizing with Mozart's music which is remote from any suspicion of trivialization: Franz Beyer's orchestration of the *Requiem* is certainly closer to Mozart than the old Süssmayr version and hence provides a service to the work. Compositions of homage which the Mozarteum have commissioned (by C. Bresgen, H. Eder, G. Wimberger and others) tackle Mozart in a variety of ways. The range of possibilities is the same, principally, as that of the different conceptions of opera production. Yet, going beyond the idea of homage, the well-known composers of today have very varied attitudes to Mozart. To praise him is, indeed, a cliché. Dmitri Shostakovich, in a memorial essay of 1956, strung together all the hackneyed, grand words and summarized them in a Pushkin quotation: 'What depth! What boldness and what elegant proportions!' The note of enthusiasm, however, with which he links all this with his own memories of childhood, is genuine and convincing. In 1960 Hans Werner Henze spoke even more emphatically about 'a god who had descended to us'; apparently Mozart provided him with a safeguard in the construction of an alternative to the avant-garde, until Henze started to seek it elsewhere, namely in the politicizing of art. Who would expect Mozart to be a model for Mauricio Kagel? And yet Kagel confesses that, since the beginning of the 1970s, the logical consistency of Mozart's music has provided a 'secret spring' for his tortuous compositional directions. The reconstruction of tradition, starting with Verdi's *Falstaff*, brings forth ever new consequences; the composer's awareness of Mozart's operas is also much in evidence in Henze's *The Young Lord*. Stravinsky's opera *The Rake's Progress* (first performance 1951) carries this eclectic play with pre-existing material to an extreme. Inspired by the pictures of William Hogarth, the poet W.H. Auden and the stage practitioner Chester Kallman created an English paraphrase of the Don Juan material with many Mozart models, particularly *Così fan tutte*. In Anne's *cabaletta*, for example, which is in one single aria, Stravinsky quotes, as well as Mozart, Handel, Gluck, Rossini, Weber and Verdi. A tendency of the age which we have come across in many manifestations is here apparent as a work of art.

History as development become a metahistory of kaleidoscopic juxtaposition. Will the future of the 'creative force' of Mozart's music lie in the recurrence and combination of images and conceptions which are always the same, instead of – as was suspected at the beginning of the chapter – in a movement forward towards an interpretative faithfulness to the text, to a survey of the total field of creativity, to an authentic picture of Mozart? A century ago Nietzsche wrote the following: 'We are late musicians. We have inherited a gigantic tradition. Our memories quote constantly . . . Our listeners enjoy the fact that we allude: it flatters them, they feel instructed here.' Is this insight fulfilled – to an unheard-of degree – now at the end of the twentieth century? Being *larmoyant* about lateness does not help a great deal. I would therefore prefer to close with a few lines from Auden's 'Metalogue to *The Magic Flute*': they cheerfully and also thoughtfully pass over all that profundity which is put on for show, and, in so doing, let something be felt of Mozart's true being:

We who know nothing – which is just as well –
About the future, can, at least, foretell,
Whether they live in air-borne nylon cubes,
Practise group-marriage or are fed through tubes,
That crowds, two centuries from now, will press
(Absurd their hair, ridiculous their dress)
And pay in currencies, however weird,
To hear *Sarastro* booming through his beard,
Sharp connoisseurs approve if it is clean
The F in alt of the *Nocturnal Queen*. . .

REFERENCES

Page

5   Stefan Zweig, 'Die zehn Wege zum deutschen Ruhm. Eine Rechenaufgabe für junge Schriftsteller', in *Der Ruf, Karneval-Heft* 1912, p. 15f.

6   Ernst Ludwig Gerber, *Historisch-biographisches Lexicon der Tonkünstler*, Pt. 1, Leipzig, 1790, column 979; also *Neues historisch-biographisches Lexikon der Tonkünstler*, Pt. 3, Leipzig, 1813–14, column 494 (reprinted Graz 1966 and 1967).

7   Johann Peter Eckermann, *Gespräche mit Goethe*, ed. F. Bergemann, Wiesbaden, 1955, p. 354 (3 Feb. 1830).

11 Walter Salmen, *Johann Friedrich Reichardt*, Freiburg 1963, pp. 189 and 314.
    Karl Gustav Fellerer, 'Zur Mozart-Kritik im 18/19 Jahrhundert', in *Mozart-Jahrbuch 1959*, p. 80ff.
    Georg Nikolaus Nissen, *Biographie W.A. Mozarts*, Leipzig, 1828, p. 633.

12 Franz Friedrich von Boeklin, *Beyträge zur Geschichte der Musik*, Freiburg im Breisgau, 1790, p. 19.
    Carl Bär, *Mozart. Krankheit-Tod-Begräbnis*, Salzburg, 1966 (in the series Schriftenreihe der Internationalen Stiftung Mozarteum, Vol. 1).
    Mozart. Die Dokumente seines Lebens. Collated with a commentary by Otto Erich Deutsch, Kassel, 1961, p. 367ff (hereafter *Mozart. Dokumente*); in addition, *Addenda und Corrigenda*, compiled by Joseph Heinz Eibl, Kassel, 1978, p. 73ff., especially p. 75 (hereafter *Mozart. Dokumente. Addenda*).

13 Joseph Haydn, *Gesammelte Briefe und Aufzeichnungen*, ed. D. Bartha, Kassel, 1965, p. 269.
    For Bossler see Walter Serauky, 'W.A. Mozart und die Musikästhetik des ausklingenden 18. und frühen 19. Jahrhunderts' in *Kongressbericht Wien 1956*, Graz, 1958, p. 579f.

14 *Mozart. Briefe und Aufzeichnungen. Gesamtausgabe.* Published by the Internationale Stiftung Mozarteum, Salzburg, collated and with a commentary by Wilhelm A. Bauer and Otto Erich Deutsch, vol. iv, Kassel, 1963, p. 175 (hereafter *Mozart. Briefe*).
    Mozart. Documente, pp. 369ff. and 379.

15 *Mozart. Briefe*, vol. vi, p. 431; Nissen, *Biographie*, p. 581; the *Pressburger Zeitung* of 31 December 1791 contains a report about the concert: see *Mozart.*

Dokumente, p. 379 (O.E. Deutsch doubts the veracity of the report, see *Mozart. Dokumente*, p. 377).

16   *Mozart. Dokumente*, pp. 391ff., 380 and 369.

17   Robert Münster, 'Zur Mozart-Pflege im Münchener Konzertleben bis 1800', in *Mozart-Jahrbuch 1978–9*, p. 159 ff.
Wolfgang Suppan, *Steierisches Musiklexikon*, Graz, 1962-6, p. 397.
Gösta Morin, 'W.A. Mozart und Schweden', in *Kongressbericht Wien 1956*, p. 420.

18   *Mozart. Dokumente*, pp. 409 and 416ff. (see also *Mozart. Briefe*, vol. vi, pp. 488 and 389).
Mozart. Dokumente, p. 416.
Mozart. Briefe, vol. iv, p. 204f.
For the genesis of the *Requiem* see Leopold Nowak's preface to the corresponding volume of the *Neue Mozart Ausgabe*.

19   *Mozart. Dokumente*, p. 424f.; *Mozart. Briefe*, vol. vi, p. 495f.
Mozart. Dokumente, p. 412.
Barry S. Brook, 'Piraterie und Allheilmittel bei der Verbreitung von Musik im späten 18. Jahrhundert', in *Beiträge zur Musikwissenschaft*, 1980, p. 217ff.

20   *Mozart. Briefe*, vol. vi, p. 454f.
Mozart. Dokumente, p. 421.
Mozart. Briefe, vol. vi, pp. 481, 484 and *passim*; Wilhelm Hitzig, 'Die Briefe Franz Xaver Niemetscheks und der Marianne Mozart an Breitkopf und Härtel', in *Der Bär, Jahrbuch von B. und H. auf das Jahr 1928*, Leipzig, 1928, p. 101ff.

21   *Mozart. Dokumente*, p. 410; *Mozart. Dokumente. Addenda*, p. 79; *Mozart Briefe*, vol. iv, p. 179 and vol. vi, p. 432f.
Mozart. Dokumente, p. 405.
Mozart. Dokumente, p. 423.
Mozart. Dokumente. Addenda, p. 88; W. Hitzig, loc. cit., p. 110.

22   Oskar von Hase, *Breitkopf und Härtel. Gedenkschrift und Arbeitsbericht*, vol. i, Leipzig, 1917, p. 158.
Mozart. Briefe, vol. iii, p. 53 (letter of 11 December 1780).
Erich Reimer, 'Idee der Öffentlichkeit und kompositorische Praxis im späten 18. und frühen 19. Jahrhundert' in *Die Musikforschung*, 1976, p. 130ff.
Hans-Christoph Worbs, 'Komponist, Publikum und Auftraggeber', in *Kongressbericht Wien 1956*, Graz, 1958, p. 754ff.

23   The Répertoire International des Sources Musicales lists the early Mozart printings that are known today (vol. A/1/6, Kassel, 1976, pp. 44–253); Richard Schaal gives a good survey in his article 'Mozart' in the encyclopaedia *Die Musik in Geschichte und Gegenwart* (hereafter *MGG*), vol. 9, Kassel, 1961, column 812ff.

25   See *MGG*, vol. 9, column 815f.
Imogen Fellinger, 'Mozartsche Kompositonen in periodischen Musik-publikationen des späten 18. und frühen 19. Jahrhunderts', in *Mozart-Jahrbuch 1978–9*, p. 203ff.

Joseph Müller-Blattau, 'Alt-Saarbrücker Hausmusik zur Goethe-Zeit', in *Saarbrücker Hefte*, 1958, p. 58ff.

Rudolf Elvers, 'Die bei J.F.K. Rellstab in Berlin bis 1800 erschienenen Mozart-Drucke', in *Mozart-Jahrbuch 1957*, pp. 157 and 160.

26 Wolfgang Matthäus, *Johann André. Musikverlag zu Offenbach am Main*, Tutzing, 1973.

27 Hans-Christian Müller, *Bernhard Schott. Hofmusikstecher in Mainz*, Mainz, 1977.

Jan La Rue, 'Mozart Listings in Some Rediscovered Sales-Catalogues, Breslau 1787–1792', in *Mozart-Jahrbuch 1967*, p. 46ff.

28 Alexander Weinmann, *Wiener Musikverleger und Musikalienhändler von Mozarts Zeit bis gegen 1860*, Vienna, 1956; reprinting of the Traeg index in *Beiträge zur Geschichte des Alt-Wiener Musikverlages*, ed. A. Weinmann, series 2, vol. 17, Vienna, 1973.

29 Otto Biba, 'Grundzüge des Konzertwesens in Wien zu Mozarts Zeit', in *Mozart-Jahrbuch 1978–9*, p. 132ff.

30 Carl Ferdinand Pohl, *Mozart und Haydn in London*, vol. 1, Vienna, 1867, p. 142f.

Leipzig *Allgemeine Musikalische Zeitung* (hereafter *AMZ*); see Eberhard Preussner, *Die bürgerliche Musikkultur*, second ed., Kassel, 1951, p. 73.

AMZ, 1802, column 346.

François Lesure, 'L'Oeuvre de Mozart en France de 1793 à 1810', in *Kongressbericht Wien 1956*, p. 344ff.

Paul Nettl, 'Frühe Mozart-Pflege in Amerika', in *Mozart-Jahrbuch 1954*, p. 78ff.

G. Morin, loc. cit., p. 417ff.

32 *Gelehrte Nachrichten*, no. xxvi, supplement to *Wiener Diarium*, 84, 1766; also in Ignaz de Lucca, *Das gelehrte Österreich*, vol. 1, Vienna, 1778, p. 311; see Kurt Blaukopf, 'Musikland Österreich', in *Musikgeschichte Österreichs*, vol. 2, Graz, 1979, p. 536.

Klaus Winkler, 'Alter und Neuer Stil im Streit zwischen den Berlinern und Wienern zur Zeit der Frühklassik', in *Die Musikforschung*, 1980, p. 37ff.

Rudolf Eller, Article on 'Leipzig' in *MGG*, vol. viii, Kassel, 1960, column 535.

E. Preussner, loc. cit., p. 73ff.

AMZ, 1801, column 549.

33 Eduard Hanslick, *Geschichte des Concertwesens in Wien*, vol. 1, Vienna, 1869, pp. 24 and 34.

34 Arnold Schering, *Musikgeschichte Leipzigs*, vol. iii, Leipzig, 1941, pp. 631 and 654.

Alfred Loewenberg, *Annals of Opera*, second ed., Geneva 1955; Elisabeth Jeannette Luin, 'Mozarts Opera in Skandinavien', in *Kongressbericht Wien 1956*, p. 391.

Alfons Rosenberg, *Die Zauberflöte*, Munich, 1964.

35 Bernhard Paumgartner, 'Eine Textbearbeitung der *Zauberflöte* von 1795', in *Festschrift O.E. Deutsch*, Kassel, 1963, p. 129ff.

Erich Valentin, 'Geschichtliches und Statistisches zur Mozartpflege', in *Neues Mozart-Jahrbuch*, no. 3, Regensburg, 1943, p. 249.

36 Hans Erdmann, 'Mozart in norddeutscher Resonanz', in *Kongressbericht Wien 1956*, p. 156ff.

Wolfgang Ruf, *Die Rezeption von Mozarts* Le Nozze di Figaro *bei den Zeitgenossen*, Wiesbaden, 1977, especially p. 137ff.

Siegfried Anheisser, *Für den deutschen Mozart, Das Ringen um gültige deutsche Sprachform der italienischen Opern Mozarts*, Emsdetten, 1938.

37 Kurt Helmut Oehl, *Beiträge zur Geschichte der deutschen Mozart-Übersetzungen*, Mainz, 1954.

Gabriele Brandstetter, 'So machen's alle. Die frühen Übersetzungen von Da Pontes und Mozarts *Così fan tutte* für deutsche Bühnen', in *Die Musikforschung*, 1982, p. 27ff., especially p. 44.

38 *Musikalische Monatsschrift*, no. 5, November 1792, p. 137.

Willi Schuh, 'Über einige frühe Textbücher zur *Zauberflöte*', in *Kongressbericht Wien 1956*, p. 571ff.

39 *Mozart. Dokumente. Addenda*, p. 80 (Goethe's letter to Wranitsky, 24 January 1796).

ibid., p. 80.

ibid., p. 84.

Mozart. Dokumente, p. 413.

40 *Mozart. Dokumente. Addenda*, p. 83f.

Dragotin Cvetko, 'J.B. Novak – ein slowenischer Anhänger Mozarts', in *Kongressbericht Wien 1956*, p. 103ff.; Karol Musiol, 'Mozart und die polnischen Komponisten des XVIII und der ersten Hälfte des XIX. Jahrhunderts', in *Mozart-Jahrbuch 1967*, p. 288.

Volker Scherliess, 'Clementis Kompositionen "alla Mozart"', in *Analecta Musicologica*, 18, Cologne, 1978, p. 308ff.

41 *Mozart. Dokumente*, p. 370.

Mozart. Dokumente, pp. 362 and 383.

Walter Serauky, 'W.A. Mozart und die Musikästhetik des ausklingenden 18. und frühen 19. Jahrhunderts', in *Kongressbericht Wien 1956*, p. 579.

42 Egon Friedell, *Kulturgeschichte der Neuzeit*, vol. ii, Munich, 1928, p. 288.

H. Erdmann, loc. cit., p. 159.

Mozart. Dokumente, p. 413.

Mozart. Dokumente, pp. 387, 406 and 409.

43 *Mozart. Dokumente. Addenda*, p. 75

Gernot Gruber, 'Introduction' and '*Die Zauberflöte* (Peroration)' to 'Opera and Enlightenment', in *Kongressbericht Berkeley 1977*, Kassel, 1982, pp. 212f. and 250ff.

Friedrich Schiller, *Briefwechsel mit Körner*, vol. III, Stuttgart, 1896, p. 117.

44 Wolfgang Seifert, *Christian Gottfried Körner. Ein Musikästhetiker der deutschen Klassik*, Regensburg, 1960.

45 Johann Georg Sulzer, *Allgemeine Theorie der schönen Künste*, second ed., Leipzig, 1793, p. 431 (reprint Hildesheim, 1967).
Carl Dahlhaus, *Die Idee der absoluten Musik*, Kassel, 1978, p. 10 and *passim*.
Der Briefwechsel zwischen Schiller und Goethe, ed. H.G. Graf and A. Leitzmann, vol. i, Leipzig, 1912, no. 394; *Goethes Briefe*, vol. ii in the Hamburg edition, ed. K.R. Mandelkow, Hamburg, 1964, p. 322, no. 675.

46 *Mozart. Dokumente. Addenda*, p. 83.
Gisela Jaacks, 'Höllenfahrt und Sonnentempel. Das Bühnenbild der Mozart-Opern', in *Mozart: Klassik für die Gegenwart*, Hamburg, 1978, pp. 99 and 108f.(contains extensive iconographic material).

47 Willi Schuh, '*Die Zauberflöte* im Mannheimer Nationaltheater 1794', in *Festschrift O.E. Deutsch*, pp. 168ff. and 174.
W. Salmen, loc. cit., pp. 55, 317 and 266.
Johann Peter Eckermann, *Gespräche mit Goethe*, Wiesbaden, 1955, p. 318 (8 April 1829).

48 W. Schuh, loc. cit., p. 181. The revision of the text by Christian August Vulpius was probably carried out without Goethe's supervision or cooperation (see Hans Löwenfeld in the new edition of the Vulpius edition, Leipzig, 1911, p. 120f). The notes that Goethe made during rehearsals also reveal that he produced *Die Zauberflöte* in two acts and not, as Vulpius had envisaged, in three (see the Weimar edition, vol. xii, p. 390f.).
Walter Weiss, 'Das Weiterleben der *Zauberflöte* bei Goethe', in *Mozart-Jahrbuch 1980–3*, p. 227ff.
Hugo von Hofmannsthal, *Gesammelte Werke, vol. iv, Prosa* (1924), p. 177.

49 Hans Georg Gadamer, 'Die Bildung des Menschen. Der *Zauberflöte* anderer Teil', in H.G. Gadamer, *Kleine Schriften*, vol. ii, Tübingen, 1967, p. 118ff.
Arthur Henkel, 'Goethes Fortsetzung der *Zauberflöte*', in *Zeitschrift für deutsche Philologie*, 1951, p. 64ff.
A. Henkel, loc. cit., p. 68.
G. Gruber, loc. cit., p. 251f.
Rheinische Musen, vol. i, see W. Schuh, loc. cit., p. 178.
Triest, 'Bemerkungen über die Ausbildung der Tonkunst in Deutschland', in *AMZ*, 1801.
Reprint, Darmstadt, 1969, pp. vii, 226 and 316.

50 Heinrich Christoph Koch, *Musikalisches Lexikon*, Frankfurt am Main, 1801, p. 441; also *Versuch einer Anleitung zur Composition*, vol. iii, Leipzig, 1793, p. 326f.

51 *Musikalische Realzeitung*, Speyer, 1790, p. 137; see W. Serauky, loc. cit., p. 579. This was not only true for Germany, but also for the international dissemination via the Parisian and Amsterdam publishers. See Karl Gustav Fellerer, 'Zur Rezeption von Mozarts Oper um die Wende des 18/19 Jahrhunderts', in *Mozart-Jahrbuch 1965–6*, p. 39ff., especially p.45.

52 Friedrich Rochlitz, 'Veranlassung zu genauer Prüfung eines musikalischen Glaubensartikels', in *AMZ*, 1801, column 677ff.

53 Friedrich Schlichtegroll, *Nekrolog auf das Jahr 1791*, Gotha, 1793; new ed.,

Kassel, 1954, with an epilogue by Richard Schaal; in the French translation: *Notice biographique sur J.C.W.Th. Mozart par Th.F. Winckler*, Paris, 1801. On Schlichtegroll see *Mozart. Briefe*. vol. vi, p. 433.

53   Franz Xaver Niemetschek (Niemczek, Němeček), *Leben des K.K. Capellmeister Wolfgang Gottlieb Mozart nach Original-Quellen*, Prague, 1789; second ed. 1808; facsimile of the first ed. with the changes and additions of the second, ed. E. Rychnovsky, Prague, 1905; further reprints; English edition, London, 1956: see especially pp. 1, 25, 30, 41, 44ff., 1, 57, 45, 58, 45f., 27, 56 and 47 (according to the Prague edition, 1905).

56   Gerhart von Graevenitz, 'Geschichte aus dem Geist des Nekrologs', in *Deutsche Vierteljahrsschrift für Literaturwissenschaft und Geistesgeschichte*, 1980, p. 131.

57   'Monumente deutscher Tonkünstler', in *AMZ*, 1800, column 417ff., especially 420. There is a reproduction of the coin in *Mozart. Klassik für die Gegenwart*, loc. cit.

61   *AMZ*, 1800, column 421; *AMZ*, 1801, columns 857, 25ff, and 52ff.

63   Alexander Hyatt King, *Mozart im Spiegel der Geschichte 1756–1956*, Kassel, 1956, p. 17.
      Berlinische Musikalische Zeitung (hereafter *BMZ*), 1806, p. 67.

64   Hugh J. McLean, 'Mozart parodies and Hayden perplexities: new sources in Poland', in *Studies in Music from the University of Western Ontario*, London/Ontario, no. 1, 1976, p. 1ff.
      Armand E. Singer, 'Don Juan in Amerika', in *Don Juan. Darstellung und Deutung*, ed. B. Wittmann, Darmstadt, 1976, p. 161 (first published in English 1960).

65   Theophil Antonicek, *Musik im Festsaal der Österreichischen Akademie der Wissenschaften*, Vienna, 1972.
      E. Preussner, loc. cit., pp. 48f. and 73.

66   *BMZ*, 1805, pp. 120 and 128.

67   Arnold Schering, 'Künstler, Kenner und Liebhaber der Musik', in *Jahrbuch der Musikbibliothek Peters für das Jahr 1931*, pp. 9ff. and 22f.
      Friederike Zaisberger, 'Mozart im Spiegel der Salzburger Presse um 1800', in *Mozart-Jahrbuch 1980–3*, p. 136ff.

68   Walter Hummel, *W.A. Mozarts Söhne*, Kassel, 1955.
      Ignaz Franz Castelli, *Memoiren meines Lebens*, Munich, 1969 (first published 1861), p. 226f.
      Carl Maria von Weber, *Kunstansichten. Ausgewählte Schriften*, Wilhelmshaven, 1978, p. 209.

69   *BMZ*, 1805, p. 6.

70   Christof Bitter, *Wandlungen in den Inszenierungsformen des* Don Giovanni *von 1787 bis 1928*, Regensburg, 1961, p. 90.
      AMZ, 1816, column 798; Karin Werner-Jensen, *Studien zur* Don Giovanni *Rezeption im 19. Jahrhundert (1800–1850)*, Tutzing, 1980, p. 155.

Johann Gottfried Herder, *Sämtliche Werke*, vol. 24, p. 336 (reprint 1967).

71 *BMZ*, 1805, p. 149ff.

F.X. Niemetschek, loc. cit., supplement to p. 47.

A.H. King, loc. cit., p. 22.

72 C . Dahlhaus, *Die Idee der absoluten Musik*, p. 68.

73 Ernst Lichtenhahn, 'Zur Idee des goldenen Zeitalters in der Musik-anschauung E.T.A. Hoffmanns', in *Romantik in Deutschland*, Stuttgart, 1978, p. 508.

Emil Staiger, Ludwig Tieck und der Ursprung der deutschen Romantik', in *Stilwandel*, Zurich, 1963, p. 175.

E. Lichtenhahn, loc. cit., pp. 503 and 506.

Nora E. Haimberger, *Vom Musiker zum Dichter. E.T.A. Hoffmanns Akkord-vorstellung*, Bonn, 1976, p. 46.

Ernst Theodor Amadeus Hoffmann, *Gesammelte Schriften* (1924), vol. xiv, pp. 50 and 55. We find the beginnings of this thought as early as Hoffmann's 1807 review of Beethoven's C major Mass (*GS*, vol. xiii, p. 135); for an opposite view see Lichtenhahn, loc. cit., who does not refer to the text concerning Mozart's *Requiem* for his argument.

74 Franz Gluck, 'Ein Don-Juan-Relief von 1787', in *Studien aus Wien*, Vienna, 1957, p. 81ff.

Rudolf Steglich. 'Über die Wesensgemeinschaft von Musik und Bildkunst', in *Musik und Bild. Festschrift Max Seiffert*, Kassel, 1938, p. 23ff. See also the representation in *Orphea*, 1825 (reproduced in *Mozart. Klassik für die Gegenwart*, Hamburg, 1978, p. 188; there are also other illustrations).

W. Salmen, loc. cit., p. 317.

Norbert Miller, 'Das Erbe der *Zauberflöte*', in *Sprache im technischen Zeitalter*, 1973, p. 62.

75 N. Miller, loc. cit., pp. 73 and 76.

Klaus Kropfinger, 'Klassik-Rezeption in Berlin (1800–1830)', in *Studien zur Musikgeschichte Berlins im frühen 19. Jahrhundert*, Regensburg, 1980, p. 325.

76 Ludwig Tieck, *Schriften*, vol. xi, Berlin, 1829, p. 53, see Roman Nahrebecky, *Wackenroder, Tieck, E.T.A. Hoffmann, Bettina von Arnim. Ihre Beziehung zur Musik und zum musikalischen Erlebnis*, Bonn, 1979, p. 72f.

Ludwig Tieck, *Schriften*, vol. xi, p. xlix.

Ludwig Tieck, *Schriften*, vol. xi, p.li.

77 See Norbert Siara, *Szenische Bauweise des Erzählers Eichendorff nach dem Opernvorbild Glucks und Mozarts*, Frankfurt/Main, 1973, p. 48.

L. Tieck, *Scheiften*, vol. xi, p. li f.

C.M. von Weber, loc. cit., p. 210.

Dorothee Sölle and Wolfgang Seifert, 'In Dresden und in Atlantis', in *Neue Zeitschrift für Musik*, 1963, p. 260ff.

78 R. Nahrebecky, loc. cit., p. 74ff.

Quoted in N. Siara, loc. cit., p. 39f.

BMZ, 1805, p. 48.

Leo Schrade, 'Mozart und die Romantiker', in *Kongressbericht Salzburg 1931*, Leipzig, 1932, p. 28f.

AMZ, 1800, column 153.

79 Jean Paul, *Sämtlicke Werke*, sec. iii, vol. 4, Berlin, 1960, p. 2 (letter to Herder, 8 October 1800).

R. Homann, article on 'Erhaben. Das Erhabene', in *Historisches Wörterbuch der Philosophie*, vol. ii, Darmstadt, 1972, columns 627ff and 631ff.

BMZ, 1805, p. 180f.

C. Dahlhaus, loc. cit., p. 66.

W. Serauky, loc. cit., p. 584.

80 Wilhelm Friedrich Wackenroder, *Werke und Briefe*, Heidelberg, 1967, p. 255.

G. Jaacks, loc. cit., p. 101.

Daniel Heartz, 'Mozarts *Titus* und die italienische Oper um 1800', in *Hamburger Jahrbuch für Musikwissenschaft*, vol. v, 1981, p. 255.

Franz Horn, 'Musikalische Fragmente', in *AMZ*, 1802, column 824.

Friedrich Rochlitz considers the comments of connoisseurs on Gluck and Mozart ('Verschiedenheit der Urtheile über Werke der Tonkunst', in *Für Freunde der Tonkunst*, Leipzig, 1824, p. 182): 'Why is there this variety of judgement, even in these circles? Where else but from the variety of those who pass them?

81 W. Salmen, loc. cit., p. 112.

BMZ, 1806, p. 11.

See the opposite view in K. Kropfinger, loc. cit., p. 327.

Hugo Riemann, *Geschichte der Musik seit Beethoven (1800–1900)*, Berlin, 1901, p. 151.

Der Sammler, 1810, p. 574.

82 E.T.A. Hoffmann, *Sämtliche Werke*, vol. v, p. 61f. and vol. iii, p. 89; Norbert Miller, 'Hoffmann and Spontini', in *Studien zur Musikgeschichte Berlins*, loc. cit., p. 460f.

E.T.A. Hoffmann, *Sämtliche Werke*, vol. xiv, p. 131.

N. Miller, loc. cit., p. 465.

83 E.T.A. Hoffmann, *Sämtliche Werke*, vol. v, p. 127.

BMZ, 1805, p. 301.

84 The illustrations under discussion may be found in the ISM Archive.

Johann Philipp Schmidt, 1814: see K. Kropfinger, loc. cit., p. 333.

Arno Forchert, ' "Klassisch" und "romantisch" in der Musikliteratur des frühen 19 Jahrhunderts', in *Die Musikforschung*, 1978, p. 408.

AMZ, 1800, column 417ff.

85 W.F. Wackenroder, *Werke*, pp. 264 and 131.

K. Werner-Jensen, loc. cit., p. 141.

86 *AMZ*, 1800, column 117.

BMZ, 1805, p. 200.

AMZ, 1799, column 146.

F.X. Niemetschek, loc. cit., p. 2.

Hermann August Korff, *Geist der Goethezeit*, vol. iii, Leipzig, 1940, p. 58ff.

W.F. Wackenroder, *Werke*, p. 25.

87 Johann Friedrich Reichardt, *Vertraute Briefe aus Paris, geschrieben in den Jahren 1802 und 1803*, pt. 3, enhanced edition, Hamburg, 1805, p. 246.

Franz Grillparzer, *Werke*, vol. iv, 1965, p. 393.

Ernst Bloch, 'Don Giovanni, alle Frauen und die Hochzeit', in *Don Juan*, loc. cit., p.81f. (first edition, 1928).

F.X. Niemetschek, loc. cit., p. 57.

Ludwig Tieck, 'Shakespeare's Behandlung des Wunderbaren', in *Ausgewählte kritische Schriften*, Tübingen, 1975, pp. 7 and 25.

88 *AMZ*, 1798, column 152.

K. Werner-Jensen, loc. cit., p. 142.

BMZ, 1805, p. 299f.

89 *AMZ*, 1801, columns 677ff., especially 684–6.

C. Dahlhaus, loc. cit., pp. 17 and 62f.

F. Horn loc. cit., column 401ff, especially 811, 423, 421, 422, 452, 423, 421, 452, 454, 844f.

90 René Wellek, *Geschichte der Literaturkritik*, vol. i, Darmstadt, 1959, p. 274.

Gernot Gruber, 'Robert Schumann: Fantasie op. 17, 1. Satz', in *Musicologica Austriaca 4*, Fohrenau, 1984, p. 101ff.

91 C. Dahlhaus, loc. cit., p. 69.

92 Quoted in L. Schrade, loc. cit., p. 31.

F. Horn, loc. cit., column 829.

E.T.A. Hoffmann, *Sämtliche Werke*, vol. i, p. 49.

93 Jean Rousset, 'Don Juan und die Metamorphosen einer Struktur', in *Don Juan*, loc. cit., p. 281f (first edition, 1967).

94 *BMZ*, 1824, p. 319.

95 N. Siara, loc. cit., p. 9.

August Apel, 'Musik und Poesie', in *AMZ*, 1806, column 449ff.

96 C.M. v. Weber, *Kunstansichten*, p. 124.

97 Alfred Einstein, *Schubert*, Zurich, 1952, p. 238.

Horst Heussner, 'L. Spohr und W.A. Mozart', in *Mozart-Jahrbuch 1957*, p. 200ff.

98 Hermann Abert, 'Mozart und Beethoven', in *Gesammelte Schriften und Vorträge*, Halle, 1929, pp. 491 and 485.

Hans Gal, 'Die Stileigentümlichkeiten des jungen Beethoven', in *Studien zur Musikwissenschaft*, 4 (1916), p. 58f.

101 Walther Vetter, *Der Klassiker Schubert*, vol. i, Leipzig, 1953, p. 154.

Gustav Gärtner, 'Eine Parallele bei Mozart und Schubert', in *Musica*, 1954, p. 117ff.

102 *BMZ*, 1806, p. 252.

AMZ, 1804, column 145f.; see K. Kropfinger, loc. cit., p. 339.

103   *BMZ*, 1805, p. 174, and 1807, p. 19.

E.T.A. Hoffmann, *Sämtliche Werke*, vol. xiii, p. 42.

Kropfinger (loc. cit., p. 366) interprets the facts in a similar manner; Gudrun Henneberg uses an exclusively Hegelian interpretation ('Der Einfluss der Philosophie Hegels auf das Mozart-Bild in der ersten Hälfte des 19. Jahrhunderts', in *Mozart-Jahrbuch 1980–3*, p. 257ff.).

104   *BMZ*, 1824, p. 447.

AMZ, 1822, and in *Für Freunde der Tonkunst*, vol. ii, Leipzig, 1825, p. 244f.

105   Franz Stoepel, *Grundzüge der Geschichte der modernen Musik*, Berlin 1821, p. 82f.

Johann Vesque von Püttlingen, *Eine Lebensskizze aus Briefen und Tagebuchblättern zusammengestellt*, Vienna, 1887, p. 16; Theophil Antonicek, 'Biedermeierzeit un Vormärz, in *Musikgeschichte Österreichs*, vol. ii, Graz, 1979, p. 238.

F. Rochlitz, *Für Freunde der Tonkunst*, vol. iii, p. 382ff. (written in 1800). Alongside the tradition of Thibaut and others who attempted to formulate the concept of Classicism with references to Palestrina and older ecclesiastical music (see Ludwig Finscher, 'Zum Begriff der Klassik in der Musik', in *Deutsches Jahrbuch der Musikwissenschaft*, 1967, p. 19f.), there were also attempts (made firstly by Niemetschek) to define Classicism using the music of Mozart.

106   Rudolf Pečman, 'Mozart or Beethoven?', in *Beethoven-Kongressbericht Berlin 1977*, Leipzig, 1978, p. 345ff.

Wilhelm Hitzig, 'Gottlieb Christoph Härtel und die Musik seiner Zeit', in *Der Bär 1929/30*, Leipzig, 1930, p. 12.

Quoted by K. Kropfinger, loc. cit., pp. 361 and 375.

107   Th. Antonicek, loc. cit., p. 231f.

G.L.P. Sievers, 'Mozart und Rossini', in *Weiner Zeitschrift für Kunst, Literatur, Theater und Mode*, 1821, p. 409f., especially p. 412.

108   K. Werner-Jensen, loc. cit., p. 167f.

Giuseppe Pintorno, *Stendhal alla Scala*, Milan, 1980, p. 128.

AMZ, 1823, column 810; see K. Werner-Jensen, loc. cit., p. 159.

BMZ, 1824, p. 318f.; K. Kropfinger, loc. cit., p. 325.

109   Clemens Höslinger, 'Mozarts Opern im Wiener Biedermeier', in *Mozart-Jahrbuch 1980–3*, pp. 100 and 102.

AMZ, 1798, column 84f.

Quoted in K. Kropfinger, loc. cit., p. 370.

Letter of 24 October 1777.

BMZ, 1805, p. 187, and 1806, p. 94.

Vossische Zeitung of 25 November 1820; see Ch. Bitter, loc. cit., p. 95.

This was announced by G.W. Fink in *AMZ*, 1839, column 477; Walter Gerstenberg, 'Authentische Tempi für Mozarts *Don Giovanni*?', in *Mozart-Jahrbuch 1960–1*, p. 58ff.

110   The texts by Toreinx are contained in *Music and Aesthetics in the Eighteenth and Early Nineteenth Centuries*, Cambridge, 1981.

111   *BMZ*, 1805, p.48.

Christoph-Hellmut Mahling, 'Typus und Modell in Opern Mozarts', in *Mozart-Jahrbuch 1968–70*, p. 145ff.

André Ernest- Modeste Grétry, *Mémoires ou Essais sur la musique*, Paris, 1789.

Romain Rolland, *Musiker von ehedem*, Munich, 1927, p.337.

BMZ, 1805, pp. 48, 28 and 115.

Rudolph Angermüller, '*Les Mystères d'Isis* (1801) und *Don Juan* (1805, 1834) auf der Bühne der Pariser Oper', in *Mozart-Jahrbuch 1980–3*, p. 32ff.

112   Herbert Schneider, 'Probleme der Mozart-Rezeption im Frankreich der ersten Hälfte des 19. Jahrhunderts', in *Mozart-Jahrbuch 1980–3*, p. 32ff.

Rudolph Angermüller, *Sigismund Neukomm*, Munich, 1977, p. 32

113   Quoted by Floyd Bradley St Clair, *Stendhal and Music*, Ph.D. Stanford University, 1968, pp. 196 and 194.

Quoted in Erich Valentin, 'Mozart in der französischen Dichtung', in *Acta Mozartiana*, 1983, p. 72.

114   H. Schneider, loc. cit., pp. 26 and 24.

115   Albert Palm, *Jérôme-Joseph de Momigny. Leben und Werk*, Cologne, 1969, pp. 53 and 250ff.

116   C.F. Pohl, loc. cit., p. 144ff.

H. Schneider, loc. cit., p. 30.

A. Hyatt King, 'Vignettes in early-nineteenth-century London editions of Mozart's operas', in *The British Library Journal*, 1980, p. 26.

117   Doris Ann R. Clatanoff, *Poetry and Music: Coleridge, Shelley and Keats and the Musical Milieu of their Day*, Ph.D. University of Nebraska, 1973.

Fl. St Clair, loc. cit., p. 187.

118   Pietro Lichtenthal, *Cenni biografici*, Milan, 1816, p. 40.

Werner Kümmel, 'Aus der Frühzeit der Mozart-Pflege in Italien', in *Analecta Musicologica* 7, Cologne, 1969, p. 145ff.; Werner Bollert, 'Mozart-Pflege in Italien 1791–1935', in *Aufsätze zur Musikgeschichte*, Bottrop, n.d., p. 3ff.

119   Giuseppe Bridi, *Brevi notizie intorno ad alcuni piu celebri compositori di musica*, Rovereto, 1827.

120   G. Morin, loc. cit., p. 419.

121   E.J. Luin, loc. cit., p. 388.

R. Angermüller, *Neukomm*, p. 20.

122   Gottfried Weber, 'Über eine besonders merkwürdige Stelle in einem Mozartschen Violinquartett aus C', in *Cäcilia*, 1832, p. 1ff.

Fellerer, 'Mozart in der Betrachtung H.G. Nägelis', in *Mozart-Jahrbuch 1957*, p. 25ff.; Arno Lemke, *Jacob Gottfried Weber, Leben und Werk*, Mainz, 1968, p. 215.

125   W.P. Griepenkerl, *Das Musikfest*, pp. xivff., 6, 60ff., 27, 67f., 245 and 297f.

127   L. Finscher, loc. cit., p. 21f.

K. Werner-Jensen, loc. cit., p. 163.

128   Friedrich Sengle, *Biedermeierzeit*, vol. i, Stuttgart, 1971, p. 350.

For Kierkegaard's Mozart interpretation see Hans Joachim Kreutzer, 'Der Mozart der Dichter', in *Mozart-Jahrbuch 1980–3*, p. 224ff.

129 Rüdiger Gierner, '*Die Zauberflöte* in Kierkegaards *Entweder-Oder*', in *Mozart-Jahrbuch 1980–3*, p. 247ff.

130 Arnold Schering, 'Aus den Jugendjahren der musikalischen Neuromantik', in *Jahrbuch der Musikbibliothek Peters für das Jahr 1917*, p. 45ff.
Karl Gustav Fellerer, 'A.W. Zuccalmaglios Bearbeitungen Mozartscher Opern', in *Mozart-Jahrbuch 1976–7*, p. 21ff.

131 Further cultural and geographical transpositions of *Così fan tutte* from the same time are to be found in Klaus Hortschansky, 'Gegen Unwahrscheinlichkeit und Frivolität: die Bearbeitungen im 19. Jahrhundert', in *Così fan tutte*, Bayreuth, 1978, p. 56.
Hans-Peter Glöckner, 'Die Popularisierung der Unmoral: *Così fan tutte* in der Belletristik', in *Così fan tutte*, p. 113f.

132 K.G. Fellerer, 'Mozart im Programm der frühen Niederrheinischen Musikfeste', in *Mozart-Jahrbuch 1962–3*, p. 32ff.

133 A. Schering, loc. cit., pp. 54f. and 50f.

134 Hans Spatzenegger, 'Neue Dokumente zur Entstehung des Mozart-Denkmals in Salzburg', in *Mozart-Jahrbuch 1980–3*, p. 147ff.
Carl Gollmick, *Feldzüge und Streifereien im Gebiete der Tonkunst*, Darmstadt, 1846, p. 139ff., especially p. 146.
Constantin Schneider, *Geschichte der Musik in Salzburg von der ältesten Zeit bis zur Gegenwart*, Salzburg, 1935, p. 173.

135 Carl Santner, *Musikalisches Gedenkbuch*, no. 1, Vienna and Leipzig, 1856.
Franz Grillparzer, *Sämtliche Werke*, Munich, 1962, vol. iv, p. 695.

136 G. Gruber, ' "Mozart, das Lieblingskind Österreichs." Musiksoziologisches zur Bildausstattung der Wiener Hofoper', in *Österreichische Musikzeitschrift*, 1980, p. 596ff.

138 F. Grillparzer, *Werke*, vol. iii, pp. 880, 252 and 236.

139 Raphael Georg Kiesewetter, *Geschichte der europaisch-abendländischen oder unserer heutigen Musik*, second ed., Leipzig, 1846, p. 97.
L. Finscher, loc. cit., p. 22.
Karl Kossmaly, *Anmerkungen zur Übersetzung von: Alexander Ulibischeff, Mozarts Opern. Kritische Erläuterungen*. Introduction by A. Kahlert, Leipzig, 1848, pp. 372 and 381; A. Schering, loc. cit., p. 55.
Josef von Heukelum, 'Stifter und Mozart', in *Die Musikforschung*, 1957, p. 137ff.
A. Forchert, loc. cit., p. 421.
F. Grillparzer, *Werke*, vol. iv, p. 145.

140 Adolph Bernhard Marx, 'Zur Beherzigung', in *BMZ*, 1825, p. 119a.
Eduard Hanslick, *Aus dem Opernleben der Gegenwart*, third ed., Berlin, 1889, p. 128; also Hanslick's *Die Moderne Oper*, Berlin, 1892, p. 30.

141 K. Werner-Jensen, loc. cit., p. 219f.

Hermann Ulrich, *Alfred Julius Becher*, Regensburg, 1974; F. Grillparzer, *Epigramm*, no. 855.

143 Jean Auguste Ingres, *Ecrits sur l'art*, Paris, 1947, p. 60.

Ludwig Lade, 'Schwind und Mozart', in *Neue Zeitschrift für Musik*, 1939, p. 477.

Walther Vetter, 'Die musikalischen Wesensbestandteile in der Kunst Moritz von Schwinds', in *Musik und Bild. Festschrift Max Seiffert*, Kassel, 1938, p. 119.

Christopher Raeburn, 'Mosel und Zinzendorf über Mozart', in *Festschrift O.E. Deutsch*, p. 156.

F. Sengle, loc. cit., vol. ii, p. 224.

144 C. Gollmick, loc. cit., p. 127ff.

145 Wolfgang Plath, 'Requiem Briefe', in *Mozart-Jahrbuch 1976–7*, p. 175.

A Mozart Pilgrimage. Being the Travel Diaries of Vincent and Mary Novello in the year 1829, London, 1955.

146 Alexander Ulibisheff, *Nouvelle biographie de Mozart, suivie d'un aperçu sur l'histoire générale de la musique et de l'analyse des principales oeuvres de Mozart*, vol. iii, Moscow 1843; German translations by A. Schraishuon, Stuttgart 1847, K. Kossmaly, Leipzig 1848, and L. Gantter, Stuttgart 1869. Quoted from the German edition 1847, p. xii, 3ff.

A. Ulibisheff, loc. cit., vol. ii, p. vii.

147 Eduard Mörike, *Mozart auf der Reise nach Prag. Erläuterungen und Dokumente*, Stuttgart, 1976; F. Sengle, loc. cit., vol. iii, p. 737ff.; H.J. Kreutzer, loc. cit., p. 219ff.

148 E. Mörike, *Werke in einem Band*, Munich, 1977, pp. 910, 944, 930 and 962.

149 E. Mörike, *Erläuterungen*, pp. 60 and 65.

Joseph Müller-Blattau, 'Das Mozartbild Mörikes und seines Freundeskreises', in *Von der Vielfalt der Musik*, Freiburg, 1966, p. 521ff.

151 G. Gruber, 'Die Mozart-Forschung im 19. Jahrhundert', in *Mozart-Jahrbuch 1980–3*, p. 10ff.

152 E. Mörike, *Erläuterungen*, p. 81f.

153 Friedrich Nietzsche, *Schriften* (Musarionausgabe), vol. vi, p. 286.

G. Gruber, 'Divergenzen und Gemeinsamkeiten in der Musikästhetik Schopenhauers und Wagners, dargestellt anhand der Mozart-Rezeption' (in press).

154 C. Dahlhaus, 'Klassizität, Romantik, Moderne', in *Ausbreitung des Historismus über die Musik*, ed. W. Wiora, Regensburg, 1969, p. 275.

Adolf Nowak, *Hegels Musikästhetik*, Regensburg, 1971, p. 156.

155 Heinrich Heine, *Säkularausgabe*, vol. vii, Berlin/Paris, 1970, p. 279.

F. Grillparzer, *Werke*, vol. iii, p. 890.

Review of the piano trio in D minor, op. 49 (1840).

156 F. Sengle, loc. cit., vol. ii, p. 274.

Letter to Zelter of 15 February 1832; see Susanne Grossmann-Vendrey, 'Mendelssohn und die Vergangenheit', in *Die Ausbreitung des Historismus*, p. 78.

Günther Weiss, 'Eine Mozartspur in Felix Mendelssohn-Bartholdys Sinfonie A-Dur, op. 90', in *Mozart. Klassik für die Gegenwart*, p. 87ff.

Franz Liszt, 'Chopin' (French version 1851/2), in *Schriften zur Tonkunst*, Leipzig, 1981, p. 155.

157 Thomas A. Regelski, *Music and painting in the Paragon of Eugène Delacroix*, Ph.D. University of Ohio, 1970, p. 167; Christina Sieber-Meier, *Untersuchungen zum 'Oeuvre littéraire' von Eugène Delacroix*, Berne, 1963.

Franz Giegling, 'Zu Robert Schumanns Mozart-Bild', in *Mozart-Jahrbuch 1980–3*, p. 263ff.

Arno Forcheret, loc. cit., p. 422.

158 Günter Katzenberger, 'Materialien zu Clara (und Robert) Schumanns Mozart – und Beethovenauffassung', in *Festschrift E. Valentin*, Regensburg, 1976, p. 61ff.

159 Imogen Fellinger, 'Brahms und Mozart', in *Brahms-Studien 5*, Hamburg, 1983, p. 141ff.

Franz Liszt, 'Mozart', in *Schriften zur Tonkunst*, Leipzig, 1981, p. 263ff.

160 Richard Wagner, *Gesammelte Schriften und Dichtungen* (hereafter *GS*), fourth ed., vol. i, p. 135.

R. Wagner, *GS*, vol. i, p. 187f.

161 R. Wagner, *GS*, vol. i, pp. 161, 140 and 148.

162 R Wagner, *GS*, vol. i, pp. 147ff and 206.

R. Wagner, *Mein Leben*. Einzige vollständige Ausgabe, Munich, 1963, vol. i, p. 284.

163 R. Wagner, *GS*, vol. iii, p. 91.

164 R. Wagner, *GS*, vol. iii, pp. 245, 247, 288 and 320.

165 R. Wagner, *GS*, vol. x, p. 97; vol. viii, p. 128; vol. ix, p. 264ff.

Johann Peter Lyser, *Mozart-Album*, 1856, p. 33.

R. Wagner, *GS*, vol. vii, p. 126.

H. Riemann, loc. cit., p. 66.

R. Wagner, *Mein Leben*, vol. ii, p. 568.

R. Wagner, *GS*, vol. x, p. 173.

166 Cosima Wagner, *Die Tagebücher 1869–1883*, vol. ii, Munich, 1977, p. 247.

C. Wagner, *Die Tagebücher*, vol. ii, p. 195.

167 R. Wagner, *GS*, vol. iii, p. 287.

Karl Jaspers, *Nietzsche. Einführung in das Verständnis seines Philosophierens* (1936), third ed., Berlin, 1950.

G. Gruber, 'Friedrich Nietzsches Aussagen über Mozart', in *Mozart-Jahrbuch 1980–3*, p. 262ff.

168 F. Nietzsche, *Schriften* (Musarionausgabe), vol. ix, pp. 431, 262 and 267.

F. Nietzsche, *Gesammelte Briefe*, Berlin, 1900, vol. v, p. 607.

F. Nietzsche, *Schriften*, vol. xvii, p. 345.

169 Pierluigi Petrobelli, 'Don Giovanni in Italia', in *Analecta Musicologica*, 18, Cologne, 1978, p. 41f.

Herbert Schneider, 'Urteile über Opernkomponisten und die Frage der Oper in den Schriften von Cornelius', in *Peter Cornelius als Komponist, Dichter, Kritiker und Essayist*, Regensburg, 1977, pp. 219ff. and 106 and 130.

170 Rudolf von Freisauff, *Mozart's Don Juan 1787–1887*, Salzburg, 1887, pp. 71, 74 and 105ff.; Ernst Possart, *Ueber die Neueinstudierung und Neuinszenierung des Mozart'schen Don Giovanni (Don Juan) auf dem Kgl. Residenztheater zu München*, Munich, 1896, pp. 4 and 7.

171 R. v. Freisauff, loc. cit., pp. 75 and 179.

C. Bitter, loc. cit., pp. 106f. and 111f.

172 Charles Gounod, *Mozarts Don Juan. Autorisierte Uebersetzung von Adolf Klages*, Leipzig, 1891, p. 119f.

173 George Bernard Shaw, *Musik in London*, Berlin, 1957, p. 41.

Quoted in R. v. Freisauff, p. 178.

Ch. Gounod, loc. cit., p. 2.

Johann Evangelist Engl, *W.A. Mozart in der Schilderung seiner Biographen*, Salzburg, 1887, p. 52ff.

G. B. Shaw, loc. cit., p. 63f.

Heinrich Adolf Köstlin, *Geschichte der Musik im Umriss*, second extended ed., Tübingen, 1880, p. 307ff.

Ferdinand Adolf Gelbcke, 'Classisch und Romantisch' in *Neue Zeitschrift für Musik*, 1881, p. 187ff.

174 F. Sengle, loc. cit., vol. iii, p. 738.

Jacob Burckhardt, *Weltgeschichtliche Betrachtungen*, Stuttgart, 1955, pp. 220f. and 226.

Friedrich von Hausegger, *Unsere deutschen Meister*, Munich, 1901 (on Mozart, pp. 53–93).

Johann Gustav Droysen, *Historik*, Munich, 1960, p. 291.

176 Georg Feder, 'Gounods "Meditation" und ihre Folgen', in *Die Ausbreitung des Historismus über die Musik*, p. 106.

Franz Zagiba, *Tschaikovskij. Leben und Werk*, Zurich, 1953, p. 258ff.

177 Winton Dean, *Georges Bizet. His Life and Work*, London, 1965, pp. 239f. and 250.

Otakar Šourcek/Paul Stefan, *Dvořák. Leben und Werk*, Vienna, 1935, p. 67f.

C. Wagner, *Tagebücher*, vol. i, p. 198.

178 G.B. Shaw, loc. cit., p. 67f.

R. v. Freisauff, loc. cit., p. 174.

179 Loewenberg, *Annals*, loc. cit.; A. Hyatt King, loc. cit., p. 27.

183 *Mozart's Bäsle-Briefe*. Edited with a commentary by Joseph Heinz Eibl and Walter Senn. With a preface by Wolfgang Hildesheimer, Kassel and Munich, 1978.

184 E. Possart, loc. cit., especially p. 36.

Heinrich Bulthaupt, *Dramaturgie der Oper*, second improved ed., vol. i, Leipzig, 1902, p. 231f.

Alfons Ott, 'Die Münchner Oper von den Anfängen der Festspiele bis zur Zerstörung des Nationaltheaters', in *Musik aus Bayern*, 1, Tutzing, 1972, p. 314ff.

185 Carl Hagemann, 'Münchens Mozart-Renaissance', in *Oper und Szene*, Berlin, 1905, p. 207ff.

186 Bernhard Paumgartner, 'Gustav Mahlers Bearbeitung von Mozarts *Così fan tutte* für seine Aufführungen an der Wiener Hofoper', in *Musik und Verlag*, Kassel, 1968, p. 476ff.; Robert Werba, 'Mahlers Wiener Mozart-Taten', in *Mozart-Jahrbuch 1979*, p. 246ff.

188 Felix Weingartner, 'Zurück zu Mozart?' in *Akkorde. Gesammelte Aufsätze*, Leipzig, 1912, p. 108ff.

Paul Hirsch, 'The Salzburg Mozart Festival 1906', in *Music Review*, 1946, p. 149ff.

Ferruccio Busoni, 'Mozart-Aphorismen zum 150. Geburtstag des Meisters', in *Von der Einheit der Musik*, Berlin, 1922, p. 78ff.

189 Joachim Herrmann, 'Mozart und die Musik der Gegenwart. Das Mozart-Bekenntnis Ferrucio Busonis', in *Acta Mozartiana*, 1956, no. 2, p. 2ff.

F. Busoni, loc. cit., p. 1ff.

Alfred Heuss, 'Das dämonische Element in Mozarts Werken', in *Zeitschrift der Internationalen Musikgesellschaft*, 1906, p. 175ff., especially p. 177.

Siegmund von Hausegger, 'Stiefkinder', in *Süddeutsche Monatshefte*, 1905, p. 563ff.

Bollert, loc. cit., p. 32.

190 Roswitha Vera Karpf, 'Beiträge zur österreichischen Wagner-Rezeption im 19 Jahrhundert', in *Richard Wagner 1883–1983*, Stuttgart, 1984, p. 234.

Paul Zschorlich, *Mozart-Heuchelei. Ein Beitrag zur Kunstgeschichte des 20. Jahrhunderts, Leipzig*, 1906, especially pp. 14 and 97.

191 Hermann von der Pfordten, *Mozart*, Leipzig, 1908.

192 Richard Beer-Hofmann, *Gedenkrede auf W.A. Mozart*, Berlin 1906, p. 15f.

Carl Krebs, *Mozart. Rede zur Feier des Allerhöchsten Geburtstages seiner Majestät des Kaisers und Königs am 27. Januar 1906 in der öffentlichen Sitzung der Königlichen Akademie der Künste*, Berlin, 1906, especially p. 5.

193 Hermann Abert, *W.A. Mozart* (revised and extended edition of Otto Jahn's *Mozart*, Leipzig, 1919–1974: seventh ed., Leipzig, 1955).

H. Abert, loc. cit., p.v.

196 Erich Valentin, '"Wir brauchen nötigst viel, viel Mozart"', in *Acta Mozartiana*, 1973, p. 1f.

197 Wolfgang Schmidt, 'Der "konservative Revolutionär" Arnold Schönberg. Ein Schüler W.A. Mozarts', in *23. Deutsches Mozartfest Augsburg*, 1974, p. 42ff.

Alan Walker, 'Schönberg's Classical Background', in *Music Review*, p. 285ff.

198 F. Busoni, loc. cit., pp. 191, 304 and 349ff.

Kurt Weill, *Ausgewählte Schriften*, Frankfurt, 1975, pp. 39 (Zeitoper), 42 (Über den gestischen Charakter der Musik) and 30 (Bekenntnis zur Oper).

262

199 Helmuth Osthoff, 'Mozarts Einfluss auf Richard Strauss', in *Schweizerische Musikzeitung*, 1958, p. 409ff.; Hans Mayer, 'Hugo von Hofmannsthal und Richard Strauss', in *Ansichten*, Hamburg, 1962, p. 9ff.; G. Gruber, *Die Zauberflöte* and *Die Frau ohne Schatten* (in press).

Josef Kaut, *Die Salzburger Festspiele 1920–1981*, Salzburg, 1982, especially p. 35ff.

201 Rudolf Flotzinger and G. Gruber, 'Einleitung', in *Musikgeschichte Österreichs*, vol. i, Graz, 1977, p. 19f. (Max von Millenkovich-Morold, *Die Österreichische Tonkunst*).

203 Friedrich Herzfeld, *Magie des Taktstocks*, Berlin, 1959, p. 66.

204 Edward J. Dent, *Mozart's Opera*, second ed., London, 1947, p. ix f.

William Mann, 'Test-Match Opera', in *Glyndebourne Festival*, 1984, p. 109ff.

205 Paul Alfred Merbach, 'Die deutschen Übersetzungen und Bearbeitungen des *Don-Juan*-Textes', in *Die Scene*, 1917, p. 102ff.; Max Kalbeck, 'Zur Frage des deutschen *Don Giovanni*', in *Der Merkur*, 1918, no.2, p. 59f.

Karl Eberts, 'Der Mannheimer *Don Juan*', in *Die Scene*, 1917, p. 129ff.

Eugen Schmitz, 'Zur Inszenierung von Mozarts *Don Giovanni*', in *Allgemeine Musik-Zeitung*, 1924, p. 507ff.

Eugen Kilian, 'Mozart Probleme', in *Neue Züricher Zeitung*, 1 October 1917.

206 Hans Loewenfeld, 'Gedanken zu einer nicht ausgeführten *Don-Juan*-Inszenierung' in *Die Scene*, 1917, p. 131ff.

C. Bitter, loc. cit., p. 129ff.

207 Wilhelm Weber, 'Max Slevogts bildnerische Interpretationen Mozartscher Musik', in *Mozart und Slevogt*, Exhibit Zweibrücken, June 1966, p. 5ff.

208 Karl Kraus, 'Beim Anblick eines sonderbaren Plakats', in *Die Fackel*, 1915, p. 149f.

209 Ernst Bloch, *Geist der Utopie* (reprint of second version, 1923), Frankfurt, 1973, especially pp. 73, 173, 113f. and 63f.

210 Hermann Hesse, *Der Steppenwolf, Erzählung*, Frankfurt, 1974, especially pp. 148, 65, 49, 51, 34, 70 and 222ff.

212 *W.A. Mozart* (for the Mozart-Week of the German Reich. Edited by Walter Thomas in collaboration with the Reichsministerium für Volksaufklärung und Propaganda und dem Reichsstatthalter in Vienna, Leipzig, 1941).

213 Hermann Cohen, *Die dramatische Idee in Mozarts Operntexten*, Berlin, 1915, especially pp. 21 and 113.

Wilhelm Dilthey, *Von deutscher Dichtung und Musik*, Leipzig, 1933, especially p. 286.

W.A. Mozart, loc. cit., p. 96.

Richard Benz, *W.A. Mozart. Gedenken zu des Meisters 150. Todestages*, Dortmund, 1941, p. 4.

214 Werner Erdmann-Böhme, 'Mozart in der schönen Literatur', in *Kongressbericht Salzburg 1931*, Leipzig 1932, pp. 257f. and 275f.

215 *Mozart in XX. Jahrhundert. Ausstellung Salzburg 1984* (compiled by R. Angermüller), especially p. 55f.

See the list of performances drawn up by Hans Jaklitsch in J. Kaut, loc. cit.,
p. 241ff.

216 Walter Hummel, *Mozart in aller Welt. Die Weltfeier 1956*, Salzburg, 1956.

219 Otto Rank, 'Die Don-Juan-Gestalt', in *Don Juan*, p. 32ff. (first ed. 1922).
Brigid Brophy, *Mozart the Dramatist*, New York, 1964, p. 242ff.
Klaus Geitel, 'Luftschutz-Lemuren und Don Giovanni als Batman', in *Don Juan*, p. 411ff.

220 ' "Rekonstruktion". Liebe im Amazonas. "Spiegel" – Rezension', in *Don Juan*, p. 419ff.

221 Arthur Drews, 'Mozarts *Zauberflöte* und Wagners *Parsifal*', in *Richard-Wagner-Jahrbuch 1906*, p. 326ff.
See the papers on *Die Zauberflöte* in *Werk und Wiedergabe. Musiktheater exemplarisch interpretiert*, Bayreuth, 1980, p. 99ff.
Stefan Kunze, '*Die Zauberflöte*. Möglichkeiten und Grenzen der Interpretation', in *Werk und Wiedergabe*, p. 147.
Dale Harris, 'The Chagall-Rennert staging of *Die Zauberflöte* at the Metropolitan Opera House', in *Werk und Wiedergabe*, p. 172.

222 R. Angermüller, '*Die Zauberflöte* manieristisch, maschinistisch, unverschlüsselt', in *Werk und Wiedergabe*, p. 150ff.
Karl Schumann, 'Mozart – Abgott und Spielball', in *Deutsches Mozartfest Augsburg*, 1960, p. 22.

224 Stephan Stompor, 'Mozart als Musikdramatiker heute', in *Musik und Gesellschaft*, 1955, p. 283ff.

227 *Neue Zeitschrift für Musik*, 1982, no. 10, p. 51.
Recordings: Fricsay/Deutsche Grammophon (1953) 2535 709; Walter/Philips AO1271L; Böhm/Deutsche Grammophon 138815; Collegium aureum/Harmonia mundi 1CO65-99673Q.

228 B. Paumgartner, loc. cit., p. 476.
Nikolaus Harnoncourt, *Musik als Klangrede*, Salzburg, 1982; also *Der musikalische Dialog. Gedanken zu Monteverdi, Bach und Mozart*, Salzburg, 1984.
Yehudi Menuhin, *Unvollendete Reise. Lebenserinnerungen*, Kassel, 1979, p. 124.
Österreiche Musikzeitschrift, 1969, p. 435.
N. Harnoncourt, *Klangrede*, p. 268.

229 *Die Presse*, Vienna, 15/16 December 1984, *Spektrum*, p. iv.

230 Glenn Gould in conversation with Bruno Monsaingeon, 'Mozart aus persönlicher Sicht', supplement to the recording (CBS 79501). Gould did, in fact, make Mozart recordings.
Wolfgang Plath, 'Der gegenwärtige Stand der Mozart-Forschung' in *Kongressbericht Salzburg 1964*, vol. i, Kassel, 1964, p. 47ff.; *Symposium*, ibid., vol. ii, Kassel, 1966, p. 88ff.

231 A. Diemer, article on 'Geisteswissenschaften', in *Historisches Wörterbuch der Philosophie*, vol. iii, Darmstadt, 1974, column 211ff.

233 Wolfgang Hildesheimer, *Mozart*, Frankfurt, 1977, especially p. 319ff.

234 Wolfgang Hildesheimer, 'Die Subjektivität des Biographen', in *Das Ende der Fiktionen*, Frankfurt, 1984, p. 123ff.
236 Annette Kolb, *Mozart*, Vienna, 1937, p. 18.
237 Joyce Carol Oates, *Marriages and Infidelities*, London, 1974, p. 489ff.
Karl Barth, *W.A. Mozart 1756–1956*, Zollikon, 1956.
Thrasybulos Georgiades, 'Aus der Musiksprache des Mozart-Theaters', in *Mozart-Jahrbuch 1950*, p. 76ff.
Hans Küng, *Christ sein*, Munich, 1974, p. 540f.
Hans Urs von Balthasar, 'Das Abschieds-Terzett', in *Mozart-Aspekte*, Olten, 1956, p. 279ff.
238 Martin Staehelin, 'Mozart und Raffael', in *Schweizerische Musikzeitung*, 1977, p. 323.
Hans E. Valentin, 'Mozart heute. Aspekte aus der Literatur', in *Mozart. Klassik für die Gegenwart*, p. 130ff.
Walter Wiora, 'Mozarts *Don Giovanni* in der seltsamen Deutung Kierkegaards und Thomas Manns', loc. cit., p. 120ff.
Erich Valentin, *Die goldene Spur. Mozart in der Dichtung Hermann Hesses*, Augsburg, 1966.
239 Ingeborg Bachmann, 'Ein Blatt für Mozart', in *Acta Mozartiana*, 1973, p. 54f (see also *Gedichte, Erzählungen, Horspiel, Essay*, Munich, 1964).
Věra Linhartová, 'Requiem für W.A. Mozart', in *Geschichten*, Frankfurt, 1965.
Peter Shaffer, *Amadeus* (German version by Nina Adler), Frankfurt, 1982.
Kurt Pahlen, *Das Mozart-Buch*, Zurich, 1985.
242 Volkmar Braunbehrens, *Mozart in Wien*, Munich/Zurich, 1986.
Heinz Gärtner, *Mozarts* Requiem *und die Geschäfte der Constanze M.*, Munich, 1986.
243 Erich Valentin, *Mozart, Weg und Welt*, Munich, 1985.
Joachim Kaiser, *Mein Name ist Sarastro. Die Gestalten in Mozarts Meisteropern von Alfonso bis Zerlina*, Munich/Zurich, 1984.
Ivan Nagel, *Autonomie und Gnade. Über Mozarts Opern*, Munich/Vienna, 1985.
Stefan Kunze, *Mozarts Opern*, Stuttgart, 1984.
Gunthard Born, *Mozarts Musiksprache. Schlüssel zu Leben und Werk*, Munich, 1985.
Klaus Umbach, 'Amadeus – das Ferkel, das Feuer speit', in *Der Spiegel*, no. 38/1985, p. 238ff.
244 Francis Carr, *Mozart and Constanze*, London, 1984 (German version, Stuttgart, 1986).
245 Dmitri Shostakovich, 'Über Mozart', in *Musik und Gesellschaft*, 1956, no. 3, p. 14f.
Ernst H. Flammer, *Politisch engagierte Musik als kompositorisches Problem, dargestellt aus Beispiel von Luigi Nono und Hans Werner Henze*, Baden-Baden, 1981, p. 116f.
Mauricio Kagel, 'Wut bisher unbekannter Art', in *Journal. Musikhochschule Köln*, 1984, no. 1, p. 1.
Robert Herold Danes, *Stravinsky's* The Rake's Progress: *Paradigm of Neoclassical Opera*, Ph.D. Washington University, 1972.
Friedrich Nietzsche, *Werke*, viii/3, Berlin, 1972, *Nachgelassene Fragmente*, p. 36.
Wystan H. Auden, *Collected Shorter Poems 1927–1957*, London, 1966, p. 276ff.

INDEX

Note The abbreviation M is used when referring to Mozart in subheadings

266

267

and Niemetschek, 56–7; and Schumann,
    157–8
Clementi, Muzio, *Musical Characteristics*, 40
Clemenza di Tito, La (opera; K.621),
    arrangements, 51, 131; Classicist view,
    46; composers' views, 163; dissemination,
    15, 19, 24; performances: early, 18, 33, 34;
    1800s, 116, 117, 118, 119, 120, 121, 136;
    1900s, 204, 215, 216, 218; popularity, 38,
    84, 108; stage sets/costumes, 46, 47; and
    sublimity, 79–81, 82, 83; writers' views,
    56, 88, 90
Cohen, Hermann, *Die dramatische Idee in
    Mozarts Operntexten*, 212–13
Coleridge, Samuel Taylor, 117
collections, *see* dissemination; *Oeuvres
    complettes*
commercialization, 189, 242–4
concert performances, 17–19, 29–31, 33, 66,
    215–16; 'Historical Concerts', 146;
    memorial, 177, 178; *see also* festivals; *and
    under individual works*
concertos, piano, 23, 66, 107; D minor
    (K.466), 107, 178; dissemination, 24–5; E
    flat major (K.482), 187, 230; post-1945
    concerts, 215
concertos, violin, 24, 156, 191
Copenhagen, 34, 67, 120, 121
Cornelius, Peter, 169, 177
Così fan tutte (opera; K.588), arrangements,
    51, 179; composers' views, 163;
    dissemination, 24; influence on other
    composers, 188, 245; interpretations, 75,
    223, 224, 226; parody on, 64;
    performances: early, 34; 1800s, 114, 116,
    118, 119, 120, 121, 184, 185; 1900s, 186,
    205, 215; recent reassessment, 217;
    popularity, 36, 38, 116, 117; quintet
    arranged by Gounod, 176; stage
    sets/costumes, 46; translations, 37–8; used
    in Lyser's *Singspiel*, 131; writers' views,
    76–7, 83, 88–9, 140, 165, 213
costumes, *see under individual operas*
Cotta (publisher), 150
cycles, Mozart, 178
Czechoslovakia, 36, 39, 216; *see also* Prague

Da Ponte, Lorenzo, 94, 116, 170, 184,
    219
Damisch, Heinrich, 202
dances, 24, 26
d'Andrade, Francesco, 187, 203, 205, 207
Daphnis and Chloe (Tchaikovsky), 177

Dargomyzhsky, Alexander S., *The Stone
    Guest*, 130, 176
Davidde penitente (oratorio; K.469), 33, 65,
    115, 132, 136; performed by Brahms, 158
Debussy, Claude, 197
Deiters, Hermann, 152
Delacroix, Eugène, 156–7
Denmark, 120–1; *see also* Copenhagen
Deutsch, Otto Erich, 232
Deyerkauf, Franz, 17, 18, 57
Dibdin, Thomas, 64
Dilthey, Wilhelm, 212, 231; *Von deutscher
    Dichtung und Musik*, 213
Dingelstedt, Franz von, 132
dissemination, 23–29, 31, 32, 62–3, 110, 116,
    152
Dissonant Quartet (K.465), 11, 12, 122
Dittersdorf, Carl Ditters von, 32
Divertimento (K.563), 24
Domgraf-Fassbänder, Willi, 205
Don Giovanni (opera; K.527), 82, 83;
    arrangements, 51, 112, 133; compared
    with Shakespeare, 88, 90; composers'
    views, 162, 163–4, 165–6, 176, 189;
    demonic elements, 189, 206–7, 217;
    dissemination, 24, 62, 63; Don Juan
    theme, 128–30, 172; duet *Giovanette che fate
    all*, 148; in film plot (*Ariane*), 215;
    influence on other composers, 97, 100–1,
    169; interpretations, 70, 73–4, 88, 110,
    170–2, 219–20, 222, 224; parodies on, 64;
    performances: early, 35; 1800s, 112, 114,
    115, 116, 118, 119, 120, 121, 122, 136, 170,
    179, 183–4, 185; 1900s, 185, 186, 187, 203–
    4, 205–7, 208, 214, 215, 216, 219;
    popularity, 38, 65, 115, 207, 218–9;
    translations, 36–7; Schwind's drawings,
    143; and Slevogt (artist), 207, 208; stage
    sets/costumes, 46, 69, 208; writers' views,
    42–3, 45, 76, 81, 93–4, 108, 115, 140, 143,
    147, 148, 149, 155, 175, 214, 238
Don Juan (Lizst), 159
Donath, Augustinos Erasmus, 41
Donna Giovanna (feminist production), 220
Dörbeck, Franz Burchard, 83–4
Dornau, Friedrich, 141
Dramatische Monaten (Schink), 42
Drews, Arthur, 221
Droysen, Johann Gustav, *Historik*, 174–5
Dublin, 121
Dülberg, Edwald, 221
Dumaine, Marc, 242
Dvořák, Antonin, 177

268

270

271

272

273